International Human Resource Management

Text and Cases

INTERNATIONAL HUMAN RESOURCE MANAGEMENT

Text and Cases

Second Edition

S C GUPTA

TRINITY PRESS

(An Imprint of Laxmi Publications Pvt. Ltd.)

An ISO 9001:2008 Company

BENGALURU • CHENNAI • COCHIN • GUWAHATI • HYDERABAD
JALANDHAR • KOLKATA • LUCKNOW • MUMBAI • RANCHI • NEW DELHI
BOSTON (USA) • ACCRA (GHANA) • NAIROBI (KENYA)

INTERNATIONAL HUMAN RESOURCE MANAGEMENT

Printed and bound in India

Typeset at : Sri Krishna Graphics, Delhi

First Edition : 2006, *Reprint* : 2006-2008 (Three times), *Second Edition* : 2006, *Reprint* : 2014, 2015

ISBN : 978-93-5138-055-9

Published in India by

TRINITY PRESS

(An Imprint of Laxmi Publications Pvt. Ltd.)

An ISO 9001:2008 Company

113, GOLDEN HOUSE, DARYAGANJ, NEW DELHI-110002, INDIA

Telephone : 91-11-4353 2500, 4353 2501

Fax : 91-11-2325 2572, 4353 2528

www.laxmipublications.com info@laxmipublications.com

Branches

Bengaluru	080-26 75 69 30
Chennai	044-24 34 47 26
Cochin	0484-237 70 04, 405 13 03
Guwahati	0361-254 36 69, 251 38 81
Hyderabad	040-27 55 53 83, 27 55 53 93
Jalandhar	0181-222 12 72
Kolkata	033-22 27 43 84
Lucknow	0522-220 99 16
Mumbai	022-24 91 54 15, 24 92 78 69
Ranchi	0651-220 44 64

C—9808/015/02

Printed at : Ajit Printing Press, Delhi.

Preface

Twenty-first century is dominated by multinationals, and as a consequence Indian organizations too are increasingly going global. Even firms that do not go global are experiencing the competitive pressures from other international organizations. The role of HR function has significantly changed in international organizations having large numbers of subsidiaries, which are operating in different countries and cultures, as compared to the domestic companies. Organizational systems, which include HR practices, processes, organization structure and culture, constitute a significant part of organizational core competency and contribute to gaining competitive advantage and organizational performance to multinational firms. In fact organizational culture and HR processes are the key resources that bind and propel global organizations. Their success, however, depends on managing cultural diversity.

All over the Far East organizations encountered the contrasts in approaches between the Oriental ways of managing and the Western ways. In many areas, such as production management and finance, the Western techniques have penetrated deeply and with little resistance. It is in the area of human management that most of the resistance is felt and it is in the area of human management that most organizations succeed or fail. There is little doubt that cultural factors affect organizations, as they have such a great impact on the way people relate to each other. Research has still not penetrated the mysteries of the process of co-operation in sufficient detail for us to understand them precisely, but the average practising manager knows full well that he cannot ignore local ways of doing things and local sensitivities. In IHRM, we try to seek the right balance between successful global HR practices and implementing them with local adaptation and sensitivities.

In most books on international human resource management (IHRM), the focus is mainly on HR processes but how these processes are conditioned by national cultures, organizational cultures and structures, to deliver organizational performance not so well made out. Therefore, a serious attempt has been made in this book to spell out interrelationship of these vital people-related dimensions. Further, how corporate governance, communication, ethics and negotiation process are influenced by national cultures has been the focus of this book. In the process of evolution of firms to become transnational organizations, they require different HR strategies and structures. This book is expected to provide guidance to industry managers to effectively lead such changes.

IHRM is an emerging discipline and its knowledge is scattered across textbooks and journals in various fields of international management. In this book the author has tried to collect together in a single volume all the essential topics connected with IHRM to present the topics clearly and concisely in an informative and readable way, supported with large numbers of business examples and cases.

The structure of this book has been altered, organising it into three parts. The first part consisting of seven chapters focuses on HR processes, practices and policies of multinationals. The second part, again consisting of seven chapters, encompasses relevant material on cross-culture and diversity management, which makes all the difference between domestic HRM and IHRM. The third part consisting of six chapters deals with employee relations, organizational structure and ethics and corporate governance, which affect the performance and service to stakeholders. The first edition has been thoroughly revised, updated and provided with the new study material in the area of employee relations and corporate governance. The book contains both short and long case studies, examples of industry practices in many global firms, including companies like, the IBM, Shell, Scandinavian Airlines, Praxair and Lucent Technologies.

This book focuses on the performance and outcome of multinational companies, primarily from the people-related factors which are as under:

- Human resource policies, practices and procedures.
- Cross-culture and organizational culture.
- State of industrial relations in major economies of the world.
- Organization structure and human resource strategies for gaining sustainable competitive advantage.
- Vision, corporate strategies and management philosophy.

I have been teaching PGDBM and MBA courses for the past several years and the need was felt for a comprehensive textbook on this subject. This book is the outcome of my teaching effort, research, executive development programmes conducted and interviews with HR executives of multinational firms. With ever-increasing globalization of business, and increasing percentage of knowledge workers, the art and science of international human resource management is playing a crucial role in multinational's success. I hope that this book will serve this vital need of academics and industry. The framework of the revised edition of IHRM is presented hereunder, highlighting the newly added chapters.

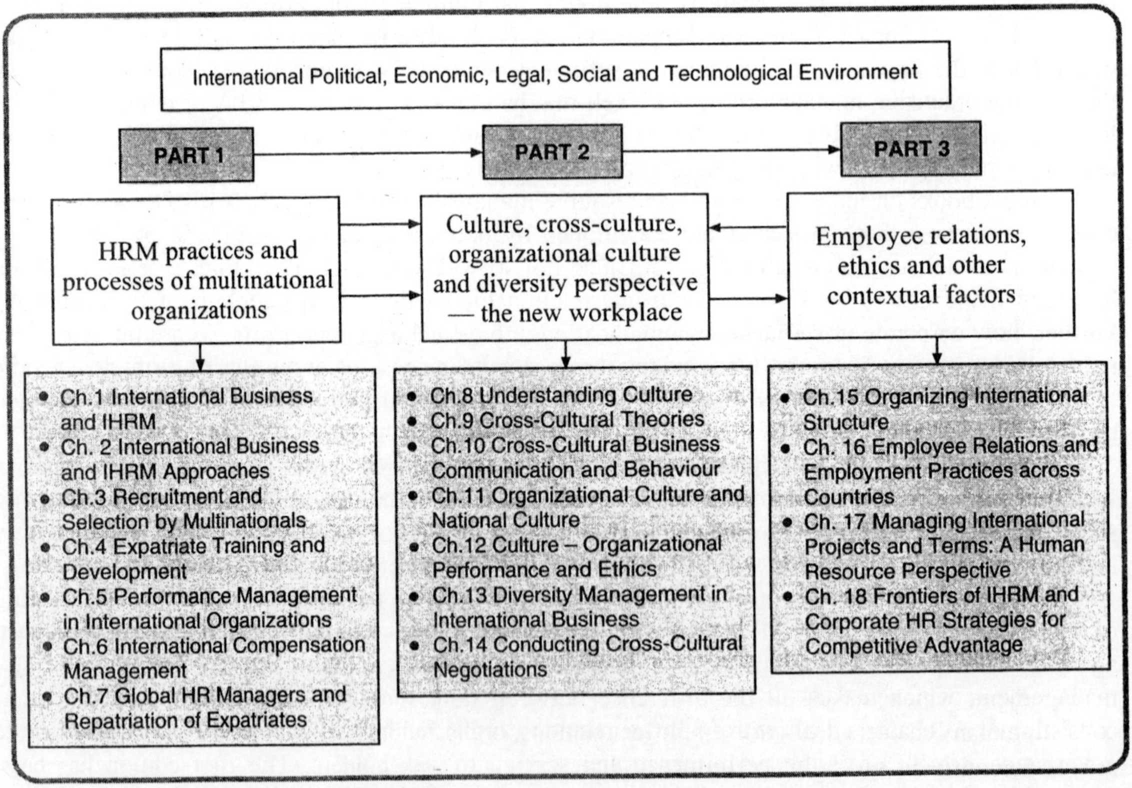

S C Gupta

CONTENTS

PART 2

PART 3

PART 1

1. International Business and IHRM
2. International Business and IHRM Approaches
3. Recruitment and Selection by Multinationals
4. Expatriate Training and Development
5. Performance Management in International Organisztions
6. International Compensation Management
7. Global HR Managers and Repatriation of Expatriates

Chapter 1

International Business and IHRM

LEARNING OBJECTIVES

After studying this chapter, you will be able to:

- *Understand the scope of IHRM (international human resource management)*
- *Learn the concept and approaches to the study of IHRM*
- *Understand what constitutes IHRM and how it is different from domestic HRM*
- *Learn interrelationship of human resources processes through human resource cycle*
- *Understand various factors that influence the IHRM practices in organizations*
- *Learn differences between domestic managers and international managers.*

OPENING CASE
IHRM (International Human Resource Management) Challenge

The Bonne Mare Group's CEO, Pierre Trollop, sits at his desk one afternoon reading his firm's recent press release in the local paper.

'The Bonne Mare Group has posted a 23 per cent increase in its 2006 earnings to a record of $ 41 million. The company based in Southern France sold 620 more boats in 2005, up 21 per cent from the previous year. The company exports to more than 40 countries with a total revenue of $ 350 million in 2006.' Bonne Mare Group's CEO is quite happy with his firm's performance as it is now firmly set in global business and its products are known for innovative design, quality and stability in even the roughest seas.

The Bonne Mare Group prides itself on combining personal craftsmanship with the latest technology. Currently, the boats are manufactured at the firm's Aix en Provence plant. Its five-year-growth plan includes steps to further increase its overseas markets while maintaining the flow of a new high quality boats for its customers. Despite this excellent news, Pierre Trollop is little troubled. During his visit to Germany he had been approached by three agents, one from Russia and two others from China and India respectively, who pointed out that economies of these countries were making significant gains. A growing number of individuals are getting rich and wealthy. They suggested to Trollop to open export offices in St. Petersburg, Beijing and Mumbai. Upon his return to office, Trollop asked his staff to provide a market research study about these emerging markets for expansion and also to think of part overseas manufacturing to further reduce labour and transport costs.

One problem that Trollop faces is how to staff these offices and manufacturing facilities in these countries. Given the characteristics of Bonne Mare's luxury products, and the unfamiliar nature of Russian, Chinese and Indian markets, he finds it more feasible to have his own people to head these overseas offices and plants – at least in the beginning. Unfortunately, no one in the Bonne Mare Group has any real knowledge about them. It is vital that managers deputed in these countries have extensive knowledge of Bonne Mare's custom cruisers, including technical manufacturing aspects. They must be able to 'mix, mingle and network' with wealthy and political figures as the cruisers sell for an average price of $ 600,000. Thus, potential buyers will represent a significant segment of these countries. Although these managers are experts in the technical performance features but no one speaks the languages of these countries or has knowledge of their culture, language and legal framework. Majority of these managers have working spouses thus making it difficult to send them alone for 2–3 years' assignment.

He called a meeting of his managers and discussed the issue with them. Everyone agreed about the growing opportunities in these markets but the questions as to how to quickly staff these markets with right people and select right entry strategies and implement them remain unanswered.

He felt an acute need for an IHRM expertise in his management team.

INTRODUCTION

Never in the history of mankind, goods, services and people have been moving across the countries at such a high rate. Globalization has thrown large opportunities and risks as well as challenges in global business. And this requires a new kind of organizational capability – having global managers who can operate in different countries, cultures, political, economic and legal environments where managers can mix, mingle and influence people to achieve organizational objectives. And people both inside and outside the organization are at the centre of this unique organizational capability. People play a key role in any type of business activity but their role has become very critical in new economy and services sector. Multinationals have emanated mostly from developed economies, which now control, about 50 per cent of world trade and 75 per cent of global GDP and dominate the service sector (60 to 80 per cent). Therefore, how multinationals manage their human resources, a vital resource (acquire, allocate, utilize and reward) becomes an important field of study and analysis. The direct cost of employing an expatriate manager is around 3-4 million dollars per annum and their cost of failure is very high taking into account indirect cost from business loss. This apart from the HR processes in international business are influenced by some additional factors, requiring high degree of coordination and integration. This area of study has come under the purview of International Human Resource Management.

THE CONCEPT OF INTERNATIONAL HUMAN RESOURCE MANAGEMENT

International Human Resource Management (IHRM) is the procurement, allocation, utilization, and motivation of human resources in the international business. In multinational organizations, the human resources managers deal with multiculturalism, performance management, dispersion, international taxation, relocation and foreign culture orientation in selecting and developing expatriate managers.

Whether one is conducting business in another country, competing against foreign firms at home, or hiring recent immigrants, he must deal with foreign cultures and languages. Every aspect of business is affected by cross-culture particularly, Human Resource Management. All of these increase the exposure and liabilities for HR managers creating new demands for internationally focused competencies.

IHRM requires, cultivation of ethical, performance oriented organizational culture, shared vision in all the subsidiaries so as to bring out synergy from all networked units. Perhaps the most important challenge is to foster such HR practices in all subsidiaries and business units that support differentiation and integration of the organization in a balanced manner with empowerment and support of all line managers. Another challenge for IHRM is the management of performance in all the networked subsidiaries.

Firms operating in international markets, face very different kind of conditions and competition. Multinationals are characterised by an interdependence of resources and responsibilities across all business units regardless of national boundaries. These companies try to cope with the large flows of components, products, resources, people and information among its subsidiaries, while simultaneously recognizing the distributed specialized resources and capabilities. As such, it demands a complex process of coordination and cooperation involving strong cross-unit integrating devices, a strong corporate identity and a well-developed worldwide management perspective. Since they look for opportunities in every country (markets, cheaper cost of capital, labour and raw materials) and react to threats by various means including fast withdrawal of resources, they have to necessarily deal with the national governments, which control entry and impose conditions of doing business in their territories, often safeguarding the interests of local firms and consumers. Hence the way multinationals do business requires high external focus and internal responsiveness.

In this perspective, national cultures also play a critical role by influencing the values, beliefs and behaviour of employees and customer preferences. Thus culture affects both internal and external perspectives of management, including the cost of doing the business and its results.

Since national cultures crucially influence these people management processes – motivation and decision-making, including negotiations and diplomacy – its study has also become necessary to understand the subject of IHRM.

The next approach to IHRM is the study of industrial relations and labour management practices and policies in different countries. Study of industrial relations in a country is very much reflective of its state of society, its historical evolution, power relationships between different groups, class struggle that is going on, its political framework and prevailing labour laws and its national culture. Industrial relations are also influenced by the strategies of major firms and their approach to labour management. This is a very wide field and encompasses the third approach to IHRM.

Since global managers are responsible for strategic responsibilities and policy making, IHRM is very close to strategic HRM.

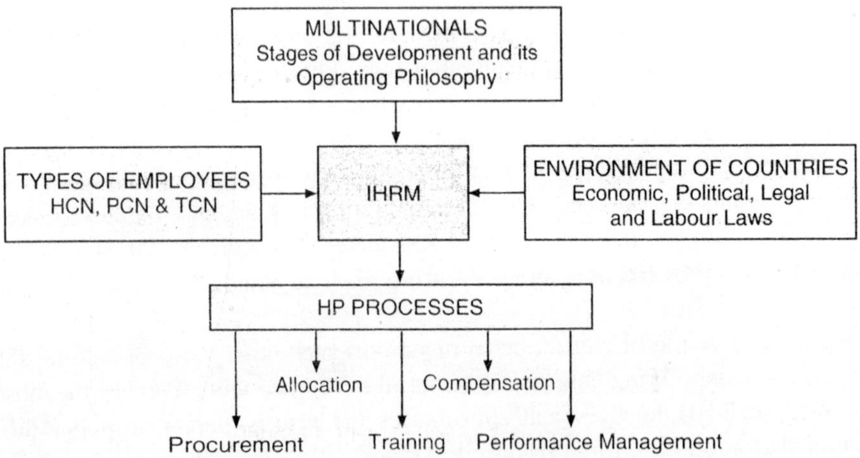

Fig. 1.1 Model of IHRM Showing its Important Dimensions

As Morgan has rightly defined IHRM is the process of procuring, allocating and effectively utilizing human resources in a multinational organization with an interplay of three dimensions:

1. Types of employees,
2. Country environments: political, economic, social, cultural and legal,
3. HR processes for recruitment, selection. training, development, compensation, performance management, employee relations, etc.

Types of International Employees

- *Parent country nationals:* Employees from the parent headquarters assigned to the venture, usually in the upper management positions.
- *Host country nationals:* Employees directly recruited and employed by the venture and are nationals of the host country. They may occupy all levels in the organization; however, initially they are usually not found in the upper management levels.
- *Third country nationals:* Employees who are nationals of neither the parent country nor the host country.

Apart from three types of employees, there is high degree of diversity at workplace due to gender, age, ethnicity, colour, backgrounds, religion and languages. This aspect makes IHRM much more complex in developing a shared vision, teamwork and designing of HR policies and planning for providing high employee satisfaction, conflict resolution methods and team-building processes.

The cultural aspect is so important that it is discussed in detail in Chapters 8, 9 and 10 in this book. The character of multinationals, their stage of development, their strategies and philosophy and predisposition are discussed in Chapter 2.

P. Morgan had presented a similar model of International Human Resource Management which is shown in Fig. 1.2.

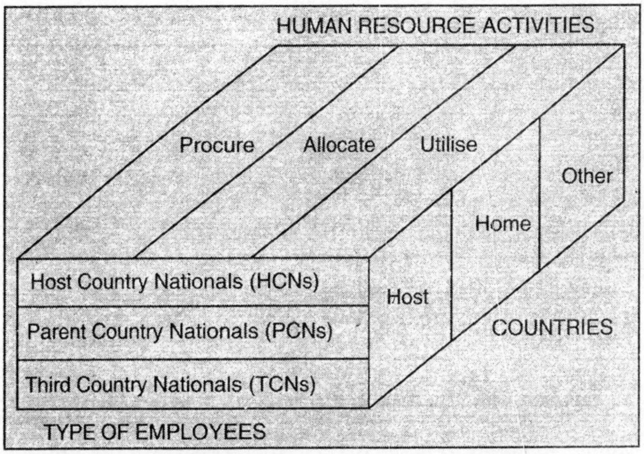

Fig. 1.2 Morgan's IHRM Model

Source: Adapted from P.V. Morgan, 1986. International human resource management. Fact or fiction, Personnel Administrator, vol. 31, no. 9, p. 44.

POLITICAL, ECONOMIC, SOCIAL, LEGAL AND CULTURAL ENVIRONMENT

Environment affects both domestic and international HRM but much more IHRM. The organization structure design in different subsidiaries and corporate whether mechanistic or organic depends upon environmental uncertainty and complexity. HR processes such as compensation design, employee and industrial relations depend mostly on the political and economic development of the country concerned.

In case of IHRM, the cultural diversity plays most critical impact. Social environment influences product design, marketing and their pricing. Environmental differences in different countries restrict development of uniform IHRM policies and organization culture at the headquarter and subsidiaries. For example, policies limiting employment of expatriates (Malaysia) and requiring extensive employment of host country nationals may be in place to encourage MNC to hire, train and develop local employees for senior positions. In developing countries the educational system may be rudimentary and local government views the presence of MNCs in the country as a means of developing local expertise. The per capita income and standard of living prevailing in any country decides the wage level and, therefore, the compensation structure to be adopted.

Contextual Factors that Influence IHRM

What makes the IHRM practices in various multinationals different? Of course, it is their strategic objectives and strategies they are pursuing to achieve them – which comes in the purview of strategic HRM. Apart from this, following factors also result in differences:

1. **The nature of industry:** Industries differ in having degree of competition. In some industries the competition is mostly from local firms and in others it is from global firms. Where the competition is mostly from local firms, the MNC can adopt HR processes and compensation structure similar to local firms. But in industries where competition is between global firms the HR processes and reward systems have to be much more sophisticated and performance oriented. Examples of such industries include semiconductors, aircraft, copiers, etc.
2. **Managerial and technological talent availability:** An MNC opening subsidiaries in Europe faces a much different IHRM challenge than one opening subsidiaries in say, western Africa.
3. **Reliance of MNC on home country markets:** Some MNCs such as General Motors have major market and dependence on its home country market, i.e. the US. Other MNCs such as Nokia, ABB, Electrolux and Nestle have their revenues coming mostly from their subsidiaries. MNCs which depend primarily on their home markets and marginally on subsidiaries are likely to impose their corporate HR processes elsewhere. While MNCs which depend primarily on their subsidiaries are likely to provide much more flexibility to their subsidiaries, e.g., Unilever.
4. **International experience of the firm:** Firms with extensive international experience have had the opportunity to develop more diverse methods of maintaining coordination and control over their foreign operation. Thus, they may focus less on centralized control of HR functions than do firms with little international experience. Newcomers to the global market place may view the international business environment as more unpredictable, higher in ambiguity and perhaps more threatening than more experienced global players. Not only the experience of the MNC as a whole but also that of its specific subsidiaries will affect the IHRM approach used. More the international experience, more confidence it is likely to place on host country nationals and decentralized HR policies.
5. **Method of business development:** In case of joint ventures and strategic alliances, the HR framework is likely to be greatly influenced by the business partner's HR approaches. On the other hand, wholly owned subsidiaries are likely to adopt corporate HR framework.

6. **Technology and the nature of products:** For technologically sophisticated products or services, the need to maintain specific production standards and quality control necessitates a greater degree of centralization of IHRM functions at the MNC's headquarters and home-country managers and technical personnel to monitor these standards. Similarly, competent employees may be selected, trained and posted more closely by headquarters while following a very decentralized HR policies for other group of employees. For example, the firm Interbrew adopts a very selective approach towards technical brewer function which it considers its core competency.
7. **Organizational culture:** Regardless of the national culture of a firm, each organization develops its own organization culture to integrate its subsidiaries and develops an image of one company. Unified culture also facilitates coordination and control and shared vision apart from employee transfer and decision-making process. Organizational culture is greatly influenced by HR practices and policies which in turn is influenced by desired corporate culture. Organizational culture is how people think, behave with each other and how things gets done. Shuttle differences come in organizational culture because it is primarily influenced by national cultures. This is again taken up in detail in Chapter 11.

DIFFERENCES BETWEEN INTERNATIONAL AND DOMESTIC HRM

Some would say that there is not much difference between HRM and IHRM and that essentially it is doing the same things, but doing them in a wider arena. The truth is not quite so. The international dimension brings with it a host of issues, which the domestic HR function would not normally get involved in. The practice of HRM in the international context is different from its domestic counterpart in a number of ways. These include:

1. **More activities:** Being responsible for a greater number of functions and activities, such as the selection, cross-cultural and diversity training, management of international assignees including repatriation, etc. Additional responsibilities like translation of language, both at headquarters and at the subsidiary level, organising schooling and housing for expatriates and providing administrative services.
2. **More expertise and knowledge:** Having to expand one's area of expertise to include a much broader knowledge of foreign country employment laws and global organization designs. Management of differential compensation due to variety of allowances and adjustments to compensate for different employment conditions and currency fluccuations.
3. **More involvement:** Having to get much more closely involved with employees' lives as the firm moves employees to foreign assignments. For example, collecting information and furnishing to visa authorities about Aids and other diseases or marital status of employees and looking after their interests and keep them informed about corporate news, developments, etc. when they are abroad.
4. **Handle wide nature of issues and problems:** Being involved with a greatly expanded and constantly changing mix of employees (from the host country and foreign locales), adding considerable diversity and complexity to the HR tasks.

5. **Manage more external pressures and responsibility:** Having to cope with more external influences, for example, having to consider the impact of foreign cultures and laws. Having to face greater exposure to problems and liabilities (for example, making mistakes in expatriate assignments can cost as much as US$ 4 million per assignee). The accumulated direct and indirect costs can be huge.
6. **Change in emphasis:** More emphasis on activities like international relocation and orientation, both pre-departure and post-departure cultural training. Knowledge of international taxation, rate of inflation and cost of living, including currency fluctuation. Diversity management, like managing people from different cultural and political backgrounds and gender differences.
7. **Strategic and coordination role:** More contacts with government officials for obtaining visas, tax certificates, fixing of meetings, and so on. Actively participate in strategic planning and implementation. More coordination and travel to assess performance of expatriates and solve problems.
8. **More risk management:** As there are increasing threats from terrorists, kidnappers and protecting intellectual property rights of firms, the IHR department may have to organize emergency evacuations from highly volatile locations like Middle East. Unfair hiring practices and promotions may result in a firm being charged with violation of legal provisions and facing media trial on people related and human right issues.
9. **More public relations work:** To enhance the multinationals image and deal with human rights and other NGOs and interest groups operating in different countries. IHR managers have to present the organization to different stakeholders and represent the company on important occasions and coordinate research in human relations and behaviour.

DIFFERENCES BETWEEN DOMESTIC AND INTERNATIONAL MANAGERS

Difference between domestic and international HRM can be better understood if one learns the differences between the competence level required in domestic and international managers, which are required to be procured and developed. To develop and manage a global business implies developing and managing people who can think, lead, and act from a global perspective, and who must possess a global mind as well as global skills. Not a dozen international specialists, but a multitude of executives, managers, and professionals are needed to form the core of a global firm. The characteristics that differentiate an international manager from a domestic one are:

1. Greater need for a 'global mindset'.
2. Have technical and people/communication skills.
3. Balance contradictions and live with conflict.
4. Oriented toward a process of continual change.
5. Be receptive to learning experiences and be skilled at exchanging information to others in the organization.
6. Know the potential for culture shock, and attempt to minimise its severity while taking advantage of the resulting adaptation.
7. Managers in subsidiaries usually have broader duties than do managers of similar-sized home-country operations.
8. International experience is often a necessity for career advancement with MNCs.

9. Political, economic and social sensitivity and knowledge of many countries.
10. Leadership and team-building should be of high order, so as to take decisions independently, keeping company as a whole in mind.

STRATEGIC ROLE OF INTERNATIONAL HR DEPARTMENT

As mentioned earlier that international HRM department has to participate and contribute in creating global strategies and implementing them in following areas:

1. Linking HRM strategies and processes to corporate strategic objectives and strategies.
2. Building a global culture, to encourage the development of managerial mindset and attitudes to make an integrated, networked organization which can cope with global competition.
3. Developing the leadership and management capability and structure to support global strategies and operations.
4. Gaining management support and involvement in human resource management.
5. Ensuring sufficient quality and depth of global managers to serve global customers.
6. Ensuring managers have the technical and managerial competence to work effectively at the global level.
7. Identifying and retaining highly qualified managers.
8. Developing global and local approaches to all HR processes as appropriate.
9. Ensuring management succession.
10. Sustaining and improving performance at all levels in all areas of the company.
11. Implementing global human resource systems for recruitment, performance management, training and development, succession planning, remuneration and benefits with geo-centric approach.
12. Establishing a total quality culture, and changing people's attitudes to quality.

The IHRM department's main objectives and role are to create a multi-cultural organization where diversity is valued as an asset and efforts are made to lookafter the interests of everyone irrespective of any bias of gender, colour, or nationality, age, background, etc. The department is actively engaged constantly in organization design and development to meet the changes in macro-environment and interests of all stakeholders. The prime task is to add values and enhance sustainable competitive advantage of all subsidiaries and headquarters. Thus IHRM plays a cutting-edge function if not the critical one.

HUMAN RESOURCE CYCLE

It was mentioned earlier that human resource processes remain basically same in domestic and international HRM. What are these processes and how are they different? In fact, the whole book is about these processes conducted in multinational business environment. Let us visit briefly the basic HR processes here which are to be dealt in great detail in multinational environment in this book.

They are best represented by Human Resource Cycle, which explains the main HR processes that contribute to organizational performance, be that domestic or international. In the human resource cycle presented by Tichy, Fombrun and Devenna, 'Selection Process', employee development process and reward system are the main variables that influence directly the 'performance' of any organization. The four generic processes; selection, performance-appraisal, rewards management and human resource development reflect sequential managerial tasks. The dependent variable in this cycle is performance and other elements in the cycle are designed to impact performance at the individual, team and the organizational level. Performance in other words, is a function of all the human resource components: selecting people who are able to best perform the job defined by the structure: motivating employees by rewarding them judiciously, training and developing people for future performance; and appraising employees in order to justify the rewards. In addition, performance is a function of organizational context and resources surrounding the individual. Thus, strategy and structure also impact performance through the ways the jobs are designed, how the organization is structured and through how well services and products are planned to meet environmental threats and opportunities. These basic human resource processes can be done at three levels: *strategic level* which deals with policy formulation and goal setting; *managerial level* which is concerned with the availability and allocation of resources to carry out the strategic plan, and at operational level to carry out day-to-day activities.

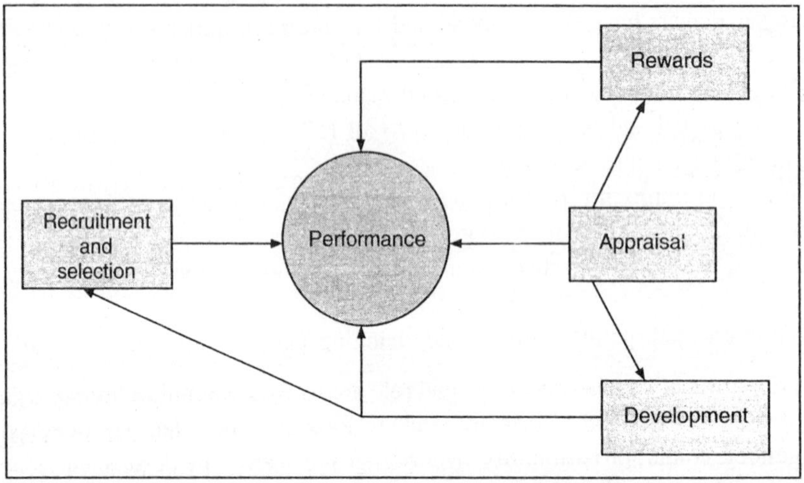

Fig. 1.3 Sequential Managerial Tasks: The Human Resource Cycle

All the HR processes are interrelated and influence each other. It is this interrelationship that should be realized in designing HR policy framework. In IHRM, the main focus is on achieving performance of entire network of subsidiaries as a whole and also individually. But whole organization is the main objective of IHRM.

Most multinationals are high performance organizations and their HR architecture is special as described by Pfeffer enumerates who enumerates seven human resource practices that seem to distinguish between high-achieving firms and poor performers. They are as follows (Universalism Concept of HRM):

1. **Hiring the right people:** It means more than just securing employees who possess the knowledge, skills and abilities required to perform a particular job; these people must also be able to acquire new knowledge and skills as jobs and environment change. In addition,

employees must find that the work is satisfying and that overall organizational climate and reward structure meets their needs. They spend great amount of resources and effort in selecting the best and better than their competitors. They select people for values and culture compatibility too. This is their core competency and in labour markets where there is shortage it results in 'war for talent', which they (labour markets) always win.

2. **Incentive pay:** If employees are expected to behave in extraordinary ways and add value to the firm, sharing the gain with employees meets the workplace justice and fairness. Some form of performance-contingent pay is required if employees are expected to be persistent in their efforts to add value to the firm. If employees believe that their contributions are instrumental in enhancing firm performance and increasing profitability, they will want to share in the benefits. How this is done, is again strategic and important. (Individual level or group level or unit level or company level and in what proportion?). We believe the key is to link rewards to the particular behaviours required of employees and to make sure that all relevant behaviours – like dependability, quality and quantity of output, generation of new ideas or cooperation – are encouraged.
3. **Employee ownership:** Employees can share the ownership of firm by holding company's stock. By making employees shareholders of the company, the conflict between capital and labour gets reduced. This puts the performance – pay contingency at organizational level.
4. **Training and skill development:** High-performing firms display a greater commitment to training and skill development than their counterparts. This core HRM activity is related to 'Kaizen'. However, knowledge and skill acquisition will not lead to improved firm performance unless employees are allowed and encouraged to use job-related knowledge and skills when performing their job. Thus, firms must take care to select people who are willing to learn and adopt and also establish rewards that encourage employees to participate in training.
5 **Cross-utilization and cross-training:** Training and development should also lead to 'flexibility' so that employees are utilized even during production slowdowns. When people are able to perform multiple jobs, or are multi-skilled, they represent a reserve of talent and are more likely to appreciate how their work and output levels affect the work of other employees in jobs related to their own.
6. **Symbolic Egalitarianism:** If the goal is to increase communication between and across organizational levels, a case can be made for reducing sub-divisions in job grades and other areas of inequality. Firms must signal with practices and policies that all are equal.
7. **Wage compression:** The relative pay differences between people at various organization levels can have profound effects on employee perceptions. These perceptions in turn, can affect wide variety of employee attitudes and behaviours. Current theory and empirical evidence suggest that if the goal is to increase the level of cooperating and team orientation, pay differences between jobs should be reduced. Note that this concerns pay distinctions at the level of job, not at the level of individual. That is, incentive pay is distinguished from pay hierarchy compression. This of course depends on HR strategy to be adopted.

In fact, the organization culture of all high-performing organizations is people-centric and team-centric where people are highly valued and empowered.

ISSUES IN IHRM

Before 1986, most written material on international HR focused on managing international assignments, usually from an American perspective. Many current books and articles are still written from a domestic point of view, but the literature is becoming considerably broader in scope. The quantity and quality of such material have increased dramatically in the past five years. The following topics have been most prevalent:

- **Managing international assignments:** This continues to be the most popular topic. Articles about the selection, training, compensation and repatriation of expatriates abound, as do discussions on the causes, costs and frequency of expatriate failures. Many articles refer to expatriate management as the major concern of HR managers in multinational corporations.
- **Selecting the right person for a foreign assignment:** This is critical for success. Expatriates must be personally adaptable and their families capable of adjusting to new and unusual challenges. Orientation and training are enormously valuable in helping expatriates and their families adjust to the new culture and learn a new language. Compensation plans for expatriates are usually complex and expensive because of the taxes, allowances and premiums. Repatriation can be traumatic and difficult for returning executives, and the transition back home needs to be planned as carefully as the move abroad.

BOX 1.1 IHRM BECOMEING MORE COMPLEX

Mr. Iwata is a Japanese citizens who served as chairman and president of Matsumoto from October 1, 1996 to November 1997. Matsumoto a Japanese subsidiary of Striker, is a distributor of medical products exclusively in Japan. Mr. Iwata was living in the US as a resident alien when he was hired by Matsumoto, then moved back to Japan to serve as the company president. He lived in Japan until he was dismissed by Matsumoto in November 1997. At this time Mr. Iwata moved back to US as a resident alien and filed a Title VII suit claiming a race and national origin discrimination as well as age discrimination under Age Discrimination in Employment Act. The defendant Striker and Matsumoto, had challenged the district court's subject-matter jurisdiction. Does the Civil Rights Act of 1991 allows extra territorial application of Title VII and ADEA?

The Court's Decision

The US district court found that it did not have subject-matter jurisdiction over Mr. Iwata's claim. The Civil Rights Act 1991 which amended Title VII of 1964 states that "with respect to employment in a foreign country , such term (employee) includes an individual who is a citizen of US". Language in the ADEA which defines a covered employee is identical. Mr. Iwata was at no time a citizen of US, the court concluded that Mr. Iwata was not a protected employee under Title VII or the IDEA. Thus the court rejected Mr. Iwata's claim.

- **Culture, communication and language:** International HR professionals are expected to understand the implications of cultural differences between countries and their interplay with differing corporate cultures. They often are responsible for seeing that expatriates are trained to adapt to cultural differences and overcome culture shock. Also, HR professionals play an important role in resolving 'cultural wrinkles' in international joint ventures, mergers and acquisitions. Expatriate managers must learn the foreign language or rely on interpreters to communicate with the local workforce. Parent company officials may struggle to communicate with local managers in foreign subsidiaries. Because human resource professionals are often expected to foster international communication, they must understand that effective communication involves more than just speaking the same language: To communicate effectively, individuals must share the deeper meanings that are often tied to cultural norms and traditions.

- **Legal aspects:** Because of multi-country employment by MNCs IHRM has become more complex as a case of Mr. Iwata in the box describes. Companies should carefully analyze the status of employees and subsidiaries to determine whether they are covered under home country or host country Acts.

Challenges to Effective Global HRM

There are a number of unique problems that global companies face while trying to implement consistent practices across their global HR networks. These problems act as effective barriers to effective Global HRM. These are:

- *Variation in country environments:* The biggest challenge is also the most obvious: the worldwide variations in social, political, and economic circumstances. An HR practice that works in one country may be unacceptable in another. Fluctuations in currency, government regulations, compensation expectations, job security, and learning styles are just a few examples of the local variations a global HR professional faces. Currently, there's European legislation that prohibits a company from sharing employment records across geographical boundaries without the employee's permission – a potential threat to global staffing.
- *Perception of HR:* Another global challenge is that the perceived value of HR function varies across locations. In one country, HR may be perceived as a true business partner, working with high-level managers on critical strategic assessments. In another country but within the same company, HR may be viewed as a transactional personnel department that handles administrative work.
- *Attitude and actions of headquarters toward HR:* These help determine how seriously the HR function is viewed locally. The position of the corporate chief HR officer also sends a strong signal to local units on the importance of the HR function.
- *Resistance to change:* The rate of change is much higher in multinational organizations. Hence a major challenge facing global HR practitioners is that different locations have their own way of doing things and resisting change. If an HR initiative that is viewed as corporate is imposing on the local HR staff, then it can be difficult to gain acceptance from the field. That's true regardless of whether it's a US multinational 'forcing' initiatives on its local business or a German company 'forcing' policies and practices on its international businesses.
- *Balance:* International companies must strive to achieve the appropriate balance between global and local HR systems and practices. It is such firms that put into application the best practices and create a benchmark for others to follow. Some of such best practices are:
    - Establishing common systems in all locations, including accounting, distribution, marketing, and management information systems.

- Creating an organizational mission based on inputs from individuals or teams in all locations.
- Providing management education in all locations about how the company wants to conduct business.
- Creating a written manual about how parent organizations will institute and manage unique corporate identity.
- Communicating to all locations that the parent organization is attempting to create a common corporate culture with shared values, mission, goals and more.

- *Diversity:* Consider diversity as an asset and cross-cultural aspects as a challenge.

Review Questions

1. Explain the concept of international human resource management as distinct from domestic human resource management.
2. What are the major issues and barriers to IHRM?
3. Explain the scope of activities of HR managers in global organizations.
4. Explain various factors that influence IHRM practices amongst MNCs.
5. Discuss the scope of IHRM subject and its approaches.
6. Explain how international HRM is different from domestic HRM and what are the approaches for study of this subject?

Assignment

In groups, study any two websites out of the following useful websites and present your research and insight gained in the class.

1. http://www.shrm.org
2. http://www.shrmglobal.org
3. http://www.albworld.org
4. http://www.chrim.org
5. http://www.ipma.hr.org
6. http://www.fcdee.com/index.com
7. http://www.windhemint.com
8. http://www.meridianglobal.com
9. http://www.expat.repat.com
10. http://www.livingabroad.com
11. http://www.ilo.org

Chapter

2

International Business and IHRM Approaches

LEARNING OBJECTIVES

After studying this chapter, you will be able to:

- *Explain various growth stages through which domestic firms evolve into transnational corporations*
- *Understand what challenges IHRM faces in various growth stages*
- *Human resource management strategy and practices in a firm's international evolution*
- *Comprehend how human resource management policies and practices influence organizational performance and effectiveness of global companies*
- *Learn the qualities required in executives managing global enterprises.*

OPENING CASE
How Does One Define a Global Company?

Ask ten different executives the question 'what is a global company?' and, more likely than not, you are likely to get ten different answers. Some might argue that a global company is one that is pursuing customers in all major economies – North America, Europe and Asia. Others might argue that you are not really global unless you put down roots in every major market in the form of producing locally what you sell locally. Yet others might suggest that the real test of globalization lies instead in whether your business unit headquarters are globally dispersed, whether your top management team consists of individuals from different nationalities, and so forth.

There are two problems with each of these perspectives. *First*, each definition overlooks the fact that globalization is a multidimensional phenomenon and, like the proverbial elephant, can never be understood fully from just one perspective – be it market presence, production bases, composition of the top management team or any other. *Second*, each definition overlooks the fact that globality is a continuous variable along a spectrum from low to high rather than a categorical binary variable with only two extreme values, global vs. non-global.

I believe that the concept of 'corporate globality' should be viewed as a four-dimensional construct based on the premise that an enterprise can be more or less global along each of four major characteristics: globalization of market presence; globalization of supply chain; globalization of capital base; and globalization of mindset (see Fig. 2.1).

The first dimension – globalization of market presence – refers to the extent to which the company targets its customers in all major markets within its industry throughout the world. Even within the same industry, globalization of its market presence can range from very low to very high. Table 2.1 presents a comparative data on the inter-regional dispersion of sales for selected firms in the information technology industry. As the data indicates, in 1993, NTT of Japan was the least globalized company on this dimension. In comparison IBM, Sun Microsystems and Cannon appeared to be among the most globalized companies.

The second dimension – globalization of supply chain – refers to the extent to which the company is accessing the most optimal locations for the performance of various activities in its supply chain. It is entirely possible for a company to have a fair local or regional market presence and yet a highly globalized value chain, or vice versa. For example, in 1999, as a key element of the turnaround strategy for British retailer Marks & Spencer, CEO Peter Salesbury announced plans to set up a global supply chain for apparel goods with manufacturing hubs in Portugal, Morocco and Sri Lanka. Toyota is another good example of a company with a global supply chain. At the end of 1995, Toyota produced about two-thirds of all its cars in Japan; the remaining one-third were produced in wholly or partially owned affiliates in 25 foreign countries spread over the Americas, Europe and Asia. Furthermore, the company exported 38 per cent of its domestic production to foreign markets. Aside from this flow of capital, goods and know-how between Japan and affiliates, Toyota also engaged in significant intra-firm flows among the affiliates. For example, within its South East Asian regional network, it exported diesel engines from Thailand, transmissions from Philippines, steering gears from Malaysia and engines from Indonesia.

The third dimension – globalization of capital base – refers to the extent to which the company is tapping into the most optimal sources of capital on a worldwide basis. The Hong Kong-based Internet Service Provider China.com represents a good example of how it is possible for a company to be quite 'local' along the dimension of the market presence as well as supply chain, and yet have a highly globalized capital base. In 1999, China.com's market base and operations were centred primarily around Hong Kong and China. Yet, during that year the company chose to get itself listed on the US-based NASDAQ. A listing on NASDAQ could potentially yield many benefits for China.com, including less expensive capital, enhanced ability to use stock options for attracting top talent and enhanced ability to make stock based acquisitions.

Last but not the least, the fourth dimension – globalization of corporate mindset – refers to the extent to which the corporation collectivity reflects an understanding of diversity across cultures and markets coupled with an ability to integrate across this diversity. The state of any enterprise's corporate mindset depends on the minds of individuals who lead the enterprise as well as the organization that determines how these individuals interact, what information is collected, how it is processed, and how decisions are made.

General Electric serves as a good example of a company with an increasingly global mindset. All GE businesses are managed through a global line of business structure, investment opportunities are identified and assessed on a global basis. Corporate leaders push hard to globalize 'the intellect of the company', which has a strong worldwide corporate culture, the composition of the leadership itself is becoming increasingly diverse in terms of nationalities.

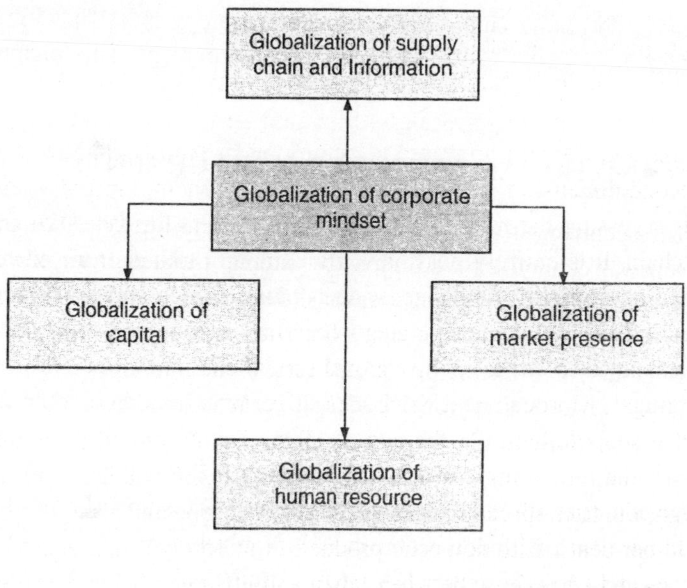

Fig. 2.1 Schematic Showing Assessment of Corporate Globality

Table 2.1 Inter-Regional Distribution of IT Sales for Selected Companies, 1993 (figures are in per cent of total company sales)

Comapny	*North America*	*Europe*	*Asia*
IBM	41	33	16
Fujitsu	6	26	65
Hewlett-Packard	51	34	9
NEC	6	4	88
Compaq	45	38	5
Cannon	30	29	37
Sun Microsystems	51	24	23
NTT	0	0	100
Microsoft	56	30	9

INTRODUCTION

With the advancement of transport systems and convergence of telecommunication, internet and information technology, the world has become a global village. International agreements on trade and tariffs at WTO and the end of cold war have accelerated the globalization process. Indian economy and business is also integrating fast with world economy after India has embarked on liberalization and privatization. Many companies in different countries are going global and in this process, management of human resource has a crucial role to play. To be successful in international business, organizational structure, corporate culture and corporate strategy must fit with each other and must enable the organization to respond fast to the external environment. This chapter will discuss these aspects.

GLOBALIZATION AND HUMAN RESOURCE MANAGEMENT

A fundamental shift is occurring in world economy, politics and lifestyle. We are moving away from a world in which national economies were closed systems, isolated from each other by barriers to cross-border trade and investment for many reasons. These trade and non-trade related barriers are slowly disappearing due to the realization that cooperation and not confrontation is the answer to global prosperity. Regional or bilateral free-trade agreements have become important aspects of a country's trade policies. Over 300 regional trade agreements and free trade areas are currently in different stages of negotiations. Trade theories had an impact on this thinking, and as a result of WTO, world trade in goods and services has increased much faster than world production every year (nearly US$ 1 billion worth trade is taking place everyday). This upsurge in global trade has thrown unprecedented opportunities and threats to business organizations.

Organizations, being open systems, have to continuously adapt and respond by processing information faster, making sense of randomly occurring global events, mastering new technologies by developing or hiring appropriate skills, bringing out new products and services faster with improved quality and at competitive prices.

Appropriate response by organizations to globalization requires empowerment of people, flexible structure, adaptable organizational culture and right type of human resource policies and practices, which are in congruence with corporate strategy both at multinational's headquarter and at a subsidiary level.

The subject of organization culture and structure have been covered in separate chapters in this book. The case of strategy at 'Hewlett-Packard' brings out the close relationship between corporate strategy, structure, organizational culture and human resource practices and policies.

Figure 2.2 starts with an analysis of the environment within which an organization exists, and which it seeks to control or survive in through certain strategies. These strategies once defined, require certain desired behaviours if they are to be achieved. If, for example, a bank is planning to move to more customer-focused, sales-driven approach, and away from an emphasis on regulations and procedures and central bureaucratic control, then the attitudes, skills and behaviours of its staff will have to change. These desired behaviours will be produced by certain human resource strategies. People have to know what to do, develop a desire to do it and be able to do it. In case of the bank, this change will require changes in training (for customer care skills), in job description (which will now specify business and performance targets), in management style (greater discretion) and direction (towards new business), in internal assessment procedures (the use of assessment centres), in organizational structure (more decentralized), and in culture (away from rule-compliance towards a more commercial, entrepreneurial approach).

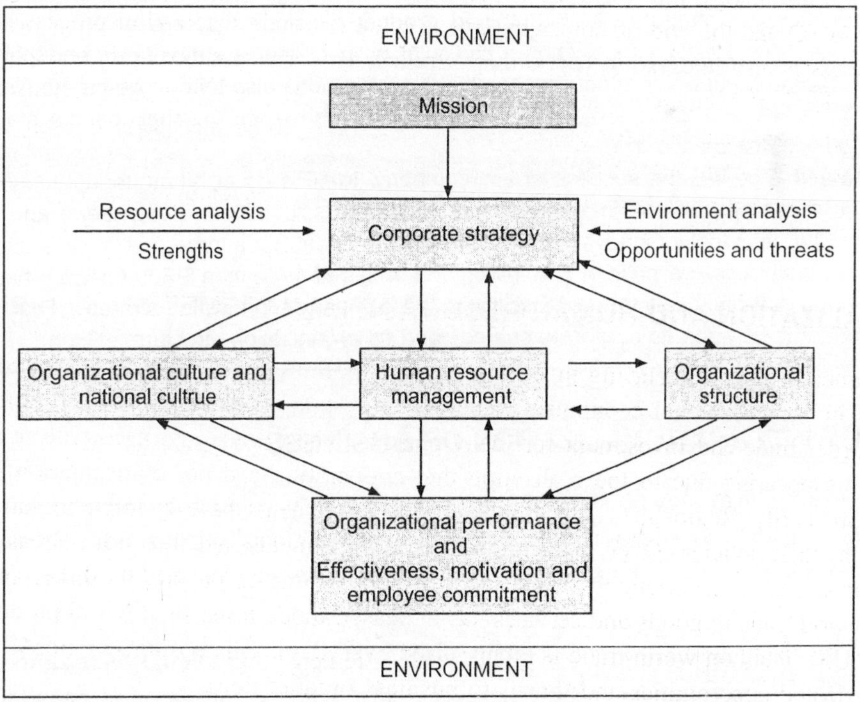

Fig. 2.2 Factors Influencing Organizational Performance

As can be seen in Fig. 2.2, environmental opportunities and threats influence corporate strategy design. This in turn influences three internal constituent variables, which subsume all aspects of organization, which have an impact on employee behaviour: structure, culture and human resource practices, and one fundamental conceptual assumption – that of integration or appropriateness. If these are 'appropriate', they will produce the desired behaviour. The degree of 'fit' achieved will affect the relationship between behaviour and strategy, and the level of achievement of organization goals. In practice, it is difficult to achieve this integration. In case of IHRM an overarching dimension of national cultures prevails, which influences all the variables of performance shown in the model in Fig. 2.2.

BOX 2.1 STRATEGY AT HEWLETT-PACKARD

Hewlett-Packard (HP) is the world's largest manufacturer of test and measurement instruments as well as a major producer of electronic calculators and computers. From its very beginning, HP has pursued a strategy that brings products of scientific research into industrial application while maintaining the collegial atmosphere of a university laboratory. The firm has concentrated on advanced technology and offers mostly state-of-the-art products to a variety of industrial and consumer markets. HP's strategy is to pursue actively a given product line and market as long as the company has a distinctive technological or design advantage. But when products reach the stage where success depends primarily on low costs and highly competitive prices, HP typically moves out of that market and turns its attention to a new design or an entirely new product.

HP's strategy of technological innovation is supported by a highly flexible organization structure. It is organized around integrated self-contained product divisions that are given a great deal of independence. New divisions arise when a particular product line becomes large enough to support its continued growth out of the profit it generates. New divisions also tend to be created when single divisions get to about 2,000 people. HP has found that above this number, people start to loose identification with the product line.

A lot of factors go into the success of any company. In HP's case, it has undoubtedly been very effective at identifying profitable markets, hiring competent scientists and engineers, and creating a corporate culture that fosters innovation and high performance. But a large part of HP's success – as typified by annual sales in excess of $ 10 billion and profits of more than $ 830 million – has been the development of a flexible structure that facilitates the company's innovation strategy. That is, HP has found the right fit between its corporate strategy and its organization structure.

STAGES OF INTERNATIONALIZATION OF BUSINESS

A domestic firm evolves slowly, starting from exporting to becoming an international company, a multinational, a global organization and then into a transnational organization. By no means this growth is always sequential; firms can jump stages. These stages are identified by certain characteristics (Fig. 2.3).

Domestic firms: Many well-known firms like Nestle, Siemens, and Digital were domestic firms to start with. Many scholars consider this as a necessary stage where companies understand their markets, customers, perfect their technologies and products, and learn to operate business.

International firms: A domestic firm begins the internationalization process when it is involved in direct and indirect exporting, importing, and licensing, franchising, manufacturer's contract, technical agreements or joint ventures. At some point after this stage is reached, a firm gains experience of markets through interactions with foreign businesses and knowledge of local cultures and customs, resulting in increase in its risk-bearing capacity. It remains categorized as international until it begins to invest directly in wholly-owned foreign subsidiaries. The orientation of firm is erhnocentric.

Multinational firms: Here the company needs the ability to understand markets in several countries and develops expertise to suit its business and products to the requirements of these markets. At this stage resource commitment is at a bigger scale and involvement with governments and politics on a higher plane.

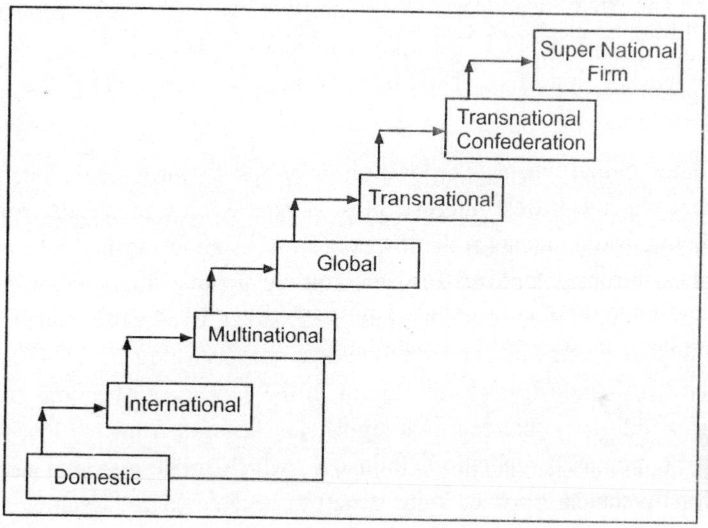

Fig. 2.3 Stages of Internationalization

Different writers have suggested number of criteria to categorize a company as a multinational. These are listed as follows:

- A corporation that conducts business in two or more countries in such volume that well-being and growth rest in more than one country and management must make decisions on the basis of multinational alternatives.
- A non-financial enterprise with base of operations in one country and more or less with integrated (producing-servicing) subsidiaries located in several foreign nations.
- A manufacturing company that does business in several countries: it has a substantial commitment to its resources in international business, it engages in international production in a number of countries, and it has a worldwide perspective in its management.
- A multinational firm that allocates company resources without regard to national frontiers but is nationally based in terms of ownership and top management.

- A company that seeks to operate strategically on a global scale.
- Any firm that performs its main operations in at least two countries.
- A firm that owns income-generating assets in more than one country. To qualify for this label, a company should operate in six or more countries and its business should be important enough to influence its overall politics and actions. In practice, multinationals whose annual sales is less than one billion dollars can be ignored.

Strategically, a multinational corporation (MNC) competes with other MNCs and local competitors on a market-by-market basis. Each individual subsidiary competes in its home country as an essentially autonomous operation. Control is largely decentralized and it is expected to make decisions on local R&D, production, distribution and marketing. Its success is measured by its actual versus expected earnings and growth. The MNC headquarter exercises worldwide financial control and coordination as well as postings of key personnel in different subsidiaries. They exhibit polycentric orientation. Singer is perhaps the world's first MNC (1862-63) and Bata is the first MNC that set up operations in India (1921).

Global: A firm becomes global when a corporation develops a coordinated system that searches the world to borrow money at the lowest interest rates, purchases raw materials from anywhere at the lowest price, manufactures components at the lowest cost, sells goods at the highest profits and invests its gains for the highest returns. A global firm acts on the premise that the entire world is a single entity. It emphasizes global operations over the domestic market. It selects best people for management regardless of nationality. It locates its corporate headquarter anywhere in the world.

The nature of the firm's industry is a key factor in the decision to become global. Globalization is most appropriate for industries that can gain significant benefits from worldwide volume in terms of reduced unit cost or increased reputation. Industries which fulfil customer needs common to all cultures and countries by standard products are suited to become firms. Examples of such industries include automobiles, steel, chemicals, petroleum, cement, agricultural commodities, pharmaceuticals, banking, insurance, computers, publishing, telecommunication and commerce.

Strategically, the global manufacturer cuts costs and increases price competitiveness by developing a worldwide production configuration that maximizes comparative advantage and economies of scale. The global enterprise 'rationalizes' its operations by creating an optimal synergetic mix in which each subsidiary specializes in a part of the production (for example, components may be produced in subsidiaries where labour is cheapest or taxes are low).

The global marketer bases the firm's marketing strategies on a few standardized world markets rather than on many customized markets. The corporation offers globally standardized products that are advanced, functional and reliable and above all, relatively low priced. The global firm does not completely reject product customization and differentiation, but adjusts to differences in product preferences only after exhausting all efforts to retain standardization. The global firms views the world as homogeneous where technological advances have reduced transportation and communications costs, softened governmental constraints, and narrowed national, social and economic differences. They adopt geo-centric orientation.

Transnational firms: Transnationalization is an advanced stage of multinationalization in which nationals of different countries hold shares of the company. While multinationals are nationally owned and managed, transnational enterprises (TNEs) are internationally owned and controlled. In these enterprises, national identities are transcended, thus eliminating home country bias in decision-making.

Firms pursuing the transnational strategy focus on the simultaneous attainment of local and experience economies, local responsiveness, global learning, multidirectional transfer of core competency or skills. They are centralized in some functions like finance and R&D but decentralized in marketing, distribution and procurement. Three frequently used criteria for assessing the globalization levels of a business unit are:

1. Share of foreign assets,
2. Share of sales beyond the national boundaries, and
3. Percentage of employment of foreign nationals.

The difference between a transnational and global firm is that a transnational lays equal emphasis on national responsiveness and global economies of scale. It is able to combine the advantages of both. It exihibits both geo-centric and region-centric orientation.

Transnational confederations: The most successful future business companies may be small- or medium-sized companies rather than giant corporations. Known as 'transnational confederations' they will ideally be located close to the market and using the economy of scope to produce great varieties of relatively customised products at remarkably low prices.

The characteristics of transnational confederations are as follows:

- Primarily organized around technology, design and marketing.
- A small- or medium-sized company, rather than a large company.
- Stages of production performed by subcontractors, rather than by subsidiaries or branches.
- Primarily a managing or marketing company.
- Composed of two parts, one that designs and markets product worldwide and the other that manufactures the products.

A super national firm would be a transnational firm that is legally denationalized by becoming incorporated through an international agency. The primary role of the world corporation will be the coordination of a transcultural, total-mankind-oriented approach to shaping the human system of living. The world corporation will link governments, businesses and universities to marshal the resources of science and technology to redesign the society's resources. The evolution of international business from simple export-trading companies into world organizations may neutralise the destructive competitiveness among-nation states by working for the common good of mankind.

The evolution or growth of a domestic firm through different stages requires different HR architecture and organization structure. Thus IHRM is characterized by faster rate of change management consequently leadership style.

Table 2.1 Comparison of Different Approaches

Structure and Control	*International*	*Multinational*	*Global*	*Transnational*
Centralization of decision-making	Core competencies centralized, rest decentralized	Decentralized	Most functions centralized	Mix of centralization and decentralization
Horizontal differentiation	Worldwide product based	Worldwide geography based	Product- and market-based matrix	Informal matrix
Need for coordination	Moderate	Low	High	Very high
Integrating mechanism	Few	None	Many	Many
Performance ambiguity	Moderate	Low	High	Very high
Cultural conflict	Moderate	Low	Very high	High

INDEX OF TRANSNATIONALITY

The United Nations Conference on Trade and Development (UNTAD) in its annual survey of foreign direct investment, calculates what it refers to as an index of 'transnationality', which is an average of ratios of foreign assets to total assets; foreign sales to total sales; and foreign employment to total employment. The top ten multinationals are as follows:

1. Rio Tinto (UK/Australia)
2. Thomson Corporation (Canada)
3. ABB (Switzerland)
4. Nestle (Switzerland)
5. Britis American Tobacco (UK)
6. Electrolux (Sweden)
7. Interbrew (Belgium)
8. Anglo American (UK)
9. AstraZeneca (UK)
10. Philips Electronic (The Netherlands)

MANAGEMENT ORIENTATION OR APPROACH

Corporate management orientation or approach decides how a firm views the world in relation to itself and how it wants to manage human resources in different countries. This mindset of a company (paradigms) can either help or inhibit a firm's ability to conduct global operations. Corporate culture and management philosophy, to a great extent, decide the formulation and implementation of corporate and operational strategies and their evolution into various stages of internationalization. Companies involved in world trade and investment can be divided into four types based on their management approach and corporate philosophy:

- Ethnocentric
- Polycentric
- Regiono-centric
- Geo-centric

They are present in different stages of evolution of a multinational firm.

ETHNOCENTRIC ORGANIZATION

Companies which are in the international stage of evolution exhibit ethnocentrism. Their motto is: 'this works in my country; therefore, it must work in other countries also.' In ethnocentric orientation, the home-country's culture and work practices are sought to be imposed on subsidiaries. The MNC tries to impose its HR policies and practices of headquarters on all other business units. These are home-country oriented organizations. For example, when a Japanese corporation invests in Mexico, Japan is the home-country and Mexico is the host country. If the Japanese corporation is ethnocentric, it will expect Mexicans to accept the inherent superiority of Japan. Investments will be made on the condition that Mexico accepts the Japanese methods of conducting business. Ethnocentric corporations believe that home-country nationals are more intelligent, reliable and trustworthy than foreign nationals. They centre all key management positions in the domestic headquarters and recruit home-country nationals for all international positions. Foreign managers and employees are second-class corporate citizens. When rewards are distributed, home-country nationals receive the lion's share.

Many internal and external influences foster this approach. Owners' and stockholders' perceptions may limit the CEOs' powers. Labour unions may pressurize in favour of domestic employment. Home-government policy may force emphasis on domestic markets.

The staffing policy of these companies is to fill all key positions by parent-country nationals. This practice was very widespread at one time. Firms such as Proctor & Gamble, Philips NV and Matsushita originally followed it. Even today in most Japanese and South Korean companies such as Toyota, Matsushita, and Samsung, key international postings are held by home-country nationals. There are three reasons why companies follow this policy. One is their belief that the host country lacks qualified individuals to fill senior management positions. Second, the firm may see an ethnocentric staffing policy as the best way to maintain a unified corporate culture. Third, if the firm is trying to create value by transferring a core competency to a foreign operation, it may believe that the best way to do this is to transfer parent-country nationals, who have knowledge of that competency, to the foreign operations.

This approach is not only reflected in the staffing policy but in all other areas such as performance appraisal where evaluation format is designed and administered by parent-nationals and new product development is done in the home country.

Many international companies exhibit this ethnocentric philosophy. They have difficulty in communicating in different languages and accepting cultural differences. But ethnocentrism limits strategic alternatives to entry modes, such as exporting, licensing and turnkey operations.

POLYCENTRIC ORGANIZATIONS

Polycentrism is an outward-oriented culture where individuals follow the St. Ambrose maxim 'When in Rome do as the Romans do. When you are elsewhere live as they live elsewhere.' Organizations following this philosophy are host country oriented. They see profit potential in a foreign country but find the foreign market difficult to understand. The polycentric message is: 'Local people know what is best for them. Let us give them some money and leave them alone as long as they make us a profit.' Polycentrism means that MNC seeks to adapt to the local cultural needs of subsidiaries by modifying the product and management policies even rules to suit local needs.

The polycentric firm is a loosely connected group with quasi-independent subsidiaries as profit centres. Home-country nationals staff headquarters, while local nationals occupy key positions in their respective local subsidiaries. No foreign national can seriously aspire to a senior position at headquarters. Headquarter keeps check through financial and posting of key persons.

Governmental pressures and foreign laws often necessitate polycentric approach. The local government may be a major customer and insist on local ways of doing business and local standards to be adopted. Many multinationals adopt this approach because they face heterogeneous environments in which product preferences may be the deciding factor and strategies are to be developed on a market-by-market basis.

There are several advantages in following a polycentric staffing policy. It is economical and executives in subsidiaries understand the culture and customs as well as how to go about managing government, suppliers and customers. However, there may be resentment among the senior executives, as they cannot get corporate positions at headquarters and will be restricted in posting to their home-country only. There are problems in coordination between units and transfer of core competencies from one unit to another or from home-country to host country. The federation that may result from a polycentric approach can also result in inertia within the firm. After decades of polycentric staffing policy, food and detergent giant Unilever found that shifting from multi-domestic strategic posture to a transnational posture was very difficult. Unilever's foreign subsidiaries had evolved into quasi-autonomous operations, each with its own strong national identity. These 'little kingdoms' objected to corporate hindquarter's attempts to limit their autonomy and to rationalise global manufacturing.

REGIONO-CENTRIC ORGANIZATION

These are regionally oriented organizations. A corporation implements a regional strategy when synergistic benefits can be obtained by sharing functions across regions. The corporation believes that only regional insiders can effectively coordinate functions within the region. For example, a regiono-centric organization might select a Japanese subsidiary to manage its Asian operations and a French subsidiary to manage its European operations. The regiono-centric message is, 'Regional insiders know what neighbouring countries want.'

The regiono-centric firm is integrated on a regional basis. Regional headquarter organizes collaborative efforts among local subsidiaries; it is responsible for the regional plan, local research and development, local executive selection and training, product innovation, cash management, brand policy, capital expenditure and public relations. The headquarter manages world strategy, country analysis, basic research and development, foreign exchange, transfer pricing, inter-company loans, long-term financing, selection of top management, technology transfer and establishing corporate culture.

GEO-CENTRIC ORGANIZATION

These organizations are world-oriented. The ultimate goal is creation of an integrated system with a worldwide approach. The geo-centric system is highly interdependent. Subsidiaries are no longer satellites and independent city-states. The entire organization focuses on worldwide and local objectives. Every part of organization makes a unique contribution using its unique competencies. The geocentric message is: 'All for one and one for all. We will work together to solve problems anywhere in the world.'

Geocentrism requires collaboration between headquarters and subsidiaries and also between subsidiaries to establish universal standards with permissible local variations. Geocentric organizations integrate diverse regions through global decision-making, making possible flow of ideas between countries. They allocate resources on a global basis, erase geographical boundaries, and globalize functional and product lines.

Within legal and political limits, the corporation seeks the best people to solve problems. Competence is what counts, not national origin. The reward system motivates managers to surrender national biases and work for worldwide objectives.

The geocentric firm overcomes political barriers by turning its subsidiaries into good citizens of the host nation. It hopes the subsidiary will become a leading exporter from the host to international community. Furthermore, the geocentric organization provides underdeveloped countries hard currency, new skills and advanced technology.

TRANSFORMATION TO A GEO-CENTRIC ORGANIZATION

For geocentrism to work, corporate culture must override national cultural differences. This is not easy. People are reluctant to learn new problem-solving skills when they already have effective cultural maps for their local environments. Inexperience, mutual distrust, nationalistic tendencies and immobility of top managers impede development of a geocentric perspective. Geocentrism requires total commitment on the party owners, managers and employees. The greatest responsibility falls on the shoulders of the CEO who must visit and review as many markets and subsidiaries as possible and remain in contact with middle managers, suppliers and respective governments. The subsidiaries must make sure that the information given to the CEO does not reflect national bias. For geocentrism to work, the CEO must be knowledgeable of critical world events and continually monitor subsidiary understanding of social, political and economic objectives in the host country.

Problems may arise in creating a geocentric corporate culture. National culture and traditional corporate culture may clash with the assumptions underlying geocentrism. In the face of growing globalization and homogenization, countries and cultures may try to strictly preserve their religious, cultural, linguistic and national identities. There are both fears and hopes from growing globalization. On the one hand, managers may loose their national identities and become corporate mercenaries, on the other hand they may become social architects by building global outlook-oriented organizations. The various approaches to IHRM discussed above are compared in Table 2.2.

Table 2.2 Four Approaches to IHRM

Aspects of Enterprise	*Ethno-centric Orientation*	*Polycentric Orientation*	*Regiono-centric Orientation*	*Geocentric Orientation*
HR strategy	Uniform strategy across all subsidiaries	Diverse strategies across subsidiaries	Regional integration of strategy, but differentiation across regions	Global overarching strategy on key corporate issues but differentiated policies on more local issues.
Performance criteria evaluation and control	By home-country headquarter	By local subsidiary management	Coordination across countries in the region, control by regional headquarter.	Global as well as local standards and control
Information and resource flow	Mainly from headquarter to local subsidiary	Little among subsidiaries, little between subsidiary and headquarter.	Little between subsidiary and headquarter, medium to high among subsidiaries in region	Inflows and outflows between and among headquarter and subsidiaries is very high
Staffing mix	Home-country managers	Host-country managers	Host country and third country nationals from within the region	Best people from anywhere in the world where they can be best used
Career development	Home-country managers developed to work anywhere	Mostly within the subsidiary career paths and development	Regional career paths and development	Managers everywhere developed to work anywhere
Purpose of socialization process	Gain loyalty, commitment and understanding of headquarter	Gain loyalty and commitment to the subsidiary	Gain loyalty and commitment to the region	Gain loyalty, commitment and understanding of the total firm and its diverse units.

COMPETENCIES REQUIRED IN INTERNATIONAL MANAGERS

A successful international business manager would need all the skills that are needed in domestic business operations. He or she must have operational knowledge of the different facets of the industry in which the company operates. Each country having its own ethos, values, business and social culture, he or she has to be a generalizing specialist as well as a specializing generalist, adding depth to the breadth of the knowledge and ability to synthesize specialist functions into general management, as one moves from one country to another.

In international business there is room for both cooperation and competition. More than a series of mechanical tasks, managing is a set of human interactions. Global managers operate in a matrix-like structure that demands cross-functional, cross-cultural, cross-product/service, international often multi-regional interactions.

Knowledge of One's Own Country

To understand the culture of other countries better, one should know one's country well. Appreciation of one's history and cultural values, understanding of current social and political issues and business situation are necessary. To gain respect from others, one has to have respect for oneself. Self-esteem as an individual, a citizen, representative of a country and a business manager is essential requirement for positioning oneself in the competitive global business.

A Global Perspective

The world is often referred to as a global village. Notwithstanding the differences in culture and value systems, many issues and concerns are global. We live in an interconnected, interdependent world economy. A global business manager must have a global business perspective and an understanding of how the world works. Learning, unlearning and relearning are integral parts of the knowledge-intensive global business. Besides acquiring thorough knowledge of the business operations in his or her chosen field of operation a global manager must be willing to listen and learn in the global arena.

Aspiring global managers have to be mentally ready to cope with surprises, mistakes, misunderstandings and even blunders in their cross-cultural interactions. Some mistakes are avoidable but some are a part of the hands-on learning of international business operations. Differences in cultural nuances often crop up at the most unexpected and critical times. Mistakes may occur in any area of business interaction, ranging from selection of cross-cultural partners to location of international business sites, name of products or translation of business promotion messages to choice of management strategies. Mistakes in international business may occur due to ignorance or carelessness; over enthusiasm or attaching additional meaning to spoken words, tone or gestures; improper use of idiom, or telling a wrong joke at the wrong time to the wrong person. Cross-cultural mistakes may also occur in simple things such as use of personal or family names or doing simple transaction giving wrong gifts at the wrong time to the wrong person; in accepting or in rejecting a cup of tea or an invitation. At times the mistakes or misunderstandings may prove to be embarrassing and very costly. Knowing what to do in another country is as important as knowing what not to do.

Global Mindset

A global manager must develop a global mindset – the capacity to appreciate the beliefs, values, behaviours, and business practices of individuals and organizations from different parts of the world. Cross-cultural mistakes cost money and may cause long-term damage to the company.

Global managers have to constantly deal with the other cross-country, cross-culture business managers. The ability to speak the language of the host country, adapt to the given environment, motivate the team, negotiate and understand other cultures is a competitive advantage in the global marketplace.

Knowledge of Other Countries

It takes two to communicate. As stated earlier listening with ears as well as eyes are integral parts of communicating and learning in the international business arena. To communicate effectively, one must have knowledge of the culture of the country one is going to operate in. This involves knowledge not just business practices but also its history, arts, values, political system, social issues and cultural sensitivities, their way of thinking, living and working. A curiosity to know and understand the other country and its people and thus educate oneself about its social, cultural and business environments are essential.

It is important to remember that cultures are not right or wrong, good or bad, just different. Perception is a person's view of reality. How people see reality varies with the position of their individual cultures. Sometimes, international success is hindered by the failure to understand how cultures differ. The international business manager should understand the cultural nuances and give full respect to the customs and social values of other countries. As in other games, in the international business game also, being adaptable and flexible is essential. It does not imply being weak. Adaptability and flexibility are important strategic tools and should be used as such.

It is also necessary to monitor how the trade pattern and policies of countries are changing, the reasons for the same, and how it is going to affect business rules.

Understanding of International Business Environment

To do business in other countries, one must know the rules of the market, acquire in-depth knowledge of the stated and prevailing practices of the business. One must acquire thorough knowledge about the other country in areas such as tax rules, labour laws, social benefits to be provided to the employees, government and public attitude towards foreign business executives and workers, foreign business investment and foreign business ownership.

To be successful in global business, one has to have a clear understanding of global business rules and develop global business mindset.

Understanding International Business Partners

Business relationships are held together by mutual confidence. For confidence building, it is essential that one should be able to communicate effectively and for this one should know the subject of interest of other party and what one likes to listen and talk about most. Each relationship has to be carefully cultivated by inviting business partners to home-country on important occasions. One should keep in touch with their development goals and strategies.

Knowledge of Customers

Like individuals, customers differ in their experiences, outlook, expectations, purchasing methods and decision-making. Each set of customers in each country must be understood from their individual economic, social and cultural backgrounds. Markets have to be redefined for each segment of each individual country.

Knowledge of the Silent and Spoken International Language

Silence is a form of speech. Spoken and silent languages are the main channels of communication in any culture. While each country may have one or more official languages, there are many variations in the use of spoken and silent languages within regions of each country.

Knowledge of Business Etiquettes of the Host Country

This has been covered in detail earlier. Business units operate in a social and cultural milieu. Each country has its own social, historical and cultural sentiments. Each business representative has his or her own values. Business opportunity may be lost because of a wrong social act.

BOX 2.2 INDIAN EXECUTIVES HIGHLY ACTION-FOCUSED BUT, TO ACHIEVE GLOBAL STANDARDS, NEW COMPETENCIES ARE NEEDED: KORN/FERRY SURVEY

While Indian executives match the business leaders in the West in their strategic thinking, they are more hierarchical like their counterparts in Asia. They demonstrate remarkably different leadership styles and emotional competencies from their western counterparts while proving to be just as strategic in terms of their decision-making and thinking styles, according to a Korn/Ferry International-IMA Leadership Study.

The study found that as managers move up an organization, they typically adopt less formal leadership styles to encourage knowledge sharing and cooperation. It shows a significant difference between the leadership styles of C-level Indian executives and their North American counterparts, indicating that the former are much more task-focused and intellectual and less social and participative. In other words they are more hierarchical and less concerned about building consensus. On this count, Indian leaders ranked most closely to executives assessed earlier from the 'Four Dragon' countries (Hong Kong, Korea, Singapore and Taiwan).

The study revealed that Indian executives are highly action-focused, complex and creative. They take decisions considering many options with a focus on high quality. This bodes well as focusing on strategic vision was listed as the most critical Western leadership practice for Asian companies seeking to global.

'While India is well known for its entrepreneurial and highly-educated talent base, more and more attention is being paid to how it will continue to develop its intellectual and managerial talent and management practices to achieve a global standard,' said Korn/Ferry chairman Paul Reilly. 'Current styles may be appropriate for the traditional and fast evolving Indian business environment, but as Indian firms continue to globlize, they will need to develop new competencies appropriate for the world stage.'

The Indian executives' emotional competencies diverged the most from those of the West, ranking lower in terms of ambiguity tolerance, empathy, energy and confidence, all of which impact their interpersonal communication and ability to access information, which is key to success.

Review Questions

1. Explain the criteria for a firm to be called a 'multinational'.

2. Distinguish between international, multinational, transnational and global organizations.
3. Explain ethnocentrism, polycentrism, regiono-centrism and geo-centrism approaches and how they influence international business?
4. Explain any four strategic alternatives in global business and competencies required by each of them.
5. Discuss the competencies required and profile of an international manager.

Assignment

Select any multinational operating in your city and interview its managers to find out the areas and functions it is following ethnocentric, polycentric, regiono-centric and geo-centric philosophy and which approach is dominant one.

Chapter

3

Recruitment and Selection by Multinationals

LEARNING OBJECTIVES

After studying this chapter, you will be able to:

- *Identify three basic sources that MNCs can tap for filling the management vacancies for overseas operations*
- *Learn the selection criteria that MNCs use for hiring the best people for overseas assignments as well as for long-term employment*
- *Understand the selection process used in making the final decisions on the part of both the organization and individual expatriate managers*
- *Discuss the reasons for expatriates' failure and success*
- *Learn Human Resource Outsourcing guidelines and strategies.*

OPENING CASE
Cadbury-Schweppes: Making Clinical Assessments of Inter-Cultural Adaptability and Risk Factors

Cadbury-Schweppes has been running its accelerated development programme for eight years. It is designed to identify and proactively accelerate the development of management talent internationally to meet the future resourcing needs of the group. Each year 16 managers go through the process. The nomination and selection processes are managed separately by each business, and selection can take place through an assessment centre or in line with the business performance or succession management process. The programme involves management development through one-year-long international assignments.

Eighteen months ago Cadbury-Schweppes made a suitability assessment of its managers undertaking overseas assignments. The number of people on international assignments is likely to be more than double over the next four years, from 120 to 300. This is a significant investment, and so it made business sense to introduce cultural adaptability assessment alongside the normal selection process.

International management is seen to revolve around the risks associated with intercultural adaptability. The recruitment process therefore attempts to assess objectively an employee's capability to perform a specific role as well as his or her suitability for an international assignment.

The process designed by Kaisen Consulting, helps employees understand the personal qualities required to work overseas and the implication of an international assignment for themselves and their families. It highlights the coping mechanisms that assist them in adapting to their new environment, and focuses on identifying the psychological 'adaptations' that take place on an international assignment.

Not all managers can adapt to living and working in a different country. The answer does not lie in managers possessing competencies that enable organizations to make yes/no decisions about their adaptability. Rather, a series of contingencies have to be managed – an individual might be able to adapt to one situation, but not to another. The approach highlights four adaptations:

- Behaviour towards others and the different norms that exist.
- Expectations about people, situations and the way things work.
- Interpretations of the situations and people's behaviour.
- Feelings about the situations, the emotional side of culture and the display of behaviours.

Rather than attempt to predict excellent performance and possession of competencies, this approach argues that it is better to pursue a selection strategy of risk reduction, i.e. identify 'risk analysis factors – the things that, if absent, will affect performance – and contraindicators – the things if present may suggest a higher level of risk associated with the assignment. It assesses such factors as a 'poly-centric mindset', 'locus of control' and 'tolerance of ambiguity'. A questionnaire is followed by a one-to-one health-screen interview which considers motivational and lifestyle issues.

Cadbury-Schweppes then considers how to structure the international assignment to reduce the risks involved. Judgments are made about three levels of intercultural adaptability:

1. Suitable for 'nowhere'.
2. Suitable for 'somewhere' (on a contingency basis).
3. Suitable for 'everywhere'.

This assessment is not used as a selection instrument. The results are considered to be valid for one year, but assessors can have a dialogue with the candidates about sensitive issues that might not otherwise be raised.

INTRODUCTION

We have seen that the need for international managers has increased more than double in four years in case of Cadbury-Schewppes, and this is the case with most other international firms. We have also seen that the success of international assignment critically depends upon selecting a right candidate. The costs of expatriates' failure are enormous, both direct and indirect. Further, there is little time between a candidate's short-listing and actual assignment. The candidate has to rush to close current job obligations and personal matters in order to prepare for the move, which, not surprisingly, creates an overload of work upon arrival in the new country and leaves little time for training. Further, the competencies required in international managers are neither easy to develop nor easy to find as discussed in Chapter 2.

TYPES OF ASSIGNMENTS

There are many types of international assignments demanding distinct role competencies. For example,

- Home-based manager but with a central focus on international markets and players,
- Multicultural team members who work on a series of international projects,
- Internationally mobile managers who undertake frequent and short visits to numerous, overseas locations for coordination, control and fact-finding,
- Employees in specialist non-management roles, which involve transfer of knowledge in the areas of sales, engineering, training and supply-chain, and
- Expatriates who set up a business and lead the subsidiary as its CEOs for longer periods.

The question is, 'Does a different set of competencies come to the fore in each of these roles? If so, the recruitment and selection process should take due care of it. Can we answer with confidence the following questions:

- Can all international competencies be developed?
- Are some competencies so complex and so rare on the ground and so time-consuming to build that the real issue is to select a core of elite managers?
- Can we identify a clear hierarchy of international management skills, from the most basic to high levels of performance?
- Do internal resourcing systems realistically make such sophisticated decisions while selecting candidates?

The consensus among HR practitioners is that it is possible to specify a set of competencies and that these can be used for the selection process, but the need for appropriate training and graded international exposure remains very much valid.

> We are not necessarily convinced that perfecting the selection process is key to creating the internationally mobile managers. It is more important to give them the exposure, the experience. It is then our ability to observe them on the job in a variety of international management events after their entry into the business, and measuring and tracking this. The best strategy is to identify the managers who have to be kept, and then directing them at the right kind of opportunities. — A HR manager

HUMAN RESOURCE PLANNING AND INFORMATION SYSTEM

Multinational companies spend huge amounts and maintain state-of-the-art information systems linking each business unit and subsidiary through its own intra-network which takes care not only of managing control system but corporate planning which includes Human Resource Information System (HRIS) and Human Resource Planning (HRP) system. HRP is the first step in the recruitment and selection process. This module provides support to Human Resource Planning in following ways:

- Matching person and job information.
- Manpower forecasting and planning, using statistical models.
- Future replacements.
- Systematic employee search and placement.
- Eligibility list of promotable candidates.
- Career planning system identifies surplus manpower for which growth in some functional areas is not possible.
- Succession planning – identifying key posts getting vacant due to retirement, promotions, etc.
- Generating surplus and deficit reports of manpower level-wise and department-wise due to new technology requirements, redeployment conditions and confidential reports.
- Maintaining records of language proficiencies of employees and their foreign experience.
- Industrial disturbance data bank.
- Maintaining records matching personality profiles of employees indicating job aptitudes.

HRIS and HRP result in reduction in HR staff levels, especially in terms of administrative staff. If implemented well, it provides an opportunity for an HR department to get a clearer profile and a better image and meet sudden requirements of staff in different subsidiaries by sourcing them from those subsidiaries which can spare them. It also helps them relocating returning expatriates properly.

RECRUITMENT AND SELECTION OF EXPATRIATES

Multinationals regard recruitment and selection as key processes and spend larger amounts of money in the global search for right candidates as compared to domestic firms. Multinationals define jobs loosely and job-related relationships are large, spread across different countries and in different cultures. The positions require an in-depth knowledge of the international environment and jobs have to be done as part of international teams in cross-functional and cross-cultural set-ups.

Recruitment is defined as searching for and obtaining candidates in sufficient numbers and quality so that the organization can select the most appropriate people to fill its job needs. Selection is the process of gathering information for the purposes of evaluating and deciding who should be employed in a particular job. In the international context, one should also look at issues of female managers, dual-career couples, equal opportunity legislation, employee diversity and high cost of expatriates' failure. Expatriates are expensive to maintain in international locations (an American expatriate costs nearly US $ 3 million per year). A recent study estimated that the average cost of expatriates is three to four times that of locals.

Certain individual personality traits directly influence some organizational outcomes, like job satisfaction, absenteeism, turnover, creativity and commitment. To fit between individual personality traits and the requirements of the job or responsibility is critical for employee job satisfaction and motivation, which, in turn, influence employee retention, absenteeism and commitment.

INTERNATIONAL LABOUR MARKET – SOURCES

There are three basic sources that MNCs can tap for overseas positions: (1) home or parent country nationals (PCNs); (2) host country nationals (HCNs); and (3) third country nationals (TCNs). These sources are described in detail in the following pages.

Parent Country Nationals (PCNs)

PCNs are managers who are citizens of the country where the MNC is headquartered. In fact, sometimes the term 'headquarter's nationals' is also used. These managers are commonly called expatriates or, simply, expats, which refers to those who live and work away from their parent country. Historically, multinationals have staffed key positions in their foreign affiliates with PCNs. On the basis of research done in the US, European and Japanese firms, Rosalie Tung found that the US and European firms used PCNs in less developed regions. The Japanese and Koreans, however, make considerably more use of parent country personnel in all geographic areas, both at the middle- and upper-level ranks.

There are a variety of reasons for using PCNs. Tung found that the most common reason (given by 70 per cent of the respondents) was to start up operations. MNCs prefer to have their own people launch a new venture. The second most common reason (cited by 68 per cent of the respondents) was that the parent country people had the necessary managerial and technical expertise. Other reasons for using PCNs include:

- The desire to provide the company's more promising managers with international experience to equip them better for more responsible positions;
- The need to maintain and facilitate organizational coordination and control;
- The unavailability of managerial talent in the host country;
- In company's view of the foreign operation as short lived;
- The host country's multiracial population, which might mean that selecting a manager of one race would result in political or social problems;
- The company's conviction that it must maintain a foreign image in the host country; and
- The belief that a parent country manager is the best person for the job.

For example, HULL, a subsidiary of the Unilever group in India, is currently headed by an Indian. Sometimes, if a product is to be launched worldwide, PCNs may be posted to make the launch successful and then operations are handed to HCNs.

Host Country Nationals (HCNs)

HCNs are local managers who are hired by the MNC. There are many reasons for hiring them at the lower or middle-level ranks. Many countries require the MNC to hire local talent as part of opening their markets to MNCs. For example, in Brazil, two-thirds of employees in any foreign subsidiary have to be Brazilian nationals. In India also, before approving joint venture agreements, government restricts the number of expatriates to be employed, primarily to limit the foreign exchange outflow and to prepare Indian nationals to undertake the responsibility at a future time. Further, even if a multinational wanted to staff all management positions with home country personnel, the MNC is unlikely to have so many available managers, and the cost of transferring and maintaining them in the host country would be prohibitive.

PCNs fill usually top positions, but this is not always the case. For example, companies following the multi-domestic philosophy or polycentric approach would select most positions, including top ones, from the host country, but usually after starting the operations and when the business is established.

European countries prefer to keep their nationals posted in host countries for long durations, unlike American companies, which post them back to headquarters or to some other subsidiaries. Sales function is usually headed by a local person (HCN). However, the Japanese are an exception; they post a Japanese CEO and other important posts are also occupied by the Japanese. They even make it clear that if anyone has a problem with this arrangement, he is free to choose another company.

Tung has identified four reasons for use of host country managers:

1. These individuals are familiar with the culture;
2. They know the local language;
3. They are less expensive and know the way things are done, the rules of local market and how to get things done or who can influence; and
4. Hiring them is good public relations.

Third Country Nationals (TCNs)

TCNs are managers who are citizens of countries other than the one in which the MNC is headquartered or the one in which it is assigned to work by the MNC. Tung found that the two most important reasons that American MNCs use third country nationals are:

1. These people have the necessary expertise; and
2. They were judged to be the best ones for the job.

Japanese companies usually do not hire TCNs, while Phatak found that the US companies usually prefer TCNs from Europe.

TCNs are found typically in large MNCs in advanced stages of growth. A number of advantages are cited for using them. One is that the salary package is usually less than that of a PCN. The knowledge of local language, like English, was the reason for choosing British managers by the US companies in former British colonies, like India, Jamaica, the West Indies and Kenya.

Today a new breed of multilingual and multiexperienced 'global managers' has emerged. These new managers are part of a growing group of international executives who can manage across borders and do not fit in the traditional third country mould. With a unified Europe, and North America and Asia becoming business hubs, these global managers are in great demand.

Advantages and Disadvantages of PCNs, TCNs and HCNs

PCNs

Advantages:

- Organizational control and coordination is maintained and facilitated.
- Promising managers are given international experience.
- PCNs may be the best people for the job because of special skills and experience.
- Assurance that the subsidiary will comply with company's objectives and policies.

Disadvantages:

- The chance of promotions of HCNs are limited.
- Adaptation to host country may take time.
- PCNs may impose an inappropriate HQ style.
- Compensation for PCNs and HCNs may differ.

TCNs

Advantages:

- Salary and benefit requirements may be lower than for PCNs.
- TCNs may be better informed than PCNs about host country environments.

Disadvantages:

- Posting must consider possible national animosities (e.g., India and Pakistan).
- The host government may resent hiring TCNs.
- TCNs may not want to return to their own countries after the assignment.

HCNs

Advantages:

- Language and other barriers are eliminated.
- Hiring costs are reduced and no work permit is required.
- Continuity of management improves since HCNs stay longer in positions.
- Government policy may dictate hiring of HCNs.
- Morale among HCNs may improve as they see career potential.

Disadvantages:

- Control and coordination of HQ may be impeded.
- HCNs have limited career opportunities outside the subsidiary.
- Hiring HCNs limits opportunities for PCNs to gain foreign experience.
- Hiring HCNs could encourage a federation of national rather than global units.

ATTRACTING INTERNATIONAL MANAGERS

How do organizations begin to attract and engage international managers? Two processes are discussed: the use of head-hunters and advertising.

Using Head-hunters: Executive search is defined as the recruitment of senior executives and specialists with an average compensation of over $ 100,000 per year. The top 15 global search firms had a net revenue of almost $ 15 billion in 2005, 24 per cent up from the previous year. Most large head-hunting firms have been established on the reputation of outstanding consultants and charismatic business leaders. Although the personal chemistry between the head-hunter and international HR manager is still important, the ability of head-hunters to offer an integrated service with no international obstacles to cross-border cooperation has become the most important criterion.

The highest growth areas that provide talented managers are China, Malaysia, India, Taiwan, South Korea, the Middle East, Russia and Eastern Europe. There are many pragmatic reasons why international HR managers use head-hunters:

> It is about understanding the market; if we require someone there, would there be someone out there? It is about learning the prices in the market and what is happening out there. — A HR manager

Cross-national Advertising: The cost of recruitment through international advertising is higher, hence creative alternatives are being used, such as targeted outdoor poster sites, airport lounges, airline magazines and journey-to-work routes. Advertising agencies focus on:

- The location of target audience.
- The kind of market they operate in.
- Sample salaries.
- Recruitment competitors.
- Whether the job-seeking audience is active or passive.
- The desired company qualities.
- Soft cultural issues, such as what an ideal brochure should look like and the wording of adverts.

Internet: The internet offers considerable potential as a source of recruitment for international mobile managers, particularly for small firms. It is most useful for attracting MBA- and PhD-level candidates for specific roles, such as marketing and IT staff. Job-posting and CV management services screening and short listing are accessible and sifting services are now being offered. Expatriates are the most networked type of managers and advertise themselves on the internet. However, most existing service providers do not have global coverage and the web is currently not appropriate for all countries.

International Graduate Programme: Many large firms are preferring to source the fresh MBAs from reputed global institutes for long-term development as international managers. There are some problems, such as retention rates may prove to be very low and the training programme with the subsidiaries may not be up to the required standard. Visa issues mean that the cadres have to be managed for a significant length of time and many organizations are finding that graduates are becoming more reluctant to move out and quality of life issues is becoming more relevant to them.

PROCEDURE OF SELECTING EXPATRIATES

In view of the high direct and indirect costs of expatriates failure, and knowing the reasons for their failure in their assignments, MNCs spend considerable time and energy in screening employees and their families before selecting them for foreign postings. However, the criteria and the selection procedure used vary from one MNC to another, and from one country to another. It may also be noted that selection is a two-way process, between the individual and the organization. A prospective candidate may reject the foreign assignment either for personal reasons, such as family considerations, or for situational factors.

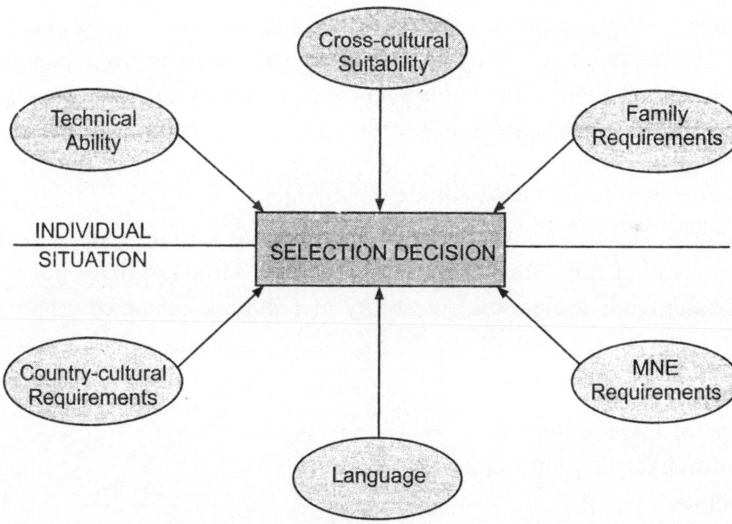

Fig. 3.1 Factors in Selection of Expatriates

Figure 3.1 indicates the factors involved in the selection of expatriates, both in terms of individuals and the specifics of the situation concerned. Figure 3.2 presents model for selecting the right person for a foreign assignment.

Technical Ability

A person's ability to perform the required jobs is an important consideration. Technical and managerial skills are, therefore, essential criteria used by all MNCs. The Price Waterhouse survey (*International*

Assignments: European Policy and Practice) of 184 European firms (nearly a quarter of which had their worldwide headquarters in the US) reports that the most important selection criteria were job-related skills (99 per cent) and leadership skills (76 per cent). Further, it is relatively easy to determine technical job-related skills and competencies based on performance in previous jobs. Past and present superiors can also be consulted to ascertain past performance.

Suitable tests can also be designed at assessment centres to evaluate candidates' relative expertise. Tung notes in her study that only 3 per cent, 5 per cent and 14 per cent respectively, of the US, Japanese, and Western European firms used tests to assess candidates' technical competence. In case of internal candidates, past performance records are available for the evaluation purpose. Of course, it is known that past performance may have little or no bearing on one's ability to accomplish a task in a foreign cultural environment. One should also note that while technical ability (or lack of it) does not emerge as a critical factor in an expatriate's failure, the job-related aspects may induce one to stay longer abroad as well as stay with the organization on return, after completing an assignment. Job autonomy is a very powerful factor in an expatriate's turnover and motivation.

Cross-cultural Requirements

An American manager who is considered an excellent communicator by his US colleagues because of his face-to-face and to-the-point style may be a disaster when required to communicate with Chinese or Japanese subordinates who value subtle, indirect forms of communication. Hence the country where the posting is to be and its culture are likely influences in the selection of the candidate. The more different the culture of the host country from the home country, the more important is this factor.

The importance of cross-cultural sensitivity in conducting business and negotiations in different countries is highlighted. According to experience and research, certain traits and characteristics have now been identified as predictors of an expatriate's success. Although these traits may not guarantee an expatriate's success, without them the possibility of failure is enhanced. These traits include:

1. Cultural empathy.
2. Adaptability.
3. Diplomacy.
4. Language ability.
5. Positive attitude.
6. Emotional stability and maturity.

Murray and Murray (1998) advocate that while managerial and technical competence is regarded as primary for an expatriate's success, effectiveness and coping skills are also necessary. Effectiveness skills is defined as the ability to successfully translate managerial or technical skill into the foreign environment, whereas coping skills enable a person to become reasonably comfortable or at least survive in the foreign environment. It is not easy to define inter-cultural competence and even more difficult is to measure it. What is needed is to measure relational ability of a person, i.e. his/her ability to relate with another cultural group, which is also a personality-related trait.

AT&T has developed formal screening procedures that help in the selection process. The questions, some of which are given below, are designed to help the candidates and their spouses to answer. The questions include:

1. Can you imagine living without TV?
2. What is your tolerance for waiting for repairs?
3. How do you feel if your driver comes late for duty or a client does not turn up on time?
4. How important is it for you to spend significant amount of time with people of your own ethnic, racial, religious and national background?
5. As you look at your personal history, can you isolate any episodes that indicate a real interest in learning about the people from other countries or other cultures?

AT&T also ensures that each person going abroad has a sponsor back home. The role of the sponsor is to stay in touch and let the expatriate know that the company is not forgetting him or her and keep him/her informed about developments in the company. The sponsor also helps in sorting out personal matters in the home country, such as filing of tax returns. The idea is that the expatriate should not feel neglected.

Family Requirements

The role of the spouse in and contribution of the family to the success of expatriates have been well documented and well researched. For example, Black and Stephens (1989) examined the influence of the spouse on an American expatriate's adjustment. They found that the adjustment of the spouse was highly correlated to the adjustment of the expatriate manager. Hence firms interview the spouse as an essential part of the selection process. Answers are sought to questions like, will you be interrupting a career to accompany your spouse on an international assignment? If a formal interview evokes resistance, then the spouse is contacted informally and attitudes ascertained indirectly through friends.

Some postings are considered 'hardship postings' – remote areas, away from major cities or major facilities with high physical risks. Accompanying family members may be an additional responsibility on such locations which MNCs may not like to bear. Similarly, there may be reluctance to select women candidates for certain Middle East or South-East Asian regions. Indeed some countries do not issue work permits for female. These factors may result in the selection of HCNs rather than expatriates.

Requirements of MNCs

Apart from expatriate-related factors, there are situational factors, such as management philosophy and approach of the MNC – whether it is ethnocentric, polycentric, regiono-centric or geocentric. The status of the MNC – whether it is an international, multi-domestic, transnational or global company – also influences this decision to a great extent. These factors have been explained in earlier chapters. Other situational factors include:

- The mode of operation involved: Selecting staff to work in an international joint venture may involve major input from the local partner, and constraints imposed by the JV agreement terms.
- The duration of the assignment: Family members tend not to accompany an expatriate when the assignment is for a short duration, so family may not be a strong factor in the selection.
- The amount of knowledge transfer inherent in the expatriate's job in foreign operation: If the nature of the job is to train local staff, then the MNC may include training skills as one of the selection criteria.

In short, the business environment of the host country in which the expatriate has to work and the goals the multinational is pursuing will very much influence the selection process.

Language Skills

Language skills are critical for some expatriate positions, but lesser for others. Tung (1987) considers 'knowledge of host country's language is important for functional heads and operative jobs, whereas communication skills, rather than specific language skills are more important for top management positions. However, it is generally agreed that lack of knowledge of the host country's language is a major barrier in an expatriate's performance in any position. A Price Waterhouse study places language skills as the third most important selection criterion. The UK-German study by Marx (1996) ranks language skills as number five (after social competence, openness to other ways of thinking, cultural adaptation and professional excellence). Table 3.1 shows that the reasons of expatriates' failure can vary from one culture to another and from one company to another.

Table 3.1 Reasons for Expatriates' Failure in the US and Japanese Firms (in descending order of importance)

US Firms	*Japanese Firms*
Inability of the spouse to adjust.	Inability to cope with larger international responsibility.
Manager's inability to adjust.	Difficulties with a new environment.
Other family reasons.	Personal or emotional problems.
Manager's personal or emotional Immaturity.	Lack of technical competence.
Inability to cope with larger international responsibility.	Inability of the spouse to adjust.

In conclusion, individual and specific situational factors interact with each other in terms of performance.

USE OF SELECTION TESTS

Selection criteria are slowly shifting from the ones based on technical and intelligence criteria to the wider-range skills and personality felt appropriate for the flexible manager. The premise is that the people who seek certainty, completeness, tidiness and rational logicality are not suited to modern business cultures or an environment that demands international mobility. The ability to deal with the ambiguity of what happens next is seen as central for internationally mobile managers. The characteristics identified are derived from models of high performance competency and flexibility. International role specifications now stress that managers must be

1. actively analytical rather than taking events at face value,
2. willing to take risks,
3. action-oriented, with strong personal goals,

4. able to look at situations constructively and not defensively,
5. capable of multidimensional vision rather than having a unitary thought,
6. able to deal with information from many sources,
7. sensitive to the needs of others,
8. able to delegate work and trust subordinates, and
9. able to live with ambiguity and complexity.

Can we develop these skills and capabilities in managers? Many doubt the feasibility of it. Hence the stress is to select candidates having these traits.

Psychometric Testing

Although there is consensus among scholars and executives that personal characteristics are important, there is a considerable debate about how such personal characteristics can be reliably and accurately measured. Personality and psychological tests have been used in the selection process, but the effectiveness of such tests as predictors of cultural adjustment is questioned. For example, Willis (1984) states that if tests are used they should be selected with care and regard for reliability and validity because, while some tests may be useful in suggesting potential problems with the candidates, there appears little correlation between test scores and performance. He adds that most of the relevant

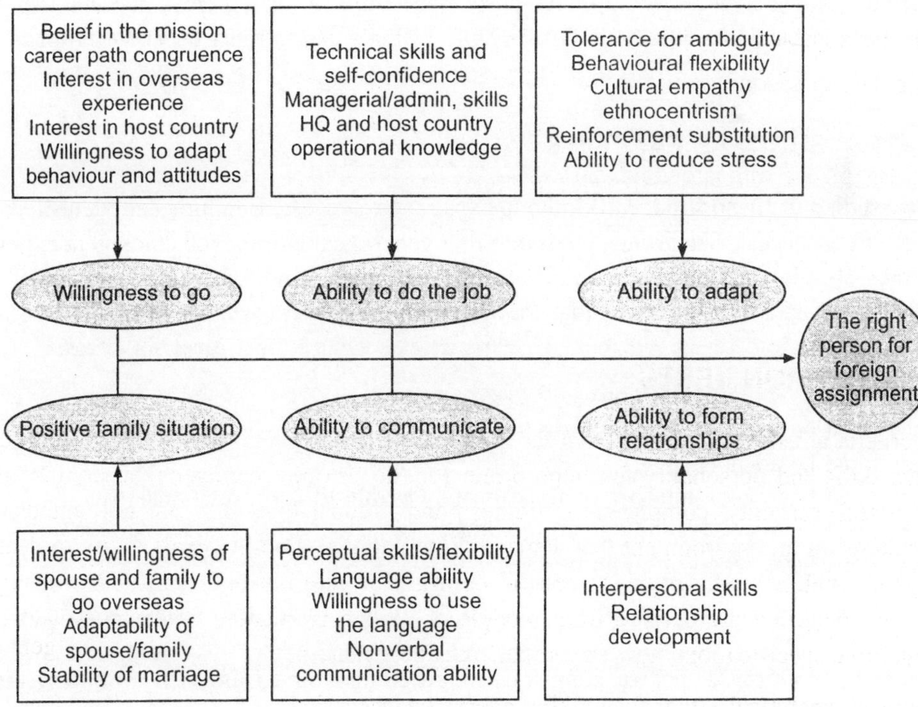

Fig. 3.2 Model for Selecting Expatriates

tests have been devised in the US and, therefore, they may be culture-bound. Use of such tests without careful modification in non-American countries adds another questionmark to their reliability and validity as predictors of expatriates' success.

Another constraint is that, in some countries (the UK and Australia), there is a controversy about the use of psychological tests. The pattern of usage of such tests differs across countries. A Price Waterhouse (1997) survey reports that only 12 per cent of the companies use formal assessment centres. Gertsen (1989) points out that personality traits are not defined and evaluated in the same way in different cultures. She states, 'the most serious problem, however, is that attitudes do not always result in implicitly expected behaviour. If a person has very positive attitudes toward a culture but is unable to express in his behaviour, it has no effect.'

Cultural adaptation problems are particularly acute in the use of personality tests. The subtle interaction between language and culture means that neither English nor simple translation is effective as an international assessment medium when the goal is to establish core individual differences. For example, the questionnaire item 'I work hard', although meaningful to British managers, is associated with the concept of toil for French managers. It is therefore seen as a negative attribute. Once the notion of 'effort' is substituted for 'work' the efficiency of the item is re-established. Then HR managers also face certain dilemmas. For example, if a French manager is coming to work in the UK, is it appropriate to test the manager against the French or UK norm group? If you test the manager in English, he or she is at an immediate disadvantage.

There are no simple answers to the issues posed by the use of testing cross-national samples, and indeed many of the issues are ultimately irresolvable. HR managers must lay more emphasis on the feedback process.

EXPATRIATES' SUCCESS FACTORS

Rosalie Tung studied the factors that contribute to expatriates' success or failure, and identified eighteen variables that affect success. She groups them into four general categories: job competence, personality traits, relational abilities and environment and family variables. Tung's variables are similar to those of Mendenhall and Oddou (1991), except that she also highlights the importance of family considerations in cultural acculturisation. Taken together, the expatriates selected must meet six criteria:

1. They must be willing and motivated to go overseas;
2. They must be technically able to do the job;
3. They must be adaptable;
4. They must have good interpersonal skills and be able to form relationships;
5. They must have good communication ability; and
6. They must have supportive families.

Factors affecting the success of expatriates can be studied under two heads: general factors and specific attributes.

The fact that many firms do not use sophisticated procedures to measure such attributes as relational skills and adaptability does not mean that they lack interest in the issues. Rather, they often assess such characteristics by using less formal methods. Some firms maintain appraisal profiles of employees, including their family situations and use them when required.

Table 3.2 Factors Contributing to the Success of Expatriates

General Factors	*Specific Attributes*
Job factors	**Technical skills** Knowledge of HQ and host country operations. General managerial skills. Administrative competence.
Relational traits	Ability to tolerate ambiguity. Behavioural flexibility. Ability to be non-judgemental. Level of cultural empathy and ethnocentrism. Interpersonal skills.
Motivational state	Belief in the mission. Congruence of assignment with career path Interest in overseas experience. Willingness to acquire new behaviour patterns and attitudes.
Family situation	Willingness of the spouse to live overseas. Adaptability and supportiveness of the spouse. Stability of marriage.
Language skills	Host country's language ability. Non-verbal communication ability.

Source: Goldstein and Associates (1989), 'Training the International Assignee' in *Personnel Administrator*, Vol. 31, 3, pp. 81–94.

ADAPTABILITY TO CULTURAL CHANGE

Overseas managers must be able to adapt to cultural change. They also need a degree of cultural toughness. Research shows that many managers are exhilarated at the beginning of an overseas assignment. However, after a few months a form of cultural shock creeps in and they begin to encounter frustration and feel confused in their new environment. This may be a good sign, as it shows that the expatriate manager is getting involved in the new culture and is not isolating himself or herself from the new environment.

As the initial and trying period comes to an end, the expatriate's ease with conditions tends to increase. In fact, after the first two years most people become more satisfied with their overseas assignment than when they first arrived. Research also shows that men tend to adjust a little faster than women, and people over 35 years of age tend to have higher levels of satisfaction after the first year, but managers under 35 years of age have higher satisfaction during the third and fourth years. In all cases, however, these differences are not statistically significant.

Organizations prescribe a number of characteristics in determining whether an individual is sufficiently adaptable. Examples include work experience with people cultures other than one's own, previous overseas travel, knowledge of foreign language, and recent immigration. Other characteristics include:

1. The ability to integrate with different people, cultures, and types of business organizations.
2. The ability to sense developments in the host country and evaluate them accurately.

3. The ability to solve problems within different frameworks and from different perspectives.
4. Sensitivity to the subtle differences of culture, politics, religion and ethics, in addition to individual differences.
5. Flexibility in managing operations on a continuous basis, despite lack of assistance and gaps in information.

AN ADJUSTMENT MODEL

In recent years international human resource scholars have developed theoretical models that help explain the factors involved in effectively adjusting to overseas assignments. Figure 3.3 provides an example of one such model. As seen in the model, there are two major types of adjustments that an expatriate must make when going on an overseas assignment. One is the anticipatory adjustment. This is carried out before the expatriate leaves for the assignment. The other is the in-country adjustment, which takes place on-site.

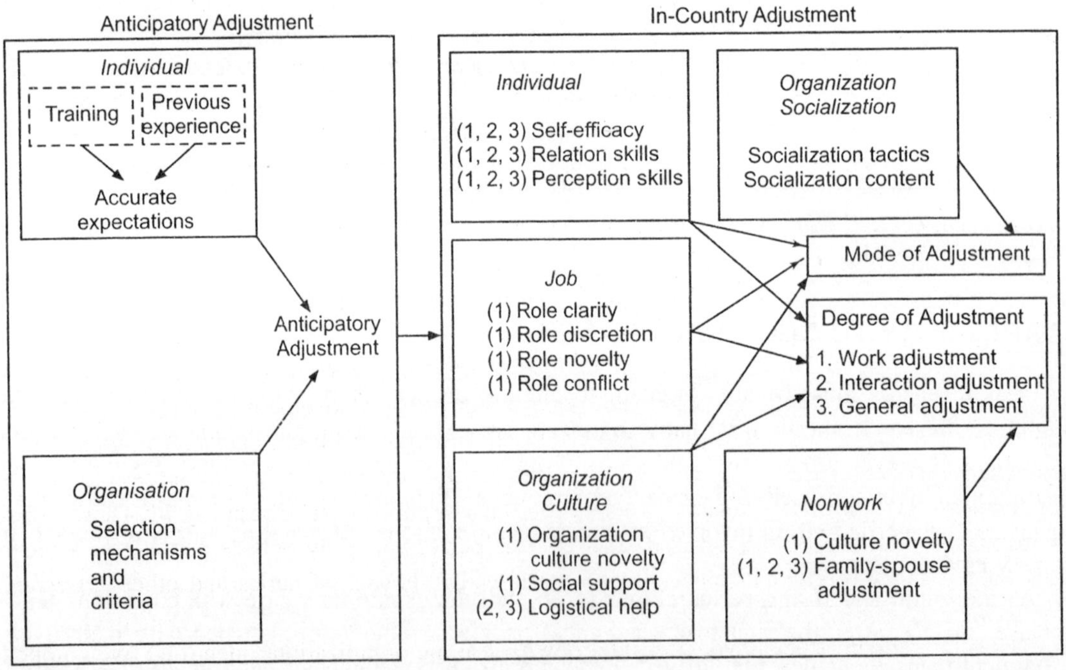

(Numbers in parentheses indicate the numbered facet(s) of adjustment to which the specific variable is expected to relate.)

Fig. 3.3 A Theoretical Model for Expatriate Adjustment

Source: J. Stewart Black, Mark Mendenhall and Gray Oddou, 'Toward a Comprehensive Model of International Adjustment: An Integration of Multiple Theoretical Perspectives' in *Academy of Management Review*, April 1991, p. 303.

Anticipatory adjustment is influenced by several important factors. One individual factor is the pre-departure training that is provided. This often takes the form of cross-cultural seminars or workshops designed to acquaint the expatriates with the culture and work-life of the country to which they will be posted. Another anticipatory factor is the previous experience the expatriate may have had with the assigned country or similar cultures. These two factors help determine the accuracy of the expatriate's expectations. The organizational inputs into anticipatory adjustment are directly related with the selection process. Earlier MNCs' relied mainly on technical competence. Obviously, technical competence is important, but it is only one of a number of skills, that will be needed. If the MNC concentrates only on technical competence as a selection criterion, then it is not properly preparing the expatriate managers for successful adjustments in overseas assignments.

Once on-site, there are a number of factors that influence the ability to adjust effectively. These include the ability to maintain a positive outlook in the face of high pressure, to interact with host nationals, and to correctly perceive and evaluate the host country's values and norms. The second factor is the job itself, as reflected by the role the expatriate plays in managing the host country's management team, the authority he/she has to make the decisions, the newness of work-related challenges and the amount of role-conflict that exists. The third factor is organizational culture and how easily the expatriate can adjust to it. The fourth aspect is the non-work factors, such as the toughness with which the expatriate faces the whole new cultural experience and how well his or her family can adjust to the rigours of the new assignment. The fifth and the final factor is effective socialisation tactics, i.e. to know 'what is what' and 'who is who' in the host's organization. These anticipatory and in-country factors influence the expatriate's mode and degree of adjustment to an overseas assignment. This explains why effective selection is so important and difficult.

HUMAN RESOURCE OUTSOURCING

Multinationals use outsourcing of many activities, including recruitment and selection, to consultants and this process is managed by the IHRM department. The increasing trend of outsourcing of HR activities (35% in 1996 in the US with total market size of $ 200 billion by 2000; source: *Hewitt Associate's Survey*) not only in developed countries but even in developing countries like India and China, create the fear that there will be no need of HR function in future. Is this phenomenon a short-term extension of the downsizing movement, started in 90's, or a permanent solution for organizational effectiveness? How are HR executives reacting to this: supporting it or resisting it? These are some interesting questions. Outsourcing is defined as 'the performance by outside parties, on a recurring basis, of HR tasks that would otherwise be performed in-house.' (Charles and others, *Academy of Management Executive*, 1996)

The authors mentioned above, after interviewing leading organizations, identified five competitive forces that are driving outsourcing, which are: Downsizing, Rapid growth or decline, Globalization, Increased competition and Restructuring. The increased focus on HR function by top management is forcing them to align HR practices and policies with corporate strategy, work more closely with line-managers to deliver more value-added services at a lower cost and further reduce their service response time to both external and internal customers. In short, top managements are examining which HR activities are needed and who can best provide them.

Many firms have also undergone changes related to re-structuring, mergers and acquisitions where some HR activities have to be done in time-bound manner by specialists, outside consultants. Companies resorting to retrenchment or firms in decline face huge pressures to reduce costs, while high-growth firms resort to it for maintaining growth pace and also to control costs. Multinational firms setting up their operations in foreign countries with little knowledge of their culture find outsourcing very attractive. The choice of activities that can be outsourced depends on whether they are deemed to be in the core competency of HR function or not. The companies like GE and other multinationals are increasingly looking for customer satisfaction, cash-flow and employee satisfaction improvement and HR function is under pressure to deliver the same and help in achieving competitive advantage. Hence HR department has to perform its tasks more efficiently than performed by outside service providers; for example, team-building activities and leadership development activities or compensation management, etc. The following areas are amenable for outsourcing which need specialized knowledge: Operation and maintenance of HR information system; compliance with regulatory requirements; organizational development; obtaining data about external labour markets or about the competitor's benefits; and reward policies. Other areas are competency mapping, training and development mostly off-the job type, and also services in head-hunting and assessment centre-related.

BOX 3.1 EMPLOYEE SELECTION AT MITSUBISHI

For the US-based Mitsubishi-Chrysler joint venture auto plant employees are selected in the Japanese way. The selection process lasts three days. On the first day, applicants are required to perform tasks that mimic factory jobs. On the second day, work-related tests are followed by a series of written, medical and drug tests and a final screening by the plant supervisors. The selection process tests individuals for high level of skills, dedication to their work, aptitude for learning new work methods and team work. Those who are selected must undergo a rigorous training programme, during which they learn technical skills, creativity facilitation and idea generation. They are taught efficiency in the spirit of Japanese philosophy of 'kaizen', or continued improvement. The basic training is followed by several weeks of on–the-job training. Later posting and promotion decisions are based on part, how well candidates do in management development seminars and in-basket exercises. In any respect, human resource management is a priority task in Japanese firms. Mitsubishi's relations with its US employees seem to be faring well, as the firm reports that over 50 per cent of its US sales are vehicles that were manufactured in the US.

Sometimes, the activities which are overwhelming in nature and the HR department is unable to cope with them, are also outsourced, for example, during wage negotiations or in the event of a strike. Outsourcing is also beneficial in conducting salary negotiations without disclosing the credentials of the firm.

Table 3.4 gives guidelines for managing the outsourcing process. Except for such core competencies, like performance appraisal or employee relationship, most HR activities can be considered for outsourcing where maintaining confidentiality or control or maintaining trust with employees is not so important.

One solid argument given by some companies is that outsourcing stimulated the thought processes of the employee and kept him in contact with consultants who had current and specialized information that could accelerate his progress on the learning curve. Outsourcing provides a big picture perspective. Another company thinks that the use of vendors improves the HR gene pool and produces new capabilities and out-of-the-box thinking. There is no doubt that outsourcing reduces career development opportunities for the HR staff. Hence outsourcing is creating opportunities, threats and challenges with the message that the HR staff should deliver value-added services, which is a specialist's function.

Table 3.4 Guidelines for Human Resource Outsourcing

Making the Outsourcing Decision

- Except for core competencies, all other HR activities should be considered as items for outsourcing.
- Determine whether the desire to outsource an activity is driven by its low contribution to core competencies or influences from external environment or poor management of the activity.
- Recognize that performance is more important than low HR Department headcounts or low costs.
- Beware of vendors that supply off-the-shelf solutions that do not fit the company's needs.
- Avoid excessive reliance on vendors.
- Decide how much control is needed for various HR activities and whether control can be retained with outsourcing.
- Identify critical benefits to outsourcing.

Selecting and Negotiating with Outsourcing Vendors

- Assign a high weighting to vendor's knowledge of the industry.
- Perform reference checks of potential vendors.
- Understand the costs involved in switching vendors for outsourced services.

Managing the Outsourcing Transition

- Expect the internal HR team to resist outsourcing and develop ways to of managing resistance.
- Anticipate conflict and develop a plan for resolving it in a manner that supports the relationship with the vendor.
- Anticipate changes to HR culture and careers.

Managing Vendor Relationship

- Develop long-term relationship with outsourcing vendors where such continuity is critical.
- Develop staff members to become effective managers of vendor relationship.
- Maintain stability of internal staff that oversee vendor relationships and understand the performance of expectations originally negotiated.
- Require competitive bidding for each outsourced service at regular intervals.

Monitoring and Evaluating the Vendor Performance

- Establish expectations, measures, and reporting relationships up front for both outsourcing parties.
- Insist on high quality performance by HR vendors.
- Insist on accurate and frequent status reporting by HR vendors and immediate reporting when problems arise.
- Establish performance targets for vendors with the help of outside consultants.
- Consider internal customer surveys for evaluating vendor performance.

Source: Jeffery A. Mello, *Strategic HRM*, p. 156.

Review Questions

1. Describe three types of employees that MNCs can tap into. Which source is more likely to be utilized, in which situations and why?

2. What are the important criteria MNCs should use when selecting expatriates? What factors may influence these criteria?
3. Discuss some theoretical dimensions that may affect anticipatory and in-country adjustment of expatriates. How can these be turned into selection criteria?
4. Imagine yourself to be the CEO of an Indian hotel chain (say, the Taj Group). You have just acquired a five-star hotel in Moscow (Russia). Which country national you will select to head the operations of this hotel? Why? If the acquiring company were to be an American MNC, which country national they would have selected?
5. Discuss the reasons for the failure and success of expatriates.

Assignment

Try to collect as many international job advertisements as you can by scanning international magazines, journals, internet and magazines circulated by airlines for its passengers. Critically examine their effectiveness and relative strengths.

CASE STUDY

Happy to be Going Home

A US family was posted to Melbourne, Australia. The expatriate's role was to assist the Australian subsidiary improve its quality control and supplier relationships. Chuck was placed in charge of purchase department. After 12 months, he had successfully established good links with the company's key components suppliers and was in the process of arranging joint company quality training programmes with these suppliers to ensure that the newly integrated just-in-time inventory procedure was on a sound footing. Chuck was enjoying his new role.

Meanwhile, 10-year-old daughter was finding it difficult to make friends in the expensive private school the company had arranged for her to attend. His wife was also finding life in Australia somewhat hard to cope with. 'On the surface, it seems so much like home, but Australians are not at all same as we Americans, and some people make disparaging remarks about us. They use terms such as 'Yanks'. I miss not being able to find similar things, such as 'brownie mix'. Both wife and daughter were very happy when circumstances provided an acceptable reason for an early end to Chuck's assignment. His elderly mother suffered a bad fall, and there was no other family member to take care of her. The family was repatriated after 14 months ending a 3-year assignment. The expatriate was replaced by another TCN.

Chapter

4

Expatriate Training and Development

LEARNING OBJECTIVES

After studying this chapter, you will be able to:

- *Understand the reasons for training and the types of training provided by multinationals to expatriates*
- *Explore the link between recruitment and selection, performance management, and training and development*
- *Learn the training process as used in international management and note that people from different cultures have different learning styles*
- *Explain how cultural assimilators work and why they are so important*
- *Explain the concept and practice of organization development as practised by international companies.*

OPENING CASE
The International Mind-set Critical factor at SWIFT

SWIFT (The Society for Worlwide Interbank Financial Telecommunication) provides a technology-based financial processing and communication service across financial markets through member banks. It supplies 24-hour global support to 6,460 financial institutions in 177 different countries, processing over 4 million traffic messages valued at over $ 2 trillion a day. It employs 1500 people, globally in numerous locations, including the Belgian HQ, the USA, Asia Pacific, Japan, Europe and Latin America. Staff comes from a wide range of nationalities, covering 35 languages.

SWIFT has recently introduced a focus on an 'international mind-set' as a part of a broader change in its organizational culture. As an organization, it was moving away from a relatively protected and technology-driven institution towards being a more client-and –business driven outfit. New management, deregulation in the sector, and a growing client base of financial institutions (that were themselves internationalizing) made it possible for SWIFT to change its resourcing approach. Teams might include employees from all parts of the world. SWIFT decided to build a 'global culture', not an Anglo-Saxon or Belgian one.

The biggest factor of failure was when people did not see where their value system was different from others', and when it did not map onto another culture easily. Although managers were united by the business language of English, it was clear that Portuguese English, or Japanese English, or many other variants that exist, are quite different one from the other. Without knowing why, communication could become blocked because of simple misunderstandings or even insults read into the language, and because of a lack of understanding of the basic values of the other person's culture.

SWIFT generated 30 corporate-wide critical success factors (CSFs) – or competencies – which can be 'permed' against any role. One CSF deemed unique to international roles is called 'international mind-set'. This is used selectively in key roles felt to be essential among team leaders, global account managers, and sales, consulting and executive roles.

All CSFs were tested against a cross-section of roles. Expert panels judged their importance for each role. A 'language ladder' was created for each CSF, including international mind-set, breaking it down into a series of logically graded levels.

At the simplest level, the focus of the competency is on the ability of staff to be aware of their own style and to be open to different values and styles. This is required for administrative and support functions. The second level becomes relevant for many specialists and project roles, and requires managers to be able to adapt their own behavioral style, have tolerance for the views of others and not allow their own management style and values to override the approach of others. At the third level, managers have to be able to anticipate and reconcile their own differences in styles.

The competency is used in the recruitment process, all 'end-to-end' development work that requires people to collaborate internationally, and for any manager on the executive. On an annual basis there will be typically 120 external recruits; they are all assessed against the competency. It is first applied to job communication , starting with the adverts and all basic communication. It is tested for as part of a criterion-based or situational interview. SWIFT does not feel that psychometric testing is appropriate to select for the competency.

INTRODUCTION

Today, more and more companies are spending substantial amount of money on training and development of their employees to attain long-term organizational goals. Training programmes are designed and delivered after extensive research and preparation so as to give acceptable return on investment, and to secure sustainable competitive advantage.

Most Fortune 500 companies have established their own training centres, schools and even universities. As Kamoche (1996) reminds us, 'the human resource refers to the accumulated stock of knowledge, skills and abilities that the individuals possess, which the firm has built over time into an identifiable expertise'. The real issue is how to build a team of internationally oriented, committed and competent personnel that will support the organization's strategic business and enhance its core competencies.

As discussed in Chapter 8, the cost of expatriate failure is very high. Therefore, MNCs take great pains to select the right persons and provide them with appropriate training before their departure as well as on arrival in a particular country. This cross-cultural and job-related training is also necessary because multinationals have to deal with clients and suppliers from different countries and conduct negotiations to set up joint ventures and strategic alliances and manage subsidiaries abroad. Therefore, they invest heavily on the training of all employees, particularly on expatriates.

WHY TRAINING

Training is the process of altering employee behaviour, attitudes, and knowledge in a way that increases the probability of individual and organizational goal attainment. Training aims to improve current work skills and behaviour, whereas development aims to increase abilities in relation to some future position or job, usually managerial. When expatriates are unfamiliar with the customs, cultures and work habits of the local people, they often make critical mistakes, which can be avoided by providing them with proper training. Box 4.1 provides an example.

BOX 4.1 CULTURAL IGNORANCE IS BAD BUSINESS

An American company eager to do business in Saudi Arabia sent over a sales manager to 'get something going'. The salesman began calling contacts soon after his arrival. After many disappointing appointments, the salesman ran into an old friend, who gave him an introduction to some basic rules of Saudi etiquette and how to do business with the Arabs. The salesman learned that he had repeatedly insulted his contacts by his impatience, refusal of coffee, 'business first' attitude and aggressive selling. Even incidental acts such as handling people or papers with his left hand and exposing the side of his shoe while sitting on the floor were improper Saudi customs.

Effective training can prevent many errors and minimise the impact of others. An early study that surveyed 75 organizations in UK., Holland, Belgium and Germany showed that some of the biggest complaints against expatriates revolved around personal shortcomings in areas such as politeness, punctuality, tactfulness, orderliness, sensitivity, reliability, tolerance and empathy. Effective training programmes can minimise these personal problems. Training can also improve the overall management style. Research shows that many host country nationals would like to see' changes in some of the styles of expatriates, including their leadership styles, decision-making, communication and group working. In terms of leadership, the locals would like their expatriate managers to be friendlier, more accessible, supportive and receptive to subordinates' suggestions.

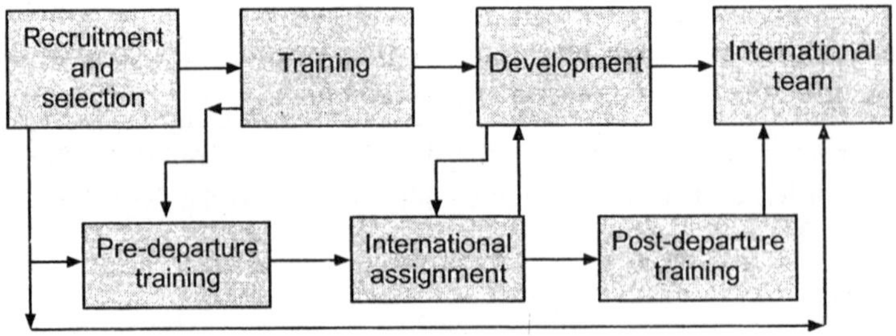

Fig. 4.1 Schematic Representation of Training and Development

Proper training can address some of these demands. It can enhance group decision-making skills, team work and leadership effectiveness. Training and development is a subset of organizational development (OD), culture change and knowledge management. Figure 4.1 is a schematic representation of training and development processes as practised by MNCs. It also shows the link with the recruitment and selection process.

New employees after their selection and old employees on their career move, receive regular training and development inputs. However, before an international assignment, it is customary to send the candidate for post-departure training before he or she assumes full responsibility as member of an international team. Candidates who have the required competency and previous experience in that country may however, be posted straight to international assignments. Initial training focuses on improving technical skills and knowledge of the company's operations and businesses. Expatriates' pre-departure training emphasises on cultural awareness and business customs of the country of posting to help cope with unexpected events in a new country. Post- departure training helps in minimising culture shock and depression that usually sets in a new country and culture.

CULTURAL INTEGRATOR

The simplest training, in terms of preparation time, is to place a cultural integrator in each foreign operation. This individual is responsible for ensuring that the operations and systems are in accordance with the local culture. The integrator advises, guides, and recommends action needed to ensure this synchronisation. The concept of integration is not new; MNCs have long tested their products in foreign markets to ensure that any necessary modifications are made before full-scale selling begins. Similarly, even though people are trained before being sent abroad, they are still not totally prepared to deal with the day-to-day cultural challenges because they lack field experience. This is where the cultural integrator comes into the picture.

He/she is responsible for handling problems between the subsidiary and host cultures. Among other things, he/she advises management on actions that can negatively affect the company's position in the host country and market, and works with the management in developing an appropriate response. Some companies send the cultural integrator from the home office; many choose a host country national who has intimate knowledge of the company's culture and can view operations from both sides. Often, the integrator can only advice or recommend a course of action; he/she has no authority to demand implementation of the action. For this reason the integrator needs proficiency in both conceptual and human relations skills. He/she must be able to envision the relationships between the MNC and the host country that will result in the best 'fit' for both. At the same time, he/she must be able to persuade the managers to accept his/her point of view.

Unfortunately, using an integrator is seldom sufficient. Expatriates must have working knowledge of local customs and known how to handle themselves in business transactions.

MANAGEMENT PHILOSOPHY AND TRAINING

The management philosophy of a company, whether ethnocentric, polycentric, regiocentric or geocentric, also influences the type of training. For example, ethnocentric companies will provide all training at the headquarters and these will be designed and delivered by home nationals polycentric. On the other hand, polycentric companies will rely on local managers to assume responsibilities for seeing that the training function is carried out wherever appropriate. Geocentric companies organize training courses in different parts of the world, where a particular function is being best carried out. Their objective is not only to organize training but also to facilitate future coordination of managers located in different parts by bringing them together and to integrate the company and introduce managers of best practices of different subsidiaries. Similarly, regiocentric companies organize training courses in different countries of the region.

BOX 4.2 HSBC CAREER

Hong Kong and Shangai banking Corporation (HSBC) has a duel career structure for its managers. It recruits graduates who specifically choose a career within their own country (residential officers) or who choose an international career (international officers). Both categories of management recruits undergo the same six-month executive development programme, with a combination of technical and interpersonal skills and the opportunity to develop cultural sensitivity and synergy. Drawing recruits from all over the world on the same programme, with as many as ten diffrenet nationalities living and working together during this initial six months, often provide contacts that last a working lifetime.

The training programme is divided into four stages . the first is an orientation and team building process over a two-day seminar designed to develop a cultural awareness. This provides the process for understanding how cultural background shapes individuals' values, attitudes and behaviour, and the way people from other cultures perceive them. The second stage is a ten-day outdoor development course designed to build team skills, culturat understanding and synergy in situations that require trust , participation and interpersonal skills. This is held in Hong Kong New Territories. The third stage is one-week course in interpersonal skills development. The fourth stage is an international assignment in order for recruits to gain experience in a branch as well as working in a different culture, reinforcing the learning undertaken in the first three stages. The main aim of this is to develop cultural sensitivity and awareness.

Therefore the approach of HSBC is to expose management trainees at an early stage in their career to cross-cultural differences, which will stand them in good stead for the remainder of their careers, whether they are to work internationally or domestically.

(Burmham, Oats, 1991)s

CULTURAL AWARENESS TRAINING

The components of cultural awareness programmes vary according to the country of assignment, duration, purpose and the provider of such programmes. Tung (1981) identified five types of pre-departure training, based on different learning processes, type of job, country of assignment and the time available:

- Area studies that include environmental briefing and cultural orientation;
- Cultural assimilators;
- Language training;
- Sensitivity training; and
- Field experience.

To decide the rigour and level of training, two factors are important: the degree of interaction required in the host culture and similarities between the home and host cultures. According to Tung:

- If the expected interaction between the individual and members of the host culture is low and the degree of dissimilarity between the home and host cultures is also low, then the training should focus on task- and job-related issues rather than culture-related issues. The level of rigour necessary for effective training should be relatively low.
- If there is going to be high level of expected interaction with host nationals and large dissimilarities exist between the cultures, then training should focus on cross-cultural skill development as well as on the new task. The level of rigour should be moderate to high.

The duration of training also depends upon these factors. It could be one to two weeks, in the first case, including focus on area briefing and sensitivity training; in the second case it can extend from two weeks to two months including language training, use of training assimilators and field experience in addition to area briefing and sensitivity training.

DEVELOPING AN INTERNATIONAL MIND-SET

Clearly, the scope of the organization's international activities will have a bearing on the skills required of international team members. However, there are certain skills and characteristics that most international teams have in common. According to Peter Smith 1992;

'Working effectively across cultures is not simply a matter of applying skills found to be effective within the culture of one's own county or organization. It requires also that one can understand and cope with the process of communication and decision-making in settings where these are achieved in a different manner.'

International teams and leaders need to change their frame of reference from a local or national orientation to a truly international perspective. This involves understanding political and cultural influences, trends, practices and international economics. Team leaders in particular need to understand and develop competitive strategies, plans and tactics that operate outside the confines of a domestic market-place orientation.

Being able to understand and lead international teams is critical. Leaders need to be able to deal with issues of collaboration and cross-cultural variances. Merely recognizing that cultural differences exist is not enough. International managers need to be able to manage those differences, if the team is to operate successfully.they need to develop processes for coaching, mentoring and assessing performance across a variety of attitudes, beliefs and standard.

Preliminary Visits

An important technique of orienting expatriates is to send them with their spouses on a preliminary visit to the host country. A Price-Waterhouse survey, (1997, 1998) revealed that 53 per cent of firms always organized a preliminary visit and further 38 per cent indicated such use in certain circumstances. The average duration of the visit was about one week. If the candidate had previous experience of this location, then the preliminary visit may not be necessary.

A well-planned overseas trip for the candidate and spouse provides a preview that allows them to assess their suitability for the job and their interest in the assignment. Such a trip also serves to introduce expatriate candidates to the members of host country management. They can also look into the type of accommodation required and schooling facilities available in the host country so that the same is organized before their arrival. This visit also helps in planning and imparting pre-departure training and initial adjustment in the host country.

The visit also helps in final selection decision by both parties. Exposure to the expatriate community during the visit and the welcome received motivates the expatriates to learn appropriate behaviours and in-country adjustment. They also become aware of the complexity of task and therefore take training seriously.

Language Skills

Language skills are an essential gateway to understanding and working effectively within the culture of the country in question. Being limited in language ability therefore runs the risk of missing out bon the subtletities that can make the difference between business success or failure. According to a report published by the Economist Intelligence Unit (Krempel 1998) businesses are looking for graduates who are multilingual and able to understand business practices and how it differs between countries. The Periperl study found that when it comes to language skills British managers compare unfavourably. Speaking on average 1.7 languages in contrast to their counterparts in 14 countries, who speak an average 2.8 languages. In the Roffey Park study, 35 per cent of the sample recognized language skills as being the main skills required, closely followed by cultural awareness and understanding.

The ability to speak a foreign language improves the expatriate's effectiveness and negotiating ability, and his/her the access to information regarding the host country's economy, government and market. Of course, the degree of fluency required depends on the level and nature of position that the expatriate holds, the amount of interaction with external stakeholders such as government officials, clients, trade officials as well as with host-country nationals. Language skills was identified as a critical component in the expatriate performance in a survey of 400 expatriates conducted by Tung-Arthur-Anderson, (1997). Respondents indicated that the ability to speak the local language, regardless of how different the culture was to their home country, was as important as cultural awareness in their ability to adapt and perform in an assignment abroad. It helped the family to find social support outside the official circle.

However, it takes long time to learn a language; therefore, its training is at times omitted. Hiring people with knowledge of the local language is one solution. For this companies have to maintain records about knowledge of languages in their staff. It is for this reason that business schools today include language courses in their curriculum.

IMPACT OF DIFFERENT LEARNING STYLES ON TRAINING

Learning is the acquisition of skills, knowledge and abilities that results in a relatively permanent change in behaviour. In organising training, it is important to know that cultural differences affect learning style. Research shows that 'Two countries may be similar in ecology, climate and may have similar language and legal, educational and governmental infrastructure, but they may be markedly different in terms of beliefs, attitudes and values.' Moreover, people with different learning styles like different learning environments, and if there is a mismatch between the preferred learning style and work environment, dissatisfaction and poor performance can result.

A recent study (Casse, 1992) investigated learning styles by giving a questionnaire to British, Indian, East African middle managers. Two dimensions of learning styles were measured: analysis and action. The analysis dimension measured the extent to which the learner adopts a theory building and test approach as opposed to using an intuitive approach. The action dimension measured the extent to which the learner uses a trial and error approach as opposed to a contemplative or reflective approach. The researcher found important differences in learning style in these three cultures. Indian managers scored higher in analysis than the other two groups; British managers in action. East African managers scored the lowest in both analysis and action.

Therefore, it is important that not only are the contents of the training programmes designed differently but the processes and learning environment also be matched according to national cultures. Further, it needs to be remembered that even if learning does occur, the new behaviours will not be used if they are not reinforced.

STANDARDISED VS TAILOR-MADE TRAINING

Some management training is standard, or generic. For example, quantitative techniques and decision-making rules can be standardised and used irrespective of where the candidate is posted. Similarly, basic behavioural concepts such as motivation, communication and leadership are often taught first with a generic programme; then a tailor-made programme is created in these areas so that the training material is made country or region specific.

Small firms usually rely on generic programmes while large MNCs have started developing and using country-specific programmes. These programmes are prepared with the help of managers who are currently working in that country and with the help of that country's nationals.

One of the most common types of training is that of self-evaluation. Participants in such training are provided personal insights about their behaviours, for example, whether their managerial style is intuitive, factual, analytical or normative. A factual style manager looks at the available information and makes decisions based on the data. An intuitive style manager is innovative and imaginative and can jump from one idea to another. An analytical style manager is systematic and logical and carefully weighs alternatives to problems. A normative style manager is idealistic and concerned with how things should be done. Every manager is a combination of all four types of styles in varying degrees, but by learning their individual preferences, participants gain insights into their own approach to dealing with people.

TYPES OF CROSS-CULTURAL TRAINING

Tung (1982) surveyed managers in Europe, Japan, and the US and found six major types of cross-cultural training programmes:

1. Environmental briefing is used to provide information about such things as geography, climate, housing and schools.
2. Cultural orientation is designed to familiarise the individual with cultural institutions and value systems of the host country.
3. Cultural assimilators using programmed learning approaches are designed to provide the participants with intercultural encounters.
4. Language training is aimed at increasing communication effectiveness.
5. Sensitivity training is designed to develop attitudinal flexibility.
6. Field experience is arranged to make the expatriate familiarise with the challenge of assignment.

Some organizations have now extended this idea to include cross-cultural training to family members, especially children as they will be accompanying their parents.

CULTURAL ASSIMILATORS

Cultural assimilator has become an important technique of cross-cultural training. It is a programmed learning technique that is designed to expose members of one culture to some of the basic concepts, attitudes, role perceptions, customs and values of another culture. These assimilators are developed for each pair of cultures: one culture where the candidate is currently working and the other culture is where he is proposed to be posted.

In most cases, these assimilators require the trainee to read a short episode of a cultural encounter and choose an interpretation of what has happened and why. If the trainee's choice is correct, he or she goes to the next episode. If the response is incorrect, the trainee is asked to reread the episode and choose another response. An example of cultural assimilator is given in Section 9.9.2 of this chapter. One of the major problems in constructing an effective cultural assimilator is deciding what is important enough to include. Some assimilators use critical incidents that are identified as important. To be identified as a critical incident, a situation must meet at least one of the following conditions:

1. An expatriate and a host interact in the situation.
2. The situation is puzzling or likely to be misinterpreted by the expatriate.
3. The situation can be accurately interpreted if sufficient knowledge about the culture is available.
4. The situation is relevant to the expatriate's task or mission requirements.

These incidents are typically obtained by asking expatriates and host nationals with whom they come in contact to describe specific intercultural occurrences or events that made a major difference in their attitudes and behaviour towards members of the other culture. These incidents can be unpleasant, pleasant or simply non-understandable occurrences.

Validation of the Assimilator

Validation means testing that the incident measures what it is intended to measure. After the cultural assimilator's critical incidents are constructed and alternative responses written, the process is validated by asking a number of people. If the majority of people agree for a particular response, it is the right one. If more than one response gets larger support than either the incident is revised or the response is revised. A second validation is to ask how important the incident is. This helps in eliminating incidents of marginal value. After this is done they are grouped so that similar incidents are placed together and presented, beginning with simple situations and progressing to more complex ones. About 75 to 100 incidents are selected for training. This is an expensive method, costing about $ 40,000 and taking roughly 800 hours to prepare. The contents remain useful for considerable time.

Example of Cultural Assimilator[1]

Situation: Sharon, a schoolteacher in Athens, was amazed at the questions that were asked of her by Greeks whom she considered to be only casual acquaintances. When she entered or left her apartment, people would ask her where she was going or where she had been. If she stopped to talk, she was asked questions like, 'How much you make a month?' or 'Where did you get the dress you are wearing?' She thought that the Greeks were very rude.

Questions: Why did the Greeks ask Sharon such questions?

Options:

1. The casual acquaintances were acting like friends do in Greece, although Sharon did not realise it.
2. The Greeks asked Sharon the question in order to determine whether she belonged to the Greek Orthodox Church.
3. The Greeks were unhappy about the way she lived and they were trying to get Sharon to change her habits.
4. In Greece such questions are perfectly proper when asked of women, but improper when asked of men.

You selected 1: The casual acquaintances were acting like friends do in Greece, although Sharon did not realise it.

Correct. It is not improper for in-group members to ask these questions of one another. Furthermore, these questions reflect the fact that friendships tend to be more intimate in Greece than in America. As a result, friends are generally free to ask questions, which would seem too personal in America.

If you have chosen any other option than you will be explained why that option or interpretation is not right.

---

[1] Fred E. Fiedler, Terence Mitchell, and Harry C. Triandis, 'The Culture Assimilator' *Journal of Applied Psychology*, April 1971, pp. 97–98.

BOX 4.3 CORPORATE PROGRAMMES TO DEVELOP INTERNATIONAL MANAGERS

- ABB (Area Brown Boveri) rotates about 500 managers around the world to different countries every two to three years in order to develop a management cadre of transpatriates to support their global strategy.
- PepsiCo has an orientation programme for its foreign managers, which brings them to the U.S. for one-year assignments in bottling division plants.
- British Telecom uses informal mentoring techniques to induct employees into the ways of their assigned country; existing expatriate managers talk to prospective assignees about the cultural factors to expect.
- Honda of America Manufacturing gives its US supervisors and managers extensive preparation in Japanese language, culture and then sends to Tokyo for up to three years to the parent country.
- General Electric likes its engineers to have a global perspective whether or not they are stated to go abroad. The company gives regularly language and cross-cultural training for them so that they are equipped to conduct business with people around the world.

DIVERSITY TRAINING

It is now well established that one of the major sources of competitive advantages for business is the effective management and development of people. Illustrative of this trend is the research report (Sparrow, Schuler, and Jackson, 1994) covering 2000 organizations pointed out that the dominant view of participants was that an organization's people provide the only realistic basis for achieving a sustainable competitive advantage. In a global setting the emphasis leads to considerations of the management of diversity and related challenges. Another major challenge facing global organizations is their ability to develop practices that balance global competitiveness, multinational flexibility and the building of worldwide learning capability. Achieving this balance requires global firms to develop cultural sensitivity in their managers and an ability to manage and leverage learning to build future capability. In looking at the dynamics involved in organizational learning and competitive success, the key role of effective team-working is highlighted.

It focuses on understanding differences – race, age, ethnicity, gender – between individuals. Diversity in organizations is a fact of life. It aims at convincing every one, how diffences can be useful to an organizations. These advantages are noted below. Effective organizations that recognize the issues involved in diversity management do something to capitalize on the advantages and at the same time deal appropriately with any negative aspects of diversity.

- *Larger applicant pool* – Maintaining an effective diverse workforce will contribute to a good reputation and more will want to join, giving better possibility of selecting better employees, which will result in better workforce.
- *Reduced costs* – An effective diverse workforce will result in less turnover, which mean less rehiring due to quits and also paying legal expenses and settling law suits for discrimination . Also the tension created in organizations where they do not deal with diversity will not be present and the outcomes of such tensions, such as low productivity, absenteeism, fighting, refusing to cooperate etc, will not be present.

- *Access to more markets* – the more diverse an organization is the more it will attract and cultivate a diverse customer base.
- *Creating problem solving* – the more diverse the group, the more diverse the ideas that are generated. Employees with different backgrounds are more likely to see issues from different perspectives, resulting in more creative ideas, which can result in better products and services.

For diversity training to conduct no training need analysis is really necessary. Further it is also necessary to align organizational systems and policies to support the diversity goals discussed in Chapter 13 – Managing Diversity. It is useful to use Lewin's force-field analysis to identify all the forces that are pushing for the status quo, i.e. resisting the diversity programme. The training can be directed to reduce those forces, attitudes that are resisting while strengthening forces that are helping change. Diversity objectives need to be reflected in management of performance appraisals. The training session should be introduced by company president highlighting the importance of diversity, in person and if it is not possible than through videotape. The best learning comes through trainees to discuss the issues facilitated by the trainer. For this small group teams be organized to discuss and present their findings to larger group. Using real cases or incidences from the company can be quite useful.

CROSS-CULTURAL TEAM BUILDING

Global organizations face a growing need to ensure that groups of managers from different nationalities work together effectively, either in management teams or in project teams addressing specific business issues. However, many organizations have found that bringing groups of managers of different cultural backgrounds together in a team can in practice be difficult. Following areas can be addressed to build effective cross-cultural teams:

- Identifying the nature and implications of national cultural differences within the team
- Establishing a basis for building understanding and awareness of national cultural differences and he ways in which they may be managed
- Formulating a framework for performing a high performing team which takes account of cultural differences and leverages the diversity present in an international team.

The first area of understanding the nature and impact of cultural dimensions are discussed in great depth in part- II, chapters 8 &9. These dimensions are: power-distance; individualism-collectivism; masculinity-femininity and low-high uncertainty avoidance. Most managers can identify the disadvantages of each cultural dimension but finding advantages of them is difficult. For example, the advantages of low and high uncertainty avoidance cultures are given below:

- Low-Uncertainty avoidance (individuals tolerance of ambiguity is low, example-Sweden)

  1. Achievement
  2. Leader as facilitator
  3. Minimum rules
  4. Open-ended learning

- High uncertainty avoidance- Germany, Us
  1. Security
  2. Leader as expert
  3. Emotional need for rules
  4. Structured learning

Hofstede further provides illustration of comparative contributions from different cultural perspectives:

Potential Competitive Advantages of Different Cultures

	LOW	*HIGH*
Power-distance	Accept responsibility	Discipline
Individual/Collective	Individual Management mobility	Collective Employee committment
Uncertainty Avoidance	Low Innovation	High Precision
Masculine-faminine	Masculine Efficiency Mass production	Feminine Personal service; custom-building

In team building training programme aims at:

1. Creating awareness of both of individual's own culture and the differences between national cultures.
2. Development of knowledge of the effect of cultural differences, and of relative strengths and weaknesses of different cultures in a management context.
3. Building of skills in the areas of managerial cultural sensitivity.

What ever the theory says, it is practice that influences organizational behavior: it is through working on real issues in a multicultural setting, using a structured framework, that skills and understanding are developed. The team building exercises are designed to:

- Build cohesion and consistency in teamworking
- Develop a shared vision and understanding
- Establish high-quality dialogue between members
- Establish full-circle feedback mechanism to review and improve team processes
- Overcoming hurdles
- Leadership behavior
- Effective pooling of knowledge and skills.

Review Questions

1. Why is training important and what are the main challenges faced in training and development of expatriate managers?
2. Identify the key aspects of successful pre-departure training programmes for expatriates.

3. Discuss how 'cultural integrators' and 'cultural assimilators' are helpful in cross-cultural training.
4. IBM is planning on sending three managers to its Zurich office, two to Madrid and two to Tokyo. None of them has any international experience. Would you suggest using a standard training programme or tailor-made programmes for each group?
5. Write short notes on following:

   - Field visits as part of pre-departure training.
   - Cultural influence on learning styles.
   - Different approaches towards training of ethnocentric, polycentric, regiocentric and geocentric organizations.

Assignment

Select any multinational and research the staffing policy and training methods practiced by it. Each group is to select a different multinational organization for this type of study. Each group should present the findings in the class and note the differences

Chapter

5

Performance Management in International Organizations

LEARNING OBJECTIVES

After studying this chapter, you will be able to:

- *Develop a framework for performance management for multinational organizations and for expatriate employees*
- *Understand various factors that influence performance management and assessment of expatriate performance*
- *Develop criteria for performance appraisal of expatriates and provide support and feedback.*
- *Discuss how culture influences performance appraisal and the feedback process*
- *Understand transactional and psychological contracts and the importance of role analysis.*
- *Learn about the importance and impact of cross-culture on the feedback process.*

CASE STUDY – PERFORMANCE APPRAISAL ACROSS CULTURES

All over the Far East organizations are coming to terms with the contrasts in approach between the Oriental ways of managing and the Western ways. In many areas, such as production management and finance, the Western techniques have penetrated deeply and with little resistance. It is in the human area of management that most of the resistance is felt and it is in the human area of management that most organizations succeed or fail. There is little doubt that cultural factors affect organizations as they have such a large impact on the way people relate to each other. Research has still not penetrated the mysteries of the process of co-operation in sufficient detail for us to understand them precisely, but the average practicing manager knows very well that he cannot ignore local ways of doing things and local sensitivities.

These contrasts in basic assumptions are keys to understanding the success or failure of appraisal systems. If you were to take apart the Western values which underlie the performance appraisal itself they would look something like the following:

1. That measured performance, or assessed performance, is the best indicator of a person's worth.
2. That a performance is attributable to a single individual.
3. That having everyone subject to similar assessment will cause the system to be perceived as fair.
4. That objectivity, neutrality and fairness are important, and the employee's relation with the organization be depersonalized.
5. That the subordinate has some recourse to appeal, if necessary, to authority other than to his boss.
6. That the responsibility for performance provides the individual with room to operate freely inside the constraints of producing the performance.
7. That people should compete in terms of performance.
8. That individual initiative and creativity (assuming they are normally possessed by high performers) should be encouraged.

All of these values are typical of individual-centred societies and there are many reasons to suggest that most of them do not transfer to the Orient. In many Oriental contexts high value is placed on smoothness of interpersonal relations, an avoidance of conflict and open confrontation. The exchange of mutual obligations, even of a highly informal kind, is a variation of the theme of paternalism. The end product is a set of fairly stable organizations, albeit usually small ones. It is, however, impossible to generalize about the response managers should make, except to say that the basic techniques are likely to need some local adaptation, if they are to work successfully.

It poses an interesting challenge for all those concerned with personal development and with management control. It should also be clearly understood that the Asian methods of management and the Asian version of the processes of management control have produced remarkably high levels of organizational efficiency and national economic performance. It should never be assumed that Western methods are automatically superior. At the same time, the development of techniques, which combine the best of both worlds, is clearly likely to have important and valuable practical consequences.

INTRODUCTION

The opening article clearly brings out the complexities in performance appraisal process due to cross-cultural factors. Due care is therefore required in designing performance appraisal system for subsidiaries located in different cultural zones with local adaptation.

Since organizations exist to achieve goals, the degree of success that individual employees have in reaching their individual goals is important in determining organizational effectiveness. The assessment of how successful employees have been in meeting their individual goals, therefore becomes a critical part of human resource management. In case of multinationals, several new dimensions; mostly cross-culture related, influence the process. The evaluation of performance of expatriates is very much linked with the performance of subsidiaries, which they are sent to manage.

Multinationals are groups of subsidiaries that are collaboratively trying to achieve sustainable competitive advantage through mutually supportive goals. The evaluation of performance of an individual subsidiary becomes complex, and this has to be taken into account while evaluating the performance of expatriates and multinational enterprises.

PERFORMANCE MANAGEMENT AND ITS LINK WITH OTHER HR PROCESSES

Performance management is the central process of the human resource cycle because it influences the following essential processes:

1. **Rewards management:** Proper design of rewards and its administration is central to employee motivation as brought out by various process theories of motivation. Rewards can be allocated in relation to performance only through the use of an appraisal system by which performance can be measured. Such appraisal systems range from subjective personal evaluations to impersonal criteria based on profitability, return on investment, market share and other quantitative measures. If rewards are to be really effective in enhancing commitment, they must be perceived to be fair, timely and valued by employees. Therefore, the appraisal system should furnish information to the management in time and about individual performance and the same should be perceived to be fair.
2. **Human resource planning:** Future requirement of human resources in any organization depends on its planned strategic growth as well as on the current inventory of skills and competencies. A current inventory of talent can be made only through a valid appraisal process that shows those who are performing well and those who are not. In addition, future human resource projections must be based on an assessment of the potential of employees, which is indicated by the appraisal process. Without this data, provided by a valid appraisal system, such forecasting is impossible, as there is no basis – making predictions. Competency mapping is also dependent on a proper appraisal of employee skills, attitudes and expertise.
3. **Training and development process:** This again entirely rests on the appraisal process. Based on an assessment of an individual's performance and potential, the individual and organizational needs can be ascertained for future training and development programmes. A weak database in this regard may lead to hit or miss training programmes and may not result in the development of human resources.

4. **Relationship with strategy:** Business strategy concerns with how objectives are set and what needs to be done to achieve those objectives. One of the main components of performance management is to set mutually supportive, organization-wide chain of objectives, which are specific, measurable, jointly set, as well as resource and time-bound. Multinationals, therefore, develop appraisal processes that are supportive of the business strategy and are in sync with organizational values and culture.

   An effective performance system at the strategic level depends upon the commitment of quality management time of senior executives, including the CEO. Perhaps the company with the best strategic performance management system is General Electric, where much time and staff work go into appraising the top 600 executives – most of them expatriates.

   It can be said that performance management is the most important responsibility of HR executives in global transnational organizations.

MULTINATIONAL PERFORMANCE MANAGEMENT

A multinational, whether it is global, transnational, multi-domestic or international, has a global strategy and goals. In this strategy, the role of foreign subsidiaries is to help achieve the overall goals of the firm, which may include supporting another subsidiary at its own cost. Therefore, individual subsidiary performance is evaluated according to the expectations and appropriate outcomes and behaviour that contribute to organizational goal attainment.

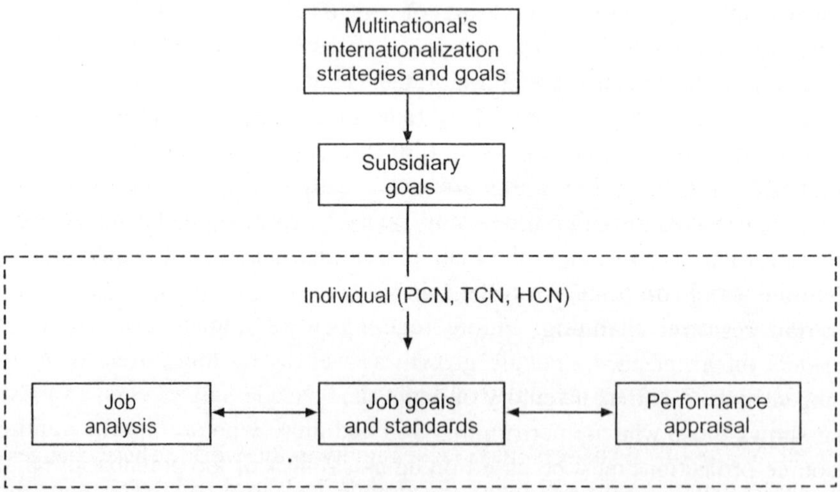

Fig. 5.1 Basic Components of Performance Management

The corporate office has specific expectations from each of its foreign affiliates in terms of market performance, raw material supplies or overall profitability and competitiveness. In this respect, the financial management of a large multinational is highly integrated and transactions between subsidiaries are netted and balance transactions are directed to a common centre, which is located in a country, providing maximum freedom for financial transactions. These transactions are so designed that maximum advantage is taken of tax arbitrage, interest arbitrage, exchange arbitrage, minimization of capital cost, and so on. Due consideration is paid to inflation rates and governmental laws controlling investments, royalty payments for patents, profits and technology transfer fees. Hence, the performance of expatriates in top positions in these subsidiaries depends on the performance of these subsidiaries. Therefore, we must understand the factors that influence or constrain the goal attainment of subsidiaries. These factors are:

Whole vs. Part

A multinational is a single entity even though it faces multiple environments in different countries and a variety of competitions. Hence, an integrated approach is a must for its success to take advantage of global opportunities and manage local as well as global threats. In this context, the good of the whole becomes more important than the good of the part, or short-term profitability of the subsidiary. Puick provides an example where a multinational establishes a subsidiary in a country to block the cash flow of its competitor by offering discounts and lower prices to customers, forcing its competitor to react in the same way. If this is not done the competitor might enter and challenge it in its major market share country. In this case, this subsidiary will be in the red but will be helping the whole company to remain profitable. Other examples are when one unit supplies components at prices lower than the cost price to minimise profits where profits cannot be appropriated or the tax rate is high. Here, again, the unit, even though doing well, incurs poor balance-sheet results. Thus, while appraising the performance of subsidiaries, these specific roles played by each subsidiary for its corporate entity must be taken into account.

Non-comparable Data

Different countries have different accounting practices, which make it difficult to compare results across subsidiaries. Subsidiaries have to comply with local accounting practices and rules. For example, in one country sales on consignment are treated as firm sales while in other countries it is based on receipt of payment, and headquarters may not be aware of this. Similarly, import tariffs may distort pricing schedules or strike in one country may hold up supplies to one of its plants in another country. Different labour laws and compensation systems in the event of lay-offs may also distort or complicate the evaluation of comparative results.

Volatility of the International Environment

Economic, social, and political changes may occur rapidly in the world. These changes directly affect the subsidiary performance results, yet they are often difficult to predict. This unpredictability in the international environment requires that long-term goals be flexible in order to respond to such environmental changes. Goals should not remain tied to multinational's pre-decided strategy and evaluated only on that consideration. For example, the Iraq war had a profound impact on oil prices and each subsidiary would have had a different impact on its balance sheet. Problems arise when subsidiary managers perceive goals and deadlines set by distant headquarters' strategy team as unrealistic and inflexible that do not take local conditions into account. If both regional and subsidiary managers are jointly involved in strategy-making and periodic review, such difficulties can be resolved or minimized.

Separation by time and distance

Time and distance make it difficult for headquarters to understand the problems or the gravity of the situation faced by subsidiaries. Higher-level managers may have little real opportunity to observe the performance of subsidiary managers unless considerable time, money and effort are expended by them in travelling to visit all subsidiary locations. Developments in sophisticated worldwide communication systems, such as video telephone, teleconference, and e-mail, do not fully substitute for face-to-face contacts between subsidiary managers and corporate staff. In some cases these facilities are also not so developed. Meeting personally is often necessary to fully understand each person's situation. For this reason, corporate managers have to travel a great deal between subsidiaries to realistically evaluate their performance in different fields.

Headquarter-subsidiary interdependence

How a subsidiary performs depends, to a large extent, on how well the multinational as a whole supports it, how much autonomy is granted in making its own strategy and implementation.

Ethical and legal issues

Many multinationals assess performance using result-oriented measures. It may be important, however, to assess how the subsidiary management is achieving its results. For example, the Foreign Corrupt Practices Act makes it illegal for American managers operating overseas to use bribes and pay-offs to achieve business advantages.

Market Maturity

Some markets are simply less developed than others. Subsidiaries in these markets, where the supporting infrastructure is not available, may perform much less well in terms of sales volume than subsidiaries in more established markets. This makes any purely bottom-line assessment of performance inappropriate. For example, at home, established brands can support new products, and new business areas can be cross-subsidized.

The productivity levels of people are very different in different parts of the world. In countries like India, infrastructural and governmental delays are so frustrating that a multinational unit may not succeed in obtaining timely clearances, resulting in long project overruns in time and cost.

In short, there are a number of significant constraints that must be considered when evaluating the performance of a foreign subsidiary and expatriates working there.

PERFORMANCE MANAGEMENT OF EXPATRIATES

Performance management is a process that enables a multinational to evaluate and continually improve individual subsidiary performance against clearly defined pre-set targets and goals. Story and Sisson (1993) emphasise four sub-processes:

1. Setting clear goals for each unit, each department and every individual employee, which are derived from the organization's and subsidiary's corporate goals. These goals must be mutually

supportive and balanced for long- and short-term needs. There must be as much participation as possible at all levels by everyone.

2. Setting standard and measurement criteria for evaluating each type of goal.
3. Formal monitoring and review of progress towards these objectives.
4. Using the outcomes of the review process to reinforce desired employee behaviour through differential rewards and identifying training and development needs.

Clark (1995) stresses one additional performance management activity – that of feeding back to the employee the result of the monitoring and recycling the objectives in the light of the feedback (Fig. 5.2).

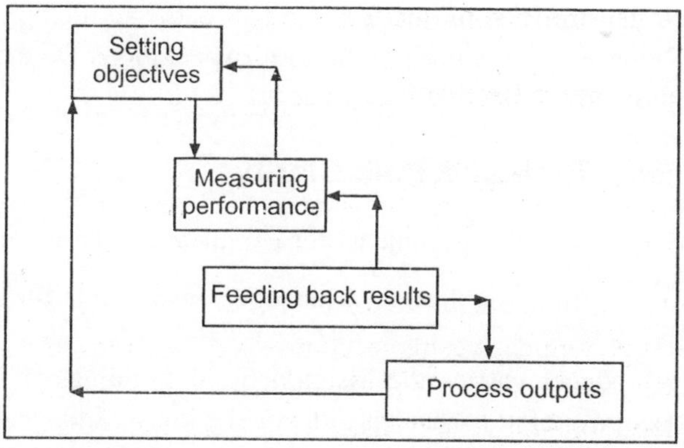

Fig. 5.2 Performance Management Cycle

Source: Adapted from Clark, 1995.

A study of performance management (Institute of Personnel Management, 1992) offers several advantages. Among these are:

1. Employees are able to meet more effectively increased local, regional and global competition in their markets.
2. A greater opportunity for employees to share and work for the achievement of the organization's vision and mission.
3. The pushing of key decisions down the organizational structure to line managers and supervisors. This creates empowerment and motivation.
4. A greater acceptance of accountability by line managers about such decisions.
5. Reward structures which forge a close link between individual and/or group performance.
6. Linking of training and development efforts with individual and organizational needs.
7. Managing organizational change.

VARIABLES THAT INFLUENCE PERFORMANCE OF EXPATRIATES

Performance can be viewed as a combination of several variables, such as motivation, ability, working conditions, clarity of goals and roles, and expectations. The following factors and their interrelationships affect performance assessment of expatriates:

- Compensation package;
- Nature of assignment (assignment task variables and role of the expatriate);
- Support from headquarters;
- Environment in which performance occurs; and
- Cultural adjustment of the individual and the accompanying family members.

Compensation Package

There are several reasons why individuals accept foreign assignments, such as additional pay and benefits, career progression, prestige and experience. Amongst these the desire to make savings for future security is perhaps the strongest reason for going abroad, sacrificing comforts of home, family and friends If compensation is not commensurate with expectations the expatriate's motivation and commitment are likely to be low, affecting performance.

Nature of Assignment, Task and Role Clarity

Hay has identified four types of task assignments for expatriates. These are:

1. The chief executive officer, or subsidiary manager, responsible for overall functioning of the subsidiary.
2. The structure reproducer carries the assignment of building, or reproducing in a foreign subsidiary, a structure similar to that which he or she knows from another part of the company. For example, he or she could be building a marketing framework, implementing an accounting and financial reporting system or establishing a production plant in another country and subsidiary.
3. The trouble-shooter is the individual sent to a foreign subsidiary to analyse and solve a particular problem.
4. The operative performs functional tasks in an existing operational structure, generally at lower-level supervisory positions.

Tahavanainen (1981) in her study of Nokia Telecommunications, identifies five categories of personnel: top managers, middle managers, business establishers, project employees, and research and development personnel. She, working on an American multinational, added a fifth category of *explorers* who identify investment opportunities in a particular sector and make direct and indirect investments.

There are differences in the way performance management and appraisal are approached in each such group. For example, middle managers play a moderate role in establishing performance objectives, whereas business establishers play a strong role in establishing their own performance goals and job descriptions.

Task variables are more under the control of multinationals than environmental factors. Because of this, task variables can be better assessed and more easily changed, depending, of course, on the level of positions and the nature of task assignment. Along with determination of task specifics, multinationals also specify roles for each expatriate and this is usually predetermined by corporate managers.

Some tasks require an individual to operate within a given structure, while other tasks demand the creation of structures. Individuals vary greatly in their ability to conceive and implement a system and in their tolerance for lack of structure and ambiguity. There are cases of expatriates, having brilliant track records in structured corporate environments but failing miserably when asked to create a structure and operate in ambiguity.

Role Clarity

A role is an organized set of behaviours assigned to a particular position. This role is predetermined by the management. For the expatriate (role recipient), the parent company or headquarters (the role sender) predetermines his/her role in the foreign assignment and this is communicated to him by senior executives in meetings before his/her departure. Sometimes, when communicating the role, cross-cultural aspects are neglected. The role expectancy is also influenced by organizational norms and values. However, even before the expatriate arrives in the subsidiary, various stakeholders have certain expectations from him and how he/she should discharge his/her responsibilities. These role expectations are in the context of organizational and national cultures. The difficulty this presents for the expatriate managers is that the role is defined in one country but performed in another. Similarly, when performance is evaluated or feedback is given, the cultural boundary is crossed and an expatriate's performance may suffer due to role conflict in trying to perform to different expectations. A study by Janssens (1994) indicated that a role conflict is likely to result in situations where the international manager has an understanding of the host-country culture and realizes that the use of headquarters' procedures and actions may lead to ineffective management. She postulated that the higher the degree of intercultural interactions, the more problems the expatriate has with role conflict.

From the perspective of the headquarters, commitment to the parent company is more important for transferring technology and doing things in company ways. If the expatriate is perceived to be identifying more with the subsidiary (the term used is 'going native'), he/she is transferred or recalled. This is also one of the reasons why a multinational restricts expatriates' service to about three years.

There is another factor known as 'role autonomy' or job discretion. In this case the expatriate has more job discretion in his/her parent organization but finds the subsidiary job tightly structured or vice versa. This again affects performance. A well-planned pre-departure training can take care of these problems.

Psychological Contract – Headquarter's Support

In understanding an expatriate's motivation and performance, we have to understand the concept of psychological and employment contracts. When an employee joins a firm he/she is provided with an explicit employment contract stating the terms and conditions of service and the job requirement. This is also known as the transactional contract. There is another component of an employment contract, known as relational or psychological contract, which are implicit expectations of employer about the morale, the support in work and quality of life – his belief regarding promises made accepted, and relied upon while accepting the job. It is based upon perceived reciprocal obligations pertaining to both formal and informal contracts and implicit agreements, and is, by nature, subjective and specific to the individual. Both transactional and psychological contracts operate within the framework of social contract, which is to work according to a set of values, beliefs and cultural norms pertaining to a society and culture. Violation of the psychological contract occurs when an individual feels that the organization has not fulfilled its obligation in return for the efforts and contributions made by him/her; this perceived discrepancy has a negative effect on commitment and loyalty to the organization.

When an expatriate takes responsibility in a distant subsidiary, he/she undergoes a process of adjustment, forming emotional and psychological impressions in his/her mind. He/she also gets cut-off from friends and family. Thus, if the expatriate perceives that the multinational has not provided the promised level of support, the perceived violation of the psychological contract may affect his/her performance and loyalty, and trigger an early recall. A perception of lack of adequate support for the family may also decrease the commitment to the point that the expatriate may resign from the organization. Thus, headquarters' support is an important variable. This responsibility usually falls on the corporate human resource personnel. Generally, each expatriate is assigned to a particular person who remains constantly in touch and provides information and needed support on behalf of the headquarters.

Environment of the Host Country

Environment is a key factor not only in the design of organization structure but in the impact it has on the performance of a subsidiary and individual jobs. In case of international business, both domestic and global environments have an impact. For instance, managing a fully owned subsidiary in China is different from managing a joint venture with a Chinese counterpart or with Chinese state-owned enterprises with continuously shifting goals. Similarly, operating in terror-affected areas or areas with racial conflicts can also affect an expatriate's performance and needs due consideration.

Cultural Adjustment

We have discussed this aspect earlier in reasons for the expatriate's failure. The process of cultural adjustment may be a critical determinant of the expatriate's job performance. The problem is that adjusting to a foreign culture is multifaceted, and individuals vary in their reactions and coping abilities. The concept of adjustment cycle is helpful in depicting the adjustment process (Fig. 5.3). The first phase is known as the 'honeymoon phase', or 'tourist phase', commencing from selection to pre-

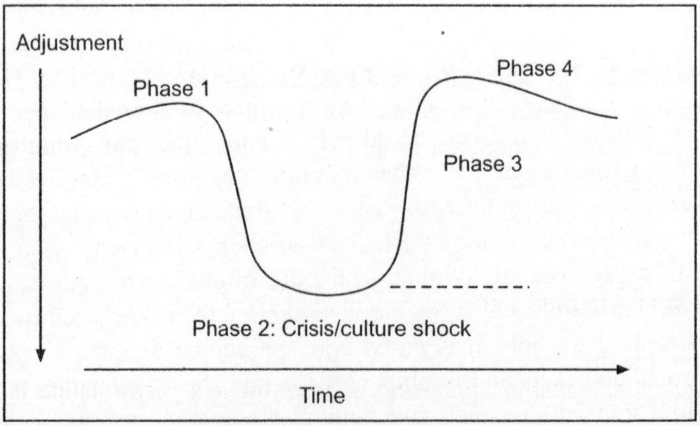

Fig. 5.3 Adjustment Cycle

Source: Adapted from H. De Cieri, P.J. Dowling, and K.F. Taylor, 'The Psychological Impact of Expatriate Relocation on Partners' in *International Journal of HRM*, Vol. 2, No. 3, 1991, p. 380.

departure training and arrival. Anxiety, challenge, hope, excitement, fear of the unknown and a sense of adventure characterise this phase. During this phase the expatriate is upbeat and has a positive approach. Then, as the novelty wears off, realities of everyday life begin to intrude, homesickness sets in, and depression takes over, leading to a period of crisis. This can be a critical time, and how the individual copes in this phase has an important outcome in terms of success or failure. Once past this crisis as the expatriate comes to terms with the new environment, there is a 'looking up' in phase three. It is likely that the expatriate and his family members undergo these cycles individually, but not all members of the family face the same mood at the same time. Certain personality factors, along with support from headquarters and spouse, and pre-departure and post-departure training can shorten the period of depression and thus help in improving the performance.

CRITERIA USED FOR PERFORMANCE APPRAISAL

First, against the company's long- and short-term goals, the expatriate's job goals and standards are fixed; achievement of these goals is measured using the standards. The goals and objectives should be specific, measurable, resource- and time-bound, previously discussed and mutually agreeable.

Goals can be further divided into hard and soft goals. Hard goals are quantifiable and can be measured such as market share, return on investment, profits earned for parent company and so on. Soft goals tend to be relationship-based, such as leadership style or interpersonal skills. Contextual goals take into consideration factors that result from the situation in which performance occurs. For example, multinationals commonly use arbitrary transfer pricing for transactions between subsidiaries in order to minimise foreign exchange risk exposure and tax expenditures. Thus, soft goals and contextual goals complement the hard goals. Periodic review and appropriate and timely feedback help in the expatriate's performance management.

Every manager has multiple obligations, not the least of which are certain kinds of relationships with peers, subordinates, suppliers, consumers, financial institutions and the government and public. Some of them are more important than others, and some need to be handled with much greater skill and aplomb than others. Because static job descriptions define behaviour in gross terms, crucially important differentiated aspects of behaviour are lost when performance appraisals are made. In a progressive company's PAS, the manager works out his own job description, prepares a mission and role statement of what he is supposed to do according to the guide which specifically directs him to concentrate on the what and the when, not on the why or the how. The guide instructs him to divide his mission into four general areas:

1. Innovation,
2. Problem-solving,
3. On-going administration, and
4. Personal.

In another company, a manager appraising a subordinate's performance is asked to describe an employee's accomplishments, neglected areas, goals and objectives. The manager is told to recognize good work, suggest improvement, get agreement on top priority elements of the task, clarify responsibility, verify and correct rumours, and talk about personal and long-range goals.

In another company's outstanding performance appraisal guide, which reflects great detail and careful consideration, the categories are: work, effectiveness with others, problem-solving, decision-making, goal setting, organization planning, developing subordinates, attending to self-development, and finding initiatives. Each of these categories is broken down into example statements such as:

- Exhibits high level of independence in work.
- Identifies problems and deals with them.
- Appropriately subordinates departmental interest to overall company goal.
- Gives people genuine responsibility, holds them accountable, and allows them freedom to act.

Some experts have suggested role analysis techniques to cope with static job description. Even these techniques are of limited use because they do not specify required behaviours. Nowhere the individual is told what behaviour is expected of him in a range of contexts. Who are the sensitive people with whom certain kinds of relationships have to be maintained? What are the specific problems and barriers? What have been the manufacturing blunders or frictions? How should union relationships and union leaders be dealt with? What are the specific integrative problems to be resolved and what are the historical conflicts? These and many more similar pieces of behaviours will be the true bases on which a person will be judged, regardless of the questions an appraisal form asks. This is the background of techniques, 'behaviourally anchored rating scale' (BARS) and 'behaviour observation scale' (BOS). In order for performance appraisal to be effective for coaching, mentoring, teaching, and changing those aspects of an employee's behaviour that are amenable to change, an employee needs to know about each piece of behaviour that is good as well as that which for some reason is not acceptable or needs modification. Hence it is utmost important to keep appropriate database about an employee's strengths and weaknesses and skills and regularly track it and use it, as brought out in Box 5.1 'EMI Music'.

It is important that there should be more than one individual to assess the performance. Besides self-appraisal there should be inputs from his subordinates as well as from one's super-boss (boss of the immediate superior). In practice, home-office managers often write performance evaluations after receiving inputs from on-sight managers. In such cases, it is recommended that a former expatriate who has served in the same location be involved in the appraisal to help reduce bias.

PERFORMANCE FEEDBACK

Feedback refers to the information provided about work behaviour and outcomes. Feedback controls the work behaviour of employees by directing actions where they are needed through timely on-going feedback. In addition, feedback promises rewards for future behaviour and thereby provides motivation. It also helps the management to understand the situation better. Hence, feedback is a vital part of performance management system.

In case of MNCs the task of providing feedback is compounded by time and distance. Interaction between the head-office staff and the subsidiary managers is less frequent and a reporting system adds to its cost. One can suggest that advancements in telecommunication facilities, such as fax, e-mail, internet and video-conferencing, help overcome the constraints of time and distance. Although such facilities help in collecting and transmitting information, they are no substitutes for the face-to-face communication. Feedback is not only to communicate facts, it is about finding the problem that has prevented higher performance about finding the solution which is mutually acceptable and about reclarifying roles and goals. The feedback activity is a great opportunity to enhance relationships and motivation. It is for this reason that international managers and IHRM executives travel long distances and spend considerable time interacting with subsidiary managers. Performance feedback has a development aspect, as it brings out the need for training and development as well.

An important aspect of an effective performance management system is the provision of timely feedback of the evaluation process. One of the problems with annual appraisal is that employees do not receive consistent and frequent feedback considered critical to maintain or improve performance. Cultural factors must be taken into account if the person giving feedback and the person receiving it come from different cultures.

CULTURAL IMPLICATIONS OF FEEDBACK PROCESS

When the two managers come face-to-face during the feedback process, their cultures also interact. Collectivist and individualistic cultures differ in the way goals are designed and assigned. In a collectivist society goals are decided for the group in consultation with them. Since a large number of employees are involved in decision-making, not only better decisions are made, they are implemented fast and in a more coordinated manner as everyone is aware of the assumptions made and the strategy chosen. It ensures more commitment and responsibility on the part of employees. On the other hand, in individual cultures the goals are decided mutually and responsibility is fixed on individuals. Since rewards are linked to performance, individuals try their best to achieve the goals. Higher individual initiative and creativity are brought on the tasks.

In low context, Western culture's (please see Chapter 9) direct communication is preferred during the feedback process. Written reports are welcome as they help in mutual understanding, but in high context, Oriental culture's written reports are feared by subordinates and indirect oral communication is preferred. In Western societies feedback can be at closer interval, but in Oriental societies it should be at longer intervals. Western societies seek feedback while Oriental societies fear feedback. The case at the end of this chapter highlights the importance of the feedback problem between managers from differing cultural backgrounds.

USE OF PERFORMANCE DATA

Performance appraisal data has multiple uses for training and development as well as for reward management. EMI Music is using the same for tracking skills availability for marketing development as mentioned in Box 5.1.

PERFORMANCE MANAGEMENT – INDUSTRY EXAMPLES

Exxon

The Compensation and Executive Development (COED) system at Exxon is designed to ensure a disciplined approach to the development of managerial talent for the company. The system is directed from the top, where the COED committee is headed by the CEO, and is made up of members of Exxon's board. The committee is in-charge of reviewing the development and placement of the top 250 Exxon executives (many of them expatriates). Meeting nearly every Monday, the COED committee

BOX 5.1 USING PERFORMANCE EVALUATION FOR SKILL DATABASE TRACKING SYSTEM AT EMI MUSIC

EMI Music has over 9,000 employees worldwide. It is not a labour intensive or HR-intensive organization. The role of international HR function is more to do with negotiation of individual contracts and retention of the key staff. HR resources are therefore strategically located around the business. The market for international managers operates in a similar fashion as that at the top of investment banking. The business skills and knowledge of the managers and the strength of their relationship with the local artists and consumers are as important as the possession of a set of international skills. Very specific and individual skills are required to build up relationships, markets and promotion, and to develop an individual artist. Artists, international managers responsible for developing local repertoire, and managers in marketing roles are invariably seen as a handful of people in the industry who have these particular skills. Being sensitive to the needs of the managers, the evaluation of their strengths and weaknesses is critical.

The role of assignment planning, tracking systems and skills databases has become critical. An internal database and the tracking process help ensure that EMI music is constantly in tune with the issues that restrict the motivation and enthusiasm of managers to be internationally mobile and assist subsequent internal assessment decisions and planned moves. Three hundred managers' performance evaluation data is tracked worldwide, of which 50 are expatriates and 90 high-potential managers; the majority are classified as internationally mobile managers.

Data is gathered by the line managers annually as part of the local appraisal process. Information generated in the Organization and Management Review (*OMR*) is extracted from this into a common format, which is 'calibrated' by the headquarter to ensure consistency of assessments. The *OMR* database contains much qualitative information, such as an employees' expressed wishes and concerns and personal issues that have been discussed such as dual-career concerns and cost issues.

Systematic customization of the fields means that the performance evaluation database plays a critical role, because it can be searched to look at 'soft issues' associated with human resource management. The case highlights the importance and usefulness of performance evaluation database in successfully managing a services-based global organization.

carefully reviews the performance of executives and examines their developmental needs. To ensure that there is a continual flow of managerial talent for the company and that all positions have back-up candidates, the committee then compares the performance of executives and makes decisions according to their future development needs.

There is also a COED system within each of the Exxon subsidiaries, where the president of each subsidiary has his own COED committee, similar to the one at the head office. This enables the COED system to reach the top 2,000 managers at Exxon. In discussion with senior Exxon managers, it is rather striking to hear the universal acclaim given to the system. Most agree that the system accounts for Exxon's overall success.

General Motors

General Motors is another company with an equally strong tradition of performance management that dates back to Alfred Sloan.

At General Motors, the Supreme Court of Executive Review in recent years has included the top six executives in the company. During the week-long sessions in the boardroom of the Detroit headquarters every February and July, the members spend long days and nights listening to the analysis of more than 600 managers from each of GM's ten vice-presidents and group executives. A variety of questions are covered to get an accurate picture of where the individual stands in his career development.

'We don't have jobs at GM, we have careers, along with performance, and the probing is centred on just what kind of potential the candidate may have.' Here are some examples. Does the executive seem to be developing at the rate expected? What is the job contributing to the person's ability? Is it rounding the person as we intended? What should be the next job for this executive? Should it be in another division or involve greater responsibility? If so, who would be put in this executive's place?

GE–360 DEGREES LEADERSHIP ASSESSMENT CHART

Characteristic	*Performance Criteria*	*MGR*	*PEER*	*Sub-ordinate*	*Others*
Vision	• Has developed and communicated clear, simple, customer-focused vision/direction for the organization • Forward-thinking, stretches horizons, challenges and imaginations • Inspires and energises others to commit to vision. Captures minds. Leads by example. • As appropriate, update vision to reflect constant and accelerating changes impacting the business.				
Customer quality focus	• Listens to customers and assigns the highest priority to customer satisfaction, including internal customers. • Inspires and demonstrates a passion for excellence in every aspect of the work. • Strives to fulfil commitment to quality in total product/service offering. • Loves customer service and creates service mindset throughout the organization.				
Integrity	• Maintains unequivocal commitment to honesty in every facet of behaviour. • Follows through the commitments; assumes responsibility for own mistakes. • Practises absolute conformance with company's policies embodying GE's commitment to ethical conduct. • Actions and behaviour are consistent with words. Absolutely trusted by others.				

(Contd.)

Characteristic	*Performance Criteria*	*MGR*	*PEER*	*Sub-ordinate*	*Others*
Accountability Commitment	• Sets and meets aggressive commitments to achieve business objectives. • Demonstrates courage/self-confidence to stand up for beliefs, ideas of coworkers. • Fair and compassionate, yet willing to make difficult decisions. • Demonstrates uncompromising responsibility for preventing harm to the environment.				
Communication influence	• Communicates in an open, candid, clear, complete and consistent manner and invites response/dissent. • Listens effectively and constantly probes for new ideas. • Uses facts and rational arguments to influence and persuade. • Breaks down barriers and develops influential relationships across teams, functions and layers.				
Shared ownership boundaryless	• Self-confidence to share information across traditional boundaries and be open to new ideas. • Encourages/promotes shared ownership for team vision and goals. • Trusts others; encourages risk-taking and boundaryless behaviour. • Champions work-out as a vehicle for everyone to be heard. Open to ideas from anywhere.				
Team builder empowerment	• Selects talented people; provides coaching and feedback to develop team members to the fullest potential. • Delegates whole tasks; empowers teams to maximize effectiveness; is personally a team player. • Recognizes and rewards achievements. Creates positive/enjoyable work environment. • Fully utilizes diversity of team members (culture, gender, race) to achieve business success.				
Knowledge expertise intellect	• Posseses and readily shares functional/ technical knowledge and expertise. Takes constant interest in learning.				

	• Demonstrates broad business knowledge/perspective with cross-functional/multicultural awareness. • Makes good decisions with limited data. Applies intellect to the fullest. • Quickly sorts out relevant and irrelevant information. Grasps essentials to complex issues and initiates actions.				
Initiative/speed	• Creates real and positive change. Sees change as an opportunity. • Anticipates problems and initiates new and better ways of doing things. • Hates/avoids/eliminates bureaucracy, and strives for brevity, simplicity and clarity. • Understands and uses speed as a competitive advantage.				
Global mindset	• Demonstrates global awareness/sensitivity and is comfortable with building diverse/global teams. • Values and promotes full utilization of global and workforce diversity. • Considers the global consequences of every decision. Proactively seeks global knowledge. • Treats everyone with dignity, trust and respect.				

CASE STUDY

The Road to Hell

John Baker, the Chief Engineer of the Caribbean Bauxite Company of Barracania in the West Indies, was making final preparations to leave the island. His promotion to the production manager of one of the large units in Canada had been announced a month before and now everything had been tied up, except the last vital interview with his successor, the able young Barracania, Mathew Rennals. It was crucial that this interview be successful and that Rennals should leave his office uplifted and encouraged to face the challenge of a new job. A touch on the bell would have brought him walking into the room, but Baker delayed the moment and gazed thoughtfully through the window, considering just exactly what he was going to say and, more particularly, how he was going to say it.

John Baker, an English expatriate, was 45 years old and had served for 23 years with this company in the Far East, several African countries, in Europe and for the last two years in the West Indies. He had not cared much for his previous assignment in Hamburg and was delighted when the West Indies assignment came through. Climate was not the only attraction. Baker had always preferred working overseas in developing countries, because he felt he had an innate knack – better than most other expatriates working for the company – of knowing just how to get along with the regional staff. However, after 24 hours in Barracania, he realized that he would need all his 'innate knack' to deal effectively with the problems that awaited him in this field.

At his first meeting with Hutchins, the Production Director, the problem of Rennals and his future was discussed. There and then it was made clear to Baker that one of his most important tasks would be 'grooming' Rennals as his successor. Hutchins had pointed out that Rennals was not only one of the brightest Barracanian prospects on the staff of Caribbean Bauxite – he was a first-class engineering graduate from London University – being the son of the Minister of Finance and Economic Planning, he also had no small political pull.

The company had been particularly pleased when Rennals decided to work for it rather than for the government in which his father held such a prominent post. The company had ascribed his action to the effect of its vigorous and liberal regionalization programme which, since the World War II, had produced 18 Barracanians at the mid-management level and given Caribbean Bauxite a good lead in this respect over all other international concerns operating in Barracania. The success of this timely regionalization policy had led to excellent relations with the government.

The relationship had been given an added importance when Barracania, three years later, became independent – an occasion that encouraged a critical and challenging attitude towards the role foreign interests would play in the new Barracania. Hutchins had little difficulty in convincing Baker that the successful career development of Rennals was of primary importance.

The interview with Hutchins was now two years old, and Baker, leaning back in his chair, reviewed his success in grooming Rennals. What aspect of the latter's character had helped and what had hindered? What about his own personality? The first item to go on the credit side would, without question, be the ability of Rennals to master the technical aspects of the job. From the start he had shown keenness and enthusiasm and had often impressed Baker with his ability in tackling new assignments and making constructive comments in departmental discussions. He was popular with all ranks of the Barracanian staff and had an easy manner that stood him in good stead when dealing with his expatriate seniors. But what about the debit side?

First and foremost, there was his racial consciousness. His four years at London University had accentuated the racial feeling and made him sensitive to any sign of condescension on the part of expatriates. It may have been to give expression to this sentiment that, as soon as he returned from London, he threw himself into politics on behalf of the United Action Party, which won the pre-independence election and provided the country with its first Prime Minister.

The ambitions of Rennals – and he certainly was ambitious – did not lie in politics. A staunch nationalist, he saw that he could serve himself and his country best – for Bauxite was responsible for nearly half the value of Barracania's export trade – by putting his engineering talent to the best use possible. On this account Hutchins found that he had an unexpectedly a easy task in persuading Rennals to give up his political work before entering the production department as an Assistant Engineer.

Baker knew that it was Rennals' race consciousness that had prevented their relationship from being as close as it should have been. On the surface, nothing could have seemed more agreeable. Formality between the two men was at the minimum: Baker was delighted to find that his assistant shared his own peculiar 'shaggy dog' sense of humour so that jokes were being continually exchanged; they entertained each other at their houses and often played tennis together, and yet the barrier remained invisible, indefinable, but ever present. The existence of this 'screen' between them was a constant source of frustration to Baker, since it indicated a weakness that he was loath to accept. If he was successful with all other nationals, why not with Rennals? But at least he had managed to 'break through' to Rennals more successfully than to any other expatriate. In fact, it was young Barracanian's attitude – sometimes overbearing, sometimes cynical – toward other company expatriates that had been one of the subjects Baker had raised last year when he discussed Rennals' staff report with him. He knew, too, that he would have to raise the same subject again in the forthcoming interview because Jackson, the senior draftperson, had complained about the rudeness of Rennals. With this thought in mind, Baker leaned forward and spoke into the intercom, 'Would you come in, Matt, please? I'd like to have a word with you.' As Rennals entered the room, Baker said, 'Do sit down,' and offered a cigarette. He paused while he held out his lighter and then went on.

'As you know, Matt, I'll be off to Canada in a few days, and before I go, I thought it would be useful if we could have a final chat together. It is indeed with some deference that I suggest I can be of help. You will shortly be sitting in the chair doing the job I am now doing, but I, on the other hand, am 10 years older, so perhaps you can accept the idea that I may be able to give you the benefit of my longer experience.'

Baker saw Rennals stiffen slightly in his chair as he made this point. Consequently, he added in explanation, 'You and I have attended enough company courses to remember those repeated requests by the personnel managers to tell people how they are getting on as often as the convenient moment arises and not just the automatic "once a year" when, by regulation, staff reports have to be discussed.'

Rennals nodded in agreement, and Baker went on, 'I shall always remember the last job performance discussion I had with my previous boss back in Germany. He used what he called the 'plus and minus' technique. His firm belief was that when a senior, by discussion, sought to improve the work performance of his staff, his prime objective should be to make sure that the latter left the interview encouraged and inspired to improve. Any criticism must, therefore, be constructive and helpful. He said that one very good way to encourage a person – and I fully agree with him – is to tell him about his good points – the plus factors, as well as his weak ones, or the minus factors. I thought, Matt, it would be a good idea to run our discussion along these lines.'

Rennals offered no comment, so Baker continued, 'Let me say, therefore, right away, that, as far as your own work performance is concerned, the plus far outweighs the minus. I have been most impressed, for instance, with the way you have adapted your considerable theoretical knowledge to master the practical techniques of your job – that ingenious method you used to get air down to the fifth shaft level is a sufficient case in point – and at departmental meetings I have found your comments well-taken and helpful. In fact, you will be interested to know that only last week I reported to Mr Hutchins that, from the technical point of view, he could not wish for a more able man to succeed to the position of Chief Engineer.'

'That's very good indeed of you, John,' cut in Rennals with a smile of thanks. 'My only worry now is how to live up to such a high recommendation.'

'Of that I am quite sure', returned Baker, 'especially if you can overcome the minus factor which I would like now to discuss with you. It is one that I have talked about before, so I'll come straight to the point. I have noticed that you are more friendly and get on better with your fellow Barracanians than you do with Europeans. In fact, I had a complaint only yesterday from Mr Jackson, who said you had been rude to him, and not for the first time either.

'There is, Matt, I am sure, no need for me to tell you how necessary it will be for you to get on well with expatriates because until the company has trained sufficient people of your calibre, Europeans are bound to occupy senior positions here in Barracania. All this is vital to your future interests, so can I help you in any way?'

While Baker was speaking on this theme, Rennals sat tense in his chair and it was some seconds before he replied, 'It is quite extraordinary, isn't it, how one can convey an impression to others so at variance with what one intends? I can only assure you once again that my disputes with Jackson – and you may remember also – have had nothing at all to do with the colour of his skin. I promise you that if a Barracanian had behaved in an equally peremptory manner I would have reacted in precisely the same way. And, again, if I may say it within these four walls, I am sure I am not the only one who has found Jackson and Godson difficult. I could mention the names of several expatriates who have felt the same. However, I am really sorry to have created this impression of not being able to get along with Europeans – it is an entirely false one – and I quite realise that I must do all I can to correct it as quickly as possible. On your last point regarding Europeans holding senior positions in the company for some time to come, I quite accept the situation. I know that Caribbean Bauxite – as it has been doing for many years now – will promote Barracanians as soon as their experience warrants it. And, finally, I would like to assure you, John – and my father thinks the same too – that I am very happy with my work here and hope to stay with the company for many years to come.'

Rennals had spoken earnestly. Although not convinced by what he heard, Baker did not think he could pursue the matter further, except to say, 'All right, Matt, my impression may be wrong, but I would like to remind you about the truth of that old saying, "What is important is not what is true but what is believed", and let it rest at that.'

But suddenly Baker knew that he didn't want to 'let it rest at that'. He was disappointed once again at not being able to break through to Rennals and having yet again to listen to the bland denial that there was any racial prejudice in his make-up. Baker, who had intended to end the interview at this point, decided to try another tactic.

'To return for a moment to the "plus- and minus-technique" I was telling you about just now, there is another plus factor I forgot to mention. I would like to congratulate you not only on the calibre of your work but also on the ability you have shown in overcoming a challenge which, I as a European, know, is of typical commercial enterprise, admittedly a big one, which is a product of the eonomic and social environment of the United States and western Europe. My ancestors have all been brought up in this environment for the past 200 or 300 years, and I have, therefore, been able to live in a world in which commerce (as we know it today) has been part and parcel of my being. It has not been something revolutionary and new that has suddenly entered my life.' Baker went on, 'In your case the situation is different because you and your forebears have had only some 50 or 60 years in this commercial environment. You have had to face the challenge of bridging the gap between 50 and 200 or 300 years. Again, Matt, let me congratulate you – and people like you – once again on having so successfully overcome this particular hurdle. It is for this very reason that I think the outlook of for Barracania and Caribbean Bauxite are so bright.'

Rennals had listened intently and when Baker finished, he replied, 'Well, once again, John, I have to thank you for what you have said, and, for my part, I can only say that it is gratifying to know that my own personal effort has been so much appreciated. I hope that more people will soon come to think as you do.'

There was a pause and, for a moment, Baker thought hopefully that he was about to achieve his long-awaited breakthrough, but Rennals merely smiled back. The barrier remained unbreached. There continued some five minutes of cheerful conversation about the contrast between the Caribbean and the Canadian climate and whether the West Indies had any hope of beating England in the fifth test match before Baker drew the interview to a close. He was glad that the interview had run along in this friendly manner and, particularly, that it had ended on such a cheerful note.

This feeling, however, lasted only until the following morning. Baker had some farewells to make, so he arrived at the office considerably later than usual. He had no sooner sat down at the desk than his secretary walked into the room with a worried frown on her face. Her words came fast, 'When I arrived this morning, I found Mr Rennals already waiting at my door. He seemed very angry and told me in quite a peremptory manner that he had a vital letter to dictate that must be sent off without any delay. He was so worked up that he couldn't even keep still and kept pacing about the room, which is most unlike him. He wouldn't even wait to read what he had dictated. Just signed the page where he thought the letter would end. It has been distributed, and your copy is in your tray.'

Puzzled and feeling vaguely uneasy, Baker opened the confidential envelope and read the following letter:

From: Assistant Engineer
To: Chief Engineer 14 August
Caribbean Bauxite Limited
Assessment of Interview between Baker and Rennals

It has always been my practice to respect the advice given to me by seniors, so after our interview, I decided to give a careful thought once again to its main points and make sure that I had understood all that had been said. As I promised you at the time, I had every intention of putting your advice to the best effect.

It was not, therefore, until I had sat down quietly in my home yesterday evening to consider the interview objectively that its main purport became clear. Only then did the full enormity of what you said dawn on me. The more I thought about it, the more convinced I was that I had hit upon the real truth and the more furious I became. With a facility in the English language which I, a poor Barracanian, cannot hope to match, you had the audacity to insult me (and through me every Barracanian worth his salt) by claiming that our knowledge of modern living is only a paltry 50 years old, whereas yours goes back to 200 or 300 years, as if your materialistic commercial environment could possibly be compared with the spiritual values of our culture. I fervently hope your culture of commercialism will never come to Barracania. By what right do you have the effrontery to condescend us? At heart, all you Europeans think us Barracanians to be 'just down from the trees'.

Far into the night I discussed this matter with my father, and he is as disgusted as I. He agrees with me that any company whose senior staff think as you do is no place for any Barracanian, proud of his culture and race – so much for all the company 'clap-trap' and specious propaganda about regionalisation and Barracania for the Barracanians.

I feel ashamed and betrayed. Please accept this letter as my resignation, which I wish to become effective immediately.

Cc: Production Manager
Managing Director

Case Question

What went wrong with the feedback given to Rennals by Baker? If you were Baker, how would you have conducted this interview?

Review Questions

1. Discuss the framework and importance of performance management in multinational organizations.
2. What difficulties can arise in assessing the performance of expatriate managers?
3. Discuss the major factors associated with the appraisal of executive managerial performance.
4. Discuss how the cultural adjustment process influences the commitment and performance of expatriates.

Assignment

Try to collect information about the performance appraisal approach and format of two multinationals, one being a Japanese MNC and the other a US MNC. Analyse the differences and similarities in the approaches of the two organizations and explain the possible reasons for the same.

Chapter

6

International Compensation Management

LEARNING OBJECTIVES

After studying this chapter, you will be able to:

- *Study various factors that need to be taken into account in designing appropriate compensation and benefits policy for expatriates*
- *Learn key components of international compensation programmes*
- *Understand two approaches to international compensation and their merits and demerits*
- *Find out how culture and business strategy influence salary decisions in global organizations.*

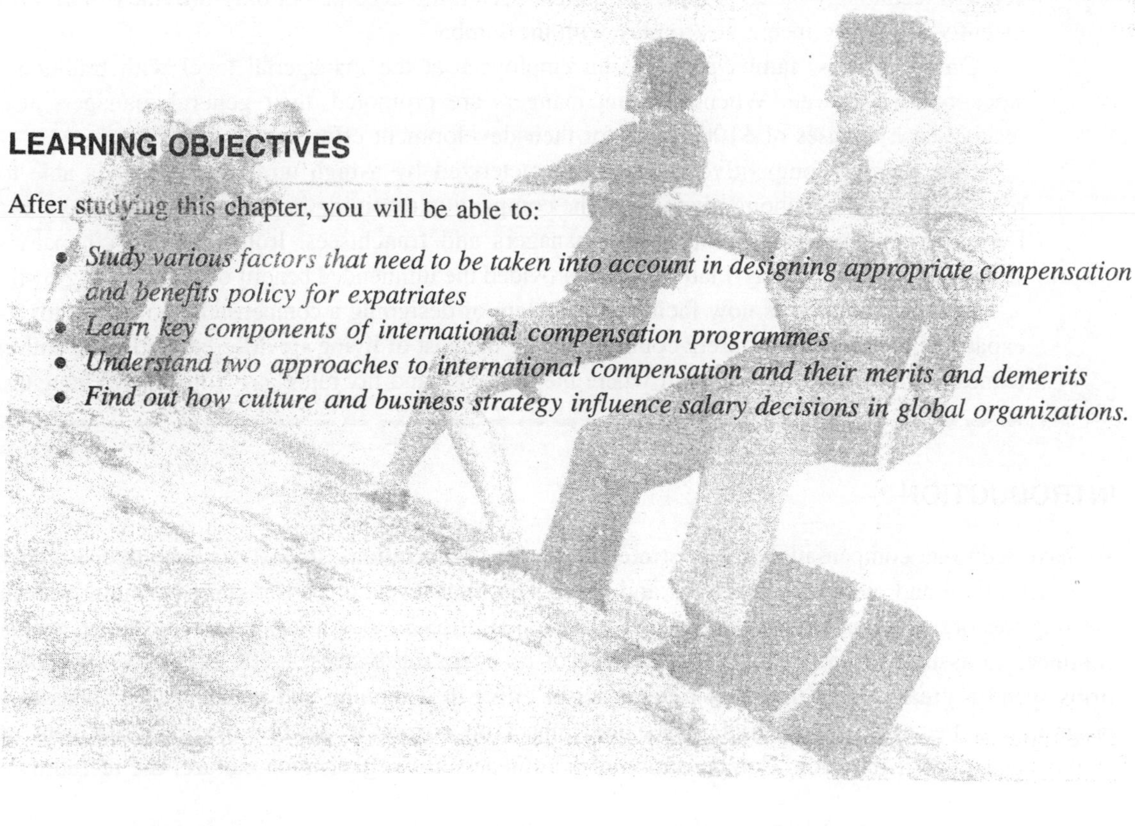

CASE STUDY – JAMBA JUICE

Jamba Juice, founded in 1990, in San Francisco, has expanded to 300 stores that employ more than 4,000 workers in 15 states and is now planning to go global. Jamba is a leading retailer of blended-to-order fruit, fresh squeezed juice, healthful soups and bread. Since its inception, one of Jamba's chief challenges has been finding and retaining qualified managers. In a high-growth company that has intense competition within the industry, Jamba is additionally challenged by its location which provides many other career opportunities to younger employees Jamba recruits. A large number of these employers are technology-based and offer more generous financial incentives than the typical food retailer.

In order to expand, Jamba must attract and retain these workers. To assist them in this objective, Jamba has developed an innovative compensation policy, which allows it to compete not only within the growing juice industry but also with the technology-based employers who attract the same young employees. Jamba's 'Pay-Plan' allows general managers to receive a percentage of the stores' cash flow, predicted on the basis of the financial performance of their business. To keep good managers on board, Jamba provides opportunities to general managers to share in the stores' profits over a three-year period. When general managers increase year-to-year sales in their operation, money accrues in a retention account which is payable only in a three-year-cycle. Much like stock options that vest in over three or five years in technology-based companies, Jamba's retention account not only provides short-term incentives but also incentives to stay with the Jamba.

On top of this, Jamba provides all employees at the managerial level with traditional stock options as well. When assistant mangers are promoted, their general managers also receive cash bonuses of $1000 each for their development efforts.

In a fiercely competitive industry, characterized by a high turnover, Jamba is able to reduce the turnover among managers. The company is receiving inquiries from Australia and Europe from prospective employees, managers and franchisees. Ironically, the company's strategically designed 'Pay-Plan' has also provided the unintended benefit of fuelling its growth.

But, the company is now facing the problem of designing a compensation structure for its expatriate managers in different countries where the cost of living are different and competition comes from different sectors and where the currency and tax ratess are constantly changing.

INTRODUCTION

We have seen that compensation, a key strategic area for organizations, impacts an employer's ability to attract, retain and motivate employees and ensures optimal levels of performance by employees in meeting the organization's strategic objectives. Compensation is also a key economic issue, which continues to assume an increasingly larger share of its operating expenses. HR executives in global firms spend a great deal of time and make a lot of effort in designing and managing compensation programmes, because of their high costs and impact on corporate performance, commitment of employees and their retention. Compensation also influences the organization culture, the recruitment and selection of competent employees, their motivation and performance. A survey by the Conference Board[1] found that 29 per cent of the firms reported the expatriates cost 2 to 2.9 times their salary in the parent country, and 50 per cent reported, 3 to 3.9 times salary, and 18 per cent reported 4 to 4.9 times salary. A senior US expatriate in India (in 2001) cost around US $ 3,00,000, with the base salary of $ 1,30,000 and the rest as allowances and benefits. This was higher in countries like Japan where the cost of living is higher than in the US. Then there are issues in designing compensation programmes, such as parity between HCNs and PCNs, state of labour markets and relevant national laws and practices.

FACTORS INFLUENCING COMPENSATION PROGRAMMES

Compensation decisions are strategic decisions and play a key role in achieving performance and sustainable competitive advantage for international firms. These policy decisions should be consistent with the overall strategy, structure and business needs of the multinational. Second, the policy should attract and retain the best staff in those areas where the firm needs them most and affords opportunities and where its core competency lies. Third, the policy must facilitate the transfer of international employees in a cost-effective manner. Fourth, the policy should give due consideration to equity and ease of administration. It should reduce the cost of operations and enhance commitment of employees. It should also facilitate international posting and transfer of employees.

These policy decisions regarding compensation and benefits require the knowledge of employment and taxation laws, customs, costs of living index, environment, employment practices of various countries, and so on. Without such comprehensive knowledge and database, the corporate HR executive will not be able to advise expatriates regarding avoidance of double taxation or to reimburse the actual costs or decide about incentives that will encourage employees to take up foreign assignments.

In addition, the knowledge of labour markets and industry norms regarding benefits and compensation is also necessary. Labour market is the availability of required skills and demands for those skills and competencies, and the going rate at which they are available for hiring in each country or globally. For higher levels of skills and competencies, international firms tap international labour markets, and for lower levels of skills, local labour markets provide the required resources. Hence, the knowledge of both the labour markets is necessary. In order to ensure equity with PCNs, the salary of expatriates has to be adjusted to foreign currency fluctuations of the two countries unless they are paid full salary and allowances in the home-country currency. If the expatriates are paid in local currency, then their salary should also be adjusted to the rise in cost of living in that country from time to time. Hence HR managers have to continuously watch foreign exchange rate fluctuations and monitor the rate of inflation or the cost of living index in different countries. It should also be kept in mind that all currencies are not floating freely and some countries keep their currencies pegged at controlled rates.

It is also necessary to find out which locations are relatively difficult, staying where living would qualify for hardship allowances. These are the locations where the climate is harsh or modern facilities are not available.

One should also be aware of the vision and mission of the company, its philosophy regarding managing human resources, its strategy of growth or stability, and the strategy of its business units

[1] The Conference Board, *Managing Expatriates' Return: A Research Report*, No. 1148–96 RR, New York, 1996.

regarding the cost, leadership, differentiation and innovation. The lifes cycle stage of each unit in each country also plays a part in taking compensation decisions. One should factor in the strength of local unions and their influence on compensation decisions. Finally all these decisions are to be adjusted according to changing political, economic and social conditions in different countries. Hence taking these decisions may require services of specialised consultancy firms or experts.

CONSTITUTION OF TOTAL COMPENSATION PACKAGE

How a total compensation package is constituted is significant. For example, executives can be paid higher basic salary with lower benefits and incentives, but it may not motivate them to perform better if high taxes take away a major portion of the pay. On the other hand, a lower basic pay and a large portion in benefits and incentives related to performance may also not encourage the employee if his net savings remain low. Then there are options regarding issuing company stocks for encouraging employees and senior managers not to sacrifice long-term objectives of growth and profitability for earning bonuses and incentives, which are linked to short-term targets and objectives. Thus, there are many complexities in the international compensation programme as all objectives are difficult to meet and therefore require high degree of expertise. The main elements are as under:

Base Pay

It is the main element that decides the rank or grade and upon this all other elements are built and retirement benefits calculated both in domestic and international compensations.

Incentives

To motivate employees for higher performance and to undertake foreign assignments, various incentives are given. In fact, the proportion of incentives in the total pay has been increasing over the years.

Retention and Referral Bonuses

Retention of trained and talented employees has become a critical issue for all organizations, particularly for MNCs. Referral bonus is paid when employees bring qualified new employees who meet the selection criteria. This reduces the recruitment cost and time of the organization, hence the payment of referral bonus. Money does not alone help retention and there are many aspects to it. For example, the quality of work-life, flexibility of work timings, challenging assignments, compatible work group, transport and other benefits and the most important being career rise and responsibility and autonomy.

Allowances

There are numerous allowances to compensate expatriates for many difficulties that they undergo. These allowances include shipping allowance, house furnishing allowance, leave travel allowance twice in a year, children's education allowance, spouse assistance allowance, club membership allowance, relocation allowance, company-provided housing and chauffeur-driven cars, etc.

Benefits

They are also known as indirect compensation and their purpose is to minimize tax payments and enhance quality of life. Their list includes use of health clubs, medical treatment to family, upkeep of house, servants, books and gifts that they are supposed to be giving in the course of their duty, etc. Hardship allowance is discussed separately in this chapter.

Taxes

They take substantial part of the salary to governments of both host and home countries. Hence MNCs follow **tax equalization policy,** according to which the expatriates pay only the taxes required to be paid in the home-country and what is paid to the host country is paid by the MNC. For this purpose, services of chartered accountant firm are used. Expatriates are required to obtain tax clearance certificates from the host government before they are allowed to leave the country. **Tax protection policy** is also adopted, which means that the employee pays up to the amount of taxes he or she would pay on compensation in the home-country. In such a situation, the employee is entitled to the difference of balance amount if total taxes are less in the foreign country than in the home-country. At times, the employee is left on his own to pay his taxes if his salary is fixed as a whole package. Table 6.1 indicates maximum marginal federal rates of taxes in some countries.

Table 6.1 Tax Protection Policy

Country	*Federal Rate of Taxes (%)*
1. USA	39.6
2. UK	40
3. Japan	37
4. France	53.5
5. Sweden	25
6. Italy	46
7. Germany	51
8. Singapore	28
9. Malaysia	29
10. China	45

Long-term Benefits

They include retirement pension, gratuity, stock-options of various kinds, medical care, insurance, etc.

The total pay depends upon the capacity of the MNC to pay, competitor's policy, labour market, company's pay policy and government regulations and others.

PAYING EXPATRIATES

The structuring of compensation systems for expatriates presents some of the following unique problems:

- Discrepancies in pay between the parent-country, host-country and third party-nationals.

- The need to vary the expatriate's compensation, depending on the 'lifestyle' of the expatriate's family (e.g. children in schools and colleges).
- Compensation issues related to re-entry into the parent country organization.
- Using compensation programmes that have not changed sufficiently over time to deal adequately with the new international business environment.

Most expatriates' compensation plans are designed to achieve five major objectives:

1. Attract employees who are qualified and interested in international assignments.
2. Facilitate the movement of expatriates from one subsidiary to another, from home to subsidiary, and from subsidiary back to home.
3. Maintain a consistent and reasonable relationship between the pay levels of employees at headquarters, domestic affiliates and foreign subsidiaries.
4. Be cost effective by reducing unnecessary expenses.
5. Make easily intelligible and easy to administer.

APPROACHES TO EXPATRIATES' COMPENSATION

There are two main approaches – 'the going rate approach' (also known as the market rate approach) and 'balance sheet approach' (also known as the build-up approach). These are discussed below:

Going Rate Approach

In this case the base salary on international transfer remains linked to the salary structure of the host country. For this, the required information is obtained through compensation surveys and published information from this country. The firm then has to decide whether local nationals (HCNs) or expatriates of the same nationality or expatriates of all nationalities will be the reference points in terms of benchmarking. For example, an American company operating in India has to decide whether its reference point will be the local Indian salary or other US companies operating in India or all foreign companies operating in India. If the location is a low-pay country, the multinational usually supplements the basic pay with additional benefits.

The advantages of this system include:

1. Equality with local nationals;
2. Simple approach to administer and easily intelligble;
3. Expatriates able to identify themselves with the host country;
4. Often equity among expatriates of different nationalities; and
5. Attracts the nationals of PCN and TCN if the location is a high-pay country, like the US or Japan.

There are, however, some problems with this system, particularly with transfers from a developed country to a developing country where the salary differences as well as the tax rates makes a substantial difference to one's salary. Further, there will be a substantial difference in compensation amongst persons of the same nationality and working in similar positions in different countries in the same firm. This will cause in-fighting for getting favourable postings and resisting low-pay-country postings.

defeating the company's strategic objectives and needs. Further, there will be problems when the expatriate is repatriated to the home-country. This problem arises especially when developing countries' nationals return from the US or other high-pay locations after a few years' service and are likely to be demotivated with salaries in their native country. A survey by Towers Perrin (*Worldwide Total Remuneration* 1997; www.Towers.com) of compensations for CEOs around the world reported following results: US: \$ 901,801; Singapore: \$ 572,414; France: \$ 523,511; UK: \$ 489,710; Australia: \$ 476,700; Germany: \$ 423,898, Malaysia: \$ 342,151 (See Table 6.2 for more details.)

Table 6.2 Compensation for Four Positions in 26 Countries (in US $)

Country	*CEO*	*HR Director*	*Accountant*	*Manufacture Employee*
Argentina	860,704	326,874	63,948	17,884
Australia	646,316	235,316	57,129	29,703
Belgium	655,390	286,222	63,883	34,366
Brazil	597,454	287,683	44,605	10,480
Canada	742,228	188,070	44,866	36,289
China	93,393	58,278	14,552	3,021
France	540,260	224,112	69,554	34,741
Germany	421,622	189,785	61,375	36,934
Hong Kong	635,186	211,321	56,711	16,691
Italy	567,685	254,138	59,388	29,469
Japan	545,233	235,536	59,107	51,997
Malaysia	350,558	130,771	24,522	7,453
Mexico	648,695	239,028	41,582	14,302
Netherlands	621,153	217,142	48,838	27,892
New Zealand	258,114	111,803	38,382	15,931
Singapore	621,871	239,376	51,733	16,912
South Africa	406,263	179,268	43,234	7,974
South Korea	194,421	109,637	41,365	17,904
Spain	399,423	196,305	56,332	22,746
Sweden	440,265	166,312	43,438	32,564
Switzerland	448,422	175,008	66,121	41,104
Taiwan	179,484	102,491	30,652	11,924
Thailand	145,173	98,120	19,175	6,293
UK	719,665	268,302	107,839	28,874
US	1403,899	306,181	66,377	44,680
Venezuela	609,097	272,212	41,192	11,221

Source: 'Towers Perrin and Mereer examine pay lows and increases in 26 countries' in *Iomes Report on Salary Surveys*, January 2001, pp. 2–4.

This policy, however, is very much favoured by polycentric organizations where subsidiaries are given autonomy to decide compensation for their employees according to local laws, customs and economic conditions.

Balance Sheet Approach

This is the most widely used approach for international compensation. Its objective is to 'keep the expatriate whole', which means maintaining relativity to PCN colleagues and compensating for the costs of international assignments and maintaining home-country living standards. Thus, it links the salary of expatriates and TCNs to the home-country salary structure. The key assumption is that foreign assignees should not suffer financially due to transfers. The salary package is divided into four parts:

1. *Goods and services*: Home-country outlays for items such as food, personal care, clothing, household furnishing, recreation, transportation and medical care.
2. *Housing*: Major cost associated with host country.
3. *Income taxes*: Parent-country and host country income taxes.
4. *Reserve*: Contributions to savings, payments for benefits, pension contributions, education expenses, social security taxes, and so on.

When costs associated with the host country assignment exceed equivalent costs in the parent country, the firm and expatriates together meet these costs to ensure that parent-country equivalent purchasing power is achieved. For example, if a US national is posted in India and suppose the dollar exchange rate is, \$ 1 = Rs 50 and Mack index or Cola index is 5, then the break-up of the annual pay will be as shown in the following table:

Item	*Amount in \$ per year in US*	*Paid in \$ in India*	*Paid in Rs in India*
Base pay	100,000	60,000	200,00,00
Cost of living allowance	10,000	nil	5,00,000
Overseas allowance	20,000	20,000	nil
Hardship allowance 5%	5,000	5,000	nil
Housing deduction 10%	10,000	10,000	nil
Income tax deduction @ 30%	30,000	30,000	nil
Total pay	\$ 95,000	\$ 45,000	Rs 25,00,000

Thus, he gets \$ 45,000 or Rs 25,00,000. The American firm pays for housing in India on an actual basis. It also pays the difference in taxes if they are higher in India.

The premium for overseas service can be paid in several ways. In some cases, a one-time payment of 30–35 per cent of the salary is made to encourage the employee to go abroad. In other cases, a constant premium is paid each year, or the premia/premiums are paid in decreasing amounts until they is phased out after a certain number of years.

When an employee takes an assignment in an undesirable location, a hardship allowance is often paid, the amount varying according to the level of hardship. Determining this level is not easy. ICI, a British MNC, used the services of Employment Conditions Abroad (ECA) to determine the amount of hardship amount to be given. ECA used following dimensions:

(1) Distance from Britain; (2) ease of travel to and from Britain; (3) difficulty of learning the local language; (4) climate; (5) health consideration (e.g. the types of diseases that are prevalent); (6) the quality of local health care facilities; (7) availability of English language schools; (8) quality of education; (9) availability of goods and services and recreation facilities; and (10) risk to expatriates and their family due to terrorism or other crimes.

To mitigate the hardship, firms may even provide two home trips per year or paid holidays for the family (Table 6.3 explains how the hardship evaluation of Uruguay has been calculated). Finally, there is a group of allowances provided to cover differences in the costs of living in home and foreign countries and to cover additional expenses associated with setting up of home in a new location. Paying a one-time allowance of certain amounts of sum covers these.

Table 6.3 Hardship Evaluation – Uruguay

		Max. Marks	*Location Score*
1.	**Assessment of physical threat**		
	A. Potential or actual violence in the area	15	3
	B. Hostility of local people	10	2
	C. Prevalence of disease	15	3
	D. Medical facilities and availability of services	10	3
	Total threat category	50	11
2.	**Assessment of discomfort to family**		
	A. Difficult physical environment	10	2
	B. Geographic location	10	4
	C. Cultural/psychological isolation	10	2
	Total discomfort	30	8
3.	**Assessment of inconvenience**		
	A. Shortcomings in local education system	5	2
	B. Availability of low quality housing	5	2
	C. Limited recreational facilities	5	2
	D. Poor quality: availability of consumer goods	5	2
	Total inconvenience factor	**20**	**8**
	Total (all categories)	**100**	**27**

Source: www.air-inc.com (sample from the *Expatriate Compensation Report.*)

Housing costs vary a great deal in different parts of the world. A recent Survey Reference indicated annual housing costs (in US $) in different cities:

- Tokyo $ 1,18,200
- Hong Kong $ 84,645
- Paris $ 71,359
- London $ 51,634
- Frankfurt $ 46,083
- Rio de Janeiro $ 38,195
- Chicago $ 28,894

Since public schools are not suitable for the children of expatriates, companies often provide funds to allow expatriates to send their children to private schools.

There are several advantages of the balance-sheet approach. First, it maintains parity in involvements for foreign assignments and also between expatriates of the same nationality but posted in different countries. Second, no problems arise when one returns to the home-country. Third, it is easy to administer and explain. Fourth, it facilitates transfers to diffirent countries.

The disadvantage of the approach is that considerable disparity of pay may occur between the nationals of the host country and expatriates, resulting in demotivation. Second, there may occur differences in pay among the different nationals doing the same type of jobs, because their basic pay is determined according to the pay in their parent country. So Americans may be paid higher pay for the same job by American firms than an Indian posted in the US and paid by an Indian firm.

TOTAL BUSINESS COST

It may be proper to look at the total business costs rather than at the living costs of expatriates, because multinational firms are interested in the overall cost of doing business with a particular country, as well as in the micro-issues of the expatriate's salary. The Economic Intelligence unit[2] has estimated this for 27 countries taking into account the wages, air travels, corporate taxes, costs for Expatriate staff, rents, road transport and perceived corruption levels. Based on this study, the top five most expensive countries in the world (1997) are:

1. Germany,
2. The United States,
3. Belgium,
4. Britain, and
5. France.

Clearly, compensation management is a complex task for international human resource executives.

CULTURAL IMPACT AND COMPENSATION POLICY

- National cultural differences also play a significant role in determining a firm's compensation policy. For example, Linchon Electric, one of the first companies to successfully implement the productivity-linked incentive system in the US, attempted to introduce the systems of piece-rate, the end-of-year bonus and continuous employment in its establishments in other countries.

While this was wholly introduced in Australia and partly in Mexico, it met with stiff resistance in European countries.

- In high power-distance cultures, the compensation system should reflect hierarchical differences in the firm. Pay should reflect the status and job differences between the employees of different levels. Compensation to local managers should be linked to their positions.
- In low power-distance cultures, the salary fixation system should be more egalitarian and performance-based. Pay and compensation should reflect seniority as well as consideration of family needs in countries with high power-distance cultures.
- In individualistic cultures rewards should be individual-based and in collectivist cultures they should be team-based.
- In cultures, with masculinity, companies should pursue a compensation strategy that recognises and rewards competitiveness, aggressiveness and dominance. In cultures, with low masculinity, compensation should focus on social benefits, quality of work-life and equity.
- In cultures, with high uncertainty avoidance, structured and consistent pay plans are preferred. Decisions regarding salary and benefits should be centralised, with no variable plans or discretionary allocations. Where uncertainty avoidance is low, pay should be linked to performance. In addition, the salaries of local managers should be competitive in order to retain talent.
- In high uncertainty avoidance cultures, it is better to have a centralised pension system with multiple controls and safeguards.
- Low uncertainty cultures would be more open to defined contribution pensions with flexible plan implementation.
- In masculine cultures, with moderate to high uncertainty avoidance, policies designed to protect job security would be welcome.
- Employees, with feminine cultures and moderate to high uncertainty avoidance, would prefer policies designed to protect income security.
- Employees from feminine cultures prefer family-friendly practices as well as other policies designed to maximise quality of work-life.
- Employees from individualistic and low power-distance cultures prefer flexible benefits programmes.

TERMINATION OF CONTRACT

One aspect of compensation that varies from country to country and has important implications for both subsidiary HR managers and HQ-based managers is the issue of what happens if the MNC decides to quit a foreign country or another firm takes over the management and is not interested in doing business in that country. When such a decision is made, termination liabilities may result in significant payoffs to employees. By tradition or law or union contract the MNC may be required to pay up to two years' salary to employees whose contracts are involuntarily terminated. In some countries, firms intending to close down operations may be required to develop a systematic plan to deal with severance payments, relocation expenses, retraining, and other services for the employees who are laid off.

BOX 6.1 A FAIR DAY'S PAY

The way the companies pay their employees tells a lot about how they see their business. 'Compensation policy is central to supporting the company culture', says Albert Knab, head of compensation and benefits at the Stuttgart office of Daimler-Chrysler, a company going through a spectacular culture change. Many companies, though, have begun to use pay policy more actively. 'Compensation strategy has become central to many companies' businesses', 'says Richard Walker, who wrote the report, *Motivating and Rewarding Managers*. Firms have become, he says, 'concerned less about acquiring physical resources and more concerned about how their human resources can be efficiently exploited.' In America, pay variability has been increasing for some years. 'The average pay increase in an organization probably has not changed in the last 20 years, but the variance has reckons Mark Huslid, professor of HRM at Rutgers, the state university of New Jersey.

Variable pay is advancing in other countries too, and covering a much wider range of workers than before. 'We are extending variable pay to more and more functions, and offering specific rewards for targeted achievements', says Eckart Reamers, head of human relations at IBM in Stuttgart. German managers find this unusual, although it is less unusual than it was. The main reason is often the need to hold down the costs. 'It is interesting that variable pay has spread in Europe at a time when inflation is at its lowest level for 30 years', says Brian Dive, in-charge of remuneration at Unilever. And adds, 'It makes sense, because if your results are not good or your people don't perform, you don't have to pay them.' And indeed, one of the most useful effects of variable pay is to pass some of the risks of running a business to the employees. If profits fall, so will profit-linked bonuses. But that is not the only reason for the spread of flexibility. It also reflects realistic by many employers that they depend more than ever on a relatively small group of excellent people; and that they need to strive constantly to increase the productivity of all the workers. An example is of Levi Strauss, one of the most famous names in the clothing business. A few years back, records Steve Epstein, Levi's head of remuneration, the company went through something of a revolution. Its jeans were being squeezed off the shelves by rival brands. 'In the past', recalls Epstein in Levi's elegant office on the San Francisco's waterfront, 'we brought in people with sales experience, and they stayed until they retired. We had thousands of resumes for every job. When you are that successful, you don't have to market yourself and we would pay everyone pretty much the same.' Lulled by its fame, Levi's grew complacent. 'Now our strategy has shifted to differentiating performances. We need incentive payments that can compete.' That is a tall order for a company fishing in the same talent pool as the heavyweights of Silicon Valley. Levis is privately held, so cannot offer stock options. But harder still has been the blow to its egalitarian corporate culture, from having to acknowledge that 20 per cent of the staff probably generate 80 per cent of the profits. 'We now focus more on paying the person, not paying the job,' says Epstein.

That change is making it easier to attract bright recruits from Generation X – the 20s and 30s – who bring not just a fresh eye but also a different attitude to pay and to work. Partly to accommodate them, the company ditched its old bonus plan, 80 per cent of which automatically went to everybody. Instead, last year it introduced a new scheme, most of which goes to reward individual performance. A streak of the old culture remains: the company is shifting the decision on who gets what from individual managers to management committees to depoliticise the process. The upshot, reckons Epstein, will be smallish across the board pay increases for most people. If the bulk of the workforce got, say, 3 per cent, then people with critical skills might get 5-6 per cent and a few rising stars might put even more. The change at Levis is being echoed all over the world. It emerges in study after study by pay consultants and academics. According to Richard Meischeid of Towers Perrin, a consultancy that conducts an annual worldwide survey of compensation, 'There is still a global trend away from programmes that rewards tenure to those that allow more flexibility.'

Review Questions

1. Discuss the main objectives of multinational firms regarding compensation policies.
2. Explain the two approaches to expatriates' payments and outline the main differences between the two. Also list their advantages and disadvantages.
3. What are the main benefits and allowances that need the attention of HR executives and how are they decided?
4. Write short notes on the following:
   - Hardship allowance
   - Repatriation
   - Tax equalization
5. What are the main factors that the MNCs take into account while deciding expatriates' salary, allowances and benefits?

Chapter

7

Global HR Managers and Repatriation of Expatriates

LEARNING OBJECTIVES

After studying this chapter, you will be able to understand:

- *Competencies required in global HR executives*
- *The role and responsibility of MNC HR managers*
- *Nurturing of talent, knowledge management and right organization culture*
- *How global managers can play their role effectively*
- *Profile of a woman expatriate manager*
- *Repatriation process of expatriates*
- *Repatriation problems and issues.*

OPENING CASE
The World-Class HRM Manager

Mervyn Raphael, founder member of Performance Consulting International, believes that global HR managers have the edge when it comes to being able to see the 'big picture'. However, he says, this is an innate ability. 'We once conducted an assessment of the employees of a very large company in India. During the course of the assessment, we found that their HR head had an amazing ability to link up different events in a pattern to create a roadmap for the company's future – a real global manager. Today he is the company's number two HR person in the USA', Raphael says. A global manager is also moulded by an environment he works in, but the key characteristics of global managers are that they are holistic thinkers, can network efficiently and are performance drivers. Tharun Raja of Hay group says that the following points differentiate global managers from regular ones, and make them successful across geographies:

- The ability to dream big, envision the future of the business and get others on the same page.
- The ability to predict changes on the business front and react proactively.
- The ability to deal with uncertainty and take key calculated decisions quick and fast.
- They win the confidence of CEOs and senior line managers for whom they act as friends philosophers and guides.
- Entrepreneurial thinking and the drive to succeed in spite of adverse circumstances.
- Networking ability: professional and personal relationships to derive advantages for the organization.
- Develop long-term HR plans in line with corporate plans and highlight the key role the human capital can play in deriving competitive advantage.
- They go out of the way to seek, motivate and retain outstanding talent in the organization.

INTRODUCTION

Globalization, multinational organizations and today's information society have profoundly changed the role of a HR manager and therefore the required competencies. Human resources are the most critical asset of all global companies and successful management of the same in a network spanning diverse countries and cultures is the primary responsibility of a global HR manager. Over the last 40 years we have seen a 1500 per cent increase in world trade; currently $1.3 trillion dollars are exchanged by world currency traders every day. In short, we are witnessing an increased economic interdependence across borders. Motorola, for example, has its presence in more than 100 countries and more than 40 per cent of its revenue comes from outside the USA. More than 70 per cent of McDonald's operating income is expected to come from overseas sales. Coca Cola earns more than 80 per cent of its revenue from outside the US. Few industries, if any, will remain untouched by globalization.

What must an organization do to remain competitive in this global environment?

What role should a HR manager play in building and sustaining global competitiveness? Which habits we need to break, and which ones need to be developed? And what competencies he should possess? This is the subject-matter of this chapter.

DEVELOPING A FRAMEWORK

The title of this chapter itself describes the evolving role of a HR manager in a performance-driven, highly competitive world. If he has to succeed in this role, he must understand what each one of the terms in the title means – Global/HRM/Expatriates. The key to success is business credibility.

GLOBAL

Business credibility factor: speaking the language of global business with authority, clarity and with passion. To engage in global strategic dialogue, a HR manager must be able to articulate the why, what and how of globalization of his organization. He should be able to understand and articulate the question: to what extent the main competitors are building a global presence, achieving greater economies of scale and tempting away the key customers. He should be able to analyse the risks and opportunities that are pushing and pulling the company into the global marketplace. There are four main principles of global contact:

- *Integration*: The company seeks to act as a coordinated network – 'one company worldwide'– in order to present a consistent face to the customer, build purchasing power and exploit the potential synergy.
- *Flow*: To maximize speed and responsiveness, resources (information, innovation, capital and expertise) must be able to flow through the organization to where they can add maximum value at any point in time. Flow enables organizational flexibility in a dynamic marketplace.
- *Leverage*: To create world class efficiency and cost advantages, the company must drive towards standardization and reduction of unnecessary duplication.
- *Optimization*: In order to produce the best results for the 'total' organization, company managers must balance local responsiveness with global responsibility.
- *Collaborate and compete simultaneously in various products and markets*: This is in order to derive maximum value.

These principles generate paradoxes and tensions that need to be managed. For example, the drive to integration and leverage can be at odds with 'flow'. Integration and leverage would move the business towards centralization, whereas flow would move it towards decentralization. There is no formula for managing these tensions. What should be globally coordinated and what nationally differentiated must be determined by each business, function and task as well as by other variables. One of the main challenges for any global manager is to balance – rather than eliminate – tensions in the business.

Further, on the basis of integration, the MNCs have operated on the basis of relative autonomy of subsidiaries. This has promoted responsiveness to local market, but often at the cost of overall fragmentation. Each MNC unit has also sought to capture and protect resources, even at the cost of other business units in the same company. This has disabled the flow of resources and organizational flexibility. There has also been the tendency in MNCs to reproduce the home-country structure. Each business, therefore, tends to develop its own purchasing processes, product development methodologies, marketing capabilities, etc. finally. MNC units have looked to maximize their own results rather than optimize results for the total organization. In addition, alliances, mergers and takeovers are changing the face of competition. *The Economist* (January 1999) states:

> Fewer than half of all mergers and acquisitions add value. Most difficult are the soft issues; the same word keeps popping up, culture – people never fit together as flowcharts. Culture permeates a company; any differences can poison the collaboration and mergers. The first is the growing importance of intangible assets... most of the value can walk out of the door.

With these challenges and imperatives of the global business, are the HR managers prepared for 'global leadership'?

COMPETENCIES REQUIRED IN HR PROFESSIONALS

Terence Brake, in his book, *The Global Leader* proposes three competency clusters:

- Business acumen
- Relationship management
- Personal effectiveness.

Business acumen is defined as the ability to gain and leverage professional knowledge and skills to achieve optimal results for the company's global stakeholders. This cluster consists of following competencies:

- *Depth of field*: being willing and able to switch perspectives between local and global, functional and cross functional arenas.
- *Entrepreneurial spirit*: taking initiative and demonstrating courage; pursuing calculated risks.
- *Professional expertise*: development of one's own knowledge and skills to world-class levels.
- Stakeholder orientation: showing willingness and ability to balance the conflicting needs of global stakeholders.
- *Organizational resourcefulness*: demonstrating insight into how the business works above and beyond one's own immediate area to get the things done within and between organizational units.

Relationship management is the ability to build and influence cooperative relationships in a complex diverse global network in order to direct energy towards the achievement of business strategies. The relevant competencies are:

- *Change leadership*: creating a new and value-added way of doing things, and mobilizing others to take ownership and drive the desired changes.
- *Community-building*: showing willingness and ability to partner with others in developing interdependent relationships.
- *Conflict management and negotiation*: balancing assertiveness and sensitivity in using conflicts to generate constructive outcomes.

- *Cross-cultural communication*: identifying and working with cultural differences to facilitate the achievement of shared understandings.
- *Influencing*: demonstrating an ability to move others to action without relying on personal authority or proximity.

Personal effectiveness is the ability to attain increasing levels of maturity in order to perform at peak levels under the difficult conditions of working in a complex global enterprise. Required competencies include:

- *Accountability*: being committed to owning problems, and taking responsibilities within one's sphere of influence for the achievement of business objectives.
- *Curiosity and learning*: demonstrating a desire to undertake challenging new experiences and an openness to learn from them.
- *Improvisation*: generating creative value-added responses, often under conditions of high uncertainty.
- *Maturity*: possessing a strong and stable sense of self with the capacity for resilience when faced with crises and setbacks.
- *Thinking ability*: demonstrating willingness and ability to attack global and local problems from multiple angles while maintaining a bias towards action.

In a survey of assessing these competencies, global HR managers were asked to rate themselves on each of these 15 leadership competencies on a scale of 1= low to 7 = high. The results indicate that the five lowest-rated competencies are those under 'business acumen cluster'. One HR manager commented that those competencies are our tickets to sitting at the global strategy table! Which means that global HR managers must be capable of, and actively participate in, making corporate strategies and implementing them. Results of surveys are:

Organizational resourcefulness	4.4
Entrepreneurial spirit	4.5
Depth of field	4.7
Professional expertise	4.8
Stakeholder orientation	4.9
Maturity	5.0
Thinking ability	5.0
Cross-cultural communication	5.1
Conflict management and negotiation	5.2
Change leadership	5.3
Influencing	5.5
Community building	5.7
Accountability	5.7
Curiosity and learning	5.7
Improvisation	5.7

Are HR managers doing right things, as well as doing things right? It was found at AMCO Corporation that HR managers were spending 65 per cent of their time on administrative matters, and

25 per cent on consulting and only 10 per cent on HR planning. To refocus HR on adding value, Amoco has formulated a new HR mission, which is to:

> Provide leadership and support to management by developing, integrating and implementing HR strategies that maximize employee and organizational effectiveness in concert with Amoco's mission.

To achieve Amoco's mission, the HR manager's time on HR strategy planning has to be about 25 per cent, 50 per cent on consultative and developmental projects and only 25 per cent on administrative tasks. HR managers at Amoco are being challenged to diagnose performance problems, develop solutions and mobilize resources. In fact, they have to be doing much more strategic thinking. According to one study, senior managers spend only 2.4 per cent of their time on developing a corporate perspective on the future.

TALENT MANAGEMENT

The main success factors of talent management skills are accelerating the development of global mindsets and skills throughout the organization. Their commitment should be to hire, develop, motivate and retain talented people who have the capacity to operate and lead in a complex and demanding global business environment. The HR managers should ask these questions: What people capabilities are needed in the organization if global strategy is to be realized, and when? Where these capabilities are located? They should know where the required global talent is. How mobile is it? What skill gaps need to be filled, and where? What moves can be made to partner with functional line managers to recruit, select, assign, develop and retain local and global talent? How much technology can be leveraged to track, train and network to generate collaborative advantages? These are the times of talent war in the corporate world.

KNOWLEDGE MANAGEMENT

HR managers have to be creative in seeking ways to generate, capture, validate, transfer, apply and integrate knowledge throughout the network to leverage available intellectual capital. Talent generates intellectual capital, the most potent business resource today. This knowledge can be thought of as codified in written documents or graphical representations, or 'tacit' in informal routines and implicit know-how. Knowledge may refer to what we know (facts), how and why we know it (research and analytical methods, mental models and paradigms), and whom we know (relationship networks). The challenge for the globally competitive organization is to minimize barriers to knowledge transfer. Some of the barriers include:

- The level of tacit knowledge contained in the best practice and, therefore, the degree of ambiguity that must often be overcome;
- The unique features of the context in which the best practice works;
- Lack of motivation and incentive;
- An inability on the part of receiver to value and absorb the knowledge;
- Lack of persistence in applying new knowledge; and
- Lack of intimate relationship between units.

Why is collaboration so important? Research by A.T. Kearney, Inc. (1996), indicates that a company's ability to transfer its distinctive critical capabilities across the organization is vital to global success. Those companies with 20 per cent greater capacity to transfer critical capabilities achieved a 7 per cent improvement in global performance. The best performers rated themselves on average 22 per cent higher at transfer capacity than the low performers. The transfer of critical capabilities cannot happen without a high level of collaboration across the enterprise. Enabling and mobilizing intelligence will come from highly productive interactions at work between people and people, people and organization and people and processes. Tapscot captures this thought well when he says:

> The age of networked intelligence is an age of promise. It is not simply about the networking of technology but about the networking of humans through technology. It is not an age of smart machines but of humans, who through networks can combine their intelligence, knowledge and creativity for breakthroughs in the creation of wealth and social development. It is not just an age of linking computers but of internet and human ingenuity.

CORPORATE CULTURE

Culture refers to the dominant values, beliefs, attitudes and behaviours in the organization and in the wider environments. The talent in the organization must be able to navigate through cultural differences encountered in dealing with suppliers, customers, distributors, partners, governments and international agencies. The company must be able to derive benefits from diversity in the organization through cross-cultural dialogue and the exploration of different perspectives.

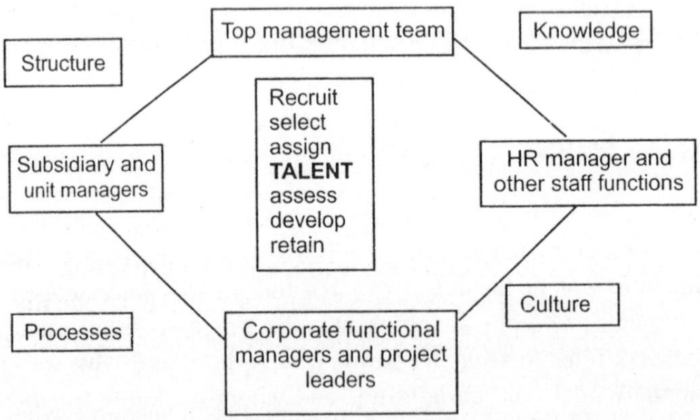

Fig. 7.1 Major Constituencies to be Influenced by HR Manager

It is equally important that the HR manager builds common working ground through the integration of shared values and accepted collaborative behaviours throughout the network. The values and behaviours the HR manager aspires to create in the organization are: teamwork, customer focus, fair treatment of employees, innovation and initiative. This requires cultural audit from time to time. There are four large constituencies that must come closer as shown in Figure 7.1.

The global HR manager should build bridges and create deep understanding with other three constituencies to be successful.

HOW A GLOBAL HR MANAGER CAN BE EFFECTIVE

A global HR manager needs to operate at several levels. First, he should partner with individual subsidiary units functional and other staff function heads for implementing their business-specific performance initiatives. Second, he should seek to identify and exploit performance synergies between related and unrelated businesses and functions. Third, he should play an advisory role and help them to manage their staff requirements by strategically linking HR processes of recruitment, selection, reward management, performance evaluation, training and retention of talent. Fourth, he should present and champion the concerns of employees to top management and simultaneously explain the rationale of management policies to employees. Next, he should lead TQM, BPR (business process reengineering), Six Sigma by organization-restructuring and other similar processes and culture improvement initiatives. He can:

1. Start by building business credibility. Be able to articulate the why, what and how of the company's global expansion. Identify the strengths and weaknesses of opportunities for and threats to your company in the global marketplace. Allocate more time for strategic thinking. Demonstrate a clear understanding of global business goals and strategies of the headquarter, as well as of all subsidiaries, (both short-term and long-term).
2. Try to understand the business environment matrix of different countries of subsidiaries and where the firm intends to enter in future. Look at the industry analysis variables and understand the customer base of the organization and how it is changing globally, regionally and locally. It is equally important to understand who are your current and future competitors and their strategies.
3. Be very sensitive to what different stakeholders – particularly key customers – perceive as value and focus all effort on collaborating with others to deliver those value propositions.
4. Study the execution capabilities of your company and how they facilitate or inhibit such business objectives as speed, quality, low cost, consistency, innovation and responsiveness. Identify performance opportunities and threats throughout the enterprise.
5. Be proactive and demonstrate leadership. Explore setting up partnerships with business functions – particularly with information technology and marketing – to produce the maximum value for the company in the shortest amount of time. It is equally important to look for performance breakthrough partnerships outside of the business with customers, suppliers and joint venture partners.
6. Review the time spent on non-value-adding activities. Outsource what you can as quickly as possible and focus on adding economic value.
7. Be visible. Measure and communicate results (create HR balance scorecard).
8. Spend some time with employee representatives and be helpful and friendly to everyone for most of the time.
9. Remember that the global business arena is rapidly becoming a battleground for talent. As economies shift from being industrial to knowledge-based, many senior managers are beginning to recognize that profits are generated from the hearts and minds of the people.

For many HR professionals, these changes will require a radical shift in mindsets and skills towards multidisciplinary high-tech and high-touch expertise.

WOMEN AND THE CORPORATE LADDER

There is a growing evidence to suggest that women are making greater strides on the international front than ever before. The 1999 global relocation survey, conducted by the Windham International and the National Foreign Trade Council, provides various measures of this trend. About 13 per cent American expatriates are women, up from 10 per cent in 1993. *Fortune* magazine summarized it by stating, 'The best reason for believing that more women will be in charge before long is that in a ferociously competitive global economy, no company can afford to waste valuable brainpower simply because wearing a skirt.'

Some argue that the numbers are small due to commonly held myths about women in business. The first is that women do not want to be international managers, and the second is that foreigners' prejudice against them renders them ineffective, whether they are nationals or not.

In a study of more than 1,000 MBAs from schools in the US and Europe, females and males displayed equal interest in pursuing international careers. As a matter of fact, only 8 per cent of the female managers surveyed said they would never relocate overseas, compared to 17 per cent of the men. They also agreed that firms offered fewer opportunities to them pursuing international career than to those pursuing domestic career. Women expatriate managers agreed that convincing superiors to let them go called for patience and persistence.

Expatriate women have generally reported numerous professional advantages to being female. Being highly visible has often been quoted as an advantage given that many women expatriates are 'firsts' for their companies. Foreign clients are curious about them, want to meet them and remember them after the first encounter. Emanuel Monogenis, a managing partner at an international search firm, observed, 'My clients now see women as equal in top global searches. In fact, more and more executives are saying they prefer women because they are willing to work harder and take less for granted than men. Many also believe women have more of a sensibility and insight into human behaviour. relationships than their male counterparts, and this is highly valued in culturally diversified workforce.'

No person will be chosen for an assignment abroad without having the necessary technical and professional qualifications. The most successful approach for female managers is to be persistent in 'educating' one's employer to be open to the possibility of sending women abroad and granting them the same status and support accorded to male peers. One female expatriate summarized her experience in this way, 'Although I am viewed as a foreigner, I still have to cope with some chauvinism but after I prove I have a brain, it is business as usual.'

Source: 'Stay-at-Home Careers', *Global Business*, January 2001, 62.

REPATRIATION

Repatriating home may evoke mixed feelings on the part of expatriates and the family. Their concerns are both professional and personal. Even in two years, dramatic changes may have occurred not only at home but also in the way the individual and the family perceive the foreign environment. At worst, reverse culture shock may emerge.

The most important professional issue is finding a proper place in the hierarchy on return. If no provision is made, the returning expatriate may be caught in a holding pattern for an intolerable length of time. For this reason, Dow Chemical provides each manager embarking on an overseas assignment with a letter that promises a job at least equal in responsibility upon return. Furthermore, because of their isolation, assignments abroad mean greater autonomy and authority than similar domestic positions. Both financially and psychologically, many expatriates find overseas position difficult to give up. Many executive perks, such as club memberships, will not be provided at home.

The family, too, may be reluctant to give up its special status. In India, for example, an expatriate family is provided with servants for most of the tasks they have to do themselves at home. Many longer-term expatriates are shocked by the increase in prices of housing and education at home. For many managers who want to stay abroad, this may mean change of company or even career – from employee to independent business person. According to one study (Nancy J. Adler), 20 per cent of the employees who complete overseas assignments want to leave the company on their return.

Loss of internationally experienced managers is not liked by the company because they report improvements in their managerial and cross-cultural skills and self-confidence. Therefore, planning for repatriation is necessary. A four-step process can be used for this purpose. The first step involves an assessment of foreign assignments in terms of environmental constraints and corporate objectives, making sure that they are realistically defined. The second stage is preparation of the individual for an overseas assignment, which should include a clear understanding of when and how repatriation will take place. During his duty abroad, the manager should be kept abreast of developments at the headquarter, especially in terms of career paths. Finally on return, he should receive intensive organizational reorientation, reasonable professional adjustment time, and counseling for the entire family on matters of, for example, finance. A programme of this type allows the expatriate to feel a close bond with the headquarter regardless of geographical distance.

THE REPATRIATION PROCESS

On completion of the foreign assignment, the MNC asks the expatriate to report back to headquarter at home-country for next position. Some expatriates are treated as global managers and after a brief stint at home are given another foreign assignment to a different country. During this stint at home, they get updated with the corporate strategy and new developments. They also settle their personal needs of their family and children's schooling, etc. In any case all global managers get repatriated before retirement.

The process of repatriation takes place in four stages:

- *Preparation* involves planning for the future and gathering all information about the new position. The firm gives a checklist of activities that need to be completed before departure, such as closure of bank accounts, settling bills; making a detailed report to hand over the charge etc. This phase is similar to pre-departure training and preparation.
- *Physical relocation* involves packing and moving, selling of some assets and goods, which he does not want to carry home. Specialized agencies are hired to assist in smooth relocation.
- *Transition* living in temporary accommodation, till permanent residence gets ready, renewing driving licences, finding job for the spouse, purchasing cars, opening bank accounts, etc.
- *Readjustment* requires at several levels. First is career anxiety. When they take foreign assignment and achieve success under difficult conditions, they expect promotion and higher responsibility. Further, during their stay abroad, they have lost vital links and contacts with the top management, which are so essential for career success. It is also possible that power centres have changed or company's management has changed.

Further, the social network of friends and associates has changed and distance is created psychologically and socially. This adjustment is needed on the part of every family member and takes time to build social, emotional and psychological links. Even children have to adjust to new school environments and friends, what affects their performance.

PREDICTORS OF REPATRIATION MALADJUSTMENT

Five factors can be considered as predictors of maladjustment in order of importance, which MNCs can address in some measure. They are:

1. *Length of time abroad* – longer period of stay abroad does change a person. It affects his self-efficacy (the degree to which an individual believes that he or she can execute a set of behaviours and self-confidence to face odds of life and take initiative). In addition, the new expatriate position is much more demanding. The extent of change depends upon the personality, age and country where he had worked. It also depends upon the communication level maintained by headquarters with the expatriate and how often he visited headquarters during his assignment and support provided by HR department to him. Workplace changes may also affect the readjustment process. He may encounter that the organization has been restructured, altering role, reporting and communication channels. Technological changes in work processes may also baffle him.
2. *Loss of status and pay* – expatriates in their assignments abroad enjoy a great deal of autonomy and power to take decisions as they often head the subsidiaries or occupy top positions and high status there. On return, they get positions lower in the hierarchy and have to function within the prevailing bureaucracy. Thus their powers, autonomy and status are reduced, requiring change in the style of functioning. In addition, pay is less and facilities and perks, including the type of bungalow enjoyed abroad, are not available, requiring change in lifestyle. This is not an easy situation and affects their readjustment process.
3. *Social factors* – have been mentioned earlier which require building new social network for self, wife and children as well. They are all undergoing the adjustment process, compounding the pain in early phase. Keeping connected through Internet, e-mails and phones with social network at home, not only keeps them abreast with developments at home but helps in getting adjusted better on return.
4. *Effect on the partner's career* – long absence from work when the spouse is abroad with him, she may not find a suitable job on return. Negative experiences during job search may compound her readjustment. Given that dual-career couples are on the increase, and that more females expect overseas assignments, the issue of partner's career is likely to become a major issue, determining availability of global managers.
5. *Multinationals' response* – some MNCs take a number of steps in advance to help expatriate before his return. First, they keep him constantly informed about developments in the company as well as in the country and help in looking after his parents and property. Second, they hold workshops on problems faced and how best they can be managed. Third, they may help him in finding a job for the spouse and a suitable home. Fourth, allow time to start judging his or her performance on the new job or give some exposure before delegating full responsibility.

It must be remembered that expatriates bring wealth of knowledge and experience and MNCs must make full use of them in planning operations abroad and training new expatriates. HR departments no doubt play an important role in this regard.

Review Questions

1. Explain the challenges to and opportunities for global HRM managers in a global, information society.
2. What competencies are desired in a successful global HR manager of a transnational organization?
3. What a newly appointed global HR manager should be attempting to be an effective and efficient HR manager?
4. Discuss the process of repatriation of expatriates, its importance and the problems they face on return. Suggest what steps can an MNC take to help them in readjustment back home on the new job that may not offer a higher position.

Assignment

Try to seek an interview with any three international HR managers as high in the corporate structure as possible and learn what type of challenges they are facing and how they are coping them with it. Present your findings to the class.

PART 2

Chapter 8

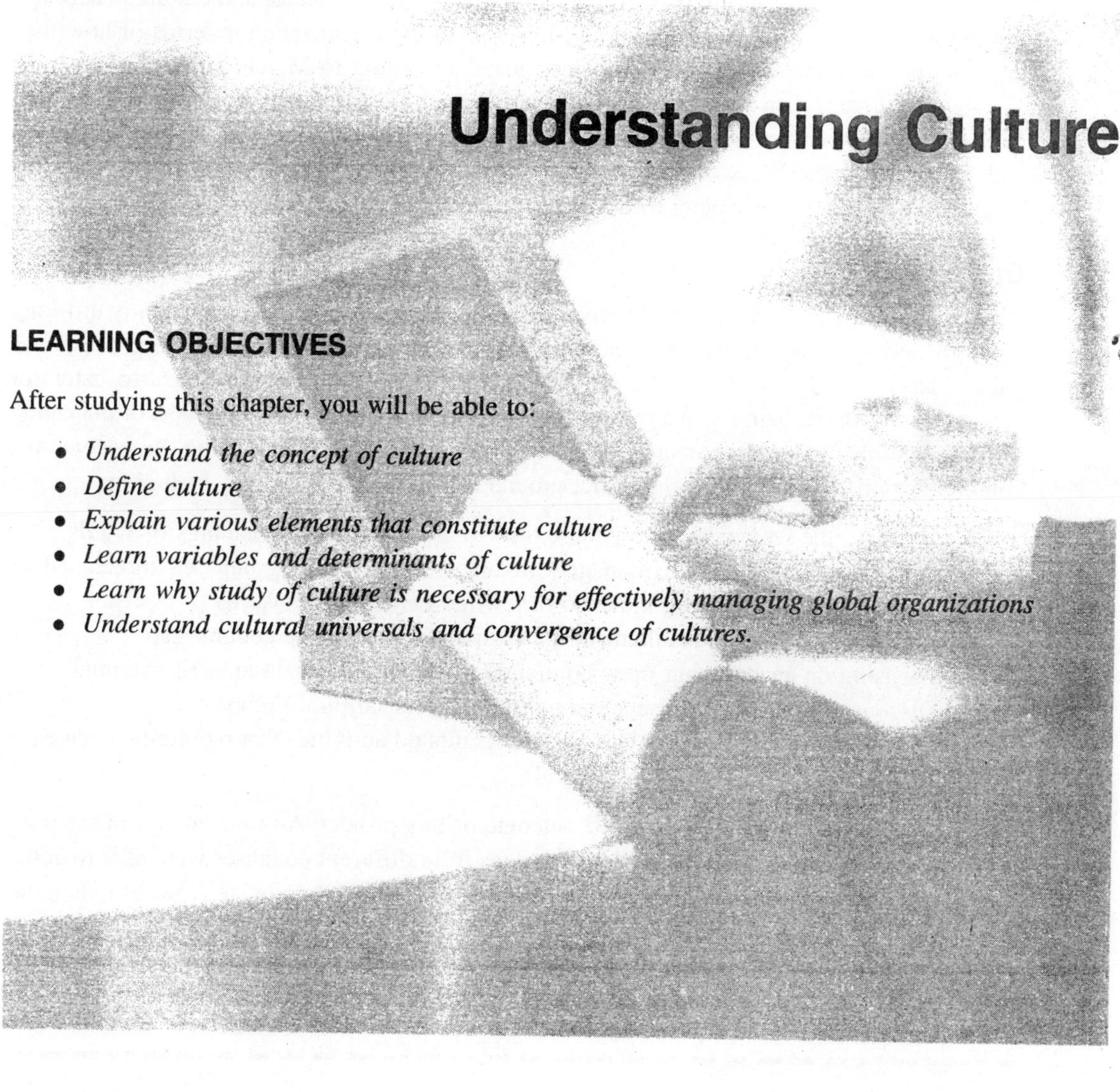

Understanding Culture

LEARNING OBJECTIVES

After studying this chapter, you will be able to:

- *Understand the concept of culture*
- *Define culture*
- *Explain various elements that constitute culture*
- *Learn variables and determinants of culture*
- *Learn why study of culture is necessary for effectively managing global organizations*
- *Understand cultural universals and convergence of cultures.*

OPENING CASE
Sometimes East is East and West is West – A Mercer Case Study

Here is a client example of how – either because of personality clashes or cultural clashes – the Western managers in this organization did not function well in Asia.

Client Situation

This company has its regional headquarters in a country in South East Asia. The company's operations span Singapore, Thailand, Malaysia, Indonesia and Vietnam. This company has a very strong market share in Japan and Asia. Its management team in S.E Asia consists of members from vastly differing backgrounds in terms of their language and culture. There is a distinct gap between the Japanese and non-Japanese in the organization in terms of how they view the organization's culture and business goals, according to Mercer consultants.

As this organization wants to move towards a high-performance organization structure, clarity is needed between the Japanese and Asian offices. Asian direction needs to be aligned with the head-quarter's goals as well as the goals of the local market. In this project we helped this company's managers to develop a mission statement and vision for the future.

Our Experience

It was a challenge to align a culturally diverse management team, as there were many differing opinions and agendas, expressed through different languages and cultures. The process was painful and slow. To overcome the language issue we created new processes to cater for language and cultural barriers. We realized we had to get around the complex task of managing group dynamics. Mercer consultants had to proceed slowly in setting the scene for communication. We also had to lay strict ground rules at these meetings, including:

- Stopping the session to give people time to cross-reference meanings of words.
- Flashing red cards when managers involved in the focus group felt threatened or when they felt personally attacked (a few red cards were flashed)
- Assigning an Asian consultant in the sessions to bridge the cultural gap.
- Focusing on encouraging open communication, and an 'open-minded listening'
- Discouraging "silo" mindsets among the different cultural groups.
- To get around the language barriers, we facilitated activities that require less sentence structures than we would normally do.

It is still too early to assess the full outcome of this project. An immediate impact from this exercise was that the various leadership teams from different countries were able to come to terms with the company's shared values and mission. This was major step toward in helping the region office align with the direction of the head-office.

Source: *Mastering Business in Asia-Human Resource Management*, Huge Bucknall & Reji Ohtaki, Wiley. p, 26,27.

INTRODUCTION

According to Peter Drucker, if management is an organ of society, culture is its very nature. Therefore, for organizational excellence, management must take care of the sensitivities of societal culture. This extends to setting of objectives, formulation and implementation of strategies, designing organization structure and communication or displaying type of leadership roles or reward systems. Human behaviour, in organizational settings is conditioned apart from other factors by societal and organizational culture which influence all other areas of business processes like communication, decision-making, diplomacy, negotiations and so on. The overwhelming success of Japanese companies in the eighties is primarily attributed to its unique national culture. In fact, every national culture can contribute something unique to the field of management and business.

Globalization, which is said to be the 'second industrial revolution', is fast changing how our society conducts business and trade. Global trade has increased from US$ 55 billion in 1974-75 (GOI, Economic Survey) to more than US$ 6,000 billion in 2000. The foreign exchange market has been growing at a rapid pace too, reflecting a general growth in the volume of cross-border trade and investment. In March 1986, the average total value of global foreign exchange trading was about US$ 200 billion per day. By April 1998 it had reached US$ 1490 billion per day. There are more than 80,000 multinationals operating around the globe. There are several global corporations, like GE, Shell, IBM and GM with sales exceeding the GDP of some nations. Increasing global interaction in business, sports, arts and culture demands that international managers be thoroughly groomed in the study and practice of cross-culture.

THE CONCEPT OF CULTURE

What then, is the concept of culture? George Peter Murdock in the article, 'The Science of Human Learning, Society, Culture and Personality' makes some profound observations. He emphasises that except in the case of man, what the 'individual' of a species learns dies with it. There is no consolidation and transmission of behaviour excepting in the broad context of genetic biological evolution. But in man, however, he says, 'most of the behaviour acquired by any individual, in whatever part of the world or period of history he may live, has been previously learned and found adaptive by other and older members of his own society, and he in turn transmits this behaviour, together with any adaptive modifications acquired through his life experience, to other younger members of his social group. The interaction of learning within a society, thus produces in every human group a body of socially transmitted behaviour, which appears super-individual, because it is shared, because it is perpetrated beyond the individual lifespan, and because in quantity and quality it so vastly exceeds the capacity of any single person to achieve by his own efforts. The term 'culture' is applied to such systems of acquired and transmitted behaviour. Since cultures change with the varying and cumulative experience of individuals in social groups, it is possible to say of man, as of no other species, with the hereditary capacity to learn, that societies as well as individuals learn. Social learning is synonymous with cultural evolution.

To the question, why do men organise themselves into societies? Plato answers, 'To give the members of society (all the members), the best chance of realising their best selves.' Thus, culture is the process of social learning and a society's adaptation to its changing environment – because human society is an open system. Human society becomes more social in order that individuals may become more individual.

CULTURE DEFINED

Culture is easier to recognise than to define. Scholars have never been able to agree on a simple definition of culture. In the 1870s, anthropologist, Edward Taylor, defined culture as 'that complex whole which includes knowledge, belief, art, morals, law, custom, and other capabilities acquired by man as a member of society.' Since then hundreds of definitions have been offered. Geert Hofstede, an expert on cross-cultural differences and management, defined culture as, 'the collective programming of the mind which distinguishes the members of one human . Culture, in this sense, includes systems of values;?group from another. . . and values are among the building blocks of culture.'

Other definitions of culture come from sociologists Zvi Namenwirth and Robert Waber who see culture as a system of ideas and argue that these ideas constitute a design for living. Ford, refers to culture as, 'Traditional problem-solving through accepted responses that have met with successes. It consists of learned problem solutions.' Robert A. Kluckhohn and D. Leighton define it as, 'habitual and traditional ways of thinking, feeling and reacting that are characteristic of the ways a particular society meets its problems at a particular point of time.' Therefore, culture is a group problem-solving tool that enables individuals to survive in a particular environment.

Culture is like air that we breath, we cannot live without it, but we cannot see it directly; culture is like gravity, we do not experience it until we jump 6 feet into the air (Trompenaars, 1993); culture is human made environment (Herskovits, 1995); culture is the systems of shared meaning placed upon events (Smith& Peterson, 1984). Despite the diverse definitions of culture, there are certain common features that constitute the essential parts of a culture.

At the core, culture consists of 'assumptions', about how things happen or get done, or are related to each other. These assumptions are taken for granted to the extent that they generally drop out of awareness (Schein, 1987). Assumptions are expresses in beliefs that people hold about things, persons, ideas and the way they are interrelated (for instance, human beings are born selfish, God exists, and money can buy anything). Assumptions are beliefs manifest themselves through values that reflect what people consider to be important and desirable (such as peace of mind, achievement and money). Values are distilled from norms that are the standards to judge what is right or wrong (for example, the right way to earn money is to do hard work) or what people do in particular situation (such as everyone cuts corners to make money). Assumptions, beliefs, values and norms are interrelated and together they influence human behaviour (for example, working hard to earn money) that in turn creates physical artifacts (such as setting up a company) and social institutions (e.g. forming business associations) that influence behaviour as well as in decreasing order norms, values, beliefs and assumptions.

Thus, culture is the totality of all these entities that enables people to maintain continuity across generations and yet adapt to changing internal and external demands. Internal demands arise from inconsistent or contradictory forces within the culture while external pressure is like the layers of onion. The layers have to be peeled to be able to reach its beliefs and values that are held at the conscious level and yet are abstract enough to be manifested in a variety of human behaviours, physical artifacts, and social institutions (Sinha, 2000) cultures are, therefore understood through their values and beliefs.

In this book, we follow both Hofstede and Namenwirth and Waber by viewing culture as a system of values and norms that are shared among a group of people and that, when taken together, constitutes a design for living. By values, we mean abstract ideas about what a group believes to be good, right and desirable. Values are shared assumptions about how things ought to be. By norms we mean social rules and guidelines that prescribe appropriate behaviour in particular situations. By society we mean a group of people who share a common set of values and norms.

ELEMENTS OF CULTURE

Important cultural elements are values, norms, attitudes, folkways and customs. **Values** form the bedrock of a culture. They provide the context within which a society's norms are established and justified. They may include a society's attitude towards such concepts as individual freedom, democracy, truth, justice, honesty, loyalty, social obligations, collective responsibility, marriage, sex and so on. Values are not mere abstract concepts; they are invested with considerable emotional significance. People argue, fight and even die for values. Values are often reflected in the political and economic systems of society. One may not be able to express one's values but most often one behaves according to them.

Norms are further subdivided into two major categories: Folkways and Mores Generally, folkways are actions of little moral significance. Rather, they are social conventions concerning things such as the appropriate dress code in a particular situation, good social manners, eating with correct utensils, neighbourly behaviour and like. While **folkways** define the way people are expected to behave, violation of folkways is not normally a serious matter. People who violate folkways may be thought of as eccentric or ill mannered, but not evil or bad ones.

Mores are norms that are seen as central to the functioning of a society and to its social life. They have much greater significance than folkways. Accordingly, violating mores can bring serious retribution and punishment. Mores include such factors as indictments against theft, adultery, etc. For example, eating cow's meat is viewed critically by Hindu society. While drinking is common in the US, the same is prohibited in Saudi Arabia and is a punishable offence. Certain norms have also been enacted into the **law.**

Cultural traits are unique aspects of individual cultures. A cultural trait may be a custom such as men opening the door for women, a gesture such as *namaste* or an idea such as existentialism, which clearly distinguishes a particular culture. ***Enculturation*** is the process of acquiring cultural traits. One acquires cultural traits naturally within one's culture. However, culture can also be acquired in other ways such as contact with other cultural groups or living abroad or marriage to someone from another culture or even by training.

Diffusion is the process through which cultures change. Each society borrows cultural traits from others, particularly if a newly learned trait seems better than a traditional one. New scientific discoveries, innovative technology, and current media events and films cause cultural change. However, some sectors of society resist such changes. This is known as ***cultural lag***.

If contacts between societies are prolonged, ***acculturation*** may occur. Traits that have been borrowed over the short-term become permanently adopted. New customs, devices, gestures and ideas irrevocably change both interacting cultures. For example, Mughal rule in India changed many customs of Hindu society.

Assimilation occurs when immigrants or other newcomers adopt the culture of the society in which they have settled. This cultural borrowing is often one-sided. The assimilated minority group eventually loses the cultural traits that had set it apart.

When people leave their own culture to enter another, they must grapple with unfamiliar and unpredictable events, relationships and objects. Some of these may cause a phenomenon called ***culture shock***. Alvin Toffler (1970) describes how culture shock begins:

Here is an interesting example:

> *My third day in Israel, accompanied by a queasy stomach, I ventured forth into the corner market to buy something light and easy to digest. As yet unable to read Hebrew, I decided to pick up what looked like a small yogurt container that was sitting near the cheese. Not being one hundred percent sure it contained yogurt, I peered inside; to my delight, it held a thick white yogurt-looking substance. I purchased my 'yogurt' and went home to eat – soap, liquid soap. How was I to know that soap came in packages resembling yogurt containers, or that market items in Israel were not neatly divided into edible and inedible substances as practiced in U.S. My now 'clean' stomach became a bit more fragile and my confidence waned.*

Culture shock is what happens when a person suddenly finds himself in a place where yes may mean, no, where a fixed price is negotiable, where to be kept waiting in an outer office is no cause for insult, where laughter may signify anger. It is what happens when the familiar psychological clues that help an individual to function in society are suddenly withdrawn and replaced by new ones that are strange or incomprehensible.

The effects of culture shock vary from individual to individual. It is common for people to suffer from anxiety, confusion and apathy when they are pushed into an unfamiliar environment. The emotional stress of the situation can easily lead to emotional and intellectual withdrawal. This has significant impact on business performance.

CULTURE, SOCIETY AND NATION STATES

We have defined society as a group of people that share a common set of values and norms; that is, people who are bound by common culture. However, there is not a strict one-to-one correspondence between a society and a nation. Nation states are political creations. They may contain a single culture or several cultures. For example, Canada has at least three cultures – Anglo culture, French culture and native American culture. India is composed of many distinct cultural groups. Similarly, we can speak of cultures that embrace several nations. For example, Islamic society or culture is shared by several nations in the Middle East.

CONVERGENCE OF CULTURES

A number of factors have encouraged the convergence of certain aspects of culture among nations, notably:

- Improvements in transport, communications and a huge increase in the number of people, who visit foreign countries.
- Globalization of media, with similar or even same television programmes and newspapers and magazine articles appearing in all nations.
- Similarities in the tastes and consumption patterns of young people.
- The operation of multinationals across the world, supplying standardised products, and using similar marketing strategies.
- Worldwide increase in consumer's willingness to accept fresh ideas and try new products.
- Adoption of similar technologies in several countries, creating common work experiences and working methods.

CULTURE CHANGE

Apart from convergence of culture, national cultures change over time, possibly in consequence of the following factors:

- Rising living standards,
- Urbanisation of population,
- Immigration and emigration, especially if the population coming in has a different religion and lifestyle than members of the existing population,
- Economic and political destabilisation that happened say in Europe or during the Partition of India,
- Improvements in the education system and increase in literacy,
- Opening of foreign trade and the influx of new ideas from other countries, and
- Introduction of new technologies, which necessarily change working practices and relationships.

CULTURAL UNIVERSALS

In 1945, G.P. Murdock published a highly influential study of what he referred to as 'cultural universals', i.e. aspects of culture supposedly found in all societies. To the extent that cultural universals exist, societies can be regarded as essentially the same and cultural difference between them less important. Examples of cultural universals are interest in sports, bodily adornment, courtship, household hygiene, gift giving, status differentiation, sexual taboos and so on.

DETERMINANTS OF CULTURE

National cultures are constantly evolving. Factors that influence the evolving pattern are prevailing political and economic systems, the social structure of society, dominant religion, language, aesthetics and education.

Religion may be defined as a system of shared beliefs and rituals that are concerned with the realm of the sacred. Most ethical systems which guide and shape human behavior, are the product of religion. The relation between religion, ethics and society is subtle, complex and profound. While religion influences values (which are the bedrock of culture), yet countries with the same religion have different cultures, for example, Bangladesh and Pakistan. Hence, religion is a weak determinant of culture. What is important for management is how religion shapes the attitude of a society towards work and entrepreneurship. In this regard, the *Bhagavad Gita*, a holy book of the Hindus propounds a unique philosophy towards selfless work, which suggests a way of life. Different religions send different messages, which create values and moral standards in a given society.

Social Structure

A society's social structure refers to its basic social organization. Although social structure consists of many aspects, for study of cultural differences, two aspects of it are more important. The first is the degree to which the basic unit of social organization is the individual, as opposed to the group. An individual is the basic unit in western societies and therefore individual achievement gets primacy. In most other societies the group is the basic unit of social structure and an individual considers himself first as part of his family or the company for which he works. It is the degree of relative importance to individualism or group that differentiates different cultures.

Social Mobility

This refers to the extent to which individuals can move out of the strata, caste or class in which they are born. The class system is less rigid than the caste system which is prevalent in India. While most societies have a class system, social mobility within it varies from society to society. For example, Britain has a more rigid class system than certain other western societies. Britain has three classes: the upper class which is associated with power and wealth, the middle class which consists of professionals and clerks, and the working class. The division of society into class or caste creates disharmony and industrial strife.

Language

Language is an essential element of culture for it reflects its nature and riches. It is language which distinguishes one culture from another. In countries such as Canada and Switzerland, two or more languages are spoken. In counties like China, India and Nigeria with a diversity of populations, several languages are spoken. Although language could be said to reflect the nature and values of a culture, this is not always the case. English is the official language of many countries, such as Australia and Singapore, but the two countries are culturally diverse. English tends to be the business language, while French is seen as the language of diplomacy.

In business communication, the translation from one language to another can result in inaccuracies. A literal translation may change the meaning. For example, some of the more famous translation blunders are 'Body by Fisher' which is translated as 'Corpse by Fisher' or 'Rendezvous lounge' translated into Portuguese as 'Meet your mistress lounge'. The same language may have different terms for the same word, for example, in American English, petrol (British English) is called gasoline and biscuits as cookies. An Indian generally would not understand the word 'downtown' frequently used by Americans for city centre.

Communication goes beyond the formal written and oral structure of language. Language is also symbolic communication in terms of space, time and friendship, and marketers need to be aware of these 'silent languages'. In the UK, a person with a large office is important in the hierarchy. But in

Japan, many high executives share offices. Much business communication also depends on non-verbal messages. Body language differs from culture to culture. For example, nodding of the head one way may mean 'yes' in one culture and 'no' in another.

Education

Learning and sharing cultural values happens through the education system. The educational system can take many forms and it is important to understand the differences because it can indicate the type of consumer market available and the quality of human resources available for employment and training.

Aesthetics

The aesthetics of a culture refers to designs, forms, colours, shapes, sounds – things conveying the concept of beauty and good taste. These are reflected in the music, art, and architecture of a society. The aesthetics of a culture can affect a firm's marketing strategy, diplomacy and management of human resources.

Colours, for example, are often used to identify brands and for product differentiation. Colours tend to have different connotations and more symbolic value in international than domestic markets. Red, for example, is a good-luck colour for many oriental cultures, while white is associated with death in Islamic countries. The design of products and packaging should take into consideration local preferences.

WHY CULTURAL SENSITIVITY IS IMPORTANT?

International managers need to know about cultural differences among nations in order to :

- Communicate effectively with customers, suppliers, business associates and partners in other countries and with foreign employees,
- Conduct negotiations and understand the nuances of the beginning postures of the other parties into a negotiation,
- Predict trends in social behaviour likely to affect the firm's foreign operations,

BOX 8.1 WHY CULTURE IS IMPORTANT FOR MANAGERIAL EFFECTIVENESS

- The chief executive officer of a leading Thai conglomerate, for instance, said that he had tried for five years to institute a feedback mechanism and failed.

  Asia's performance Challenge McKinsey Quarterly, 2001 Number 3
- "We spent US $ 1 million rolling out our new business planning and systems development model. The Indians tore it to shreds; The Chinese got bored with it. What is actually happening?

  A MERCER Client situation report- p23
- "We have opportunities in 11 Asian countries-80% staffed by locals, 15 % are intra-Asian staff, and 5% Western expatriates. Staff doesn't cooperate and our western managers can't seem to build effective teams.

  A MERCER Client situation report- p23

- Understand ethical standards and concepts of social responsibility in various countries,
- Predict how cultural differences will affect consumer reactions to advertisements and other promotions,
- Foster relationships between union confederations and employee associations requiring cultural empathy,
- Understand local government policies and influence it for business promotion,
- Conduct efficient meetings in different countries and encourage employee participation in management,
- Understand how people interpret market research and other information.

HOW CULTURE AFFECTS MANAGEMENT APPROACHES?

There are many ways of examining cultural differences and their impact on international management. Culture can affect technology transfer, managerial attitudes, managerial ideology and business-government relations. Perhaps most important is how culture affects people's thinking and behaviour. Following are the ways in which culture directly affects management.

- *Centralised vs decentralised decision-making*: In some societies, top managers make all important organizational decisions. In others, these decisions are diffused throughout the organizations and middle and lower level actively participate in, and make, key decisions.
- *Safety vs risk*: In some societies, organizational decision-makers are risk aversive and have great difficulty with conditions of uncertainty. In other societies, risk-taking is encouraged, and decision-making under uncertainty is common.
- *Individual vs group rewards*: In some countries, personnel who do outstanding work are given individual rewards in the form of bonuses and commissions. In other countries, cultural norms require group rewards, and individual rewards are frowned upon.
- *Informal vs formal procedures*: In some societies much is achieved through informal means. In other societies, formal procedures are set forth and followed rigidly.
- *High vs low organizational loyalty*: In some societies, people identify very strongly with their organization or employer. In other societies, people identify with their occupational group such as that of engineers or doctors.
- *Cooperation vs competition*: Some societies encourage cooperation between people, while others encourage competition.
- *Short-term vs long-term horizons*: Some nations focus most heavily on short-term horizons such as short-range goals of profit and efficiency. Others are more interested in long-term goals such as market share and technological development.
- *Stability vs innovation*: Some cultures encourage stability and resistance to change, while others put high value on innovation and change.

The example of Samsung shows that competition has produced the movement of people, goods and capital in international business. Underpinning this is the requirement to appreciate and understand the social-cultural environment that will assist successful implementation of multinational strategy. Samsung, although not always guaranteed to achieve its aims, shows an understanding of the differences in culture and uses them for its advantage and those of its employees, suppliers and customers.

For all the examples of good practice, there are many *faux pas* made by companies who fail to explore the effect of their advertising campaigns, management approaches and relations with suppliers and retailers. These firms suffer losses either because they have to withdraw from a market or rectify problems at heavy costs – because fast- changing markets are not matched by changes in behavioural patterns, values and attitudes.

Box 8.2 describes how electronics major Samsung manages its international operations with cultural sensitivity.

BOX 8.2 SAMSUNG: SYNTHESISING MANAGEMENT STYLES

Samsung, the South Korean conglomerate, runs business right across Europe, from Hungary where TVs are produced to Portugal where microchips are made to Germany where cameras are produced. There are operations in the UK and in Slovakia. How can a Korean company be successful in these vastly different cultural climates?

Samsung has developed a synthesis of management styles, taking the best from the European and Korean approaches. For example, in Germany the emphasis is given to individual workers as the company recognises that individual ability is high. In South Korea, on the other hand, emphasis is placed on teamwork. A further difference appears when looking at the structural design adopted by the company. A bureaucratic approach is followed in its home country, something that would not find favour in Europe. Hence in UK and other European countries, the company's structure is flat and authority devolved. Creating an indigenous management style is also part of the company's strategy to make its European operations self-sufficient, based on the need to have fast response time to market changes.

CASE STUDY

Run Silent, Run Shallow

Very few managers write a-bout management. Many are not capable of it; some can but are too lazy; most won't because speaking up involves taking risk – the risk of saying something out of turn or of revealing what should stay hidden, the risk of offending someone significant. The Asian manager compared with the Western manager is even more risk averse.

Despite the fact that 'the strong silent hero' is a Western stereotype, their culture sets up leaders those who have something to say, and who speak out loud and clear. Alfred Sloan, Jr would probably have been known only as one of the more notable of General Motors' string of chairmen had he not written the book, *My Years with General Motors*. David Ogilvy was only one of the many creative advertising men until he authored *Ogilvy on Advertising*. And would Lee Iaccoca be the best known and most admired managers in the world if he had not written his best selling autobiography?

Asian culture, on the other hand, does not seem to offer the same incentives. Confucius said: 'I wish I did not have to speak at all.' Tzu Kung asked, 'But if you do not speak, Sir, what will we disciples pass on to others?' Confucius replied: 'Look at the heaven there. Does it speak? The four seasons run their course and all things are produced. Do they speak?' In Java, halus the ideal man speaks softly and moves with dignity. The leader in Asia, traditionally, is marked by the effort his followers exert to understand what he means from what he has not said; with a look, with a faint smile, a frown, he conveys volumes, and they strain to read his message because he is their leader.

Western management is effective because it is open. Western managers are articulate about their experience: they document their problems and solutions, they study and analyse their successes and failures, and they abstract, generalise and draw conclusions from them that they then publish widely. Because of this free flow of ideas, their management technology grows in effectiveness, efficiency and influence. Fredric Taylor, 'father of modern management science' was a production manager continually in search of the best way to get things done on the shop floor; he then started writing his insights.

Henry Fayol, who first tried to analyse the functions of managers, was the CEO of a large mining conglomerate when he wrote *General Principles of Management*. The West has a long line of professional managers who have written about their practices of management and thereby contributed greatly to the development of its technology.

There is too much secrecy among Asian managers. We keep things to ourselves; we distrust each other; we refuse to help and to learn from one another. And because we do not document our experiences, analyse it and generalise from it, we have a very shallow understanding about what works and does not work in Asian organizations. Instead, we read books from the West and attempt to apply to our situation the 'principles' that Western managers and academics have developed from their experience with Western workers in Western organizations. And then we bemoan the fact that their rules of thumb, their current best practices, their surefire prescriptions usually do not work for us; that somehow, the results they bring do not quite fit our needs, circumstances and culture.

Case Question

Discuss how much western management literature is relevant for India and other Asian countries.

Review Questions

1. Why is culture so important an issue for international business?
2. Discuss and define the concept of culture.
3. Outline the main elements of 'culture'.
4. What is cultural universal?
5. What forces are causing convergence and culture change?

Assignment

Develop a cultural profile for one of the countries in the following list. In small groups interview people who have visited these countries or served there and ask their experiences apart from net surfing and reading about their culture. Present this study before the class.

China
Japan
France
Italy
Brazil

Chapter 9

Cross-Cultural Theories

LEARNING OBJECTIVES

After studying this chapter, you should able to:

- *Understand Hofstede's landmark study of cross-culture and its four dimensions*
- *Understand country clusters based on cultural variables suggested by Ronan and Shenkar*
- *Understand the 'orientation approach' of Kluckhohn-Strodthbeck in explaining cross-cultural differences*
- *Understand the interpretation of communication by its context, as explained by Hall*
- *Understand Andre Laurent's research in ascertaining managerial assumptions and approaches in different cultures*
- *Evaluate Trompenaar's work in understanding cultural differences while doing business in different countries*
- *Analyse and understand the significance of values in different cultures.*

OPENING CASE
Cultural Misunderstandings Threaten not only Work Environment but also Bottom Lines

Arvind joined a firm in Japan as senior manager, on the first day he was asked to pick up his recruitment letter and other forms. He recalls, 'It seemed like a suggestion, so I said I would do so later.' This casual remark cost him a job. Suggestions are meant to be interpreted as commands in Japan, he learnt later.

Preeti was preparing to receive her husband's Chinese boss for dinner. She ordered special Chinese lanterns to welcome him. But when he arrived, he took one look at the lanterns, bowed and took leave. Preeti ruefully recalls, 'The Chinese use different lanterns for different social occasions. I had decorated my home with funeral lanterns!' Both these cases show cultural misunderstandings can cause problems at the workplace. With more and more Indians working abroad and liaisoning with foreigners, these misunderstandings can cause companies not just goodwill but business. She recalls a joint construction project of an Indian firm and an American firm. The American firm was checking and cross-checking the modalities required to finish the project. This irritated the Indian engineers who felt that the Americans were questioning their competency, while the Americans felt that they were trying to be clear, thorough and transparent.

Cultural misunderstanding nearly derailed an Indo-Japanese project of constructing a bridge. An Indian firm sent a detailed list of technical questions to their Japanese counterparts. They panicked when no reply was forthcoming. What had happened? Was the deal off? Three weeks later the Japanese responded. Unlike in India or the West, the Japanese take the feedback from everyone and then only respond. This takes time. But they present a full picture and a well-considered reply. This concept is alien in India or the US, where e-mail etiquette to reply next day prevails.

Late Mark McCormack, founder of the international sports marketing group, IMG, related in his book 'The 100 per cent solution' how one of his executives visiting a Chinese firm in the afternoon found everyone asleep. The nap which lasted half-an-hour is said to be a routine practice. In China, even the law allows it.

Source: *TOI*, dated 7 May 2007, by Ashwin Ahemad.

INTRODUCTION

In the previous chapter, we learnt that culture influences both thinking and behaviour of individuals, which in turn influence the managing of institutions, businesses and negotiations. In this chapter, we will review the work of several researchers in this field, who have tried to measure or develop dimensions or characteristics criteria through which cultural differences in different countries and parts of the world can be assessed or understood. Geert Hofstede, Kluckhohn-Strodthbeck, Andres Laurent, Hall and Trompenaar have done the most important work in this area. There are some similarities and some differences, but together, their work helps us understand national differences in culture. Based on their work, suitable cross-cultural training programmes can be designed and delivered.

HOFSTEDE: CULTURE AND WORKPLACE

Geert Hofstede, in his book, *Cultures and Organizations: Software of the Mind*, focuses on the 1980, 1984, and 1991 versions of his IBM studies, involving 1,16,000 employees in 70 counties and 3 regions, namely East Africa, West Africa and Saudi Arabia. By restricting research to one company, he tried to eliminate the impact of changing organizational cultures and analysed the influence of different national cultures.

This findings demonstrate that:

- Work-related values are not universal;
- Underlying values persist when a multinational company tries to impose the same norms on all its foreign interests;
- Local values determine how the headquarter's regulations are interpreted;
- By implication, a multinational that tries to insist on uniformity is in danger of creating morale problems and inefficiencies.

The four well-known dimensions that Hofstede examined were:

- Power distance;
- Uncertainty avoidance;
- Individualism;
- Masculinity.

Comparisons between different cultures are plotted across these four dimensions, largely independent of each other.

Power Distance

It is 'the extent to which less powerful members of organizations accept that power is distributed unequally'. It is the distance between individuals at different levels of hierarchy. Countries in which people blindly obey the orders of their superiors have high power distance. Examples would include Mexico, South Korea and India. In such societies, lower-level employees tend to follow orders as a matter of procedure. Even at higher levels, strict obedience is the practice. Hofstede found that power distance is greatest in Malaysia and least in Austria and Israel. This dimension shows desirability of equality and inequality in the society or dependence versus interdependence. Organizations in low power-distance countries are usually decentralised and have flatter structures. The proportion of supervisory personnel is less and the workforce often consists of highly qualified people in high power-distance countries. The salary gap between different levels is higher. Power is reflected through status symbols. Status is highly valued and has higher motivational appeal. Management is more by control than by participation.

The employees in low power-distance cultures expect to be consulted and treated more as equals, expecting their managers to be supportive. They feel more able to control their own destiny and expect to be in control of their career, making their own choices and decisions.

Uncertainty Avoidance

It is 'the extent to which people feel threatened by ambiguous situations, and have created beliefs and institutions that they try to avoid these'. This dimension measures how far cultures prepare or socialise their members into accepting ambiguous situations and tolerating uncertainty about the future. High uncertainty-oriented nations tend to have a high need for security and a strong belief in experts and their knowledge. Examples include Germany, Spain and Japan. Members in such countries are more anxiety-prone and have high job stress. Employees place high premium on job security, career planning, health insurance and retirement benefits. Clear rules and regulations are welcomed and those managers who decide and give clear instructions are highly respected.

Countries with low uncertainty culture are more entrepreneurial and innovative and exhibit less emotional resistance to change. They are likely to feel more comfortable with ambiguity, uncertainty and uncertain and unstructured situations. Swedes, for instance, suppress emotions and see shyness as a positive trait and talkativeness as a negative one. In business they opt for the rational course rather than the emotional course.

Swedes are avid appliers of new technology and are ruthless in scrapping what is old and inefficient. Trade unions, which find a place on the board, accept job cuts if they find rational arguments in favour. In such countries managers are of a lower average age in higher-level jobs. Little value is attached to loyalty to the boss. Generalist careers are preferred over specialist careers. Inter-organization conflict is considered natural and compromise is an accepted route to reconciliation. The manager breaks formal rules and bypasses authority, if necessary. Organizations in such countries have less restructuring activities, fewer written rules and more risk-taking managers. They encourage personnel to use their own initiative and to assume responsibility for their actions. Sweden, the US and the UK are examples of countries with low uncertainty avoidance.

Individualism

Individualism is the tendency of people to look after themselves and their immediate families only. Hofstede measured this cultural difference on a bipolar continuum with individualism on one end and collectivism on the other. Collectivism is the tendency of the people to belong to groups and to look after each other in exchange for loyalty. Individualist cultures stress individual achievements and rights and expect the individual to focus on his/her needs. Competition is expected. Americans, high on individualist score, readily go to court against authority and each other to claim their rights. Individual decisions are valued over group decisions and individuals have the right to differ from the majority opinion. The manager aims for variety rather than conformity in work and does not have strong emotional bond with the company. He/she is loyal for so long as it suits his/her interests. Social philosophies reflect universalistic concerns with the society rather than with the need of any particular group or family. There is the sense that one should be fair to all.

Individualism cannot be equated with greed. Distinction between individualism and collectivism can be best understood by knowing who makes the decision, individual or the group, and how this affects performance.

In collectivist cultures, children are taught to think in terms of 'we'. Employer and employee are seen as members of one family; relationship prevails over task and duty. Promotions and advancements are often based on seniority and loyalty rather than on performance. Employee performance is better when he/she works in an in-group than when working alone or in an out-group.

Hofstede found that wealthy countries had higher individualism scores and poorer countries had higher collectivism scores. Countries, like the USA, Canada, Denmark, and Sweden had high individualism and higher gross national product. Japan was an exception. Conversely, countries like Pakistan or those in Latin America had low individualism (high collectivism) and low gross national product.

Masculinity

Masculinity is defined by Hofstede as 'a situation in which the dominant values in society are success, money, and things'. Hofstede measured this dimension on a continuum, ranging from masculinity to femininity. Contrary to some stereotypes, femininity is the term used by Hofstede to describe 'a situation in which the dominant values in society are caring for others and the quality of life'. Countries like Japan, with a high masculinity index, place great importance on earnings, recognition, advancement and challenge. Individuals are encouraged to be independent decision-makers, and achievement is defined in terms of wealth. The workplace is characterised by high job stress and managers believe that their subordinates don't like working, hence requiring some amount of control.

Countries like Norway, with a low masculinity index, tend to place great importance on cooperation, friendly atmosphere, and employment security. Individuals are encouraged to be group decision-makers and achievement is defined in terms of human contacts and living environment. The workplace has a cordial atmosphere and managers give more credit to employees and freedom to act.

Cultures with a high masculinity index like Germany and Spain favour large-scale enterprises. Economic growth is more important than conservation of environment.

Table 9.1 Countries and Regions Used in Hofstede's Research

ARA	Arab countries (Egypt, Lebanon, Libya, Kuwait, Iraq, Saudi Arabia, UAE)	JAM	Jamaica
		JPN	Japan
		KOR	South Korea
ARG	Argentina	MAL	Malaysia
AUL	Australia	MEX	Mexico
AUT	Austria	NET	Netherlands
BEL	Belgium	NOR	Norway
BRA	Brazil	NZL	New Zealand
CAN	Canada	PAK	Pakistan
CHL	Chile	PAN	Panama
COL	Colombia	PER	Peru
COS	Costa Rica	PHI	Philippines
DEN	Denmark	POR	Portugal
EAF	East Africa (Kenya, Ethiopia, Zambia)	SAF	South Africa
		SAL	Salvador
EQA	Equador	SIN	Singapore
FIN	Finland	SPA	Spain
FRA	France	SWE	Sweden
GBR	Great Britain	SWI	Switzerland
GER	Germany	TAI	Taiwan
GRE	Greece	THA	Thailand

(Contd.)

Table 9.1 Contd.

GUA	Guatemala	TUR	Turkey
HOK	Hong Kong	URU	Uruguay
IDO	Indonesia	USA	United States
IND	India	VEN	Venezuela
IRA	Iran	WAF	West Africa (Nigeria, Ghana, Sierra Leone)
IRE	Ireland		
ISR	Israel	YUG	Former Yugoslavia
ITA	Italy		

Source: Adapted from Geert Hofstede, *Cultures and Organizations: Software of the Mind,* McGraw-Hill Ltd., UK, 1991, p. 55.

Young men expect to have careers, and do not often view themselves as failures. Fewer women hold higher-level jobs and they often find it necessary to be assertive. Industrial conflict is common.

Cultures with high femininity tend to favour small-scale enterprises and place great importance on conservation of environment. The school system is designed to teach social adaptation. Many women hold higher-level jobs and they do not find it necessary to be assertive. Industrial conflict is less and workplace has less stress (Table 9.2).

Table 9.2 Four Dimensions of Culture

Countries	*Power Distance*	*Uncertainty Avoidance*	*Individualism*	*Masculanity*
Argentina	49	86	46	56
Australia	36	51	90	61
Brazil	69	76	38	49
Canada	39	48	80	52
Denmark	18	23	74	16
France	68	86	71	43
Germany	35	65	67	66
UK	35	35	89	66
Indonesia	78	48	14	46
India	77	40	48	56
Israel	13	81	54	47
Japan	54	92	46	95
Mexico	81	82	30	69
Netherlands	38	53	80	14
Panama	95	86	11	44
Spain	57	86	51	42
Sweden	31	29	71	5
Thailand	64	64	20	34
Turkey	66	85	37	45
U.S.A.	40	46	91	62

INTEGRATING CULTURAL DIMENSIONS

A description of the four dimensions of culture is useful in helping explain the differences between various countries. But Hofstede has gone beyond this to show how countries can be described in terms of pairs of dimensions. Figure 9.1, which incorporates power distance and individualism, provides an example. In this figure, the US is located in the lower left quadrant. Americans have very high individualism and relatively low power distance. They prefer to do things for themselves and are not upset when others have more power then they have. In fact, Americans are taught that everyone is equal, so individuals having important titles or jobs do not overly impress them. Australians, Canadians, the British, New Zelenders have the same basic values and therefore can be clubbed together in one cluster.

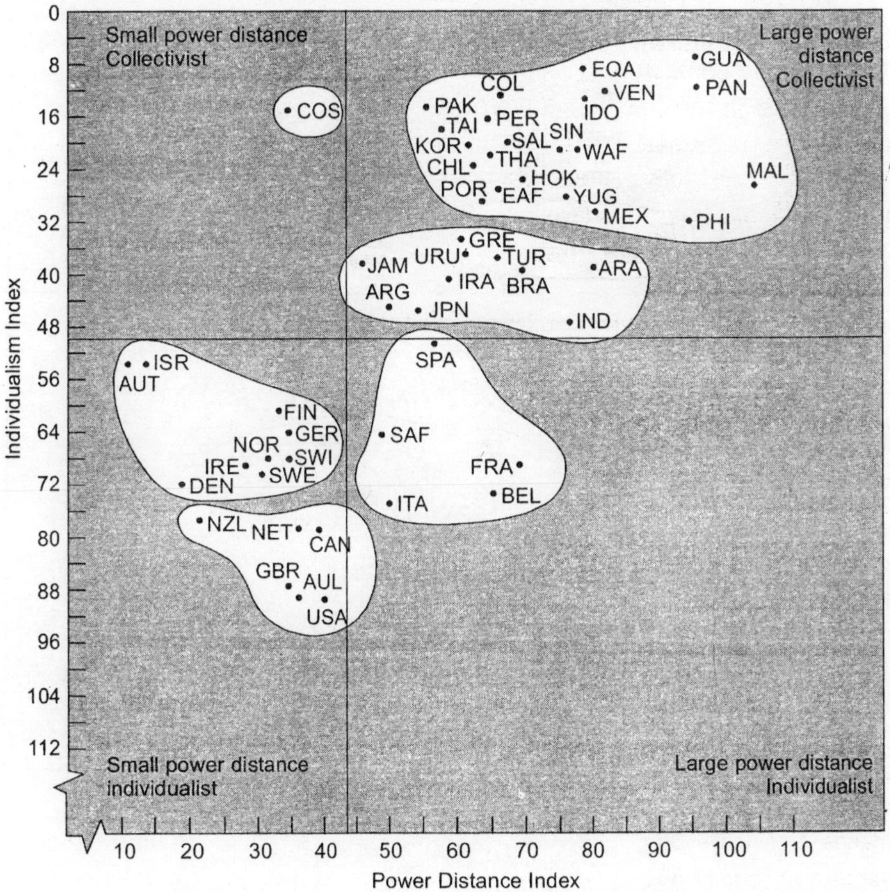

Fig. 9.1 A Power Distance and Individualism-Collectivism Plot

Source: Geert Hofstede, *Cultures and Organisations: Software of the Mind*, McGraw-Hill Ltd., UK, 1991, p. 54.

Table 9.2 plots the uncertainty avoidance index for 53 countries against power distance. Once again there are clusters of countries. Many of the Anglo nations tend to be in the upper left-hand quadrant, which is characterised by low power distance and weak uncertainty avoidance. Similarly, Figure 9.3 plots 53 countries in terms of uncertainty avoidance and masculinity and femininity.

The integration of these cultural factors into a two-dimensional plot explains culture's effect on behaviour. A number of dimensions are at work and sometimes they do not all move in the anticipated direction.

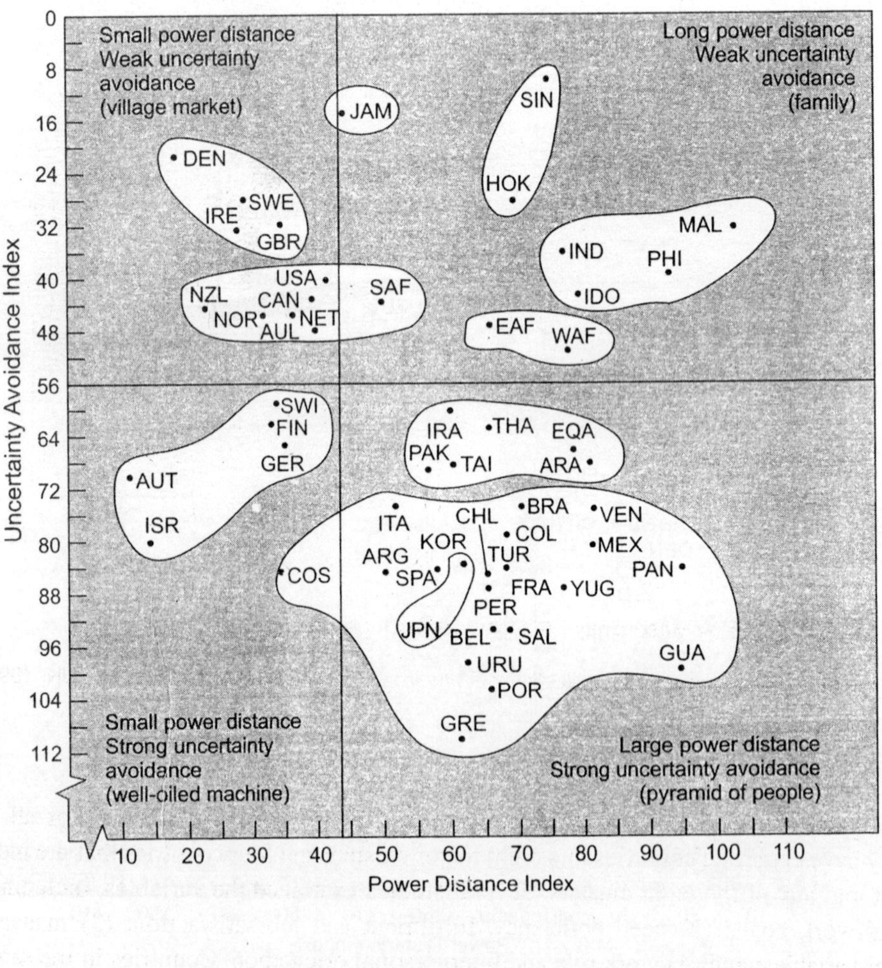

Fig. 9.2 A Power Distance and Uncertainty Avoidance Plot

Source: Geert Hofstede, *Cultures and Organizations: Software of the Mind*, McGraw-Hill Ltd., UK, 1991, p. 141.

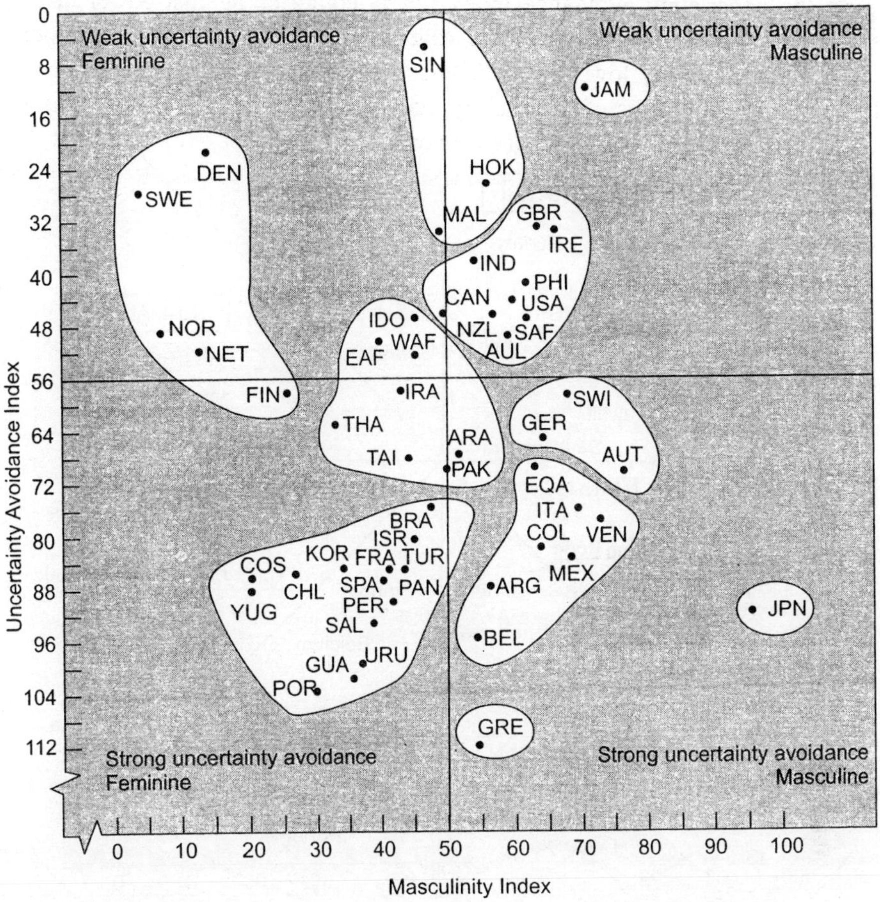

Fig. 9.3 A Masculinity-Femininity and Uncertainty Avoidance Plot

Source: Geert Hofstede, *Cultures and Organizations: Software of the Mind,* McGraw-Hill Ltd., UK, 1991, p. 123.

COUNTRY CLUSTERS

To date, perhaps Ronen and Shenkar have provided the most integrative analysis of all available findings. They have classified countries into eight major clusters and four countries that are independent and do not fit into any of the eight clusters. Several studies examined the variables, including: (1) the importance of work goals; (2) need deficiency, fulfilment and job satisfaction; (3) managerial and organizational variables; and (4) work role and interpersonal orientation. Countries in the same cluster are culturally similar and countries in any given cluster closer to the centre are higher in gross national product. Not everyone agrees with the synthesis presented above. Some researchers place India and Israel in the Anglo culture cluster because of the strong Anglo ties of these countries. Others combine the Nordic and Germanic clusters into one cluster. Still others believe that some Latin European countries, such as Italy, Portugal and Spain, are culturally much closer to those of the South American culture and would cluster them there. Nevertheless, Figure 9.4 does provide a useful mode.

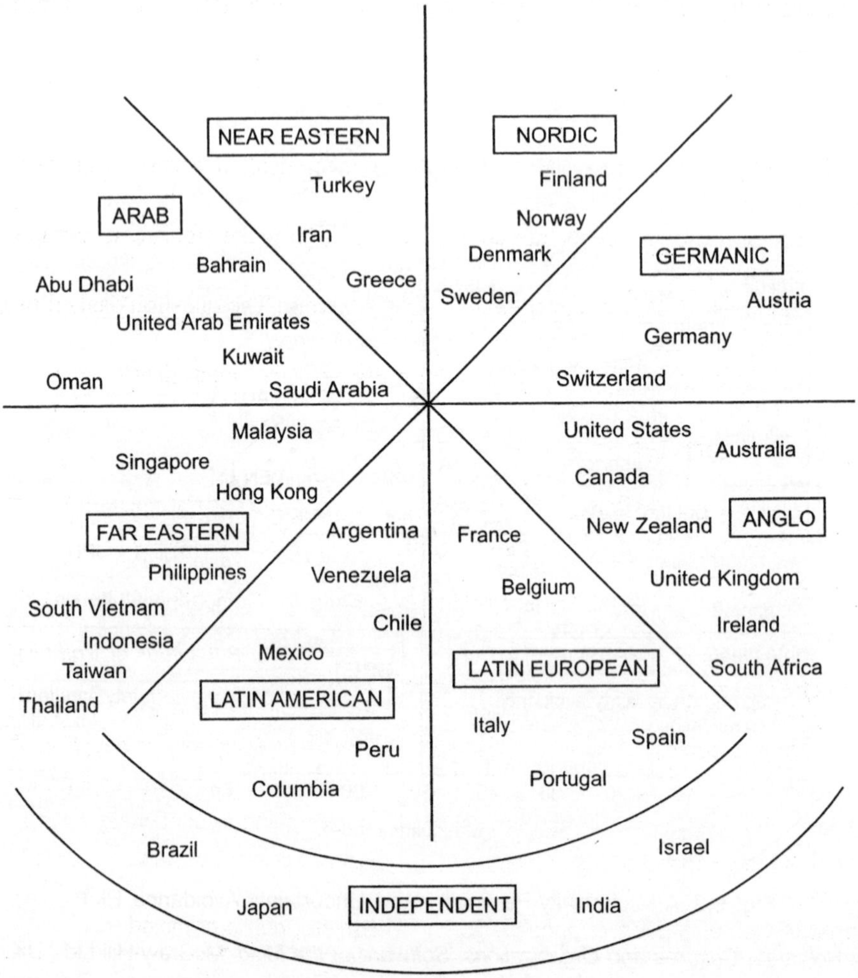

Fig. 9.4 A Synthesis of Country Clusters

Source: Simcha Ronen and Oded Shenkar, 'Clustering Countries on Attitudinal Dimensions: A Review and Synthesis', in *Academy of Management Journal*, September 1985, p. 449.

EVALUATION OF HOFSTEDE'S WORK

Weaknesses

Three problems have been identified in Hofstede's work. First, like all national cultural studies, it assumes that national territory and limits of culture correspond. It is not so in the case of smaller countries, and in case of bigger countries there are sub-cultures. Second, Hofstede's respondents worked within a single industry and a single multinational. Here, the objection is that unskilled manual workers are not taken into account, who may form bulk of the population of that country. Third, some of the dimensions suggested overlap. For example, some traits of low-power distance are similar to the femininity dimension.

Strengths

- The information population (IBM employees) is controlled across countries, which means comparisons can be made.
- The four dimensions tap deep into cultural values and make significant comparisons between national cultures.
- The connotations of each dimension are highly relevant. The questions asked of the informants relate to issues of importance to international managers.
- No other study compares so many national cultures in so much detail.

KLUCKHOHN-STRODTHBECK

This theory is based on the 'patterns of behaviour and thinking' in different cultures. The researchers distinguish and compare cultures based on the dimensions listed in Table 9.2.

Table 9.2 Kluckhohn-Strodthbeck's Criteria for Comparing Cultures

S.No.	*Orientation of People*	*Pattern of Behaviour or Thinking*
1	What is the nature of people?	Good, evil or mixed
2	What is a person's relationship to nature?	Dominant, harmony, or subjugation
3	What is a person's relationship to others?	Hierarchical, collectivist or individualistic
4	What is the modality of human activity?	Doing, being or containing
5	What is the temporal focus of human activity?	Future, present or past
6	What is the conception of space?	Private, public or mixed

What is the nature of people? This question explores the assumptions of people in different cultures about human nature, which could be good, evil or mixed.

Douglas McGregor wrote *Human Side of Enterprise* in 1960 in which he described his famous Theory X and Theory Y assumptions of human nature. Those who subscribe to Theory X assume that people are lazy, lack ambition, dislike responsibility, are self-centred, indifferent to the organization's needs, resist change, and need to be controlled or coerced. Those who subscribe to Theory Y assume that people have the potential to develop, to assume responsibility, and to pursue organizational goals, if given the chance and the social environment to do so. The task of management is to change organizational structures, management practices and the human resource practices, including organizational culture, to allow individual potential to be released. His Theory Y corresponds to assumptions of human nature being good, while Theory X corresponds to assumptions that human nature is basically evil and therefore people at work require controlling. It is easier to build teams and delegation of authority is more common in countries where the orientation to people and organizations is 'good'. Democracy is a preferred way of life in such countries. In countries where the orientation to human nature is 'mixed', there is more use of middleman and business contracts are made more specific. In such countries legal profession is a flourishing trade. America and India are nations with mixed orientation, while Saudi Arabia and Japan are countries where orientation towards human nature is good. Americans are optimistic about other people's motivations and capacities.

The second orientation is about relationship to nature, which relates to locus of control – whether it is internal or external. Americans, with an orientation for being 'dominant' (locus of control – internal), believe that man can control nature and spend huge amounts on space research, weather control, biotech and so on. In such dominant countries, conflict is not disapproved of and differences in views are encouraged. Organizational change is easier to implement. There is quicker response to environmental change by restructuring organizations. Consultants play an important role.

The eastern countries, with an orientation towards harmony, believe that there should be peace between man and nature. There is also a desire to avoid conflicts. Countries in the Middle East and India, with an orientation for subjugation, believe that destiny and God control everything. People believe in astrology and assign all success and failure to God. People usually resist change.

The third orientation – a person's relationship to others – is about the importance of hierarchy or respect for seniority on the basis of age, sex, familial or official position. In countries, like Thailand, China and Indonesia, there is more followership than leadership. Organization structures are taller and communication is more top-down. Seniors are obeyed and differences are avoided. Employees say what their superiors expect them to say. In countries, with an orientation towards 'collectivism', the needs of the group are uppermost and people strive towards consensus. In 'individualist' countries like the US, people strive towards individual excellence and this is valued by society.

Industrialist Americans, and the more collectivist Saudi Arabians' response to the feat of a Saudi pilot in the 1991 Gulf War showed very different attitudes towards individual achievement. The US television networks 'lionised' Sharmani, the Saudi pilot, who was thought to have shot down two Iraqi planes. But in the Arabic media, the pilot was unnamed and his feat was hidden in the official military communication.

The fourth orientation is the modality of human activity. When it is towards 'doing' as in the case of Americans, Germans or the British, self-identification is achieved through action and performance. Everyone in these countries is trying to develop a better mousetrap, so the rate of innovation is very high. Companies spend a great deal on research and development. One's achievement should be visible and measurable to be recognized by society. Where the orientation is towards 'being', people are more philosophical and spend time in abstract thinking. In countries of the Middle East, and in India and China, status in life is derived from birth, age, sex, family, and social connections more than through one's achievement. In such cultures, feelings are valued more than logic. Planning is often short-term, and spontaneity is appreciated. Where the orientation is towards 'containing' (Japan, Thailand), focus is on self-control. Striving is for balance between feelings and doing – there is more of self-enquiring.

The fifth orientation is the temporal focus of human activity. When it is 'future-oriented', as in the case of the US, the belief is that a better future can be planned and controlled. Past performance is less important; there is greater focus on career planning and training. Change is valued. On the other hand, if the orientation is towards the 'past', like in India, Pakistan and the Middle East, people base their decisions on lessons learned from the past.

The last orientation is the concept of space in the minds of people – how much people value privacy. If people think space is 'public', then a notice that a meeting is in progress is interpreted as a request to stay out. In countries, like China, space is more 'public' when doors are closed. People suspect something fishy. They will generally walk in without knocking. Open-space layout and public meetings are preferred in these countries. In the Western countries, on the other hand, space is more 'private'. People like their own chambers and always knock before entering others' rooms.

The Kluckhohn-Strodbeck model has weaknesses so far as the manager is concerned:

- The research was not carried keeping in mind the implications for the management.
- The orientations and variations are imprecisely defined.
- Interpretations are bound to be subjective.

Nevertheless this model is very useful for comparing cultures.

HALL'S THEORY OF CULTURAL CONTEXT

In interpreting messages, the context in which the message is framed is very important. The same utterance can have different meanings if understood in different contexts. We interpret and create messages with reference to our pre-existing shared information base. This shared information base includes values which link members of a culture group and influence how they refer to their contexts when maintaining relationships. Different culture groups respond to their contexts differently. An analyst interested in the behavioural priorities of a particular group must understand the contexts and how members experience those contexts.

Hall distinguishes between high-context and low-context cultures. Members of high-context cultures depend heavily on the external environment, situation and non-verbal behaviour in creating and interpreting communications. Members of this culture group learn to interpret the covert clues when they communicate – so much meaning is conveyed indirectly. These high-context cultures are Arabic, Chinese, and Japanese, in which the indirect style of communication and the ability to understand the same are highly valued.

In low-context cultures, like the US, Sweden and Britain, the environment is less important, and non-verbal behaviour is often ignored. Therefore communication has to be explicit and clear. A direct and blunt style is valued and ambiguity is disliked in managerial communication. People pay more attention to words then to gestures. People publish their experiences, which are widely read and commented upon. In the East, experiences are not published but passed on to close individuals.

High-context cultures have the following characteristics:

- Relationships are relatively long-lasting and individuals feel deep personal involvement with each other.
- Communication is mostly in 'shared codes'; hence it is economical, fast and efficient.
- People in authority are personally responsible to the actions of subordinates. This places a premium on loyalty to subordinates and superiors.

- Agreements between members tend to be spoken rather than written. This means that written agreements are just best guess and further modifications are expected as per the situation. This is disliked by Americans who belong to the low-culture group.
- 'Insiders and outsiders' are closely distinguished; outsiders include first non-members of the family, clan, organization, and foreigners.
- Cultural patterns are slow to change.

The characteristics of low-context cultures are:

- Relationships between individuals are of relatively short duration, and deep personal bonds with others is not greatly valued.
- Messages are explicit; the sender depends less on the receiver to understand the message from context.
- Authority is diffused throughout the organization and personal responsibility is difficult to pin down.
- Agreements are always written and expected to be binding on both parties. Parties are expected to be compensated for any breach of contracts. There is greater reliance on the legal system to resolve disputes, which is reflected in the size of the judiciary in these countries: the 1987 data recorded 279 lawyers per 1,00,000 people in the US, 114 in the UK, 77 in Germany, and 29 in France against only 11 in Japan.
- Insiders and outsiders are less closely distinguished. This means foreigners can adjust more easily in such cultures.
- Cultural patterns are faster to change.

Hall's model is built on qualitative insights rather than an quantitative data and does not rank different countries. In general, high-context cultures include Japan, China, Korea, Vietnam and other Asian countries, countries around the Mediterranean, and the Middle East. Low-context cultures include the US, Scandinavian countries and Germany. France exemplifies a mix of high- and low-context cultures. This model is useful in understanding how members of different cultures develop business relationships, negotiate with insiders and outsiders and implement contracts.

ANDRE LAURENT'S STUDY OF CULTURE, STATUS AND FUNCTIONS

This research by Laurent was directed to bring into focus some of the implicit management and organizational assumptions that managers are known to have; it is not so much to explore national differences. Laurent analysed the values of managers in nine European countries and the US in 1983, and in 1989, along with Adler and Campbel, collected data on China, Indonesia and Japan. Laurent used four parameters: perceptions of the organizations, authority systems, role formulation systems and hierarchical systems. The research treated management as a process by which managers express their cultural values. It examined following points:

- To explore how far a manager carries his/her status into the wider context outside the workplace; it framed the following question in its survey: 'Through their professional activity, its managers play an important role in society?' The percentages in agreement were as follows:

Denmark	32%
United Kingdom	40%
Netherlands	45%
Germany	46%
US	52%
Sweden	54%
Switzerland	65%
Italy	74%
France	76%

These findings show that in France and Italy managers carry their status into activities outside the workplace. But Danish and British managers are less able to apply their organizational status to influence their non-workplace relationships. This means a British manager can easily play under his subordinate in a club match than a French or Italian manager. In contrast, in Eastern and Middle-Eastern societies managers are expected to behave as managers even outside their workplace.

Bypassing Hierarchy

The values ascribed to hierarchical structuring affect what information is communicated, how and to whom in an organization. In response to the statement, 'In order to have efficient relationships, it is often necessary to bypass the hierarchical line,' the national groups responded thus in disagreements:

Sweden	22%
UK	31%
US	32%
Denmark	37%
Netherlands	39%
Switzerland	41%
Belgium	42%
France	42%
Germany	46%
China	66%
Italy	77%

This means that Swedish employees bypass hierarchical lines when direct contact with knowledge sources outside the organization promises greater efficiency and speed. Similarly in the US, it will be perceived as lack of initiative on the part of the subordinate if he does not contact sources in other units directly. In contrast, Italian and Chinese managers would perceive this as lack of respect for the hierarchy and feel threatened. Hence in Italy and China companies have vertical structures with clearly differentiated ranks and power centres, while Swedish companies may have a number of decision-making power centres.

Manager as Expert vs Manager as Facilitator

Adler et al (1989) asked managers from 13 countries to respond to the statement, 'It is important for a manger to have at hand precise answers to most of the questions that his subordinates may raise about their work.' Percentages in agreement were:

Sweden	10%
Netherlands	17%
US	18%
Denmark	23%
UK	27%
Switzerland	38%
Belgium	44%
Germany	46%
France	53%
Italy	66%
Indonesia	73%
China	74%
Japan	78%

In traditional Asian businesses, the superiors should be able to provide answers to technical questions. This is because subordinates cannot easily challenge their superiors' advice. They tend to value it above suggestions given by peers, whatever its quality.

The Asian manager who cannot provide answers loses status. This is viewed seriously as unity of the group depends on maintaining the superiority of one's hierarchical position. And losing one's status means endangering the security of the group.

At the other extreme, say in Sweden, it is more important that the manager be able to tap sources of expert power, perhaps elsewhere in the company, than give all the technical answers himself/herself. This means that a Swede working for an Indonesian company is frustrated by what he/she perceives as inefficiency when an Indonesian co-worker refuses to ask an outsider for help. And when he/she does make an advance, he/she is censured by co-workers for lack of loyalty and respect. While the Swede uses the hierarchical structure to facilitate problem-solving, the Indonesian values it as a means of signalling who has authority over whom. So, when planning a project, the Swede first identifies necessary functions, and then looks for the right people to perform them. But the Indonesian places most value on social harmony and assesses the potential of the project on the basis of who will be involved in the different positions. In the Indonesian context, a group which does not observe social priorities and protect group interests, places individual interests in jeopardy, and the members cannot work together efficiently. This affects not only the project at hand but also future relationships.

Prof. Andre Laurent carried out this landmark study by asking managers from different European countries undergoing successive courses of management development training at INSEAD (The European Institute of Business Administration), in France. Typical survey statements read as follows:

- The main reason for having a hierarchical structure is, so that everyone knows who has authority over whom.

- Most managers seem to be more motivated by obtaining power than by achieving objectives.
- It is important for managers to have at hand precise answers to most questions that their subordinates may raise about their work.
- In order to have efficient work relationships, it is often necessary to bypass the hierarchical line.
- Most managers would achieve better results if their roles were less precisely defined.
- An organization structure in which certain subordinates have two direct bosses should be avoided at all costs.

The questionnaire asked from the respondents their degree of agreement/disagreement with these statements. When their responses were analysed, it appeared that the most powerful determinant of their assumptions was by far their nationality. Overall and across 56 different items of inquiry, it was found that nationality (culture) had three times more influence on the shaping of managerial assumptions than any of the respondents' other characteristics such as age, education, function, type of company and so on.

The conception of organizations was shown to vary widely across national cultures as did the conception of management. From a sample of ten Western national cultures, managers from Latin cultures (French and Italian) more consistently perceived organizations as systems of social relationships monitored by power, authority and hierarchy than managers from the UK and the US did.

American managers held an instrumental view of the organization as a set of tasks to be achieved through a problem-solving hierarchy where positions are defined in terms of tasks and functions and where authority is functionally based.

The overall research findings by Laurent and his associates led to the conclusion that deep-seated managerial assumptions are strongly shaped by national cultures and appear insensitive to the more transient culture of the organizations.

LORANGE'S CROSS-CULTURE RESEARCH

P. Lorange tried to identify what managers perceived as being most important for career success. This led to a list of 60 criteria. National groups of managers were then asked, in a systematic survey, to select from among these 60 criteria those they saw as most important for career success within the firm.

For American managers, the single most important criterion to have a successful career with the company was 'ambition', drive and a pragmatic, individualistic, achievement-oriented assessment system. For the French the single most important criterion was 'being labelled as having high potential', a more social and political reading of the same system. German managers more than others believed that creativity was essential for success. In their mind, the most successful manager is the one who has right individual characteristics. Their outlook is rational: they view the organization as a coordinated network of individuals who make appropriate decisions based on their professional competence and knowledge.

British managers hold a more interpersonal and subjective view of the organizational world. According to them, the ability to create right image and get noticed for what they do is essential for success. They view the organization primarily as a network of relationships between individuals who get things done by influencing each other by communicating and negotiating.

French managers look at the organization as an authority-network, where the power to organize and control the actors stems from their positioning in the hierarchy. They focus on the organization as a pyramid of different levels of power to be acquired or dealt with. French managers perceive the ability to manage power relationships effectively and to 'work the system', particularly critical.

A comparative analysis across cultures brings the startling evidence that the art of managing and organising has no homeland.

TROMPENAAR'S CONTRIBUTION

Trompenaar focused on practical problems of dealing with members of other cultures in an uncertain world, where we cannot fully understand each other. He bases his arguments on questionnaire responses given by 15,000 informants, of whom 75 per cent were managers and 25 per cent, were administrative staff, representing a range of companies from 50 countries. They are as follows:

- Relationship and rules: Universalism vs Particularism. The Universalist's approach is to say that what is good and right applies everywhere; for instance, rules penalising the sales staff who do not fulfil their quotas apply whether or not an individual claims extenuating circumstances. The Particularist, emphasises the obligations of relationships; for example, a salesman failed to fill his quota because of concern for his sick son can be excused. A Universalist would not tip-off his friend about inside information, while a Particularist might.
- The group and the individual: Collectivism vs Individualism. This is more or less like Hofstede's dimension of Collectivism vs Individualism.
- Feelings and Relationships: Neutral vs Emotional. Some cultures are affective in that they show emotions; others are neutral and control and subdue their emotions. For example, Italy, France and the US, in that order, show their emotions, while the Japanese and Koreans control their emotions.
- How far we get involved, Specific vs Diffuse. In specific-oriented cultures, the manager separates the work relationships with subordinates from other dealings with them. In diffuse-oriented cultures, the superior-subordinate work relationship pervades in all other dealings.
- How we accord status. While some cultures accord status on the basis of achievement, others ascribe it on the basis of 'age, class, gender, education and so on'.
- How we manage time. Applying other researchers' work, Trompenaar distinguishes Sequential Cultures (in which time is treated as sequences of events) from Synchronic cultures (in which a number of events are juggled at the same time).
- How we relate to nature. Some cultures believe that they can and should control nature. Trompenaar characterises these as inner-directed. Outer-directed cultures go along with nature.

Trompenaars' system meets practical rather than academic needs. It draws together and applies ideas contributed by a range of scholars like Kluckhohn-Strodthbeck, Hofestede and Andre Laurent.

Trompenaars asked questions to people and based on their response, evaluated national cultures as shown in Table 9.3.

Table 9.3 Seven Countries on Ranks of Cultural Dimension

Items	*USA*	*UK*	*Sweden*	*Denmark*	*India*	*Japan*	*South Korea*
Sworn witness not lying even for a friend	1	3	2	4	6	5	7
Preference to work individually not in a group	2	3	1	4	5	6	NA
Housing not company's responsibility	2	4	1	3	5	6	7
Preference for not being dependent on family	1	3	4	2	NA	5.5	5.5
Respect for achievement, not for family concern	2	3	4	1	5	NA	NA
Belief that it is worthwhile to control nature	2	4	6	5	3	7	1
Belief that what happens is one's own doing	1	3	5	2	4	6	NA
Functional, not authority, orientation to organization	3	2	5	1	4	6	NA
Refusal to help boss in his personal matters	3	1.5	1.5	4	6	5	NA

Note: Rank 1 denotes highest value; NA means information not available.

VALUES IN CROSS-CULTURES

We looked at assumptions of managers in different countries, which guide their thinking and actions in management. Assumptions arise from values that organization members carry. Values are basic convictions that people have regarding what is right and wrong, good and bad, important and unimportant. These values are learned from the culture in which the individual is reared and they direct the person's behaviour. Values represent the deepest level of a culture. They are broad feelings, often unconscious and not discussable, about what is beautiful or ugly, rational or irrational, natural or paradoxical, decent or indecent. These feelings are present in a majority of the members of a culture.

Personal values have been the focus of numerous intercultural studies. The findings, in general, show that there are both differences and similarities in the work values and managerial values of different cultural groups. George W. England (1978) gave a personal value questionnaire to over 2,000 managers in five countries: Australia, India, Japan, South Korea and the US. The questionnaire consisted of 66 concepts regarding business goals, personal goals, ideas associated with people and groups and ideas on general topics. The results showed some significant differences between the managers in each group. The US managers placed high value on tactful acquisition of influence and regard for others. The Japanese managers placed high value on difference to superiors, on company commitment and on the cautious use of aggressiveness and control. The Korean managers gave importance to recognition by others. The Indian managers placed high value on the non-assertive pursuit of objectives. The Australian managers placed importance on values reflecting a low-keyed approach to management and a high concern for others. In short, value system across national boundaries are often different.

Value differences and similarities across cultures – Personal values have been the focus of numerous intercultural studies. The findings, in general, show that there are both differences and similarities between the work values and managerial values of the different cultural groups.

Differences in work values have also been found to be a reflection of culture of industrialization. England and Lee (1974) found the following:

- There is a reasonable strong relationship between the levels of success achieved by managers and their personal values.
- It is evident that value patterns are predictive of managerial success and could be used in selection and placement decisions.
- Although there are country differences in the relationships between values and success, the findings brought out that personal values across five countries mentioned above are quite similar.
- The pattern indicates successful managers appear to favour pragmatic, dynamic, achievement-oriented values. They regard an active role in interaction with other individuals as instrumental to the achievement of the manager's organizational goals. Less successful managers have values associated with static and protected environment in which they take a relatively passive role.

Table 9.4 American Cultural Values, Alternative Values and Management Implications

American values	*Alternative values*	*Management implication*
Individuals can influence planning and the future	Human action is determined by the will of God.	Life follows a preordained course scheduling.
Individuals should be realistic in their assumptions.	Ideals are to be pursued regardless of what is 'reasonable'.	Goal setting and career development.
We must work hard to accomplish our objectives.	As perquisites for success. wisdom, luck and time are also required.	Motivation and hard work is not the only reward system.
The primary obligation into their family and friends and the organization.	Individual employees have a commitment	Loyalty and motivation
Employees can be removed if they do not perform well.	The removal of an employee involves great loss of prestige and will rarely be done.	Promotion and removal
Company information should be available for communication anyone who needs it within the organization.	Withholding information to gain or maintain power is permissible.	Organization and managerial style
Competition stimulates career better performance. What works is important.		Competition leads to imbalances and disharmony. Development and marketing. Symbols and processes are more important than the end.

Source: Philip R. Harris, and Robert T. Moran, *Managing Cultural Differences*, Hauston: Gulf Publishing, 1991, pp. 79-80.

Do values change over time? In one of his research studies, England (1978) found that personal value systems are relatively stable and do not change rapidly. However, changes are taking place in managerial values as a result of different culture and technology and globalization.

COMMON PERSONAL VALUES

An interesting finding about successful managers around the world is that they come from different cultures, but many of them have similar personal values. Of course, there are vast differences in values between national groups. For example, some managers are pragmatic and judge ideas in terms of whether they will work; others are highly ethical-moral and view ideas in terms of right or wrong; still others have a feeling-orientation and judge ideas in terms of whether they are pleasant; some have values that are related heavily to organization's life, while others include a wide range of personal values. So there are many value patterns. However, similar overall value profiles have been found in successful managers in each group. Here are some of significant values:

US managers: Highly pragmatic; high achievement and competence orientation; emphasis on profit maximisation, organizational efficiency and productivity.

Japanese managers: Highly pragmatic; strong emphasis on size and growth; high value on competence, achievement, dedication and loyalty to organization.

Korean managers: Highly pragmatic and individualistic; strong achievement and competence orientation.

Australian mangers: High moral and humanistic orientation; low value on achievement and success, competition and risk.

Indian managers: Highly individualistic; strong focus on transition compliance and competence.

Nevertheless, these similarities are too small compared to the vast inter-country differences. That is why the ideal managerial value system in one country is often not so ideal in another country.

Review Questions

1. Discuss the significance of plotting various dimensions of Hofstede along two axes with high and low values?
2. Discuss how power distance influences organizational operations and societal values?
3. Discuss the characteristics of the four cultural dimensions of Hofstede.
4. Discuss the weaknesses and strengths of Hofstede's model.
5. Discuss how 'Individualism-collectivism' dimensions affect motivation, leadership and reward system in organizations in different countries.
6. What do you understand by the term value system in management? Are cultural values the same worldwide or are there marked differences? Are these values changing over time or are they fairly constant?
7. What are the cultural orientations of Kluckhohn-Strodthbeck? How are they useful to international businessmen?
8. Discuss the main ideas of Andre Laurent. Comment on the statement 'The art of managing and organization has no homeland.'
9. Discuss the cultural context theory of Hall. Describe main characteristics of high-context and low-context cultures.

10. Review Hall's explanation of high-context and low-context cultures and apply it to two organizations. What differences do you find in the following?
    (a) Management-staff communication.
    (b) Relations between peers.
11. Within each of the two organizations which of these is rewarded and which is punished?
    (a) An individual follows his/her job specification to the letter, whatever the task.
    (b) An individual departs from his/her job specification when it seems more efficient.
    (c) An individual follows authorised reporting procedures, whatever the task.
    (d) An individual departs from authorised reporting procedures when this seems more efficient. Explain any differences.
12. Discuss how useful are Trompenaar's idea of cultural characteristics in the international business and negotiations.

Assignment

Within which types of national culture the following of these would be rewarded? And punished?

(a) The individual follows his/her job specification to the letter, whatever the task,
(b) The individual departs from his /her job specification when this seems more efficient,
(c) The individual follows authorized reporting procedures, whatever the task,
(d) The individual departs from authorized reporting procedures when this seems more efficient.

Justify your choice.

Chapter

10

Cross-Cultural Business Communication and Behaviour

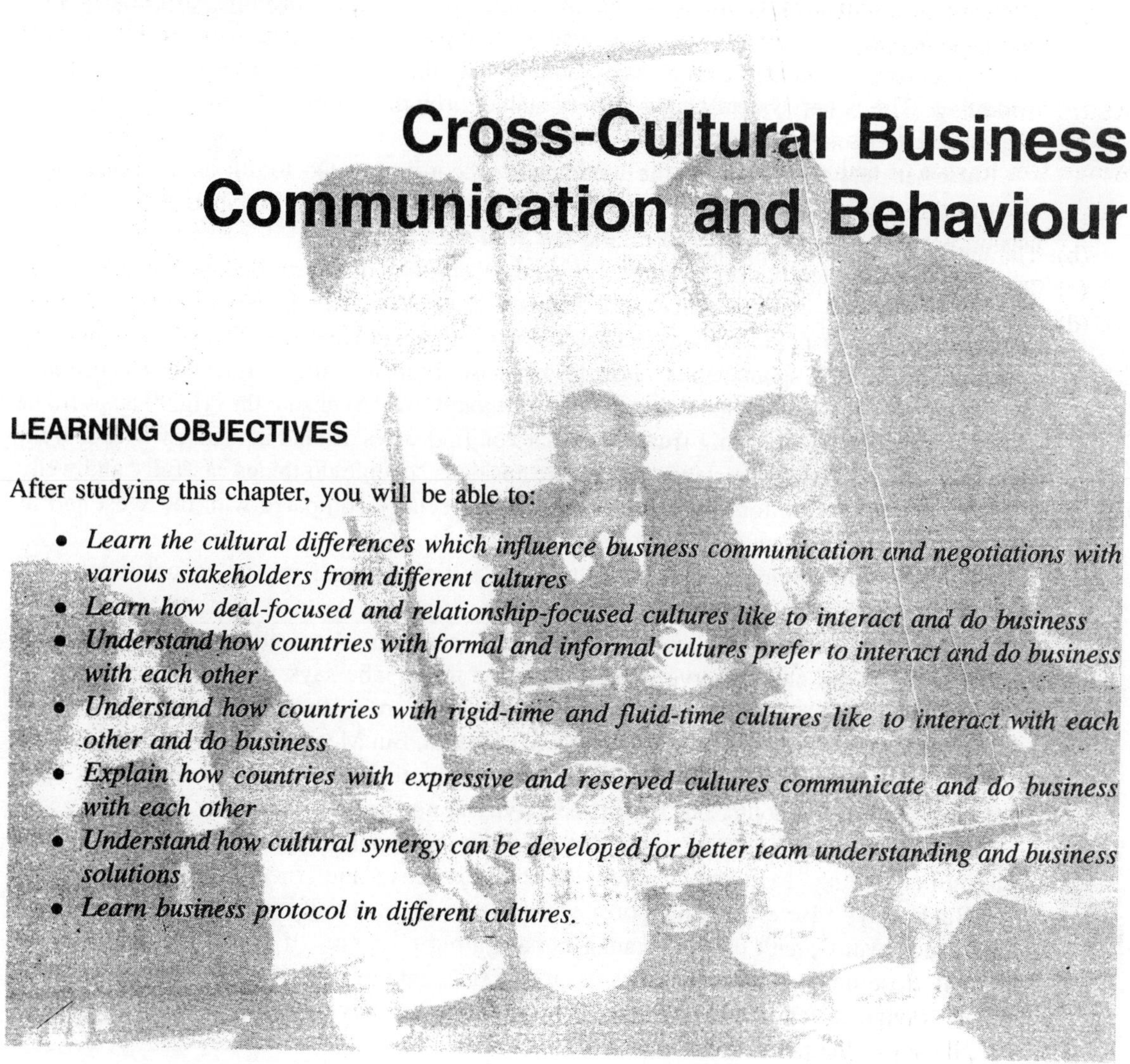

LEARNING OBJECTIVES

After studying this chapter, you will be able to:

- *Learn the cultural differences which influence business communication and negotiations with various stakeholders from different cultures*
- *Learn how deal-focused and relationship-focused cultures like to interact and do business*
- *Understand how countries with formal and informal cultures prefer to interact and do business with each other*
- *Understand how countries with rigid-time and fluid-time cultures like to interact with each other and do business*
- *Explain how countries with expressive and reserved cultures communicate and do business with each other*
- *Understand how cultural synergy can be developed for better team understanding and business solutions*
- *Learn business protocol in different cultures.*

OPENING CASE
Culture Clash

A big presentation is looming. The manager gathers his team together for an old-fashioned brainstorming session in the boardroom. Once everyone gets settled, issues, he is met with silence. The team sits and stares. Why so? Have they hit a creative drought? Are they terrified of their boss? Probably not. In some parts of Asia, this is just the way it is. In Asia, western managers not only face the obvious language issues, but also the cultural ones. One sweeping cultural rule can't be applied to Asia as a whole. Each country has its own set of beliefs.

One such hurdle – perhaps the most challenging for management – is getting people to feel comfortable enough to speak up their minds. The Chinese are ambitious but cautious when it comes to 'unsafe moves', which would include speaking up, particularly in a hierarchical situation. Tom Doctoroff, J. Walter Thompson's North-East Asia art director and chief executive of Greater China, says, adding that this is partly because of a confused worldview. The belief system keeps society stable through hierarchy, rules and regulations; the worldview is one of balance and harmony.

But what does this mean for the workplace? According to Doctoroff, an American who has lived in China since 1998 and in Hong Kong before moving to Shanghai, it creates tension between the need to conform and the need to achieve.

Emphasis is often put on having a working open-door policy to put staff at ease when they walk the plank into the office of a senior staff member. This is one of the ways which Arto Hampartsoumian, the Managing Director at Wieden and Kennedy, Tokyo, helps his staff open up and be more spontaneous. 'For the Japanese, brainstorming is difficult because they deliberate; decisions are made in a much slower, though way to ensure the "right" answer,' he says. Deliberation 'can be a big frustration' but you find ways around it, Andrew Meaden, the chief executive of Mindshare Japan, says. The upside is 'people do things carefully and well'. 'There's enormous care for how things are done, especially compared with the West and its faster turnaround,' he says.

Michelle Kristula-Green, Leo Burnett Asia–Pacific's Hong Kong-based president, adds that 'there's more of a culture to let everyone be heard in Asia, as opposed to the more aggressive West', with several people talking at the same time. 'In Asia, people are less prone to intrude. They are more reserve, which is a good thing,' she says.

Weekends are far less sacrosanct in India then they are in the West- 'You will find our office working on every weekend virtually'- Says Chopra. But Meaden points out: 'the intensity of work in Asia is less than in the U.K.,' No one can say that people in Asia don't work hard, or at least put in long hours, but their productivity is not same'.

There is also the matter of respect, 'In Australia, you assume you have respect when you walk into a meeting,' Matthew Godfrey, the chief executive and Director of South-East Asia Ufor Bates, says. 'Here (in Singapore) you have to learn loyalty, and that takes time.' If respect and loyalty aren't earned, managers have a big problem: 'If they think you're racist, they will close up and eat you alive,' Doctoroff says, adding that if you come across as an arrogant foreigner, staff will follow orders in a passive-aggressive manner. 'But if you establish trust', he says, 'the possibilities are endless.'

There are other ways of preempting the cultural conundrum. For Hampartsoumian, it meant calling in a Feng Shui master when he ran BBDO Singapore to create some balance and harmony in the workplace. The agency was having a new office built in the city-state that blends Chinese, Malaysian and Indian cultures. While an expensive project, it was all done 'to protect the health of the agency,' he says.

Source: 'Brand Equity' in Economic Times, 28 July 2004.

INTRODUCTION

Moving from one country to another, whether for business or pleasure, almost invariably causes culture shock, and the severity of the shock is directly proportional to the cultural distance between two countries. Richard, in his book, *Cross-Culture Business Behaviour* (2000) has put into workable categories the cultural dimensions of Hofstede, Hall, Laurent, Robert Moran and others. They used four dimensions to divide the countries on the basis of cultural divide which is most relevant for business communication and negotiations perspective. These four dimensions are:

- Deal-focused vs relationship-focused cultures.
- Formal vs informal cultures.
- Rigid time vs fluid time-based cultures.
- Expressive vs reserved cultures.

DEAL-FOCUSED VS RELATIONSHIP-FOCUSED CULTURES

Deal-focused (DF) cultures are task-oriented, while relationship-focused (RF) cultures are more people-oriented. Conflicts arise when DF managers or marketeers communicate or negotiate with RF business persons. Many RF managers find their DF counterparts pushy, aggressive and offensively blunt. On the other hand, DF managers often consider their RF counterparts dilatory, vague and inscrutable. RF people prefer to deal with family, friends and persons or groups well known to them – people who can be trusted. They are uncomfortable doing business with foreigners. As seen in Box 10.1, most countries are RF and like to assess and know the other party before talking business.

In contrast, in DF cultures found in northern Europe, North America, Australia and New Zealand, people are relatively open to doing business with strangers. This means, in DF countries one can straightaway talk business and get down to facts. The US is highly DF, perhaps because Americans are raised in a mobile immigrant society. Hence they are open to discussing business possibilities with people they don't know. The success of telemarketing illustrates this openness. All one has to do is, fix an appointment and convince an American about the value of the deal to get the business.

This approach, however, will not work in Japan. Here, the best method is to first arrange for a right person or organization to introduce you to the prospective client. The ideal party to provide introduction is a person or organization of stature who is known to both parties, banks, commercial section of the country's embassy in the target country or through the Chamber of Commerce. In RF

BOX 10.1 CATEGORIZATION OF COUNTRIES BASED ON DEAL/RELATIONSHIP FOCUS

DEAL-FOCUSED CULTURES

Nordic and Germanic Europe, North America, Australia and New Zealand

MODERATELY DEAL-FOCUSED

United Kingdom, South Africa, Latin Europe, central and eastern Europe, Chile, southern Brazil, northern Mexico, Hong Kong and Singapore

RELATIONSHIP-FOCUSED

Arab world, most of Africa, Latin America and Asia

countries, people get things done through relatives, friends, business contacts and personal connections. The Chinese call this 'guanxi', a word well known throughout East and South-East Asia. It means 'pull' or 'clout'. This is also seen as the only way to break bureaucratic delays. One has to have

FORMAL VS INFORMAL CULTURES

BOX 10.2 CATEGORIZATION OF COUNTRIES BASED ON FORMAL/INFORMAL CULTURE

INFORMAL CULTURES

Australia
USA
Canada
New Zealand
Denmark
Norway
Israel
Iceland

FORMAL CULTURES

Most of Europe and Asia
Mediterranean region
Arab world
Latin America

Source: R.C. Richard, *Cross-Cultural Business Behaviour. Marketing, Negotiating and Managing Across Cultures*, Copenhagen Business School Press, Denmark, Indian Edition 2000 (Viva Books Pvt. Ltd.)

patience dealing with RF companies. For example, it took nine years for Volkswagen to negotiate with the government of China on the opening of an automobile factory. And it took twelve years for McDonald to work out an agreement with the then Soviet government to open the first Golden Arches restaurant in Russia.

DF cultures value a direct, frank and straightforward language, while their counterparts often favour an indirect, subtle and roundabout style. They give priority to maintaining harmony and avoid saying anything that may cause embarrassment or loss of face to the other party. The Japanese, for instance, never say the word 'no' but use other means to indicate the same.

Formal cultures tend to be organized in steep hierarchies, which reflects major differences in status and power. In contrast, informal cultures value more egalitarian organizations with smaller differences in status and power. These contrasting values cause conflict at the conference table. Formal ways of addressing people and maintaining proper protocol are ways of showing respect to people. Box 10.3 gives an illustration of this.

BOX 10.3 HOW TO INSULT A MEXICAN CUSTOMER

Jose Garcia Lopez, a Mexican importer, had been negotiating with a Danish manufacturing company for several months, when he decided to visit Copenhagen to finalise the purchase contract. The meeting went smoothly. On the last day of his visit, Garcia confided that he looked forward to signing the contract after his return to Mexico.

That evening, the Danes invited Garcia out for an evening. Flemming, the 40-year-old export manager, and his 21-year-old assistant, Margrethe, hosted an excellent dinner and then took the Mexican on a tour of Copenhagen's nightspots. Around midnight, Flemming glanced at his watch and said, 'Mr Garcia, I have a very early flight tomorrow to Tokyo. I hope you will forgive me if I leave you now. Margrethe will make sure you get back to your hotel alright and then drive you to the airport tomorrow morning. I wish you a good flight.'

Next morning, on the way to the airport, Jose Garcia was uncharacteristically silent. Then he turned to the young assistant and said, 'Margrethe, would you please tell your boss I have decided not to sign the contract, after all. It is not your fault, of course. If you think about what happened last evening, I believe you will understand why I no longer wish to do business with your company.'

Source: R.C. Richard, *Cross-Cultural Business Behaviour: Marketing, Negotiating and Managing Across Cultures*, Copenhagen Business School Press, Denmark, Indian Edition 2000 (Viva Books Pvt. Ltd.)

People from egalitarian societies are often unaware of the importance of status distinctions in hierarchical cultures. They often do not know how to show respect to high-ranking persons from formal cultures, who may be easily offended by perceived slights. The lesson here is that, when dealing with government officials in formal cultures, it is important to show respect and deference, as illustrated in Box 10.4.

BOX 10.4 SWEATING HIS WAY TO SUCCESS

An American consultant with a decade of business experience in South Asia arranged for his Chicago consultant to meet with the Minister of Textiles in Bangladesh. The company had asked for a favourable decision on a complex issue involving garment quota allocations, but was not optimistic about the outcome; a competitor who had made a similar request had seen his application summarily rejected by mid-level bureaucrats in the Ministry.

It was a sweltering day in Dhaka and the Minister's air-conditioner too was not switched on. This caused the visitor considerable discomfort, because, on the consultant's insistence, he was wearing dark suit with a tie. He sat steaming and sweating while the Minister chatted away amiably, cool and comfortable in his white muslin. After an hour and a half of aimless conversation, the Minister stood up and with a broad smile and informed the petitioner that he had decided to grant his request. The consultant learnt from his contacts in the government that the Minister had deliberately not turned on the AC for the meeting. 'His Excellency may have been testing', said the contact.

Source: Narrated by a consultant friend to the author.

RIGID TIME VS FLUID TIME

Time is an important differentiator between cultures. We can broadly divide the world into rigid-time and fluid-time societies. In rigid-time societies, punctuality is critical, schedules are set in concrete, agendas are fixed and business meetings are rarely interrupted. Edward T. Hall invented the term 'monochronic' for these clock-obsessed, schedule-worshipping cultures.

BOX 10.5 CATEGORISATION OF COUNTRIES BASED ON THE TIME FACTOR

MONOCHRONIC BUSINESS CULTURES

Nordic and Germanic Europe
North America
Japan

MODERATELY MONOCHRONIC BUSINESS CULTURES

Australia/New Zealand
Russia and most of East-Central Europe
Southern Europe
Singapore, Taiwan, China, South Korea, South Africa

POLYCHRONIC BUSINESS CULTURES

Arab world,
Most of Africa, Latin America
South-East Asia

Source: R.C. Richard, *Cross-Cultural Business Behaviour. Marketing, Negotiating and Managing Across Cultures*, Copenhagen Business School Press, Denmark, Indian Edition 2000 (Viva Books Pvt. Ltd.)

In contrast, are polychronic cultures, where people place less emphasis on punctuality and are not obsessed with deadlines. Polychronic cultures do not value scheduling of business meetings. In fact, several meetings-within-meetings may be taking place simultaneously.

Orientation to time varies not only among different countries but often within a given country as well. For example, in Brazil, temperate Sao Paulo is relatively monochronic, whereas Rio de Janeiro is strongly polychronic.

Suppose you are an export marketeer scheduled to meet your German customer at 9 a.m. the next morning. It is expected that you reach his office at 8:55 a.m. The worst thing would be to show up late; tardiness signals lack of discipline and interest in business.

If the same meeting is in Rome, your local counterpart is likely to wait for half an hour after the agreed time and greet you as though nothing at all is wrong. And if the meeting is in Sicily (polychronic culture), if your Sicilian counterpart shows up on the day of the meeting, he is considered punctual!

India is also polychronic. For instance, most marriage invitations will say dinner will be served at 8 p.m. but it is most likely to start only after 10 p.m.

CROSS-CULTURAL COMMUNICATION

When a member of one culture sends a message to a member of another culture, intercultural communication takes place. The message contains the meaning intended by the sender (encoder). When it reaches the receiver, however, it undergoes a transformation in which the influence of the receiver's (decoder) culture becomes part of the meaning. Box 10.6 provides an example of international communication in which the meaning got all mixed up. Note how the attribution of behaviours differs for each participant. Attribution is the process in which people look for an explanation of another person's behaviour. When they realize that they do not understand another, they tend, say Hall and Hall, to blame their confusion on the other's 'stupidity, deceit or craziness'. In the situation depicted the Greek employee gets frustrated and resigns after experiencing communication problems with his American Boss. Cross-cultural sensitivity and training could have avoided this outcome.

BOX 10.6 CULTURAL NOISE IN INTER-CULTURAL COMMUNICATION

Behaviour	Attribution
American: 'How long will it take you to finish this report?'	American: I asked him to participate. Greek: His behaviour makes no sense. He is the boss. Why doesn't he tell me?
Greek: 'I don't know how long should it take.'	American: He refuses to take responsibility. Greek: I asked him for an order.
American: 'You are in the best position to analyse time requirements.'	American: I press him to take responsibility for his actions.
Greek: 10 days.	Greek: What nonsense; I'd better give him an answer.
American: 'Take 15. Is it agreed? You will do it in 15 days.'	American: I offer a contract. Greek: These are my orders; 15 days.

In fact, the report needed 30 days' regular work. So the Greek worked day and night but at the end of 15 days he still needed to do one more day's work.

	American: I am making sure he fulfils his contract.
	Greek: He is asking for the report.
	Both attribute that it is not ready
	American: I must teach him to fulfil a contract.
	Greek: The stupid incompetent boss! Not only he gives me the wrong orders, but he doesn't even appreciate that I did a 30 days' job in just 16 days.
	The American is surprised.
	Greek: I can't work for such a man.

Cultural differences begin as soon as communicators encounter one another. Greetings range from the bow (the lower it is, the more respectful) in Japan to the 'wai' in Thailand (pressed palms together with a head bow) and to the handshake in Europe and America. How people communicate is perhaps the most significant cultural dimension. Based on this, cultures can be divided into expressive and reserved cultures.

EXPRESSIVE VS RESERVED CULTURES

There are three types of interpersonal communications:

- Verbal communication has to do with words and the meaning of words.
- Para-verbal language refers to how loudly we speak those words, the meaning of silence and the significance of conversational overlap.
- Non-verbal communication (also called body language) is communicating without using any words.

Varying degrees of expressiveness in para-verbal and non-verbal communications cause problems for international managers and negotiators. Box 10.6 mentions which markets are expressive cultures and which are reserved cultures.

Expressive people tend to be uncomfortable with more than a second or two of silence during a conversation. In contrast, people from reserved cultures feel at ease with much longer silences. Japanese negotiators, for example, often sit without speaking, which seems like eternity to voluble Mexicans, Greeks or Americans. After three or four seconds, the latter feel compelled to say something – anything – to fill the silence.

Unfortunately the loquacity of expressive people tends to irritate the reticent Japanese, who seem to value the space between spoken words just as much as the words themselves.

Conversational overlap refers to the interruption of a speaker by another. While expressive people regard overlap as a normal part of conversation, people from reserved cultures consider overlap extremely rude. Scandinavian researchers have found that Spanish negotiators interrupt Swedes about five times as often as Swedes interrupt Spaniards. This causes problems in negotiations unless parties are aware of this cultural trait. Japanese not only take turns to avoid overlap, but also often pause a few seconds before speaking.

BOX 10.7 COUNTRIES CATEGORIZED AS EXPRESSIVE/RESERVED CULTURES

VERY EXPRESSIVE CULTURES

Mediterranean countries
Latin Europe
Latin America

VARIABLY EXPRESSIVE CULTURES

USA and Canada
Australia and New Zealand
Eastern Europe
South Asia
Africa

RESERVED CULTURES

East and South-East Asia
Nordic and Germanic Europe

Distance Behaviour

Every human being is surrounded by an invisible envelope of air, called 'space bubble', which varies from culture to culture as shown below:

- Close: 20 to 35 cms – Arab world, the Mediterranean region, Latin Europe, Latin America.
- Distant: 40 to 60 cms – Most of Asia, Europe and North America.
- If a person from the Arab world, having a close air bubble, comes too near you, you will probably step back if you are a large-bubble person. And he will certainly not like this.
- Expressive people engage in more physical contact in public than those from reserved cultures. Thus 'touch behaviour' in public can cause serious problems. Americans do much shoulder patting, elbow grabbing and backslapping to please their counterparts. Similarly 'eye contact' is also related to a given culture. Expressive people like to read the eyes and face as they talk. Direct eye contact is a critical element of body language. The extent of eye contact varies from country to country as shown below.

Intense Eye Contact: Arab world and the Mediterranean region, Latin Europe and Latin America.
Firm Eye Contact: Northern Europe and North America.
Moderate Eye Contact: Korea, Thailand and most of Africa.
Indirect Eye Contact: Most of Asia.

One should behave as expected in the circumstances of a particular culture and not be baffled by unexpected approaches.

BOX 10.8 WALKING WITH LATIN EUROPEANS

Living in Florence taught me the importance of appropriate gaze behaviour. One day I was walking to the railway station accompanied by my friend, Paolo. It was only a ten-minute stroll and I thought we had plenty of time. However, every time Paolo had something to say he would touch me on the shoulder and turn me towards him so that we could look directly into each other's eyes. Since Paolo spoke every few steps, I ended up missing my train. From that day I mentally doubled my estimated walking time when in the company of Latin Europeans.

Source: R.C. Richard, *Cross-Cultural Business Behaviour: Marketing, Negotiating and Managing Across Cultures*, Copenhagen Business School Press, Denmark, Indian Edition, 2000 (Viva Books Pvt. Ltd.)

KINESICS: NON-VERBAL BEHAVIOUR

Two aspects of kinesics are of importance to international negotiators: facial expressions and hand and arm gestures. Expressive people employ plenty of both, while people from reserved cultures hide their emotions. Expressive negotiators gesticulate to add emphasis to what they are saying. But the same gesture may mean different things in different cultures. For example, raised eyebrows send the following signals:

North America:	Interest/surprise
England:	Scepticism
Germany:	'You are clever'
Philippines:	Hello!
Arab world:	No
China:	Disagreement

What this list shows is that the same expression can have a different meaning – sometimes the opposite meaning – in another culture. The same applies to hand and arm gestures.

BUSINESS PROTOCOL

Dress Code

Climate and culture both play a role in sartorial behaviour. In the tropics and in desert countries, businessmen often wear open-necked shirts and cotton trousers. But even in these countries it is advisable to wear a suit or a blazer for the first meeting. For meetings with government officials this formality takes on greater importance. In most other parts of the world, one should wear a dark suit, conservative tie, white shirt and dark socks. Here are few culture-specific hints:

- Visits to Latin Europe and Latin America require special attention to the style and quality of both men's and women's clothes and accessories.
- In the Middle East, business contacts often judge one by the quality and price of his briefcase, watch, pen and jewellery. One should wear and carry the best one has.
- Germans feel more comfortable doing business with men whose shoes are well polished.

- Throughout Asia it is a good idea to wear slip-on shoes because custom requires you to remove your footwear when entering temples, people's homes and some offices as well.
- In Muslim countries female visitors should show as little skin as possible.

usiness Cards and Gifts

ı some cultures, the beginning of a relationship is symbolised by the exchange of business cards. In apan and Korea, people formally present their cards, at the beginning of every first meeting, to the most important member of the team first and then to other members in the descending order of importance. No further exchange with these persons should be made as giving the card a second time means that you have forgotten him or her, and this may be taken as a deliberate insult. These cultures even have an etiquette in giving and receiving cards. The card should be presented with the other person's language face-up in case of bilingual cards. After receiving the card one should read it and place it before oneself during the meeting.

Europeans invest far less formality in card presentations, and may exchange them only at the end of the meeting to serve as reminders. Germans include their full academic and professional titles, and expect to be addressed by them.

Gifts

RF cultures value exchanging gifts more than DF cultures, because it is an accepted way to build and cement strong personal relationships. Good choice gifts include quality pens, branded liquor (not in Muslim countries) or products your home country is famous for. Gifts are exchanged after the signing of an agreement in Europe, and at the end of a meeting in Japan and other Asian countries. America is not a gift-giving culture and many companies prohibit their professionals from giving or accepting gifts. In Japan wrapping of the gift is as important as the gift itself and it is received with both hands. In Europe, it is opened in the presence of the giver, while in Asia it is opened after he/she leaves.

Forms of Addresses

The more formal the culture, the more likely you will confine yourself to using the person's family name plus any applicable title or honorific. This is sometimes a problem for Americans and Australians doing business in East Asia. For example, you do not need to know the full name of your Korean customer or potential customer. 'Manager Kim' or 'Chairman Park' shows the appropriate degree of respect in this very hierarchical society. Visitors to Japan who interact with women should remember that the prefix *san* can mean 'Miss', 'Ms', 'Mrs' as well as 'Mr'. The Chinese normally have three names of one syllable each, of which the first is the family name. So your counterpart Yi Er Man should be addressed as 'Mr Yi' and not 'Mr Man'. In Spain and the Hispanic countries of Latin America, people look for two family names. Mexican Pablo Garcia Mendoza, for example, would be 'Senor Garcia'. However, if he is a university graduate, he becomes Licenciado (Licenciada for women) Garcia.

What about the more informal cultures? In the USA, the saying goes: 'I don't care what you call me just as long as you call me for dinner.' Nevertheless, physicians and surgeons are addressed as 'Doctor' on all occasions. Those with doctorates, on the other hand, are called 'Doctor' only when on duty. In Silicon Valley start-up companies everyone is called by the first name.

BRIDGING THE CULTURAL GAP

Before heading to an important series of business meetings in Indonesia recently, Aric Peters did his homework. He read up on some of the cultural norms of South-Eastern Asian nations, and he and his team came prepared. But what he saw at his client's lunch surprised him: his hosts used left and right hands while eating. 'I had read this was taboo', says Peters, who is a manager with Butler National Corporation. So I just asked, 'What is the deal with this?' They said, 'Oh, that is a very old tradition.' Live and learn. The nature of cultural differences is forever evolving. Many companies operating primarily in a home-country must be prepared to deal with cultural differences that may arise in client relationship. And as Peter's Indonesian lunch demonstrates, just when you think you have known a particular country enough, its culture surprises you. This is an important issue for business.

That has led many firms to develop ongoing strategies to manage cross-cultural issues. The Televista company, headquartered in Dallas, US, has a call centre in Mexico, not very far, but there are times when the Mexican and American cultures clash on anything from workday hours to attire. In addition to teaching the surface elements of social exchange, Televista has gone one step further, requiring managers to take lessons both in English and Spanish. This is a more than a day-long training session in cultural sensitivity. This is likely to generate more comfort in doing business with each other.

Andy Welssberg also believes in giving cultural training to pharmaceutical representatives even though many of them will never venture outside the US, because cultural issues crop up regularly between representatives and their physician customers and sometimes between those customers and their patients. 'We have to talk about how different racial and ethnic populations may respond to pharmaceuticals,' he says. 'There have been lots of studies that show that reactions can be very different and call for different behaviour on the part of sales representatives.' A key tactic, CPRI, a communication firm, has developed in an online training that allows sales people to play their role through potential culture clashes, and then follow up with questions or comments via online messaging with trainers. 'Cultural issues are not just international issues,' Weissberg says. 'They are in our neighbourhood, too.'

Review Questions

1. Discuss the broad cultural patterns that divide the world. Explain in detail how people from expressive cultures are likely to conduct business operations and negotiations with people from deal-focused, formal cultures?
2. Discuss with suitable examples the importance of protocol in conducting international business operations and negotiations.
3. Which countries are grouped as:
   (a) Relationship-focused, formal, polychronic and expressive,
   (b) Deal-focused, moderately formal, monochronic,
   (c) Relationship-focused, formal, monochronic and reserved, and
   (d) Moderately deal-focused, formal, variably monochronic.
4. Explain the components of the effective cross-culture communication with suitable examples.

Assignment

Choose any two countries that appear to be culturally diverse. Compare the cultural aspects of these countries to indicate how cultural differences influence:

1. The ease of doing business in each country,
2. The state of economic development of these countries,
3. Their business practices, and
4. Business ethics.

Chapter

11

Organizational Culture and National Culture

LEARNING OBJECTIVES

After studying this chapter, you will be able to:

- *Define corporate culture and describe its determining features*
- *Understand the impact of corporate culture on the functioning and operation of organizations and people at work*
- *Understand Harrison's typology of organizational culture*
- *Learn the classification of corporate cultures by Trompenaars and Charles Hampden-Turner based on national cultures*
- *Understand Dan Denison's work on the 'fit' between environment, strategy and culture*
- *Understand how national cultural values influence corporate cultures and change management.*

OPENING CASE
LEADING BY DESIGN- JETBLUE AIRWAYS

The airline industry is not a very happy place to be these days. Unless, that is, you are at JetBlue Airways, the fastest domestic growing carrier in the USA and the only US airlines except Southwest that is making money. JetBlue based at New York's JFK airport, grew revenues more than threefold in first four years. The company now operates nearly 300 daily flights to 29 destinations including Puerto Rico and the Bahamas. JetBlue topped the Airline Quality Rating for two years (2004-2005) and placed number 1 in the J.D.Powers' 2005 rankings of consumer satisfaction.

A large part of JetBlue's success can be attributed to its organization culture. From the beginning, JetBlue has incorporated strong customer-focused values that encourage continual adaptation. Founder David Neeleman based JetBlue's culture on the values he developed while working as a missionary in the slums of Brazil. The corporate philosophy is that the greatest satisfaction a person can achieve comes from serving others. Today every new employee is asked to make a commitment to the basic corporate commandments: safety, caring, integrity, fun and passion. JetBlue's people department actively scrutinizes all applicants to see how well they will mesh with the values, and then provides them with comprehensive training that gives them the tools they need to make good decisions and do the right thing in serving customers.

JetBlue's response to September 11, terrorist's attack in New York illustrates the values in action. When employees realized that the airport would be shutting down and passengers would be stranded, they immediately started reserving the buses and shuttling people (even customers of some other airlines) to hotels, where they were put up at JetBlue's expense. Soon after the attacks, JetBlue became the first airline to install bullet-proof, dead-bolted cockpit doors on all its aircraft, even before the Federal Aviation Administration issued the orders. Instead of encouraging Americans to shake off their fear of flying, JetBlue ran ads to tell people it was Ok to take time to heal. Yet, rather than laying off workers and cutting routes during the slowdown in the air travel, JetBlue expanded its service and picked up some new markets where large carriers had scaled off.

JetBlue does not believe in waiting around for others to determine what needs to be done; instead leaders take proactive approach and move quickly to implement changes that can provide customers with better service, greater safety and a happier flying experience. The company initially differentiated itself by offering only one class, providing assigned seats with more leg room, and installing free satellite television on the backs of all seats. But leaders continue to push the envelope in trying to give customers what they want, exploring for example, options such as airplanes internet service and phone-to-airplane communications.

When JetBlue first started flying in 2000, skeptics said it was doomed to fail. Five years later, JetBlue's adaptive, customer-focused culture has made it one of the few bright spots in the turbulent airline's industry.

INTRODUCTION

Since the Industrial Revolution, employers have faced a dilemma. On the one hand, they have to have tight control over what their staff does and how they do it – to ensure that time, resources and, materials are not wasted. On the other hand, they also needed varying degrees of employee goodwill, creative good sense, and commitment. Controlling invariably brings in rules, regulations and reporting. No factory can be run by rules and no set of rules can ensure all that is required of employees. Efforts to achieve control through rules will not succeed because they are oppressive, intrusive, unpleasant, demanding, and risk workers' commitment, on which their goodwill and common sense are dependent.

It is possible to argue that all management philosophies and approaches are nothing but a step in the direction of solving this dilemma – to achieve both control and commitment. Ultimately all solutions fail because the two ends are opposite. The only way to solve this problem is to develop a strong corporate culture, which will generate a high level of commitment and enthusiasm and bring in control through teamwork. This is no doubt a high claim. But a number of studies have established that organizational culture is the key to performance, and that it can be changed to ensure that employees are committed and compliant to respond to organizational change.

DEFINING ORGANIZATION CULTURE

Organizational culture is difficult to define. Forehand and Gilmer, have defined it as 'a set of characteristics that describe an organization and (a) that distinguish one organization from another, (b) that are relatively enduring over a period of time, and (c) which influence the behaviour of people in an organization.'

Charles Handy (1993) goes further and suggests that cultures are more than just commonly agreed ways of perceiving an organization. He states:

> In organizations, there are deep-set beliefs about the way work should be organized, what authority should be exercised, how people are rewarded and controlled. What are the degrees of formalization required? How much planning and how far ahead? What combination of initiative and obedience is desired in subordinates? Do work hours matter, or dress or personal eccentricities? Do committees control an individual? Are there rule and procedures or only results? These are all part of the culture in an organization.

We can look at some other definitions of culture. 'Organizational culture is the collection of shared (stated or implied) beliefs, values, rituals, stories, myths and specialized language that fosters a feeling of community amongst organizational members' (Smircich, 1983). Hofstede (1991) described corporate culture as the 'psychological assets of an organization, which can be used to predict what will happen to its financial assets in five years' time.'

According to Smircich (1993), a strong culture performs five important functions:

- It gives members a sense of identity;
- It encourages commitment to the organization's mission;
- It promotes organizational stability;
- It influences behaviour by helping individuals to make sense of their surroundings;
- It expedites organizational processes and ensures controls.

From this, it is clear that organizational culture is a major determinant of performance and gives guidelines to employees to understand why others behave in a particular way and how they themselves should behave. It also enables them to interpret and understand organizational activities, processes and happenings.

LIMITATION OF ORGANIZATIONAL STRUCTURE

The roots of emphasis on culture lie in empirical research as well as in theory and practice. The recognition of the limitations of organization structure, both formal and informal, to act as a social glue or provide a social mechanism for coordination or explain human behaviour at work is quite significant. Empirically, scholars working in the area of organization effectiveness had devoted research to identifying its variables and quantifying statistical construct of 'climate', by which they meant the profile of values and attitudes held in an organization (Payne, Phesysey and Pugh, 1971). In another area, discussion of power and conflict in organizations focused on the extent to which people's beliefs and interests underlie strategic and operational decisions (Abell, 1975). In yet another field, anthropology had long ago recognised the concept of culture as critical to the understanding of human behaviour. Douglas (1986) placed cultural analysis firmly on the agenda of organizational analysis. Further it was Western observation of Japanese 'economic miracle' that stimulated most interest in how culture can be created or changed. It has been argued that the secret of Japanese success lies in a homogeneous national and religious culture, which is reflected in corporate culture. Shared values of dedication, reciprocity, rights and obligations provided cultural powerhouse that became one of the engines of their corporate success.

WHAT DOES ORGANIZATIONAL CULTURE COMPRISE?

Figure 11.1 depicts how culture may be revealed and created in an organizations.

First Layer

In the centre of the model is core of shared values, beliefs, assumptions and paradigms. The relationship between the values people hold within an organization and the organization's practices, structure, technology and strategy are complex and interactive. The strategy and the values of an organization may be written down, but the underlying assumptions which make up the paradigms are usually evident only in day-to-day conversations or discussions of the people; or may be so taken for granted that they can be observed in what people actually do.

Each of the outer rings in the model is the creation of people, the subject of decision-making, the result of action taken or not taken. These actions or inactions are, we assume, to an extent reflective of the values; hence the influence from the centre. If there is value diversity within the organization, it is unlikely that everyone's values will be equally represented.

The influence shown in the model is two-way because each layer, once created, has an impact on the way values are subsequently developed. Furthermore, this model represents an incomplete as well as interactive set of influences. In reacting to and anticipating events outside the organization, the actions and decisions of its members are not guided by values alone. There are often significant external environmental influences which dictate internal actions, although of course there is also the possibility of influence coming the other way, from organizations controlling aspects of their environment.

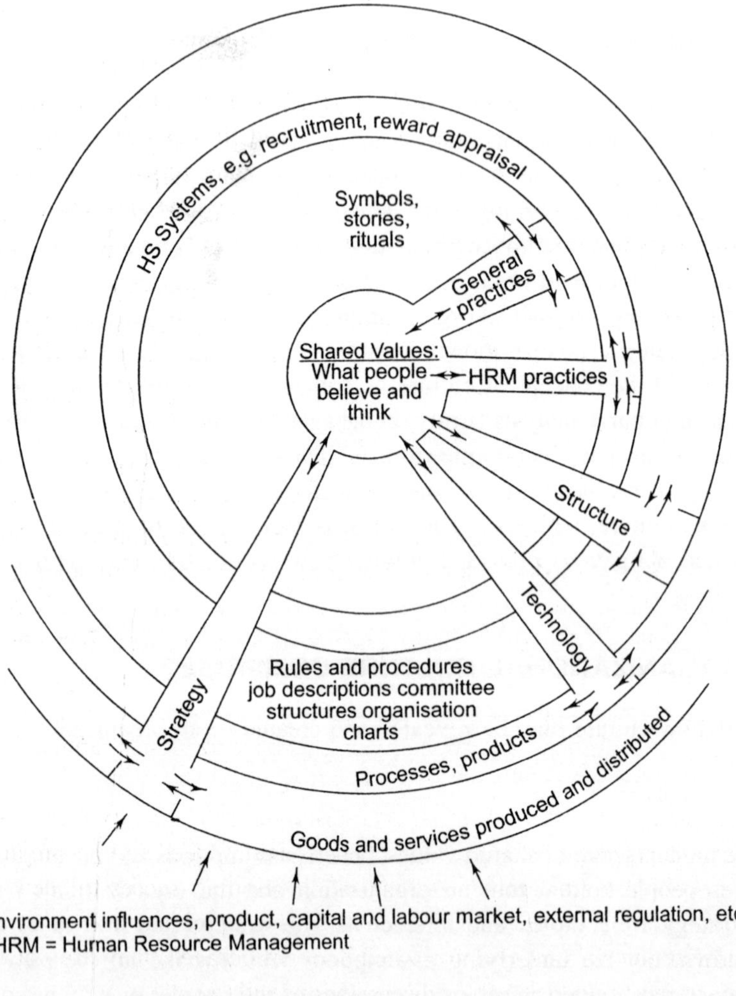

Fig. 11.1 A Map of the Corporate World: How Culture may be Revealed and Created in Organizations

Cultural Web – Second Layer

An organization's culture is like an 'iceberg'; it has both visible and invisible elements. The observable aspects include the physical setting, legends, myths, heroes and heroines, ceremonies, behaviour and dress. Above shared values and beliefs in the model, the second layer labelled 'general practices', includes the visible parts of culture known as 'rituals' stories' 'language' and 'symbols' constituting a cultural web.

Values are revealed in these symbols and yet symbols and practices shape values. The search for an attention-catching logo or signature tune or company song may easily lead to the encapsulation of the value which is either already dominant or else has been selected for serious promotion. The use and development of language reflects values: for example, Garscombke (1988) showed how, in adopting the language of militarism (e.g. defensive strategies, guerrilla marketing and counter-offensive), managers are creating a militaristic culture in their organizations.

The rituals associated with induction, retirement, the Annual General Meeting, or the annual cricket match all reveal things about values as well as being the means by which attempts are made to engineer value changes. The internal and external designs and fittings of buildings, office space and recreation facilities, and the layout design and contents of the annual report are similarly both creatures and creators of corporate values. The following examples illustrate how these rites and ceremonies are used by managers to reinforce important cultural values.

- In a leading bank, election as an officer was seen as the key event in a successful career. A series of activities accompanied every promotion to bank officer, including a special method of notification, taking the new officer to the dining room for the first time, and the new officer buying drinks on the Friday after his or her promotion. This is a 'rite of passage'.
- Tupperware holds a weekly rally at which the sales people are recognised in reverse order of sales volume. The event is associated with celebration and hoopla and reinforces the goal of sales volume held by the company. This is a 'rite of enhancement'.
- An important annual event at McDonald's is the nationwide contest to determine the best hamburger cooking team in the country. The contest encourages all stores to re-examine the details of how they cook their hamburgers. The ceremony is highly visible and communicates to all employees the McDonald's value of hamburger quality. This is a 'rite of renewal'.
- In a Western firm, every Christmas, the chairman comes down from his office on the top floor to walk through every department, shaking hands with each employee. His appearance serves as a ceremony to communicate concern for the organizational family. This is a 'rite of integration'.
- At 3M, top managers keep alive stories that describe innovative projects that were killed by the company management. The heroes of the stories worked on the projects in secret and eventually proved the management wrong by developing successful new products. These stories are repeated by top managers to enhance the entrepreneurial spirit at 3M and to let employees know that if they feel frustrated and discouraged, they are not the only ones to overcome considerable odds in the process of innovation.
- T.J.Watson, Jr., son of the founder of IBM used the metaphor 'wild ducks' to describe the type of employees needed by IBM. His point was, 'You can make wild ducks tame, but you can never make tame ducks wild ducks again.' Wild ducks symbolise the freedom and opportunity that must be available to keep from taming creative employees at IBM.

Third Layer – Human Resource Practices and Organizational Culture

Moving to the next layer shown in the model, the focus shifts to human resource management practices. The operation and contents of the reward system including pay, promotion and fringe benefits; appraisal and performance management; recruitment and selection both reveal and shape values. It is often here that disjunctions between practice and values become apparent. On the one hand, the company philosophy may talk of treating all employees equally, of placing high value on long service and loyalty, and yet employees may find separate dining and recreational facilities maintained for different levels of staff and that pay and promotions are geared to achievement of short-term performance targets. Similarly, disjunction can occur between expressed values (usually at the top of the organization) and the next layer in the structure. High value may be placed on the maintenance of internal communication system, the importance of encouraging risk-taking and the development of entrepreneurial flair, and yet procedures for authorising expenditure may remain bureaucratic.

ORGANIZATIONAL STRUCTURE AND CULTURE

Organizational structure reflects power structure and, again, delineates important relationships and emphasises what is important in the organization. In most companies, there is a strong informal network of individuals and groups, which coalesce around specific issues to promote or resist a particular view.

Charles Handy (1985), a leading writer on organization theory and practices, has described the close relationship which often exists between culture and structure. In describing four types of culture, discussed later in this chapter, Handy refers not only to values but also to the shape of the 'host' structure. Thus, his 'power' or 'club' culture, with its strong value element of 'watching the boss', is described as a network around a central point. His 'task' culture, with values of 'all hands on deck', is described as an open network without a central point. His 'role culture', with value placed on following the book/procedures, is described as a pyramid or temple. His 'person' or 'existential' culture, with value placed on human relationships, lacks any focus at all but is a collection of valued individuals or groups. Handy also finds different cultures as typical of different types of company: for example, he describes how small, family-owned firms and new start-ups have a power culture; how a role culture is most often found in large organizations in stable environments; and person culture in universities and professional practices of doctors and lawyers. The boundary between history, strategy, structure and culture in this analysis becomes blurred.

ORGANIZATIONAL CULTURE AND TECHNOLOGY

Moving to the next layer in this model, we can also consider the relationship between values and technology (as evidenced in product and process developments) and strategy (which goods to produce and sell). These decisions and outcomes may well embody and reflect central values, but may equally reflect values held only by a minority. Indeed they may reflect opportunistic and thoroughly sensible decisions in terms of achieving strategic objectives, but they may not be in tune with the values. For example, investments in new process equipment may facilitate lower unit cost and higher quality, and yet require some redundancies. What impact does this have on a cultural change programme, which emphasises creating a caring family-like atmosphere within the organization?

In this model, culture is shown at the centre of organization analysis. Sometimes culture may be the driving force, exerting a major influence on all layers of experience and outcomes. Hence, developing an appropriate culture is an essential basis for successful organization development. In other cases, environment or strategy may be at the centre of the model and culture only operating at upper layers.

At a general level there is agreement that culture refers to collection of shared values and common assumptions, which employees may not even be aware of but is reflected in their behaviour, approach and conversation. There is, however, less agreement on how culture is created, passed on to new members and how changes in culture take place in organizations.

TYPES OF ORGANIZATIONAL CULTURE (ROGER HARRISON)

Power Culture

This type of culture provides excitement and drives for some people but seems threatening to others. It depends on strong leadership from a central power source controlling and manipulating all activities within the organization. This culture functions mainly through subordinates looking to the boss for all decisions and clearances. In practice, those at the middle and lower levels react quickly to rumours and use the grapevine as the main source of information. Although regulations exist to control and direct behaviour they are not adhered to in practice. Decisions are made largely as a result of political strength rather than logical deduction.

Money and status are more highly valued than technical expertise. This has implications for the employees, who are likely to prosper in such organizations. People strive to get the attention of the boss as all authority flows from him. Members who wish to progress form a network of influential people to increase the information and connection they hold. This culture is usually found in small entrepreneurial organizations and in companies with autocratic bosses.

Role Culture

This type of culture places great value on functions, job specialisation, procedures and rules. Job descriptions, authority relationships, and communication procedures are formal and the role of the manager is to coordinate activities between the different functions. Anyone who performs beyond what is expected of a particular role is seen to be threatening, and new ideas and creativity are discouraged. Everyone sticks to his job description and role and any unforeseen event is referred higher up. This culture is followed in bureaucratic, mechanistic organizations where the environment is simple and stable. All government and public sector organizations have this type of culture.

Task Culture

This type of culture is job or project-oriented; the onus is on getting the job done rather than prescribing how it should be done. Task of culture attracts people who prefer to solve new problems. The style of this culture is for people to work in teams and work on problems or tasks. Great emphasis is placed on the value of group working and individual preferences are sacrificed to ensure the continued life of a team. This culture is adaptable.

Unlike role culture, formal roles and procedures have little meaning and influence, because success is based on expertise, control over an individual's work, easy working relationships and mutual respect for personal competence. Task culture is sensitive to change and adapts quickly to new situations. Control is highly decentralised and exercised by means of allocating projects to group leaders to manage people and resources accordingly. This culture is appropriate for organically structured organizations where flexibility and team working are encouraged, where the environment is dynamic and jobs are complex and need high customisation or where speedy action and quick response to the customer or environment are needed.

Person Culture

The primary objective of this culture is to serve the individuals in a group; structure, rules, procedures, and roles are only to serve the needs of individual members. Change occurs only to meet their needs and control is exercised by mutual consent of the members. The wishes of professionals are the central focus of this culture. An example of person culture would be a group of professionals like doctors or members of a voluntary organization. Such a culture will not exist in large organizations except as a sub-culture.

It is clear that according to Harrison's definition of different cultures, people will show commitment in terms of the extent to which they feel comfortable in a specific culture. People are attracted to the culture which reflects the values they hold and the ways in which they wish to work. Sometimes even if comfortable with the role, people may not feel comfortable if the culture does not match their value system.

STRATEGY AND ORGANIZATIONAL CULTURE

Strategy and external environment are big influences on corporate culture. Corporate culture should embody what the organization needs to be effective within its environment. For example, if the organization requires flexibility and responsiveness, the culture should encourage adaptability. The

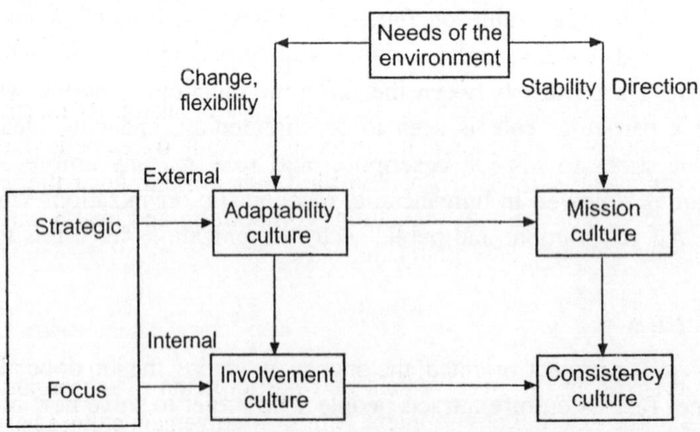

Fig. 11.2 Categorisation of Culture Based on the Fit between Strategy, Environment and Culture

Source: Based on D.R. Denison, *Corporate Culture and Organizational Effectiveness*, New York, John Wiley, 1990.

right relationship between cultural values and beliefs, organizational strategy, and the business environment can enhance business performance. Prof. Dan Denison conducted a study of culture and effectiveness and proposed that the fit between strategy, environment and culture is associated with four types of culture (Fig. 11.2). These categories are based on two factors: (a) the extent to which the competitive environment requires change or stability and (b) the extent to which the strategic focus and strength are internal or external. The four categories associated with these differences are adaptability, mission, involvement, and consistency.

Adaptability Culture

Adaptability culture is characterised by strategic focus on the external environment through flexibility and change to meet customer needs. The culture encourages norms and beliefs that support the capacity of the organization to detect, interpret and translate signals from the environment into new behaviour responses. Companies with this type of culture need to react to bid for new projects and have the capacity to restructure or adopt a new set of behaviours and processes for new tasks. Marketing, electronics and cosmetics companies may use this culture because they have to move quickly to satisfy customer needs.

An example is Detroit Edison, which experienced years of predictable growth and suddenly found itself in a decade of rapid change and external demand. The energy crisis, nuclear power, and abrupt end of energy demand required a corporate culture that reacted to these demands, and the organization had to change its culture.

Mission Culture

Mission culture is ideal for an organization concerned with serving the external environment but without the need for rapid change. Mission culture places importance on a shared vision of organization purpose. The vision provides members' work activities with meaning that goes beyond typically defined jobs and roles. Organization leaders shape behaviour by envisioning a desired future state that is important to everyone.

One example is Medtronics, manufacturer of cardiac pacemakers. Its mission is to contribute to human welfare by application of biomedical engineering. Its employees believe the organization is on a mission to serve people, to make a difference in the medical field. Over the years the environment has changed with respect to government regulation, competition and health care reimbursement, but the organization's mission remains essentially the same.

Involvement Culture

Involvement culture focuses on the involvement and participation of the organization in the rapidly changing expectations of the external environment. A high-involvement culture has a clan-type structure. More than any other type, this culture focuses on the needs of employees as the route to better performance. Involvement and participation create a sense of responsibility and ownership and hence, greater commitment to the organization. Companies in fashion and retail industries also use this type of culture because it releases the creativity of employees, enabling them to respond to rapidly changing consumer tastes.

Consistency Culture

Consistency culture has an internal focus and an orientation towards a stable environment. This type of culture supports a methodical approach to doing business. Symbols, heroes and ceremonies support cooperation, tradition and rule by well laid-out procedures and policies to achieve organization goals. Personal involvement is lower, but that is outweighed by a high level of consistency, conformity and collaboration among members. This organization succeeds by being integrated and efficient.

One example of consistency culture is Safeco Insurance Company, considered by some as stuffy and regimented. Employees take their coffee breaks at an assigned time, and the dress code specifies white shirts and suits for men and no beards. However, employees like this culture. Reliability counts; extra work is not required. The culture is appropriate for an insurance company, because it can be trusted to deliver insurance policies on time and as agreed upon.

IS CULTURE 'TAUGHT' OR 'CAUGHT'?

After the landmark study by Tom Peters and Waterman it was published in the book, *In Search of Excellence* (1982), a number of studies appeared identifying common traits of most successful companies. From these common traits, researchers are trying to find out, what type of organizations, structure, practices contribute to the organization's performance. These studies and contemporary consultancy take the view that it is a key management challenge to create an appropriate culture that will facilitate the development and implementation of a 'winning' strategy. But there is a counter-argument, which claims that deliberate attempt to create specific cultures are, in the long run, doomed to fail. Such a view is based on the assumption that the values people espouse are not open to short-term manipulation. Smircich (1983), Clegg (1990), Turner (1990), and Anthony (1990) are proponents of this approach in which culture is 'caught' and not 'taught'; in which the underlying theme of 'organizational cognition' (Thompson and Wildwsky, 1986) shapes the cognition of individual members of organizations in what are, to an extent, subconscious processes. Experience is gained and values are formed within the organizational arena. Executive policies and practices have an impact on cultural creations, but their impact is not subject to executive determination. This perspective has become popular with theorists, but as one would expect from a view which denies deliberate manipulation. One of the reasons for its development has been practitioners' concern that attempts to create a Japanese-style situation in organizations in Europe and USA were easier said than done. Even though executives could identify the cultural results they felt were desirable, they have proved very difficult to recreate (Wickens, 1987).

The view of culture as emergent rather than prescribed can most obviously be supported in situations where there is no overarching value consensus, causing subcultures (wherein different sets of values and beliefs serve as 'sense making' devices for different groups of workers) to coexist.

According to this view, values, myths and rituals are not independent variables. They are not creatable, but are generative processes that yield and shape different meanings for different groups. Events, working practices, structures and strategies create the context in which these generative processes grow and develop, but they do not determine them.

The relevance of considering these different perspectives on corporate culture is that each of them has some empirical validity. One can find corporate cultures of Canadian firms, which exactly fit

Hofstede's ideas of 'national' imprinting of values. One can find examples of Kanter's 'strong corporate cultures', and of diverse and conflicting subcultures coexisting in spite of efforts to transform them into a homogeneous culture.

Although most organizations have a dominant culture, subcultures may be structured around localised needs of the employees who interact on a daily basis and may have their own heroes, heroines and values. Studies on mergers and acquisitions illustrate the importance of recognising both subcultures and counter-cultures (subgroups that strongly resist what the organization stands for). Cultural clashes can and do occur. Understanding the visible and invisible aspects of culture and the dominant and subgroups in an organization is the first step in managing cultural change effectively.

HOW CULTURE DEVELOPS AND IS TRANSMITTED?

Change processes are not always overt, and formal; they may also be symbolic. Many of the rituals or rites of organizations are implicitly concerned with effecting or consolidating change. They can be managed proactively: new rituals can be introduced or old rituals be done away with.

Organizational culture, including the invisible elements mentioned earlier are fostered by a variety of means. Socialisation (the way employees learn, adopt and pass on knowledge and culture) is the process by which culture is passed on. Part of the socialisation process consists of rites of passage – designated occasions that reinforce particular values and create a bond among them and between employees and the organization. Table 11.1 explains such socialisation rites, with their role and examples.

FACTORS THAT INFLUENCE ORGANIZATIONAL CULTURE

Management cannot just be conceived in terms of the manipulation of techniques or tools of analysis; it is also about the application of experience built up over the years, often within the same organization or industry. This is rooted not only in individual experience, but also in group and organizational experience accumulated over time. This taken for granted nature of assumptions, values and beliefs is influenced by several factors, discussed hereunder.

Table 11.1 Some Common Socialisation Rites, Their Role and Examples

Type of Ritual (Rite)	*Role*	*Example*
Rites of Passage	Consolidate and promote social roles and interaction	Induction programmes; training programmes
Rites of Enhancement	Recognise effort benefiting organization; Similarly motivate others	Award ceremonies; promotions
Rite of Renewal	Reassure that something is being done; Focus attention on issues	Appointment of consultants; project teams
Rite of Integration	Encourages shared commitment; Reassures rightness of norms	Christmas-New Year parties

Leadership Style and Values of Founders and CEOs

The philosophies, and examples of organizations' founder and CEOs are strong influences on the formation and conditioning of corporate culture. For example, TISCO's culture is very much influenced by the vision and philosophy of Jamshedji Tata and J.R.D. Tata; this is the company that has seen no strike or work stoppage since the last 75 years. Since the last 75 years, while production has increased manifolds, productivity increased, manpower reduced, new technology and modernisation achieved making Tata Steel the cost leader in the whole world.

Another example is Walt Disney whose philosophy lives on in the company's practices and continues to shape its culture: give the people everything you can give them; keep the place as clean as you can keep it; keep it friendly; make it a fun place to be. Heroes such as Tom Watson at IBM, Ed Land at Polaroid, David Packard at Hewlett-Packard, Lee Iacocca at Chrysler, Bill Gates at Microsoft and Narayan Murthy at Infosys are enduring influences on their company's corporate culture.

NATIONAL CULTURE AND ORGANIZATIONAL CULTURE

Organizational culture is shaped not only by technologies and markets, but also by the cultural preferences of leaders and employees. Some international companies have European, Asian, American and Middle-Eastern subsidiaries, which would be unrecognisable as the same company except for the logo and reporting procedures.

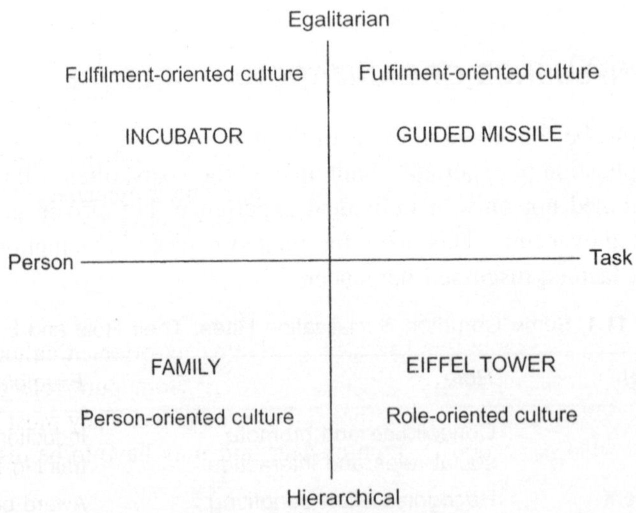

Fig. 11.3 Corporate Images

National culture influences the extent to which leadership, teams and employee activities are socially valued and supported. Studies suggest that directive styles of leadership appear culturally inappropriate in northern Europe, North America, Australia and New Zealand. An employee participation programme failed in Russia, perhaps because of the national culture's disbelief and distrust in participatory programmes. On the other hand, the cultures of Sweden and Japan strongly support employee involvement in organizational activities.

Trompenaars, and Charles Hampden-Turner have studied the impact of national culture on organization cultures by distinguishing corporate cultures along two axes's: equality, hierarchy and orientation to the person – the task. This gives broadly four types of cultures depending on how they think and learn, how they change and how they motivate, reward and resolve conflicts. The four types can be described as follows: (1) the family; (2) the Eiffel Tower; (3) the guided missile; and (4) the incubator. Each of these types of corporate culture is the 'ideal' type. In practice, the types are mixed or overlaid with one culture dominating.

Family Culture

Family culture is one, which is 'personal', with face-to-face relationships, as well as 'hierarchical' (power-oriented). The leader is not threatening but benevolent. The leader regarded as a caring father/mother who knows better than his/her subordinates what is good. Work in this type of culture is usually carried out in an atmosphere that in many respects mimics the home. The Japanese recreate the family in their corporate culture. The main business virtue is *amae*, a kind of love between persons of different rank, with indulgence shown to the younger and respect to the older. To please your superior is a reward in itself. Pressure is moral and social rather than financial or legal. Relationship with the company is for the long-term and one of loyalty. Many corporations with family-style cultures are from nations like Greece, Italy, Japan, Singapore and South Korea.

Eiffel Tower Culture

In this culture a bureaucratic division of labour roles and functions is prescribed in advance. These allocations are coordinated from the top of the hierarchy. This hierarchy is very different from that of a family. You obey the boss because it is his/her role to instruct you and he/she has legal authority to tell you what to do. The role of boss is confined to the office. If you meet him/her on the golf course, you have no obligation to let him/her play through and he/she probably would not expect it either. Careers are much assisted by professional qualifications. The bureaucracy is depersonalised and a rational-legal system is very much prevalent in Austria and Germany.

Guided Missile Culture

This culture is egalitarian, impersonal and task focused. Project-oriented culture is oriented to tasks, typically undertaken by teams or project groups. It differs from pure role culture found in most organization in that the jobs members do, are not fixed in advance. They must do 'whatever it takes' to complete a task and what is needed is often unclear and may have to be discovered.

Incubator Culture

This culture is based on the existential idea that organizations are secondary to the fulfilment of individuals. If organizations are to be tolerated at all, they should be there to serve as incubators for self-expression and self-fulfilment. The purpose of this culture is to move individuals from routine to more creative activities and to minimise time spent on self-maintenance. The incubator is both personal and egalitarian. Indeed, it has no structure at all and just some services like word-processing, coffee, heat and light provided by the organization and so on. Cultural incubators are seen not only in small innovative companies in the Silicon Valley and on Route 128 around Boston, but also in groups of doctors, lawyers, consultants and charted accountants. The difference in four types of organizational culture are explained in Table 11.2.

Table 11.2 Characteristics of Four Corporate Cultures

Dimensions	*Family*	*Eiffel Tower*	*Guided Missile*	*Incubator*
Relationship between employees	Diffuse relationships from organic whole to which one is bonded.	Specific role in mechanical system of required interactions.	Specific tasks in cybernetic system targeted upon shared objectives.	Diffuse, spontaneous relationships growing out of shared creative process.
Attitude to authority	Status is ascribed to parent figures who are close and powerful.	Status is ascribed to superior roles that are distant yet powerful.	Status is achieved by project group members who contribute to targeted goals.	Individuals exemplifying creativity and growth achieve status.
Ways of thinking and learning	Intuitive, holistic, lateral and error correcting.	Logical, analytical, vertical and rationally efficient.	Problem-centred, professional, practical, cross-disciplinary.	Process-oriented, creative, ad hoc, inspirational.
Attitude to people	Family members.	Human resources	Specialists and experts.	Co-creators
Ways of changing	Father changes course.	Change rules and procedures.	Shift aim as target moves.	Improvise and attune.
Ways of motivating and rewarding	Intrinsic satisfaction in being loved and respected.	Promotion to greater position and larger role.	Pay or credit for performance and problems solved.	Participation in the process of creating new realities.
	Management by subjective.	Management by job description.	Management by objectives.	Management by enthusiasm.
Criticism and conflict resolution	Turn other cheek, save other's face, do not loose power game.	Criticism is accusation of irrationality unless there are procedures to arbitrate conflict.	Constructive, task related, then admit error and correct fast.	Must improve creative idea, not negate it.

Source: Fons Trompenaars and Charles Hampden-Turner, *Riding the Waves of Culture,* Nicholas Brealey Pub., London, 1998, p. 179.

WHICH COUNTRIES PREFER WHICH TYPE OF CORPORATE CULTURE?

Even though 'pure types' of culture seldom exist, nevertheless in different national cultures one or more of these types clearly dominate the corporate scene. Research by United Nations' Centre for Intellectual Business with a database of 13,000 respondents from 42 countries and corporates, shows very marked distinctions. Figure 11.4 shows the results of this research. It shows highest scores for guided missile companies in the USA and UK, and highest scores for family companies in France and Spain. Sweden scores highest for incubators and Germany for Eiffel Tower. However, in general, smaller companies are likely to take the family and incubator forms while larger companies needing structure are more likely to take the Eiffel Tower form.

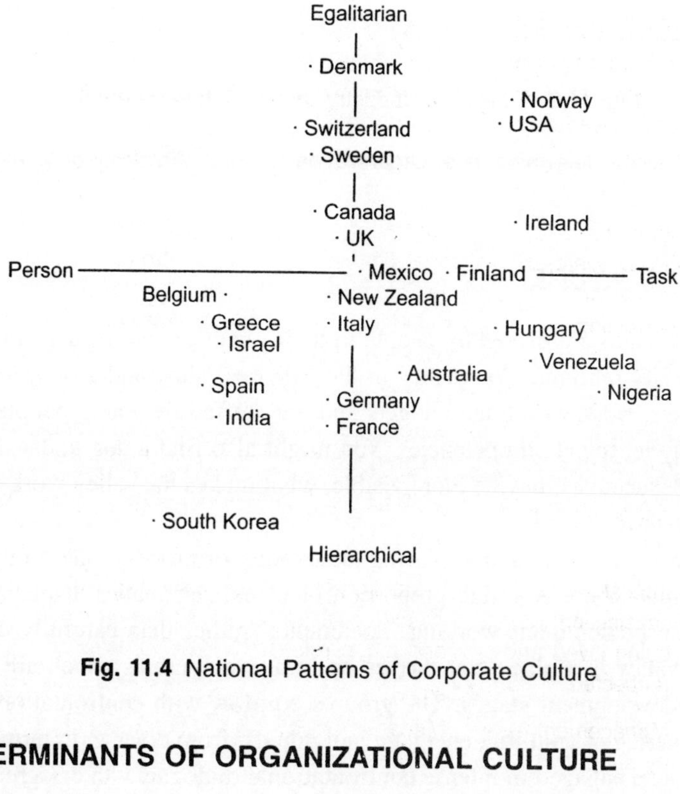

Fig. 11.4 National Patterns of Corporate Culture

INDUSTRY DETERMINANTS OF ORGANIZATIONAL CULTURE

Organizational assumptions about an industry's competitive environment, customer requirements and societal expectations also influence a firm's strategies, structure, work processes, performance and even survival. Figure 5.5 presents a model of industry-driven culture formation. 'Culture formation is neither a random event nor an action dependent solely on the personalities of founders and current leaders' (Miller). Assumptions regarding an industry's environment are made and interpreted by an organization's leadership but how the organization responds to customer requirements, competition and societal expectations depends on industry-specific assumptions.

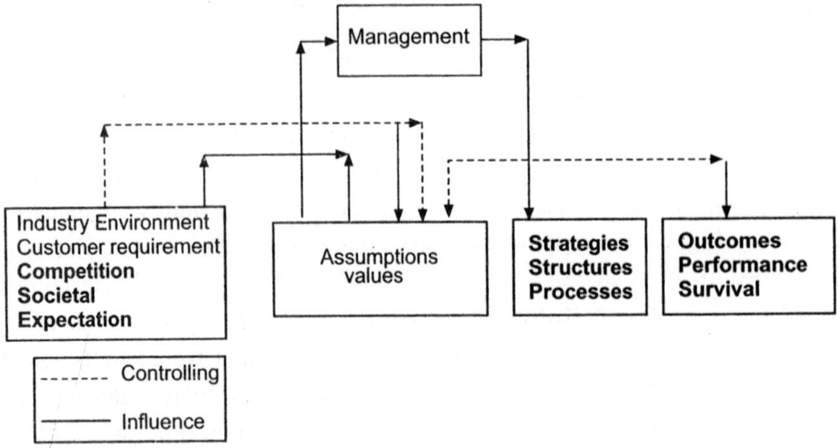

Fig. 11.5 A Model of Industry-driven Culture Formation

Source: G. Gordan, 'Industry Determinants of Organization Culture', *Academy of Management Review*, Vol. 16, No. 2, 1991.

SILICON VALLEY CULTURE

Silicon Valley project teams are driven by people in their twenties and thirties close to the knowledge base of recent university training. Companies in the Silicon Valley and around route number 128 to Boston take great risks, work with huge budgets and are staffed by young people empowered and at the peak of their early technical competencies. You might also find a dog under the conference table. Though a few senior executives may be more visible, what makes the valley work is the empowerment of young technical cadres.

The group is irreverent towards any existing technology or process. The group's language is both technical and colloquial. There is a high proportion of visual schematics displayed around the room, which seem to be the predominant working 'documents' rather than carefully constructed prose or algorithms. Silicon Valley is a place that thrives on intuitive symbols which are imprecise, being in conceptual or early development stages. The group's comfort with confrontation is impressive. It is common to see a gathering of youthful, energetic individuals, from diverse (in terms of race, nationality and gender), background engaged in intense confrontational dialogue with disagreements and differing speculations being 'encouraged' as a humus from which will spring a new approach. And it is always the 'new' that is most revere. If an existing approach is seen as efficient and economical, the group searches for ways to incorporate similar features into the 'new' as opposed to sticking with the 'old'.

It is this overriding commitment to change, to incorporate the latest, to adopt potential new designs and approaches which makes Silicon Valley a special place. The Valley sees itself as the 'incubator' of the future and wealth creating in the Valley is associated with those who obsolete the past, doing so more quickly than their competitors.

CASE STUDY

Falcon Computers

A small group of managers at Falcon Computers met regularly on Wednesday mornings to develop a statement capturing what they considered to be the 'Falcon Culture'. Their discussions were wide-ranging, covering what they thought their firm's culture was, what it should be, and how to create it. Other firms in the environment probably influenced them, since they were located in the Silicon Valley area of California.

Falcon Computers was a new firm, having been created just eight months earlier. Since the corporation was still in the start-up phase, managers decided that it would be timely to create and instil the type of culture they thought would be most appropriate for their organization. After several weeks of brainstorming, writing, debating and rewriting, the management produced a document called 'Falcon Values', which described the culture of the company as the management saw it. The organizational culture statement covered such topics as treatment of customers, relation among work colleagues, preferred style of social communication, the decision-making process, and the nature of work environment.

Peter Richards read over the 'Falcon Values' statement shortly after he was hired as a software trainer. After observing managerial and employee behaviour at Falcon for a few weeks, he was struck by the wide discrepancy between the values expressed in the document and the actual practice within the organization. For example, the 'Falcon Values' document contained statements such as 'Quality: Attention to detail is our trademark; our goal is to do it right the first time. We intend to deliver defect-free products and services to our customers on the date promised'. However, Richards had already seen reports showing that a number of defective computers were being shipped to customers. And his personal experience supported his worst fears. When he borrowed four new Falcon computers from the shipping room for use in a training class, he found only two of them working. Another example of the difference between Falcon Values and actual practice concerned this statement on communication: 'Managing by personal communication is part of the Falcon way. We value and encourage open, direct, person-to-person communication as part of our daily routine.' Executives bragged about how they arranged their chairs in a circle to show equality and to facilitate open communication whenever they met to discuss the 'Falcon Values' document. Richard had heard the 'open communication' buzzword a lot, but hadn't seen much evidence of such communication. As a matter of fact, all other meetings used a more traditional layout, with top executives at the front of the room. Richards believed that secrecy and communication that followed the formal chain of command characterised the real organizational culture that was developing at Falcon. Even the 'Falcon Values' document, Richard was told, had been created in secret.

Richards soon became disillusioned. He confided in a coworker one afternoon that 'Falcon Values' was so much at variance with what people saw everyday that very few took it seriously. Employees quickly learned what the organization truly emphasised on – hierarchy, secrecy, and expediency – and focused on these realities instead, ignoring many of the concepts incorporated in the values document. Despite his frustration, Richards stayed with Falcon until it filed for bankruptcy two years later. 'Next time,' he thought to himself as he cleaned out his desk, 'I will pay more attention to what is actually going on, and less to what the top management says is true.' Furthermore, he thought to himself, 'I guess you just can't create values.'

1. What is more important, the statements in a corporate culture document or actual management behaviour?
2. Why did Falcon executives act as they did? What type is Falcon culture?
3. Discuss the statement of Richards, I guess you just can't create values. Do you agree or disagree?
4. How can executives change the old values and culture that govern an organization?
5. Why didn't employees like Richards blow the whistle on Falcon, challenging the inconsistency between values and behaviour?

Review Questions

1. Describe the elements of an organization's culture.
2. What determines the 'effectiveness' of an organization's culture?
3. Describe how organizational culture is transmitted? Why has culture become so important?
4. Describe national and other determinants of culture.
5. Describe different types of organizational cultures and their features.
6. Discuss the different types of culture that characterise different nations.

Assignment

Work in small groups and each group to select any two organizations and prepare organization culture profile. Compare the profiles and present to class.

This instrument is designed to find out some of the values, beliefs and practices of organizations. Below are given 8 sets, containing four statements. Please read the statements in each set and then rank-order them. Give rank 1 to the statement which describes your organization most clearly or accurately. Give rank 2 to a good description of your organization; rank 3 to a statement not so true of your organization; and rank 4 to the statement which is least true of your organization. Please rank all sets. There is no right or wrong answers.

Set 1

(a) No consideration is given to values in this organization.
(b) Values are not shared in the organization.
(c) Values are shared only at the top level.
(d) Organizational values are widely shared in the organization.

Set 2

(a) The size of room and its furniture, is according to a person's rank.
(b) Each senior member has a room with a large
(c) Genearlly small tables are used by managers.
(d) Large working tables are used here.

Set 3

(a) The dominant belief is that things don't happen; you make them happen.
(b) The belief here is that most things depend upon top management.
(c) People believe that the major constraints are managerial.
(d) People believe that there are too many constraints, which are difficult to fight.

Set 4

(a) The leaders here expect to be implicitly obeyed.
(b) The leaders here are role models for their people.
(c) People are expected to follow the proper channels that have been laid down.
(d) The leaders set the standards for performance.

Set 5

(a) In mee'ings, people can sit wherever they find place.
(b) People are indifferent to meetings and try to avoid then.
(c) There is an implicit hierarchy in the seating patterns at meetings.
(d) In meetings, seats for those are fixed. Generally, meetings are not held without top management.

Set 6

(a) The customers are regarded as a most important person here.
(b) A good product is given the highest importance.
(c) Rules and regulations are given high importance.
(d) The Chief Executive is the most important person here.

Set 7

(a) Most communication is generated at the meetings of top people.
(b) All communication is in writing, and through memos.
(c) There is not much work related communication among people.
(d) People communicate with one another to solve problems.

Set 8

(a) A lot of attention is given to updating technology.
(b) The top management have parties to celebrate good performance..
(c) High performance is celebrated, with everybody joining in.
(d) People are busy streamlining rules and regulations.

Refer Udai Pareek, *Training Instruments in HRD and OD*, Tata McGraw Hill, p 806.

Chapter

12

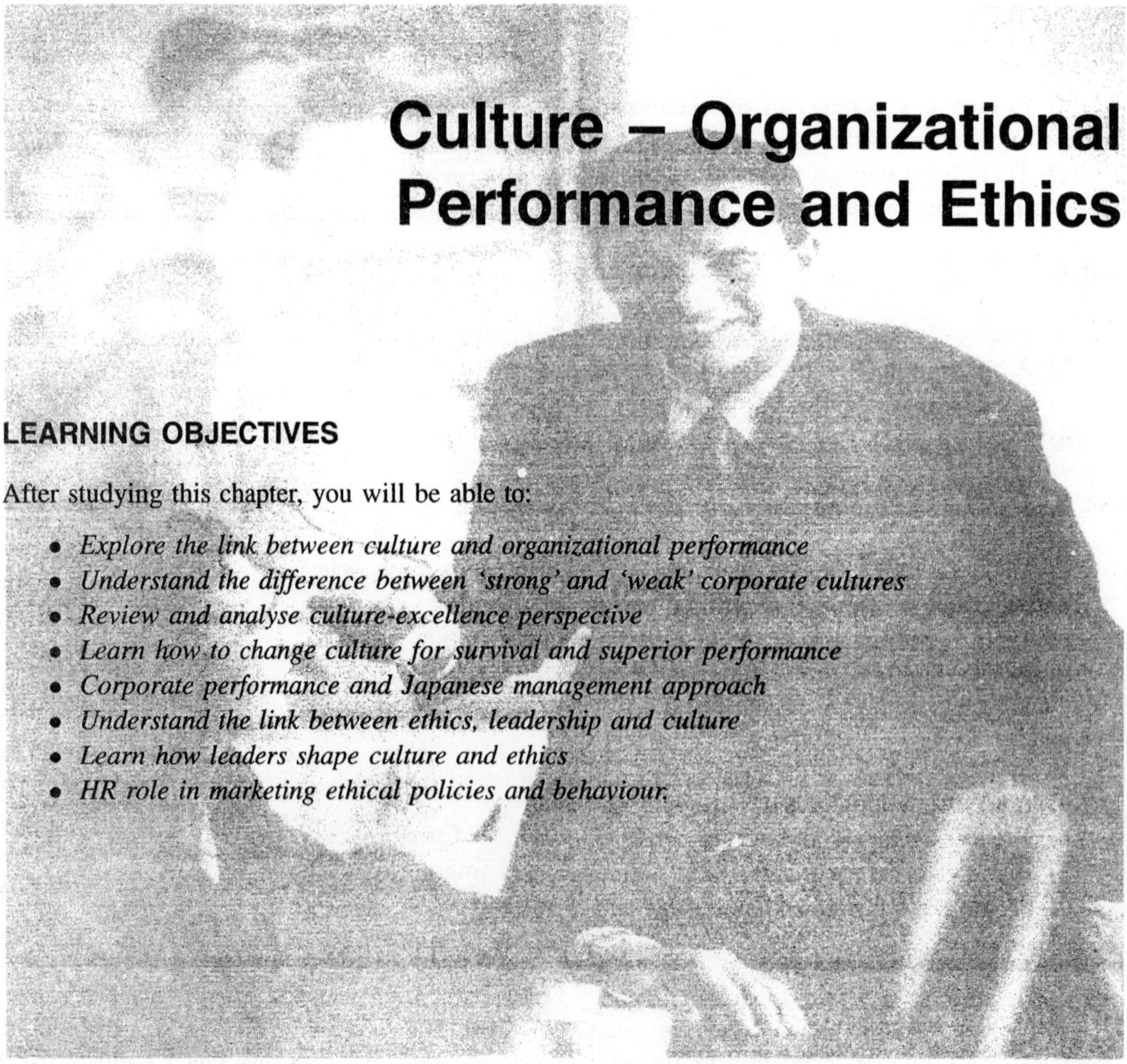

Culture – Organizational Performance and Ethics

LEARNING OBJECTIVES

After studying this chapter, you will be able to:

- *Explore the link between culture and organizational performance*
- *Understand the difference between 'strong' and 'weak' corporate cultures*
- *Review and analyse culture-excellence perspective*
- *Learn how to change culture for survival and superior performance*
- *Corporate performance and Japanese management approach*
- *Understand the link between ethics, leadership and culture*
- *Learn how leaders shape culture and ethics*
- *HR role in marketing ethical policies and behaviour.*

OPENING CASE
Creating Cultures and Changing Them – Tandem Computers

At Tandem Computers, Jim Treybig created a culture to fit his vision. At 4 o'clock every Friday afternoon, employee beer bursts were on in full swing at Tandem Computers' offices around the country. Every week, 60 per cent of the company dropped in for beer bursts for an hour, joined by visiting customers and suppliers. Employees at Tandem had neither time clocks nor name tags, but they did have flexible hours, a swimming pool, a volleyball court, locker room and showers. Despite all the fun, Treybig was serious about his five cardinal points for running a company, which defined the Tandem culture:

1. All people are good.
2. People, workers, management and company are all the same thing.
3. Every single person in the company must understand the essence of the business.
4. Every employee must benefit from the company's success.
5. You must create an environment where all of the above can happen.

Treybig was a hero. He symbolized hard work and concern for people. Without question his culture worked. Then suddenly, the party at Tandem was over. Growth slowed, profits went flat, and the stock price dropped. Treybig had to find a new strategy and change the culture to fit it. Even more important, he had to change his style. He asked his salaried workers to put in 10 per cent overtime without pay, stopped all hiring, froze salary increases and restricted travel expenditure by subjecting it to a vice-president's prior approval. Treybig also became more authoritative and acted no longer like 'one of the gang'. His new style sent signals to tighten up the internal controls. At Treybig's behest, Tandem also developed a new line of products. The strategy worked. New products now account for 75 per cent of sales, and administrative procedures are more systematic and suited to a large corporation. Tandem still has swimming pools and Friday beer bursts to encourage informal communication among people from different departments. But its new culture also fits its new strategy and competitive environment.

Analysis: At Tandem, Jim Treybig used symbols to both create an organizational culture and then to change the culture to fit the new environment. Fitting Tandem's culture to its strategy has allowed the company to be extraordinarily successful. The success of Tandem is due to its strong culture, represented by a widely shared philosophy which stresses its commitment to the importance of people. This value is 'broadcast by T-shirts, bulletin boards and word of mouth'. Another element is the lack of formal structures, roles and rules which are replaced by far more effective functional equivalents: unwritten and shared understanding. Tandem seems to maintain a balance between and autonomy and control without relying heavily on centralised or formalised procedures, or rigid status hierarchies.

INTRODUCTION

One of the most striking and pervasive claims of Strategic Human Resource Management is that an organization's culture is the key to its performance and that these organizational cultures can be manipulated to ensure that the employees are enthusiastic, committed and compliant.[1] Therefore, management of corporate culture is the central responsibility of modern managers (Legge, 1998). The subject of culture change has invited intense research, writing, debate and criticism. The outstanding growth and strength of Japanese industrial performance in the last two decades has inspired envy and emulation in the West as well as in India and much of it is ascribed to Japan's unique societal culture. Further, in the wake of several corporate scandals, organizational ethics has became a subject of global seminars and symposiums. And ethics is rooted in organizational culture. Both organizational ethics and culture are greatly influenced by organizational leadership. These are the topics of this chapter.

LINK BETWEEN CULTURE AND ORGANIZATIONAL PERFORMANCE

The positive correlation between corporate culture and organizational performance is based on the findings that organizational cultures can be assessed, managed, constructed and manipulated in the pursuit of enhanced organizational effectiveness. Employee norms, beliefs, and values can (and when necessary should) be changed so that they exhibit the appropriate behaviour, commit themselves to the organization, support the management and its strategy. This view holds that the norms and values shared by numbers of an organization create consensus, and unity and generate employee commitment.

Organizations to be affected should adapt to the external environment. External adaptation refers to how the organizations meet its goals and deal with outsiders. Culture helps guide the daily activities of workers to meet certain goals. It can help organizations to respond steadily to customer needs or to moves of competitors. Internal integration means that members develop a collective identity and know how to work effectively.[1] It is culture that guides day-to-day working relationships and determines how people communicate within the organization, what behaviour is acceptable or not acceptable, and how power or status is allocated.

When an organization's culture is strong, it can have a powerful impact, though not necessarily a positive one. Culture strength refers to the degree of agreement among members of an organization about the importance of specific values. If widespread consensus exists about the importance of those values, the culture is cohesive and strong; if little agreement exists, the culture is weak.

Strong cultures can be either adaptive or un-adaptive. Research (S. Ramnarayanan, *Organization Behaviour*, p. 338) into 200 corporate cultures found that strong culture does not ensure success unless the culture is one that encourages a healthy adaptation to external environment. A strong culture that does not encourage adaptation can be more damaging to an organization's success than having a weak culture. (refer the case of IBM). Adaptive cultures have different values and different behaviour patterns from unadaptive cultures. Strong but unadaptive cultures can be detrimental to a company's chances for success. But adaptive and strong culture is considered 'the managerial formula for success' (Jaggi, 1985). Managers understand the 'elements' that are common in all 'productivity' cultures (Akin and Hopeland, 1986). The 'right' culture may 'reap a return on investment that averages nearly twice as high as those firms with less efficient cultures' (Dennison, 1984). Sustained competitive advantage (Barney, 1986) is expected from the 'right' culture because it is not possible for competitors

---

1. Christopher Mabey, Graeme Salman, John Storey, *Human Resource Management,* Blackwell, 1998, p. 4553.

to imitate it. A strong adaptable culture is described as 'right' (Bleicher, 1983: 495)' 'rich' (Deal and Kennedy, 1982:14); 'healthy, blooming' (Ulirich, 1984: 313); 'consistent', (Hinterhuber, 1986) and 'participatory' (Dennison, 1984; Sackmann, 1990: 119).

Deal and Kennedy (1991: 22) argue, 'Since organizational values can powerfully influence what people actually do, we think that values ought to be a matter of great concern to managers. In fact shaping and enhancing values can become the most important job a manager can do. In our work and study we have found that successful companies place a great deal of emphasis on values.' In general, these companies share three characteristics:

- They stand for something, that is, they have a clear and explicit philosophy about how they aim to conduct their business.
- Management pays a great deal of attention to shaping and fine-tuning these values to conform to the economic and business environment of the company and communicating them to the organization.
- These values are known and shared by all the people who work for the company, from the lowliest production worker right through the ranks of senior managers.

Therefore, it becomes the primary task of managers to develop a shared system of beliefs and paradigms. Tom Peters (1978: 10), renowned management consultant, also supports this new role of managers.

STRONG AND WEAK CULTURES

It is important to clarify here that although various academicians and consultants have identified many common characteristics, there are no 'universal' success factors of corporate culture. Schien states, 'Do not assume that more or stronger culture is better.' What is better depends on the stage of evolution of the company and its current state of adaptiveness. Instead of implanting a strong culture it is always better to understand and use the strengths of the existing culture. The argument that cultural characteristics, whether imprinted from wider social contexts (as in the case of Japan) or nurtured and developed by management action can determine or explain corporate performance (or even national economic and industrial performance) would be gross oversimplification. Culture is only one of several human factors associated with corporate performance. Other human factors include staff capability, structure and human resource management practices. Furthermore, there are other factors, deriving from technology, market position and national, global, fiscal and economic conditions which profoundly affect performance. The notion, then, that culture and corporate performance are somehow bound together in a uni-dimensional way is unrealistic. It is multi-dimensional and culture is one of the several variables influencing, and being influenced by corporate performance.

Nevertheless, researchers have long sought to identify the elements of successful, strong organization cultures, and successful cultures are usually defined as strong.

Strong Cultures

Strong cultures have the following elements:

- A strong unifying corporate philosophy and mission;
- Trusted and trusting leaders;

- Open communication channels and access to top management;
- An emphasis on the importance of people and productivity relationships;
- An emphasis on the customer and on service;
- A general sense of accomplishment and belonging by all;
- Commonly shared rites, rituals and ceremonies;
- Employees take pride in their work and speak well about the company;
- Satisfaction with rewards, performance and effort;
- Highly ethical in their business ways.

Strong culture must have a fit with the company's corporate strategy and its external environment.

Cultures in Need of Change

Several characteristics of weak cultures that are in need of change can be identified. The managers are more concerned about themselves or some pet projects rather than about customers or employees. The senior members of the organization are critical of each other and form their own groups and support each other at the cost of the organization. They do not build any common understanding about what is important in the organization. Day-to-day life is either disorganized – everyone does his or her own thing – or are contradictory – 'the left hand and the right hand work at cross-purposes'. Weak cultures have no clear values or beliefs and cannot agree among themselves on what is important. Worse, different parts of the company have fundamentally different beliefs about what constitutes success. Weak cultures also tend to have an inward, short-term focus. Fragmentation, inconsistency and morale problems exist among groups and individuals. Finally, subcultures are in grown and clashes flare up between different groups.

ORGANIZATIONAL EFFECTIVENESS

The effectiveness of an organization's culture can be examined and evaluated from at least three perspectives. The contingency theory approach identifies effectiveness as the fit of an organization's culture with its internal systems and external environment. The goal attainment approach identifies effectiveness as the extent to which stated goals are obtained. The competing value approach is interested in how well leaders and managers adopt effective values and competences as they respond to changing environments. These perspectives should be viewed as different but complementary ways to understand cultural effectiveness. No single perspective represents the best or right way. Ideally organizational leaders should be able to mobilise organizational culture to meet all demands.

MANAGEMENT PRACTICES THAT BUILD STRONG ORGANIZATIONAL CULTURE

- The internalization of beliefs and values depends upon the perceived integrity of their managers.
- Managers believe in and practice the organization's cultural values.
- Managers are role models who take pride in what they and their co-workers do and practice together.
- Management style is modelled on high ethical standards and values.

- Managers demonstrate a positive attitude and loyalty towards the organization and fellow employees.
- Managers give others the feeling that the work they do is valued however, mundane that may be.
- Managers understand and apply the psychology of motivation to create a highly satisfying work environment.
- Group dynamics has two dimensions: Equity, equality and consensus are key factors in group cohesion both inter- and intra-group relationships.
- Managers develop leadership qualities and values to get the best performance from each group member.
- Managers develop feelings of group belonging for every individual as the basis of team spirit.
- The skills of every group member are developed individually and collectively to mutual benefits.
- Consensus is deeper and stronger than compromise. It promotes ownership of decisions and builds bridges between different points of view.
- Individuals are empowered to change group thinking in status-free and blame-free decisions.
- Consensus requires managers to listen and explain at the appropriate level of understanding.
- Behaviour should be consistent with an attractive image. Successful behaviour can change attitudes. Ethics reinforce an image to be trusted.
- Identification requires a strong, clear, attractive corporate image reinforced by management style.
- The image is reinforced by a mission statement and consistent management practices.
- Authoritative, trustworthy and reliable managers personalize (walk) the values.
- A friendly-open and accessible management style presents an influential image.

CULTURE-EXCELLENCE APPROACH

A study of the success secrets of America's 62 large companies by Peters and Waterman (1982) has given rise to much discussion and review both by managers and academicians. Their book, *In Search of Excellence: Lessons from America's Best-Run Companies* has become the best selling management book. They studied companies like IBM, Texas Instruments, and Hewlett Packard.

The authors argue that there are eight key attributes which organizations need to demonstrate if they are to achieve excellence. They believe that it is the freedom given to managers and to employees to challenge the orthodox and to experiment with different solutions, which distinguishes the excellent companies from the also-rans. 'Autonomy', 'freedom to challenge the orthodox' and 'empowerment to experiment' are certainly aspects of strong corporate cultures. Their nine attributes of 'excellence' are as following:

Bias for Action

A preference for doing something – anything – rather than sending an idea through endless cycles of analysis and committee reports.

Bias for action means appropriate and rapid response. One of the methods devised for achieving quick action is 'chunking', which means a problem is first made manageable (i.e. broken into chunks) and then tackled by a small group created especially for that purpose. The main reason for the use of such groups, variously called project teams, task forces or quality circles, is to facilitate organizational fluidity and to encourage action. The key characteristics of these groups are:

- They usually comprise no more than ten members.
- They are voluntarily constituted.
- The life of the group is usually between three to six months.
- The reporting level and seniority of membership is appropriate to the importance of the problem to be dealt with.
- The documentation of the group's proceedings is scant and very informal.
- These groups take on a limited set of objectives, which are usually determined, monitored, and reviewed by them.

'Chunking' is just one example. What is intended and encouraged is innovation and experimentation. These companies' philosophy for action is simple: do it, fix it, and try it, in small teams. Smallness induces manageability and a sense of understanding, and allows a feeling of ownership.

Close to Customer

Excellent companies reach out to the customer, while others merely talk about it. The customer dictates product quantity, quality and service. The best organizations go to extreme lengths to achieve the demanded quality, service and reliability. No part of business is closed to the customer. In fact, many of the excellent companies claim to get their best ideas for new products from listening intently and regularly to their customers. Such companies are more driven by their direct orientation to the customers rather than by technology or by a desire to be the low cost producer. They seem to focus more on the revenue-generation side of their services.

Autonomy and Entrepreneurship

Perhaps the most important element of outstanding companies is their ability to be big and yet act small at the same time. It means breaking the corporation into companies/units and encouraging them to think independently and competitively. This brings entrepreneurial spirit among the people because autonomy is pushed down the line. Product champions are allowed to come forward, grow and flourish. These champions are pragmatists who latch on to someone's idea and doggedly bring something concrete and tangible out of it. Other champions are executive champions who were earlier product champions and godfathers who back teams and are role models for other champions. These champions are provided 'sub-optional divisions', which are independent business units. These are further supported by strong reward systems. Entrepreneurship is further encouraged by no-holds barred communication, which is both informal and supported by physical and material resources. Given this support, the communication between and amongst workers is not only informal and spontaneous but also intense.

Productivity through People

It is creating in all employees the awareness that their best efforts are essential and that they will share in the rewards of the company's success. They treat their workers with respect and dignity; they refer to them as partners. This is because people, rather than systems or machines, are seen as the primary source of quality and productivity gains. Therefore, there is deep respect for the individual and the willingness to train him, to set reasonable and clear expectations for him, and to grant him practical autonomy to step out and contribute directly to his job. There is closeness and family feeling. The slogans of such companies tend to reflect this view of people: 'respect the individual', 'make people winners', 'let them stand out', 'treat people as adults'.

Hands-on, Value-driven

It means that executives keep in touch with the firm's essential business and promote a strong corporate culture. Outstanding companies are value-driven; they are clear about what they stand for and take the process of value-shaping seriously. There is an implicit belief that everyone in the organization, from top to bottom, should be driven by the values of the organization.

These values are almost always stated in qualitative, rather than quantitative, terms. When financial objectives are mentioned, they are always ambitious but never precise. Furthermore, financial and strategic objectives are never stated alone. They are always discussed in the context of the other things the company expects to do well. The idea that profit is a natural by-product of doing something well, and not an end in itself, is almost always universal.

Implanting these values is a primary responsibility of managers. They set the tone by leading from the front. Coherence and consensus must first be created among senior management by regular meetings, both formal and informal, so that the management speaks in one voice. The managers are passionate about preaching the values of the organization. They spread the excitement not in their offices but on the shop floor. Inculcating these values, however, is a laborious process and persistence is vital in achieving the desired goals.

Stick to the Knitting

This means remaining with the business the company knows best. Acquisition or internal diversification for its own sake is not the choice of outstanding companies. But when they do acquire, they do it experimentally by first 'dipping a toe in the water'. If the water does not feel good, they get out fast. Acquisitions are always in fields related to their core competency.

Simple form Lean Staff

This means minimum administrative layers, a few people at the upper levels, and one structural dimension, either product or function or geography, should have clear primacy.

The core structure remains fixed while work is done through teams and ad hoc groups that keep changing. Such a simple structure requires a small, lean staff at the top and middle levels. There are more doers and fewer administrators.

Simultaneous Loose-tight Properties

This means fostering a climate where there is dedication to the central values of the company combined with tolerance for the idiosyncrasies of employees who accept those values. A paradoxical combination of central direction and individual autonomy, it means that the management controls everything tightly, but allows individual innovation and risk-taking. This is possible only by developing a strong organizational culture.

Review of Culture-Excellence Perspective

The companies cited by Peters and Waterman (such as RMI, with its emphasis on the value of happiness and smiling faces of its workforce, and McDonald's with its emphasis on 'Quality, Cleanliness and Value') were notable for the consistency they had developed between values, practices, structures and strategies. However, the duo only gave snapshots of successful companies, whereas evidence of disjunction between the levels is more likely to emerge from a longitudinal study.

Two years after the publication of this book, articles started appearing suggesting that many of these companies were sliding from grace. HP was said to have fallen in the microcomputer and super mini-computer markets, and its 'technology-driven, engineering-oriented culture, in which decentralisation and innovation were a religion and entrepreneurship were the gods, is giving way to a marketing culture and growing centralisation'. Atachi 'was so out of touch with its markets that it failed to realise that its customers were loosing interest in video-game players and switching to home computers'. Interestingly, as their success begins to fade, far from emphasising their 'excellent' attributes, these companies revert to more conventional forms of centralised structural response.

Questions have been asked about whether the Peters and Waterman prescriptions could withstand the voyage across the Atlantic. In a debate between Waterman and De Woot (Belgian professor from the Louvian Institute), reported in the *Financial Times*,[2] the latter questioned whether European firms were ready to embrace all the elements of 'excellence'. In response, Waterman stressed that he and his co-author had not seen people, innovation, and values as alternatives to structural solutions, but that they were concerned about reviving interest in the soft 'Ss' (style, skilled staff, and shared values) on the assumption that the hard 'Ss' (strategy, structure and systems) were already well established as preconditions.

De Woot's six-year study of management at all levels in nine French and Belgian corporates showed that where there was little concept of strategic management, there was no basis for developing a Peters and Waterman scheme.

Despite the criticisms, there is no doubt that Peters and Waterman have struck a popular note with practitioners. It is commonplace to hear of companies requiring all their senior executives to read and act on the book.

CORPORATE PERFORMANCE AND JAPANESE MANAGEMENT APPROACH

Reduced to ashes, in the Second World War, Japan is now an industrial power second only to the USA. There are many reasons for its success, but the most important is its management approach. Since there are differences in the management of large and small enterprises and treatment of full-time and part-time workers and female employees, some argue that there is no such thing as 'Japanese Management' (Dale, 1986). Nevertheless, the vast majority of observers do seem to agree that it does exist (Pascale and Athoes, 1982; Holden and Burgess, 1994).

2. *Financial Times*, 26 November 1984.

The Japanese approach to management broadly revolves around teamwork, quality consciousness and flexibility (Wickens, 1987). McKenna (1988) believes that the key elements are lifetime employment, seniority principle with pay and promotion, and enterprise unionism. Pang and Oliver (1988) also draw attention to training and education, company-based welfare schemes, quality circles and methods of manufacturing, such as 'Just-in-time' production. Keys and Miller (1984) point to long-term planning, lifetime employment and collective responsibility. All these factors and more can be separated into two categories: those relating to personnel/industrial issues and those related to business/manufacturing practices.

Personnel Issues

The dedication, commitment and ability of Japanese workers are seen as major factors in the success of Japanese companies. Though much credit for this is given to the culture of Japanese society, especially its Confucian tradition of obedience and loyalty, respect and sacrifice for family, similar levels of motivation have been produced in Japanese companies operating in the West (Wickens, 1987), which would imply that other factors are also at work. Chief among these is the crucial role played by personnel policies prevalent in many Japanese enterprises, especially the larger ones. The core of the Japanese approach to personnel comprises a group of practices and policies designed to socialise and bind employees to the organization, and promote their long-term development and commitment. The principles practices and policies are;

- Lifetime employment: Many employees are recruited straight from school or university, and expect and are expected to spend the rest of their working years with the same organization. This 'guarantee', based on mutual obligation, creates an intense sense of loyalty to and dependence on the organization. Akido Morita, founder of Sony, used to write a personal letter to every new employee: 'Since you are going to spend most of your life in this company why not make it a happy place to work.' Indeed, Holden and Burgess (1994) observed that while a Japanese worker might survive the loss of his family, the collapse of his employing organization would be unbearable. No wonder that some Japanese workers have died due to over-exertion without ever complaining. Lifetime employment gives rise to a stable workforce and a stable culture. However, if a worker is fired for any reason, it is difficult for him to find another job.
- Internal labour markets: Most positions are filled from inside the company, which demonstrates to the employee that satisfactory performance will bring promotion. It also eliminates the potential for tension, which can emerge by the recruitment of outsiders.
- Seniority-based promotion and reward system: Employees are ranked and rewarded primarily, but not exclusively, on their length of service, and independent of the precise nature of the job they perform.
- Teamwork and bonding: Although Japanese employees are made to feel part of the organization, and they see the organization as an extended family, they are first and foremost members of particular workgroups or teams. The group is developed as a single entity, which takes collective responsibility for its performance. Japanese companies use a variety of techniques, both at work and social setting, for bonding team members to each other and to the organization.
- Enterprise (single company) unions: Unlike in the West, Japanese companies allow only one union to represent the interests of the workforce. Indeed, they are not trade unions but

associations where senior executives at some stage in their career are expected to serve as union officials.

- Training and education: Extensive and continuous training and education form an integral part of Japanese personnel policies. This emphasis on the continual development of employees to enable them to carry out their work better and prepare them for promotion represents a significant investment by Japanese companies in their human capital. Much of the training is done on the job and is always geared to the twin aims of improving organizational performance and individual development. Employees are also encouraged to take responsibility of their own self-development.
- Welfare of employees: Many Japanese companies provide a wide range of welfare benefits to their employees. These cover medical treatment, housing and education of children. Some of the large companies are almost mini welfare states in themselves.
- Job rotation: Most employees have to work by rotation in different departments like marketing, purchase and production before promotion to a senior post. This makes them appreciate better the demand of other employees and results in better coordination.

Many other practices and policies can be added to this list, but these appear to be at the core.

Business Practices and Work Systems

The Japanese ability to satisfy the customers, and thereby capture markets, by developing and producing products to a higher specification and lower cost than their competitors is staggering. Some of the methods used to achieve this include *Houshin kanri* (policy development); *Genba kanri* (workshop management); *Kaizen* (continuous improvement); *Kanban* (a paperless form of scheduling). Japanese business practices and work systems can be characterised by three interrelated elements: long-term planning, timeliness and quality with the involvement of Japanese workers in decision-making.

Review of Japanese Management Approach

It is not the merit of individual practices that has given Japan the competitive edge; it is the integrated and mutually supportive way of the personnel policies combined with hard aspects of management (strategy, structure and systems) that has worked. However, from the Western standpoint, Japanese companies appear to operate very oppressive and authoritarian regimes where workers are more like slaves. Whatever the merits and demerits of the Japanese approach, there is little doubt that it has a very significant impact on corporate performance; consequently attempts are being made to introduce 'Japanisation' into many Western companies (Ackroyd et al., 1988; Hannam, 1993; Pang and Oliver, 1988; Pascale and Athos, 1982; Schonberger, 1982; Turnbull, 1986).

CULTURE AND ETHICS

Of the values that make up an organization's culture, ethical values are now considered among the most important. Ethical standards are becoming part of the formal policies and informal cultures of many organizations. Ethics is the code of moral principals and values that governs the behaviour of a person or group with respect to what is right or wrong. Ethical values set standards as to what is good or bad in conduct and decision-making. Ethics is distinct from behaviour governed by law. It goes beyond law; it does not mean simply following the law. Much behaviour is not codified and managers must be sensitive to the emerging norms and values. The notion of 'social responsibility' is an extension of this idea. It refers to the management's obligation to make choices and take action so that the organization contributes to the welfare and interest of society (management is an organ of society created to serve its interests – Peter Drucker) as well as to itself. A few examples of the need for managerial ethics are as follows:

- A senior financial executive approached J.R.D. Tata, suggesting how substantial amount can be saved by a particular approach which is well within the accounting practice and law. J.R.D. asked him 'But is it good? Is it a good practice?' The executive understood and left.
- The project manager for a consulting project wondered whether some facts should be left out of a report because the marketing executives paying for the report would appear in bad light if the facts were reported.
- A retail store has planted hidden cameras to capture shoplifting and thefts. The cameras also revealed employees criticising the management or misbehaving while on duty. Should it take action against the employees?

These issues are difficult to resolve and often represent dilemmas. An ethical dilemma arises when every available alternative seems undesirable; right or wrong is not clearly identifiable. These choices can be aided by establishing ethical values within the organization as part of the corporate culture.

The standards for ethical or socially responsible conduct are inbuilt within each employee as well as within each organization itself. The forces that influence ethical decisions are shown in Fig. 12.1.

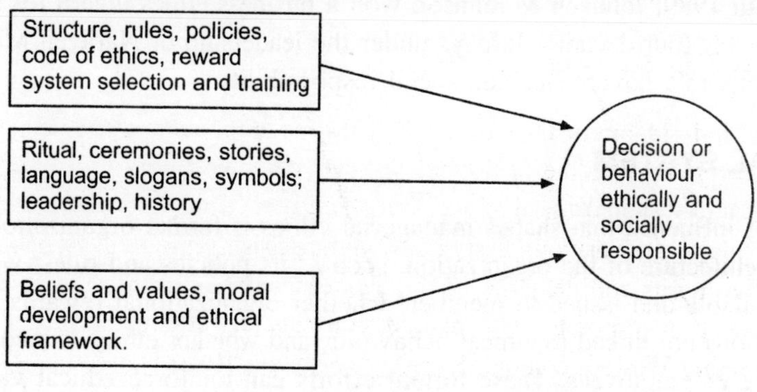

Fig. 12.1 Factors Determining Ethical Decision

Personal Ethics

Every employee brings a set of personal beliefs and values into the workplace, which gets translated into behaviour. The behaviour of individuals is an important aspect of ethical decision-making in organizations. The family backgrounds and spiritual values of managers provide principles by which they carry out business. In addition people go through stages of moral development. The first stage is to obtain rewards and avoid punishment; the second is to meet the standards of good behaviour set by colleagues and society. Most managers are at this level. At the highest level of development, people develop an internal set of standards and are driven by their conscience. These are self-chosen ethical principles that are more important than external expectations. Only a few people reach this high level, which can mean breaking laws, if necessary, and self-sacrifice to sustain higher moral standards.

The other personal factor is whether managers have developed an 'ethical framework' that guides their decisions. Utilitarian theory, for example, argues that ethical decisions should be made to generate the greatest benefit for the greatest number of people. This framework justifies business managers taking disciplinary action against some employees. The personal liberty framework argues that decisions should be made to ensure the greatest possible freedom of choice and liberty for individuals. Liberties include freedom to act on one's conscience, free speech, due process of law and right to privacy. The distributive justice framework holds that moral decisions are those that promote equity, fairness and impartiality with respect to the distribution of rewards and the administration of rules, which are essential for social cooperation.

PERSONAL AND ORGANIZATIONAL ETHICS

Rarely can, ethical or unethical business practices be attributed entirely to personal ethics of a single individual. Since business practices reflect the values, attitudes, and behaviour patterns of an organization's culture, ethics is as much an organizational issue as a personal one. Enron and Johnson & Johnson are two examples. Though Johnson & Johnson's handling of the Tylenol-poisoning crisis has sometimes been attributed to the ethical standards of then CEO James Burke, the decision actually reflected a shared set of values and guiding principles that have been deeply ingrained in the company since its early days. In 1989, Johnson & Johnson won a business ethics award for sustaining ethical decision-making for over four decades. Infosys under the leadership of Narayan Murthy has won an award in India for corporate governance and social responsibility.

ORGANIZATIONAL SYSTEM

The third category of influence that shapes managerial ethics is formal organizational systems. This includes the basic architecture of the organization, such as its policies and rules; whether an explicit code of ethics is available and issued to member; whether organizational rewards, including praise, attention and promotions are linked to ethical behaviour; and whether ethics is a consideration in the selection and training of employees. These formal efforts can reinforce ethical values that exist in informal cultures.

Today numerous companies are establishing formal ethical programme. HP familiarizes all employees with its high standards of business practice, which cover everything from conflict of interests to accepting gratitude. HP sales people are instructed to refrain from commenting on a competitor's character or business practice. At Northup, peers and subordinates, through anonymous questionnaire, rate managers on their ethical behaviour.

HOW LEADERS SHAPE CULTURE AND ETHICS?

A report issued by the Business Round Table – an association of chief executives from 250 large corporations – discussed ethics, policy and practice in Fortune 500 companies. In the experience of the surveyed companies, the single most important factor in ethical decision-making was the role of the top management in providing commitment, leadership and example for ethical values. The CEO and other top managers must be committed to specific values and must constantly lead in tending and renewing those values.

Values can be communicated in a number of ways – speeches, company publications, policy statements and most important personal actions. Successful leaders are responsible for creating and sustaining a culture that emphasises the importance of ethical behaviour in employees everyday life. When the CEO engages in unethical practices or fails to take firm and decisive action against unethical practices of others, the attitude filters down through the organization. Formal code of ethics and training programmes are worthless if leaders do not set and live unto high standards of ethical conduct.

In the words of Azim Premji,'If you consider Wipro as a successful organization, I would rate values as the foremost contributor to its success. At the outset, we decided that character is one factor that will guide all our actions and decisions. We defined a set of values and beliefs for the organization in the early '70s before it was fashionable to do so. We decided that upholding those values was more important than achieving business success. Let me also confess that upholding these values has not been easy, especially in the early years. But we struck on. And as the years rolled by, we realised that what started in the realm of idealism not only held true in reality, but also proved to be a unique, tactical competitive advantage. Customers wanted to buy from us because we honoured our commitments.'

BOX 12.1 MANAGERS SHOULD KEEP THESE GUIDELINES IN MIND

1. Pay attention to corporate culture. Understand the underlying values, assumptions and beliefs on which the culture is based as well as its observable manifestations. Evaluate the corporate culture based on rites and ceremonies, stories and heroes, symbols and language.
2. Make sure the culture is consistent with the strategy and environment. Culture can be shaped to fit the needs of both.
3. Take control of ethical values in the organization. Ethics is not the same as following the law. Ethical decisions are influenced by the management's personal background, by the organization's culture and its systems.
4. Act as a leader for the internal culture and ethical values that are important to the organization. Influence the value system through symbolic leadership, including the use of ceremonies, slogans, symbols, and stories. Communicate important values to employees to enhance organizational effectiveness.
5. Use formal systems of the organization to implement desired cultural and ethical values. These systems include an ethics committee, ethics ombudsperson, disclosure mechanisms, a code of ethics, a mission statement and training in ethical decision-making framework.

The reason for so much recent managerial interest in corporate culture is, very obviously, because of the claim that culture plays a major part in determining organizational performance. If it was not for the power and appeal of the claim there would be little need to discuss organizational cultures. There would also be little interest in writing about and researching organizational culture. Yet there is enormous interest. Stablin and Nord (1985, p. 22) note: 'Probably never before in organizational studies has an innovative areas been given so much attention so rapidly.'

Therefore, fundamental to any consideration of organizational culture is the argument that such cultures matter greatly because they affect the organizational performance. Further when organizational strategy changes, it becomes necessary to bring in corresponding structural change (structure follows strategy). As per the author of the book, merely structural changes are not enough to ensure success of strategy. What is required is also cultural change along with restructuring of organization.

ETHICS ACROSS CULTURES

Values in the culture influence ethical standards. The old Sydney Lumet movie *Twelve Angry Men* tells a story of a juror persuading his eleven colleagues in the American jury room that the accused is not guilty. Earlier eleven members of jury had believed and argued that the accused is guilty. Ultimately lone jury convinced them that accused is not guilty. In collective cultures the lone member might not go to that extent against the group.

In 1985, when Readers Digest (US) decided to close its loss-making Japanese subsidiary, it encountered savage opposition from the Japanese union and parts of the press. They portrayed the parent company as being guilty of neglect and abandonment in the face of unswerving loyalty...The union placed ads in the *New York Times* saying that the company has dumped its Japanese readers and its own employees and that the company's behaviour was unfair, unscrupulous and irresponsible (Gundling 1991). The interests of shareholders and workforce did not correspond. Whereas the Japanese recognized the interests of the workforce, the Americans prioritise the shareholders interest. Each side appears to have behaved in accordance with its own ethical norms.

Because cultures differ, behaviour considered appropriate in one culture may be interpreted differently in some other.

Ethical universalism is the concept that there is single possible ethical code, which all people should follow. Hofstede connects this with individualism: 'laws and rights are supposed to be the same for all'. Collectivist values imply that 'Laws and rights differ by group'. This implies that different standards need to be applied when evaluating the behaviour of different groups. The international managers must expect managers from other cultures to apply different criteria in making ethical decisions, and that such choices are heavily influenced by each one's culture.

HR ROLE IN MAINTAINING ETHICAL POLICIES AND BEHAVIOUR

The global HR manager has a special role in ensuring that the organization deals fairly and ethically with its employees and the employees deal fairly with one another, the clients and the organization. Some policies for organizations in this regard are:

- Respecting people and not using them solely as means to one's own ends
- Not doing any harm
- Telling the truth
- Keeping the promises

- Treating people fairly without discrimination
- Not depriving people of basic rights, such as right to speech and association.

In organizational terms, fulfilling these duties may translate into the following:

1. Instituting careful health and safety practices, informing employees of potentially hazardous conditions and taking responsibility for occupational disease and stress-related illness traceable to working conditions.
2. being truthful in recruiting.
3. avoiding the use of invalid and discriminatory selection, appraisal and promotions.
4. paying equal pay for work of comparable worth.
5. providing ways for employees to voice their concern and not illegally constraining employees to form an union.
6. following fair policies with regard to discipline, termination for cause and layoffs.

Keeping these into mind the Society for Human Resource Management (SHRM) has formulated a code to guide HR professionals, available at: **http://shrm.orgethics/code-of-ethics.asp**).

Professional Responsibility: As HR professionals we are responsible for adding values to the organizations we serve and contributing to the ethical success of these organizations. We accept responsibility for our individual actions and decisions. We are also advocates for the profession by engaging in activities that enhance its credibility and value.

Professional Development: As professional we strive to meet the highest standards of competence and commit to strengthen our competencies on continuous basis.

Ethical Leadership: HR professional are expected to exhibit individual leadership as a role model for maintaining the highest standards of ethical conduct.

Fairness and Justice: We are ethically responsible for promoting and fostering fairness and justice for all employees and their organizations.

Conflicts of Interests: We must maintain a high level of trust with our stakeholders. We must protect the interests of our stakeholders as well as our professional integrity and should not engage in activities that create actual, apparent or potential conflicts of interests.

Use of Information: We consider and protect the rights of individuals, especially in the acquisition and dessimination of information while ensuring truthful communications and facilitating informed decision-making.

Review Questions

1. How would you set about identifying and analysing the culture of an organization?
2. From where managers derive ethical values? Do you think managers use ethical decision frameworks as part of their decision-making? Why?
3. Discuss how a strong corporate culture can be negative as well as positive for an organization.
4. Discuss the Peters Watersman's culture excellence perspective. Can it be universally applied?
5. Discuss the Japanese management approach. What difficulties do you expect if an Indian organization desires to implement it?
6. Discuss the traits of strong and weak cultures? Explain management practices that build strong cultures.

Assignment

In groups of 4-6 students, study the corporate culture; based on Tom Perters and Waterman's book 'In search of excellence' or using 'Training Instruments in HRD' by Udai Pareek, p. 791, 'OCTAPACE – the values of openness, confrontation, trust, authenticity, proaction, autonomy, collaboration and experimentation'.

Select the following types of organization.

- A manufacturing and a services organization.
- A private sector and public sector organization.
- A small and a large organization.
- A local or national organization and a multinational one.

Present in the class and discuss the differences in corporate cultures.

Chapter

13

Diversity Management in International Business

LEARNING OBJECTIVES

After studying this chapter, you will be able to:

- *Appreciate the growing importance of managing diversity at workplace for organizational effectiveness*
- *Define the dimensions of diversity and its concept*
- *Understand various approaches to manage diversity effectively including culture change*
- *Learn what global corporates are doing to liverage diversity for increased organizational performance.*

OPENING CASE
What Happened at Coca-Cola?

Coca-Cola

- is considered the world's most recognized brand name;
- controls 53% of the world's soft-drink market;
- was an international brand by 1900;
- was instrumental in the racial integration movement in Atlanta in the 1960s;
- was rated as 32nd on *Fortune's* 2002 list of 50 best companies for minorities;
- agreed to spend $200 million to settle recent racial and gender bias lawsuits.

How does a company with a history of international business, that long targeted many of its products to minority groups, that is headquartered in a state where 28% of the population is black, lose the largest racial discrimination suit (Ingram et al. the Coca-Cola Company) in US history? The case illustrates the contrast between a corporation's public image and the acceptance of racism within its organizational culture. Although Coca-Cola contributed to civil rights groups, such as Southern Christian Leadership Conference and the Rainbow Push Coalition, according to Foust (2000), 'when it came to its own workforce, the story was quite different... According to allegations filed in the discrimination lawsuit, former CEO Ivestor told a transferee, stunned by the latent racist culture, at its headquarters that it would take 15 to 20 years before Blacks would be fairly represented in the company.'

However, this was not the first time that racism at Coca-Cola had been an issue. The company's southern bottlers taunted and terrorised Coke's first Black salesman. Privately, legendary CEO Robert S. Woodruff questioned civil rights legislation in the 1960s. And if the worst excesses of the past are gone into, according to internal documents released in the lawsuit, even today the median salary for the Black employees is 44% less than that for the Whites.

Industry Background

The soft drink industry has its roots in the US when physicians in the 1800s, began prescribing the bubbling waters discovered in New York as a cure for ailments. Later, the development of artificial carbonated water and the addition of flavours like lemon and root beer and the growing popularity of local pharmacy's soda fountain as a social gathering spot led to increased demand for these products.

From its humble beginnings, the soft-drink industry enjoyed a phenomenal growth rate. One in every four beverages consumed in the US is a soft drink, which amounts to an annual consumption of 53 gallons for every man, woman and child in the country. However, due to the consumer shift to bottled waters, teas, fruit juices and product variations in coffee, the consumption rate in soft drinks has become stagnant in the US. To increase sales, soft-drink producers diversified into other products and aggressively competed in a market that is highly saturated, except in developing countries.

Company's History

The history of the Coca-Cola Company, the producer of two of the world's three most popular carbonated drinks, parallels the industry trends in terms of growth and product lines. Pioneering a sophisticated distribution system of local bottlers, who purchase the Coke syrup from the Corporation, and implementing aggressive growth strategies of 7% to 8% a year, Coke now controls 51% of the carbonated beverages sales in the world and 18% of the non-carbonated beverage market. In 2002, the Coke had $19 billion in operating revenues and netted $3.9 billion from its 300 brands sold in over 200 countries.

However, Coke had humble beginnings when John S. Pemberton began a patent medicine business in Atlanta, Georgia, in 1886, where he invented such products as liver pills, hair dye and the beverage known as Coca-Cola. With caffeine and cocaine in his sugary syrup concentrate, the product was marketed as a cure, all remedy. Pemberton grossed a mere $50 in sales during the first year. In 1891 he sold the business and its secret formula for $2300 to Asa Candler. The new owner, a druggist, improved the original formula, removed the cocaine, and hired a sales force that blanketed the US and beyond, selling syrup concentrate to local bottlers. He promoted the business, using such progressive marketing techniques as free samples and product logo premiums, and by 1900 the company had sold a million gallons of syrup, and by 1969, six billion gallons.

During World War II, General Eisenhower requested that Coke be made available to American soldiers serving in North Africa and Europe. So the company set up multiple foreign bottling plants that paved the way for a global business presence after the war. During the 1950s, the company expanded rapidly internationally and opened 15 to 20 plants per year. As early as the 1950s the company recognized the importance of minority markets and included racial minorities in its advertisements.

Although Coca-Cola was a one-product company until the 1960s, it quickly became synonymous with the American way of life. The company's advertisements never reflected the problems of the world, only a good and happy life. For Coke, the 1960s were a time of diversification, product development, and increased competition. Because Pepsi began to aggressively challenge Coke for the market share, Coke quickly bought Minute Maid and Belmont Springs Water and launched Tab, Sprite and Fresca, making significant in roads into the diet soda market. During the 1970s, Coke focused on foreign expansion, particularly into China and Russia. As a result by 1984, Pepsi outsold Coke with a 22.8% market share compared to Coke's 21.6%. Although introduction of Diet Coke, now the world's number 1 beverage, pumped up sales, the introduction of a reformulated 'New Coke' was a marketing and public relations disaster. Coke's great financial returns in the 1990s were based on the notion that it could keep increasing earnings at 20% or more per year. It cannot. (Sivy, 2000, p. 42)

Corporate Leadership and Culture

Fuelled by phenomenal marketing and financial success, Coke was run by bureaucrats and accountants focused more on getting the most out of what they had than on thinking of new ideas. Described as 'insular' and predominated by the 'good old boys' from the University of Georgia, the organization was a 'marketing machine that created desire for the Coke brand at whatever the price', rather than a sales company that gave consumers what they wanted. In some parts of the world, Coke was seen as representing American imperialism. This attitude is exemplified by former CEO Roberto Goizueta's wish that one day Coke should replace tap water. In 1997 when he suddenly died, the board replaced him with his protégé, M. Douglas Ivestor. Refusing to appoint a chief operating officer, 'investor did what accountants do best; he put his head down and carried on with the old ways of doing things.' Over the next two years, Ivestor, described as 'arrogant and insecure' (Morris and Sellers, 2000), inherited many problems, including a tainted Coke scare in Europe that resulted in the largest product recall in company's history (Europe Shuns, 1999), in a decline in earnings for two straight years, and the need to steeply increase the price of Coke syrup sales to bottlers in an attempt to bolster profits.

The Lawsuit

In 1999, just when things seemed like they couldn't get worse for Ivestor, Coca-Cola was served with lawsuit that accused the company of systematically discriminating against Black employees in promotions, evaluations, terminations and pay. Publicity surrounding the case troubled Coke, whose US customer base is disproportionately made up of African-Americans and Latinos.

Could this lawsuit have been prevented? Earlier when Black employees shared their complaints with Rev. Josheph Wheeler, president of the local NAACP, he brought these concerns to Coca-Cola officials. He was told that the company was under no obligation to talk to him because he was not a lawyer. Greg Clark, the one of the plaintiffs, said, 'That he never would have sued had he felt that his concerns were taken seriously. They ignored me, ignored me, to the point where I felt that I had no other recourse.' (Harrington, 2000, p. 188).

In response to the lawsuit, Ivestor appointed Carl H. Ware, the highest-appointed Black executive in the company as the co-chair of the Diversity Advisory Council along with senior vice-president Jack Sthal. Ware, a Harvard graduate, joined the company in 1974 to work in the area of urban and government affairs. As the VP of the Africa group were focused on cultivating African governments and bridging cultural hurdles so that company could do business, often in partnerships with local governments, he is credited with influencing Coca-Cola's decision to divest its business in South African assets in the support of anti-apartheid cause. In 1994, Ware helped in organizing Nelson Mandela's fund-raising tour in the US, which is credited with paving the way for Coke sales in post-apartheid South Africa, where Coke sales exceeded 400 million gallons a year. Having worked 26 years at the company, Ware was known for his ability to defuse problems before they became full-blown crises. In 1991, Jesse Jackson, critical of Coke's hiring record and its weak support for Black's businesses, was set to kick off a 'Don't Choke on Coke' boycott. Jackson called it off after Ware helped credit a $50 million programme to help support Black vendors.

As the lawsuit wound its way through the court system, the number of plaintiffs increased, and both sides turned up the pressure. What began with four current and ex-employees (administrative assistant Motisula Abdullah, security officer Gregory Clark, consumer information specialist, Linda Ingram, and a former director, Kimberlay Orton) eventually became a major class-action suit with approximately 2000 plaintiffs. The claim was that Coca Cola had 'systematically discriminated against African-Americans by paying them lower salaries than Whites for the same work, passing them over for promotions and subjecting them to harassment (Mokhiber, 2000, p. 30)', since at least 1995. Coincidently, 1995 was the same year that Carl Ware presented Ivestor, then Coke's CEO, with a report documenting racial discrimination in pay, performance evaluations and promotions for Black employees. The plaintiffs asked both for monetary damages and court order that required the company to change some of its employment practices. The lead co-counsel in the case was Cyrus Mehri, a 37- year-old lawyer, who had successfully won the $176 million Texaco racial discrimination lawsuit.

Coca-Cola denied the charges of discrimination, claiming that the plaintiffs' claims had nothing in common but their race. Carl Ware said, 'I think we have made great strides in developing gold standard for diversity management' and 'I myself am a good example, a proof that glass walls do not exist in Coke.' However, the company's dithering continued even after the suit was filed. For starters, rather than pursue the almost inevitable settlement, Coke first engaged in a vigorous pre-trial defence and attempted to stop the class-action status of lawsuit. The court instructed the company to add a disclaimer to company e-mails to employees about the case that read, 'The foregoing represents Coke's opinion of lawsuit. It is unlawful for Coke to retaliate against employees who choose to participate in this case'. The company did not add the disclaimers.

In October 1999, while the case was pending, Ivestor effectively demoted Ware, the company's highest-ranking Black executive by having him report to a fellow senior VP. In response Ware announced he would retire at the end of the year. The episode fuelled questions about Coke's commitment to diversity' (Smith, 200, p. 52). Although Ivestor's tenure was fraught with financial problems, the demotion of Ware seemed to be one of the catalytic events/public relations problems that moved influential board members to strongly suggest to Ivestor that he was no longer the man to run Coke. On December 5, 1999 Ivestor submitted his resignation. Morris and Sellers wrote:

Ivestor's sudden fall from one of the world's premier corporate jobs is more than just a tale of bad luck or plans gone wrong. It is a management story full of leadership lessons. It features colossal arrogance and insecurity. Its main character was blind to his own weakness and unwilling to take advice. But, the ultimate measure of a CEO is how he handles crises, and again and again, in the view of certain directors and the powerful bottling executives, Ivestor was a day late and a dollar short. He took pride in being a substance-over-style guy but that translated into taking no heed of image and perception issues, which are merely all important to a company like Coke. (2000, p. 78)

The board elected Douglas Daft, a 56-year-old Australian, with 30 years experience at Coke, primarily in their Asian and Middle-Eastern market, as president and CEO. In contrast to his predecessor, Daft was a delegator, who spoke of repositioning the company from three perspectives: building brand, thinking and acting locally in global business relations, and being seen as a model citizen. In his speech at CEO's club in Boston, he said,' I want the

Coke to be one of the most desired employers in the world. I have told our people that we are going to take our company to the head of the class when it comes to the diversity of our workforce and our business". He quickly mended fences with Carl Ware by naming him VP for Global Public Affairs, reporting directly to him and adopted two of the suggestions from Ware's 1995 report: clear support for diversity from the top executive and tying compensation increases to the achievement of diversity goals. As a result, Ware rescinded his retirement plan.

In November 2000, as a result of a court-ordered mediation, Coca-Cola settled the lawsuit with almost all the 2200 plaintiffs for $192.5 million. The agreement applied to all non-hourly, US-based employees of the company but not to employees of its bottlers. The terms of settlement called for back pay to current and former employees, future pay equity adjustments, linkage between the senior manager's compensation and the company's CEO performance and the creation of an outside seven- member task force to provide independent oversight of Coca-Cola's compliance. The task force was responsible for preparing four annual reports, evaluating the implementation of these programmes. Cyrus Mehri, head of the plaintiffs' legal team, summed up his opinion of the case:

The biggest problems at Coke were their HR practices. They had almost as many job titles as they did jobs, there was no consistent job posting, and promotional practices were not consistently applied. This gave undue discretion to managers and prevented employees from having a fair chance to compete for these positions. Coke had cultivated an image of being extraordinarily progressive and generous in the African-American community. Unfortunately, Coke like so many other companies got very arrogant and believed their own PR. They valued minorities as consumers, but not as employees.

> When asked to comment on the case, Coca-Cola media representative wrote:
> Clearly we learned a valuable lesson from the lawsuit. But, in addition to the learning around diversity, another great learning for us was that we had no documented proof, when it came to the lawsuit efforts. We did not measure the growth and development of minorities and women at the company.

After the Lawsuit

Alexis Herman, former US Secretary of Labour, chaired the Task Force that issued its first report in September 2002. Since the settlement, Coke implemented numerous systemic changes in its policies and procedures (see Exhibit 1) with measurable results (see Exhibit 2). Although the report was generally positive, the task force cited key areas that needed additional work: identification of employees for senior management positions and improvement in the perceptions of minority employees that their career opportunities are comparable to those of White employees. Currently, 'about a third of Coke's employees are minorities but most top executives are White. All minorities, the report said, are overrepresented in lower-paying support jobs.

The Task Force also chided the Corporation for missing opportunities to diversify the board of directors, which was then composed of nine White Man, two white women and one

African-American man. In 2002, when board membership was expanded from 12 to 14, two White men were selected. 'The company failed to consult with the Task Force which undermined the diversity management efforts and suggested lack of sensitivity to diversity goals.'

Shortly after the report was published, CEO Daft wrote a memo to employees that said, 'There is still work to do. Our commitment to diversity is a journey not an endpoint. Diversity is not an initiative; it is fundamental element of our business success'. In 2002, Coke began a five-year $800 million supported diversity programme. That year alone $181 million worth of goods and services were purchased from women- and minority-owned businesses. In 2003, Coke extended health benefits to same-sex domestic partners and named the first Hispanic female, Maria Elina Lagomasino, as CEO of JP Morgan Bank, to its board of directors. Coca-Cola is currently ranked number 25 on *Fortune* magazine's list of best companies for diversity and at number 18 on diversity Inc, 's survey of the top 50 companies for diversity (Dest, personal communication, November 5, 2003).

However, Coke's public relations problems with diversity were far from over, particularly about Cola's commitment to diversity in terms of the company's minority supplier programme which has been adversely commented in the press. At 2002 annual shareholders meeting some African-American employees protested because they believed that Blacks remained unrepresented in the top corporate ranks, got fired more often and were still paid less than the White employees. 'Protesters handed out material claiming that 16% of the Coke's workforce is Black but that Blacks have just 1.5% of the top jobs (White, 2002, E03). In May of the same year, some employees in Texas accused Coke of repackaging nearly out-of-date soda, making it down and then reselling it in minority neighbourhoods since 1993. Coca-Cola's management denied the allegation.

On May 24, 2002, the Coca-Cola Company, in a conciliation agreement with the US Department of Labour agreed to pay $8.1 million as back pay to over 2000 female employees. The agreement followed an audit of Federal Contract Compliance, which enforces federal rules against discrimination at companies holding government contracts. The audit revealed disparities between male and female employees between 1998 to 2000 (Bean, 2002).

EXHIBIT 1

1. Established uniform process for employee reviews.
2. Required that all job postings attract at least three candidates, one of whom must be a woman or a minority.
3. Implemented mandatory diversity training for managers and employees.
4. Conducted human resource audits and adverse impact analyses.
5. Tied performance appraisals and compensation for managers to their effectiveness in performance management.
6. Implemented a uniform compensation system based on job-related matters, including a market-based compensation structure, a common review date and additional compensation training for managers.

7. Established a mentoring programme.
8. Initiated executive briefings for senior management concerning diversity strategies.
9. Implemented a 'Solutions' programme that included an ombudsman and a hot line to resolve employee disputes.

EXHIBIT 2

Key Findings from the First Annual Report of the Task Force

- Of the 6,864 non-hourly Coke employees, 30% are minorities, up 4% since 12/00. Two thirds of the minorities are African-Americans.
- In the first 6 months of 2002, White men were promoted at the rate of 4.7%, women at 5%, and minorities at 5.7%; of the 301 new hires 29% were minorities, and 55% were women.
- Minorities make up only 20% of the workforce at the executive level and are overrepresented at 47% among the lowest-paid support personnel.

INTRODUCTION

Walk into Malik's Bakery in New York and you might think you have entered the United Nations building. In the kitchen are bakers, Hoans from Vietnam, Ideleso Oliver from Cuba, Joe Vigh from Rumania. Workers on the front counters are two women, one from Germany and the other from the Czech Republic. The popular bakery is owned and operated by Lea Malik, a native of Hungary. Like Malik's Bakery, most companies in the U.S. have a multicultural workforce and most international organizations are becoming highly diversified and multicultural.

Diversity is a challenge that has the potential to be a positive or negative influence on an organization. Ignoring the issue will drain an organization of its most vital resources. In order that diversity is valued and utilised, its knowledge must be combined to change the mindset and organizational policies and practices. While it is a fact that diversity will become increasingly present, it becomes all the more important to capitalise it as an organizational asset.

Minorities represent over one quarter of American workforce and this is projected to increase substantially in the future. Hispanic population is one of the fastest growing groups in the U.S. and is replacing African-Americans as the second largest ethnic group. Within next 50 years in the U.S. only 14% will be African-Americans, and 8% will be Asian-Americans. By 2060, non-Hispanic Whites will be a minority. Further, women now represent 50% of the paid workforce compared to just 20% a few decades ago. Similarly percentage of aged people (above 50 years) is increasing in every country.

There are many other dimensions of diversity existing in organizations. Managers need to understand how the social environment affects employees' beliefs about work and they must have the communication skills to enhance self-esteem in members of diverse work groups.

THE CONCEPT OF DIVERSITY

We discriminate between people in many respects of our life and work and this leads to 'stereotyping'. Stereotyping tends to make 'rigid judgements' about others that ignore the specific person and the current situation. Stereotyping can lead to prejudices, which are judgements about others that reinforce beliefs about superiority and inferiority. The dimensions on which people are discriminated are many. They can be classified as primary and secondary as shown in Fig. 13.1. The primary categories – gender, ethnicity, race, sexual orientation and mental/physical qualities represent those factors that are either inborn or exert extra influence on early socialisation. These factors make up the essence of who we are as human beings. They define us to others and others react to us because of them. These factors define us to ourselves. They are enduring aspects of our personality. Secondary dimensions are those features that we learn or have some control over throughout our lives, such as education, marital status, religion, etc.

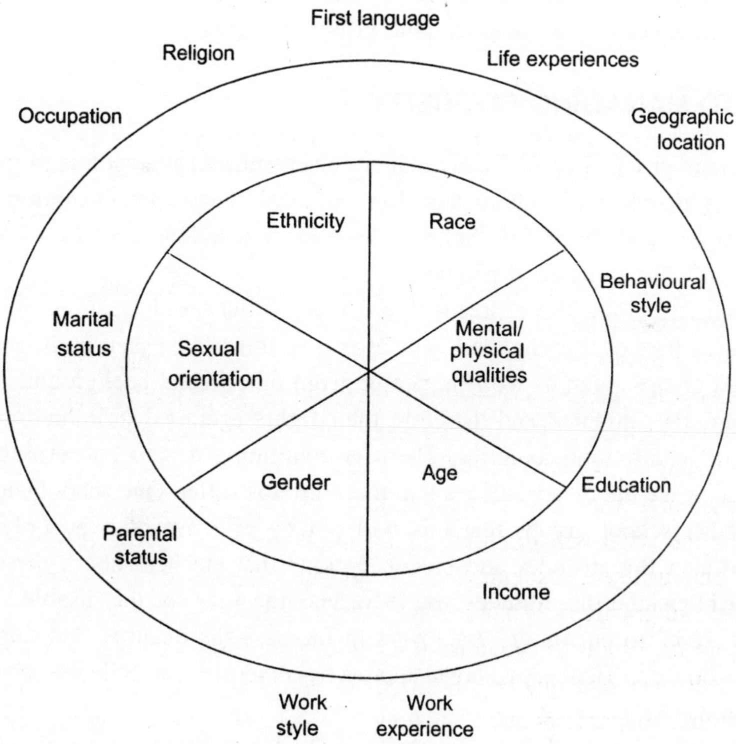

Fig. 13.1 The Primary and Secondary Dimensions of Diversity

Employees are discriminated in many ways, particularly in the selection process, promotions, rewards, postings and day-to-day dealings on the basis of the above-mentioned dimensions. Certain forms of discrimination are acceptable but others are not, and have been made unlawful. It is, therefore, necessary to arrive at some definition of diversity.

In its broadest context, diversity is defined as 'recognising, appreciating, valuing, and utilising the unique talents and contributions of all individuals' regardless of age, career experience, colour, communication style, culture, disability, education level or background, employee status, ethnicity, family status, function, gender, age, language, management style, marital status, physical appearance, race, religion, sexual orientation, thinking style, speed of learning and comprehension, etc.

Every organization must measure and monitor its diversity scorecard by looking at its workforce profile. This can be done by answering following questions:

1. What is the ethnic, racial, religious and gender composition of the workplace?
2. What is the age span of the workforce?
3. What percentage of top management are women, minorities or those who are disabled?
4. How do these percentages change when they are applied to middle management, first-line supervisors or staff?
5. Is the cultural or ethnic distribution the same from top to bottom in the organization?
6. What is the turnover rate by demographic group and age?

APPROACHES TO MANAGING DIVERSITY

There are always certain groups in any society that are discriminated against due to the prejudices and preconceptions of the people with whom they have to deal. These preconceptions are sometimes verbalised, but often not, and the people holding these preconceptions may well be unaware of the way that they see and judge things and people.

However, verbalised or not, these preconceived ideas influence the actions of the people who hold them, and the way they deal with others. The effects of this can be seen in the employment arena where disadvantaged groups, such as women, people from other racial backgrounds, disabled people and older people, are discriminated and therefore their rights against discrimination in employment are protected by law in different countries. There is continuing debate concerning the action that should be taken to alleviate the disadvantages that these groups suffer. One school supports legislative action, while the other school argues that this will not be effective and the only way to change fundamentally is to alter the attitudes and preconceptions that are held about these groups. It was hoped that law would change the attitudes and there was the year for the disabled in 1981 and the 'opportunities year, 2000' to encourage employers to increase the quantity and quality of women's participation in the workforce. Hence, two broad approaches emerged, one called as 'equal opportunities' and the other as 'managing diversity'.

Equal opportunities approaches have sought to influence behaviour through legislation so that discrimination is prevented. It has been characterised by a moral and ethical stance promoting the rights of all members of society. Management of diversity approaches, on the other hand, stresses the economic and business case for equal treatment, offering benefits and advantages for the employer if they invest in ensuring that everyone in the organization is equally valued and given the opportunity to develop their potential and make a maximum contribution. The financial benefits of retaining staff, which might otherwise leave due to lack of career development or the image of the organization as a good employer that may suffer or the value of different employee perspectives, etc. can be stressed.

The two approaches are compared in the following table.

Table 13.1 Comparison between 'Equal Opportunities' and 'Management of Diversity' Approaches

Aspect	*Equal Opportunities*	*Managing Diversity*
Purpose	Reduce discrimination	Utilise employee potential to maximum advantage
Case argued	Moral and ethical	Business case – improve profitability
Whole responsibility	Personnel Department	All managers
Focuses on	Groups	Individuals
Perspective	Dealing with different needs of different groups	Integrated
Benefits for employees	Opportunities improved for disadvantaged groups, primarily through setting targets	Opportunities improved for employees
Focus on management activity	Recruitment	Managing
Remedies	Changing system and practices	Changing the culture

A conceptual model of the relationship between quality of opportunity and managing and valuing diversity is developed by LaFasto (1993), as shown in Table 13.2. Here different types of organizations

Table 13.2 Differentiating Organizations: How they Value Diversity

Complying Type or Monolithic Organization	*Managing Diversity Plural Organization*	*Valuing Diversity or Multicultural Type*
Reacting to the pressure not to the problem, let alone the opportunity. Compliance and obligation. Keep the law out of our business. Situational ethics. Avoid legal consequences.	Diversity is important as a competitive business practice and we are here to run a business. We need to attract the best people. Job stability/continuity is important to success. Turnover costs money.	Individual self-esteem is important to performance. People who feel comfortable in their work environment are more likely to feel confident in their ability to contribute. Business, social, and moral values are one and same. Job is part of life and not vice versa. The more productive people are those who feel valued for who they are. Productive people= high performance organisation

Source: Lafasto (1992), *Baxter Health Care Corporation: Diversity in Human Resource Management*, p. 28. John Wily and Sons Ltd.

are termed as 'monolithic', plural and multicultural according to the way they look at and manage diversity. Ellis Sonnefield describes managing diversity as, 'The challenge of meeting the needs of culturally diverse workforce and of sensitising the workforce and managers to differences associated with gender, race, age and nationality in an attempt to maximise the potential productivity of all employees'. In this context, one should monitor the level of intergroup conflicts that is related to socio-cultural group differences, the group identity strength – the extent to which a person feels strong and quality of inter-group communication (frequency and effectiveness). It is also desired to measure increased rate of productivity from diverse team groups and also increased rate of innovation.

Based on these observations one can identify three types of organizations: (1) complying type or monolithic ones, (2) managing diversity or plural types and (3) valuing diversity or multicultural type. Based on this, LaFasto (1992) has brought out the following conceptual model:

The characteristics of multicultural organizations are:

1. A culture that fosters and values cultural differences.
2. Pluralism as an acculturation process.
3. Full structural integration.
4. Full integration of the informal networks.
5. An absence of institutionalised cultural bias in human resource management systems and practices.
6. A minimum in inter-group conflict due to the proactive management of diversity.

THE CULTURE QUESTION

The roots of discrimination go very deep and it is culture-conditioned. Culture is important in two ways in managing diversity: first, in respect of the whole range of approaches to managing diversity and the way an organization treats its people. Equal opportunity approaches tend to concentrate on behaviour and, to a small extent, on attitudes, whereas managing diversity approaches recognise the need to go beyond this. So changing the culture to one which treats individuals as individuals and supports them in developing their potential is critical, although the difficulties of culture change make this a very difficult task.

Second, depending on the approach to the management of diversity, the existing culture of various groups within the organization comes into play. Masreliez-Steen (1989) explains how men and women have different perceptions, interpretations of reality, languages and ways of solving problems, which, if properly used, can be beneficial to the whole organization, as they are complementary. She described women as having a collectivist culture where they form groups, avoid the spotlight, see rank as unimportant and have few but close contacts. Alternatively men have an individualist culture, they form teams, develop a profile, enjoy competition and have many superficial contacts. The result is that men and women behave differently, often fail to understand each other and experience 'culture clash'. However, the difference is about how things are done and not what is achieved. The fact that women have different cultures with different weaknesses and strengths means that they need managing and developing in a different way. They need different forms of support and coaching. A similar argument applies to different ethnic groups and it is generally from this perspective that Jackson et al. (1993) proposes a series of stages and levels that organizations go through in becoming a multicultural organization.

Level 1, stage 1: the exclusionary organization

This organization maintains the power of dominant groups in the organization, and excludes others.

Level 1, stage 2: The club

This club still excludes people but in a less explicit way. Some members of minority groups are allowed to join as long as they conform to pre-defined norms.

Level 2, stage 3: The compliance organization

This organization recognises that there are other perspectives, but doesn't want to do anything to rock the boat. It may actively recruit minority groups at the bottom of the organization and make some token appointments.

Level 2, stage 4: The affirmative action organization

This organization is committed to eliminating discrimination and encourages employees to examine their attitudes and think differently. There is strong support for the development of new employees from the minority groups.

Level 3, stage 5: The redefining organization

The redefining organization is not satisfied with being anti-racist and so examines all it does and its culture to see the impact of these on its diverse multicultural workforce. It develops and implements policies to distribute power among all groups.

Level 3, stage 6: The multicultural organization

This organization reflects the contribution and interests of all its diverse members in everything it does and espouses. All members are full participants of the organization and there is recognition of a broader social responsibility to educate others outside the organization and to have an impact on the external operation.

PROCESS OF MANAGING DIVERSITY

Ross and Schneider (1992) advocate a strategic approach to managing diversity based on their conception of the difference between seeking equal opportunity and managing diversity which is:

- Internally driven, not externally imposed.
- Focused on individuals rather than groups.
- Focused on the total culture of the organization rather than just on the systems used.
- The responsibility of all in the organization and not just of the personnel function.

Their process involves the following steps:

1. Diagnosis of the current situation in terms of statistics, policy and culture, and looking both at issues and causes.
2. Setting aims that involve the business case for equal opportunities, identifying the critical role of commitment from the top of the organization, and a vision of what the organization would look like if it successfully managed diversity. For example, the vision statement of 3M clearly shows the framework of the company to manage diversity. The statement reads: 'Valuing uniqueness while respecting differences, maximising individual potential and synerging collective talent and experiences for the growth and success of 3M.'

3. Spreading the ownership. This is a critical stage in which awareness needs to be raised via a process of encouraging people to question their attitudes and preconceptions. Awareness needs to be raised in all employees at all levels, especially managers, and it needs to be clear that diversity is not something owned by the personnel function.
4. Policy development comes after awareness-raising, as it enables a contribution to be made from all in the organization; new systems need to be changed via involvement and not through imposition on the unwilling.
5. Managing the transition needs to involve a range of training initiatives. Positive action programmes, specifically designed for minority groups, may be used to help them understand the culture of the organization and acquire essential skills, policy implementation programmes, particularly focusing on selection, appraisal, development and coaching, further awareness training and training to identify cultural diversity and manage different cultures and across different cultures.
6. Managing the programme to sustain momentum. This involves a champion, not necessarily from the personnel function, but someone who continues in his or her previous organization role in addition. Also the continued involvement of senior managers is important, together with the trade union. Harnessing initiatives that come up through departments and organising support networks for disadvantaged groups are key at this stage. Ross and Schneider also recommend measuring achievements in terms of business benefit – better relationships with

Guidelines for organisational change for managing and valuing cultural diversity

Leadership	*Research/ Measurement*	*Education*	*Culture and Management Practices*	*Follow-up*
Top management Commitment and support. Steering and advisory groups Communication strategy	Comprehensive organisational Assessment. Baseline data Benchmarking	Awareness training development of inhouse training. Orientation programmes Advanced training	Recruitment, orientation, Performance appraisal, compensation, promotion, training and development to be transformed	Evaluation process. Accountability Ensuring continuous Improvement

Fig.13.2 Framework for Managing Change for Diversity Management

(*Source*: Adopted from *Cultural Diversity in Organizations, Theory, Research* and *Practices*, San Francisco: Barrett-Koehler, 1993, p. 3-10).

customers, improvements in productivity and profitability, for example, which need to be communicated to all employees.

It is clear from the above that training for diversity needs to be far more than a one-day event. They recommend a series of workshops, which allow time for individuals to think, check their assumptions and reassess between training sessions. Key issues that need tackling in arranging training are ensuring that the facilitator has the appropriate skills; carefully considering the participants mix; deciding whether the training should be voluntary or mandatory; being prepared to cope with any backlash from previously advantaged groups who now feel threatened; and being prepared for the fact that training may reinforce stereotypes. They argue that training has enormous potential benefits, but that there are risks involved.

Organizations have a long way to go before getting to the stage of really valuing diversity and in order for them to continue to strive it is important to reinforce the business advantages. Thompson and DiTomaso (reported by Ellis and Sonnfield 1994) put it very well:

> Multicultural management perspective fosters more innovative and creative decision-making, satisfying work environments, and better products because all people who have a contribution to make are encouraged to be involved in a meaningful way....More information, more points of view, more ideas and reservations are better than fewer.

In bringing about this organizational change of mindset, the framework shown in Fig. 13.2 is useful

CORPORATE PRACTICES

HP believes that a diverse workforce encourages creativity and innovation. It helps build an exciting, stimulating work environment and provides competitive advantage in the acquisition of new businesses. HP follows following policies:

- HP has a special committee called Diversity and Inclusion Leadership Committee, made up of senior business leaders from around the world. The committee meets regularly and reviews HP's progress in the area.
- Regular workshops are organized in order to make the workforce aware of the various policies.
- The best work environment policy gives all employees responsibility for contributing to a positive, productive work environment, free of discrimination, harassment and offensive behaviour.
- The equal opportunity policy states HP will not discriminate against any employee for employment or promotion because of gender, age, race, ancestry, religion, national origin, and physical or mental disability.
- HP encourages employees to report any suspected case of discrimination or harassment, either by using open door policy or by contacting Employees Relations Executive. All allegations are investigated promptly and appropriate action is taken.

Deutsche Bank

The bank's annual report informs external stakeholders of the progress and acheivements in relation to diversity. A diversity training programme has been developed to provide managers with the necessary tools to build, retain and develop diverse teams, which also reinforces the business case for diversity management and encourages managers to be more proactive in creating an inclusive work environment. In addition, the bank runs 'managing and working with respect courses' for all employees and managers.

Egon Zehender

It is the world's fifth best HR consultancy organization. It has been a leading consultant for managing diversity at various organizations. It considers managing diversity is imperative for longer-term success. The Egon team have recently reviewed some of their practices and found seven key factors for managing diversity effectively, which are as follows:

- A clear articulation of the business case for diversity.
- A clear understanding of the current situation.
- Diversity is championed from the top.
- Diversity leadership is a stand-alone function at senior level assisted by HR function.
- Programmes are focused on culture change rather than just redressing imbalances.
- Wide employee engagement and involvement is achieved.
- Management processes, measuring goals and incentive systems underpin the change.

Review Questions

1. Why diversity management is acquiring so much importance in global business management? What are the benefits that diversity can provide and what problems it can create for organizations?
2. Explain the concept of diversity management and what are its primary and secondary dimensions? Do you think that legal course is the best option? Discuss.
3. What are the various approaches to manage diversity. Compare them.
4. Explain in detail, with corporate examples, how the organization culture that values the diversity at all levels can be changed and sustained?
5. Discuss the process of managing diversity effectively in multinational organizations. What role HR function can play in this?

Assignment

1. Select any three large companies and research about gender discrimination or any other type of discrimination being present and suggest how this can be mitigated for better performance.
2. Make guidelines for organizational change for managing and valuing cultural diversity.

Chapter

14

Conducting Cross-Cultural Negotiations

LEARNING OBJECTIVES

After studying this chapter, you will be able to:

- *Understand the anatomy of negotiations*
- *Prepare for international negotiations*
- *Plan for important cross-cultural negotiations*
- *Conduct successful international negotiations*
- *Learn negotiation styles of major cultural groups and countries.*

OPENING CASE
Cross-Cultural Negotiations within the United States

I had a client in West Virginia who bought from me for several years. He had a family business that he'd started in a small town with his grandfather, and it had now grown to be the major employer in the town. We had developed quite a close relationship. Every few months, I would make a trip up from North Carolina to see him, knowing after a while that he would need to place an order with me as lung as I spaced our visits out every few months. When we got together, at first we would talk about everything but business, catching up with each other. I would ask him about his life, the business, his family, the town. ete., and he would ask me about my work and the company and life in the big city in North Carolina when I lived and .worked. Once we'd caught up with each other. we would get down to some business, and this was often after lunch. Each and every time, it would take a few hours of this and that, but I'd always leave with all order, and it was always a pleasant break, at least for me, from my usual hectic pace.

One day I phoned in preparation I'm my next trip, to see if he would be in, to arrange a convenient day, and he told me that he'd like me to meet a friend of his next time. I was up there to visit him. His friend, lie said, was interested in some of the things my company was selling, and he thought I should meet lent, Of course I was delighted, and we arranged a convenient day for the three of us to meet.

When I arrived at my client's office, his friend Carl was already there. We were very casually introduced, and my client began explaining Carl's work, and how he thought What my company sold could be useful to him. Carl then took over and spoke a little about what he did, and I thought for a moment that we were going to go straight into business talk. However, in just a few moments, the conversation between the three of us quickly turned back to discussions of life in town, North Carolina, our respective families, and personal interests. It turned out that Carl liked to hunt, and he and my client began regaling me with stories of their hunting adventures. I'd hunted a little, and shared my stories with them. One thing led to another, and soon we were talking about vacations, the economy, baseball – you name it.

Occasionally, we would make a brief journey back to the business at hand, but it always seemed to be in conjunction with the small talk, like how the tools we manufactured were or were not as precise as the mechanisms on the tuns we used for hunting things like that. I realized that quite a lot of Information about our mutual work, my company, their needs, and their work was being exchanged in all this, even though business was never directly addressed. I remember the first few meetings my client and I had with each other many years ago – how we learned about each other this way then, too. I was struck with how quaint it felt now, how different it was from the way I usually had to sell and yet how much

Well our discussions went on this way through the rest of the mornin, weaving some business back and forth through the larger contexty of informal chit-chat about each other and our lives. Just before lunch, my client learned back and began what seemed to be a kind of informal summary of who I was and what I did and how what I did seemed to him to be just the thing that Carl and his company could use. Carl agreed and my client asked him almost on my behalf, how much he wanted to order, and Carl thought for a moment and gave me the biggest order I ever got from west Virginia. 'Now that that's done.' my client said, 'how about some lunch?' We all went to the same place we always go to when I'm in West Virginia talking about life and things and some business. By midafternoon I said I had to be heading home. We all agreed to stay in touch. We've been in touch ever since, and now I've got two clients to visit whenever I'm in West Virginia.

What Makes International Negotiation Different?

Phatak and Habib (1996) suggest that two overall contexts have an influence on international negotiations; the environmental context and the immediate context (see Fig. 16.1). The *environmental context* includes environmental forces that neither negotiator controls that influence the negotiation. The *immediate context* includes factors over which negotiators appear to have some control. Understanding the role of factors in both the environmental and the immediate contexts is important to grasping the complexity of international negotiation processes and outcomes.

Environmental Context

Salacuse (1988) identified six factors in the environmental context that make international negotiations more challenging then domestic negotiations: political and legal pluralism, international economics, foreign governments and bureaucracies, instability, ideology, and culture. (Culture has received by far the most attention by those examining international negotiation and it is discussed in a separate section later in this chapter) Phatak and Habib (1966) have suggested an additional factor external stakeholders. These factors can act to limit or constrain organization that operate internationally, and it is important that negotiator understand and appreciate their effects.

Political and Legal Pluralism

Firms conducting business in different countries are working with different leagal and political systems. There may be implication for taxes that an organization pays labor codes or standards that must be met and different codes of contract law and standards of enforcement (e.g. case law versus common law versus no functioning legal system). In addition, political considerations may enhance of detract from business negotiations in various countyries at different times. For instance, the open business environment in the former Soviet republic in the 1990s is quite different than the closed environment of the 1960s, and concluding business in China today is quite different than even 10 years ago.

International Economics

The exchange value of international currencies naturally fluctuates and this factor must be considered when negotiating in different countries. In which currency will the agreement he

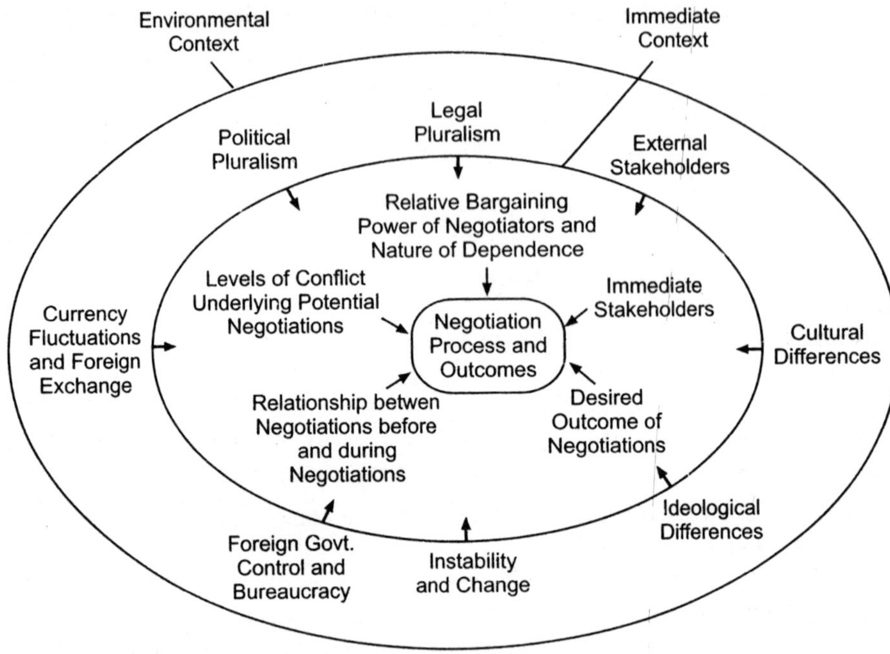

Fig. 14.1 The Contexts of International Negotiations

Source: Adapted from A.V. Phatak and M.H. Habib. 'The Dynamic of International Business Negotiations.' Business Horizon 39 (1996). pp. 30-38 and from J.W. Salacuse. 'Making Deals in Strange Plàces: A Beginners Guide to International Business Negotiation. – Negotiation Journal 4 (1988). pp. 5-13.

made? The risk is typically greater for the party who must pay in the other country's currency (Salscuse, 1988. The less stable the currency, the greater the risk for both party. In addition, any change in the value of a currency (upper or downward) can significantly affect the value of the agreement for both parties, changing a mutually valuable deal into a windfall profit for one and a large loss for the other. Many countries also control the currency flowing across their border. Frequently, purchases within these countries may be made only with hard currencies that are brought into the country by foreign parties, and domestic organizations are unable to purchase foreign products or negotiate outcomes that require payment in foreign currencies.

Foreign Government and Bureaucracies

Countries differ in the extent to which the government regulates industries and organizations. From in the United States are relatively free from government intervention, although some industries are more heavily regulated than other (e.g. power generation, defense), and some states have tougher environmental regulations than others. Generally, business negotiations in the United States occur without government approval, however, and the parties to a negotiation decide whether or not to engage in an agreement based on business reasons alone. In contrast, the governments of many developing and (former) communist countries closely supervise import and joint ventures. (see Brouthers and Bamossy, 1997; Derong and Faure, 1995; Pfouts, 1994), and frequently an agency of the government has a monopoly in dealing with foreign organizations (Salacuse, 1988). In addition, political considerations, such as the effect of the negotiation on the government treasury and the general economy of the country, may influence the negotiations more heavily than what Western businesses would consider legitimate business reasons.

Instability

Businesses negotiating within North America are accustomed to a degree of stability that is not present in many areas of the world. Instability may take many form, including a lack of resources that American commonly except during business negotiations (paper, electricity, computers): shortages of other goods and services (food, reliable transportation, portable water); and political instability (coups, sudden shifts in government policy, major currency revaluations). The challenge for international negotiators is to anticipate changes accurately and with enough lead time to adjust for their consequencs clauses in their contracts that allow easy cancellation or neutral arbitration, and consider purchasing insurance policies to guarantee cotnract provisions. The advise presumes that contract will be honoured and that specific contract clauses will be culturally acceptable to the other party.

Ideology

Negotiators within the United States generally share a common ideology about the benefits of individualism and captalism. American believe strongly in individual right, the superiority of private investment, and the importance of making a profit in business (Salacuse, 1988). Negotiators from other countries do not always share this ideology. For example, negotiators from some countries (e.g. China, France) may instead stress group right as more important than individual rights and public investment as a better allocation of resources than private investment; they may also have different prescriptions for earning and sharing profit. Ideological clashes increase the communication challenges in international negotiation in the broadest sense because the parties may disagree at the most fundamental level about what is being negotiated.

Culture

One does not have to leave the United States to see the influecne of culture on negotiations (see Box 13.1). Clearly it is challenging when the fundamental beliefs about what negotiation is and how it occurs are different. The critical role that culture place in international and other cross-cultural negotiation will be discussed at length later in this chapter.

INTRODUCTION

Every step in international business involves negotiations, be that between the governments of various countries and multinationals to allow to operate in their territories, or suppliers and customers from different cultures or between unions and employees working in subsidiaries or factories located in different countries. No skill is more required in international managers than negotiating skills.

Governments often impose restrictions on repatriation of profits and ownership of raw material sources, and require employment of local people and use of indigenous inputs. On the other hand, MNCs have resources, technology and management skills and they want tax concessions and protection of their patents and technology. Hence, the two must interact and negotiate with each other to settle terms. In this equation, the local partner and the government of MNCs home-country also participates to influence business outcomes. All this requires intense negotiations and diplomacy between different players. Hence, negotiation and diplomatic skills are essential qualities of international managers.

Negotiation skills are also required when seeking to enter a market via an agent or distributor, setting up sales network, establishing a joint venture or a production facility as well as licensing a technology or seeking technology transfer. Negotiation plays a key role in mergers and acquisitions. In international diplomacy, major breakthroughs, such as the signing of Euro tunnel agreement or the Sino-Soviet border agreement, which took several years and many rounds at different levels, are made only through negotiations. Failure to appreciate how deals are made through negotiations and diplomacy may seriously jeopardise the interest of a firm. It is also important to know how different societies and cultures influence this process. This is the purpose of this chapter.

NEGOTIATION AND DIPLOMACY

Negotiation is a dialogue between two or more parties, who are trying to work out a solution to their problem. This interpersonal or inter-group process can occur at a personal level, as well as at a corporate or international (diplomatic) level. Negotiations typically take place because the parties wish to create something new that neither could do on his or her own, or to resolve a problem or to make a deal with each other.

The parties acknowledge that there is a conflict of interest between them and think that they can use some form of influence to get a better deal, particularly when they have interlinked goals that they cannot attain independently. The nature of interdependence will have a major impact on the nature of their relationship, the way negotiations are conducted, and the outcome of these negotiations. Mutual adjustment is one of the key causes of the changes that occur during negotiation. Both parties know that they can each influence the other's outcomes. The effective negotiator attempts to understand how people will adjust and readjust their positions during negotiations, based on what the other party does and is expected to do.

The parties have to exchange information and make an effort to influence each other. As negotiations evolve, each side proposes changes to the other party's position and makes changes to its own proposals. This process of give and take is necessary if a settlement is to be reached. If one party makes several proposals that are rejected, and the other party makes no alternate proposals, the first party may break off negotiations. Parties typically will not concede much if they sense that other party is not willing to compromise. The parties must work towards a solution that takes into account each person's requirements and optimises the outcomes for both.

THE ANATOMY OF NEGOTIATION PROCESS

It is necessary to look at negotiation process and techniques before moving to cross-cultural considerations in the negotiation process. Negotiations involve two levels – one is the rational decision-making level, the other is at the psychological and social levels. Psychological and social elements are affected by culture, therefore, negotiations are as much to do with the psychological as with the rational.

Failure to optimally resolve the psychological factors that affect negotiation will include such elements as attitudes, persuasion styles, goals and expectations, perceptions and misperceptions, the need to avoid the conflict, the need to win, and so on. The ripe moment for a solution is when a deadlock seems likely and the costs of not reaching the agreement are rising for both parties. Then, an alternative emerges for achieving the original goals, and the likely cost of lost opportunity is so high that the alternative is irresistible.

PARAMETERS OF NEGOTIATION

It is important to carefully decide:

1. Where to negotiate?
2. When to negotiate?
3. Who negotiates?
4. Who has authority to decide?
5. Why negotiate?
6. How to negotiate?
7. How much time is needed for negotiations?

In theory, negotiating in one's homeland gives territorial advantage, including consultation with others in one's company and availability of information. However, meeting at the negotiating party's premises gives you insights into how they manage their operations and their capacities. It also enables one to hide from other company members should one prefer to be anonymous. Meeting on neutral territory or alternately at each other's place makes a compromise.

The timing of holding the negotiation is also critical. The parties should meet when the problem is ripe and both parties need a solution. One should avoid holidays and religious festivals, such as month of Ramadhan in Arabia, Chinese lunar New Year or Christmas in the West. Timing of the negotiation also involves planning the schedule, how often should the parties meet, and at what interval.

It is also important to estimate how much time is required for conducting negotiations. Decision-making in collectivist cultures takes longer because a consensus has to be built among interested parties within the firm. Sometimes, after a consensus has been built, negotiators may be unwilling to make radical concessions, which means creating a new consensus. Negotiators from China often demand a large amount of technical information and progress may be delayed due to this. Ghauri (1988) concludes from his study of deals between Swedish, Indian and Nigerian firms that negotiations with unfamiliar parties takes more than double the time taken with familiar parties. Time usually spent by U.S. and Japanese negotiators on various activities during negotiations, is given below:

PLANNING FOR THE NEGOTIATION

It is helpful to plan the negotiation. Know whether you are in a win-win or win-lose situation. Be sure of your goals, positions and underlying interests; then figure out the best resolution, a fair and reasonable deal, and a minimally acceptable deal. What information do you have and what do you need? What are your competitive advantages and disadvantages? What are the other's advantages and disadvantages? Give some thought to your strategy.

It is important to be clear on what is important to you. Be clear about your own as well as other party's real goals and issues. Many negotiations fail because people are so worried about being taken advantage of that they forget their own needs. People who lose track of their own goals will break off negotiations even if they have achieved their needs, because they become more concerned with whether the other side has 'won'.

It is helpful to have a min-max strategy. Have a 'walk-away' position. When entering a negotiation or conflict resolution, make sure you have answers to these questions:

1. What is the minimum I can accept to resolve the conflict?
2. What is the maximum that I can ask for without appearing outrageous?
3. What is the maximum I can give away?
4. What is the least I can offer without appearing outrageous?
5. What answers the other person is likely to have to these questions?

It is important to know your competitive advantage, your strengths and weaknesses as well as those of your competitor.

In most conflict resolution or negotiation situations, you will have a continuing relationship with the other party, so it is important to leave the situation with both sides feeling they have 'won'. It is very important that other person doesn't feel that he or she has 'lost'. When the other person feels he has 'lost', the results are often lack of commitment to the agreement or even worse, retaliation. The most common failure is the inability of negotiating parties to search for the integrative potential in a negotiating problem. Beneath hardened positions are often common or shared interests.

PREPARATION FOR NEGOTIATION

All negotiations particularly international ones, demand planning and preparation. Preparation includes collecting information about the negotiation context, which include:

- Taxation and Legal data: The transaction may be taxed in more than one country and contracts may be subject to two or more legal systems.
- Commercial data: Payment terms including an advance amount desired, guarantees, installation and trial-run, supplier's responsibility for sub-contractor, acquisition of land, obtaining permission and clearances such as environment clearance and so on.
- Financial and Economic data: Size of the economy, speed of growth, inflation, investment policies, subsidies and tax incentives, banking system, financial security, repatriation of earnings.
- Infrastructure data: Size of population, other demographic data, road and rail systems and other communications.

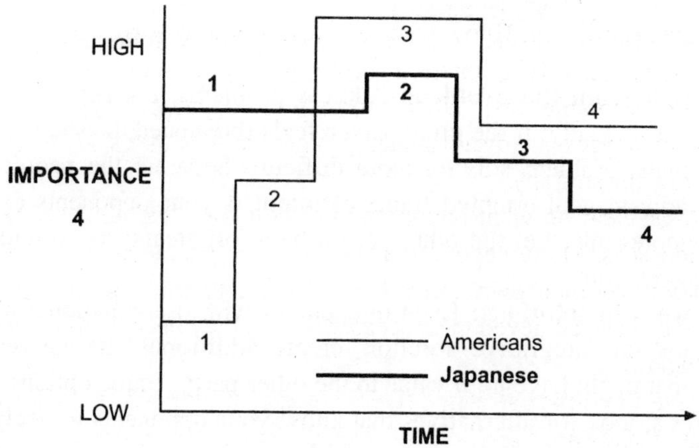

1 = Non-Task Time (Building Relationship) 2 = Information Exchange
3 = Influence Building 4 = Conclusion & Agreement

Fig. 14.1 Relative Importance given to Different Stages of Negotiation by US & Japanese Businesses

- Labour force data: Skills available, education standards, training facilities.
- Political data: Who has power and who supports and oppose your plan at national, regional and local levels.
- Trade unions: How they will react to negotiation settlements.
- Cultural data: What the other party considers important.

From this diagram it is clear that Japanese's assign very high importance to relationship building and take longer time than Americans. On the other hand, Americans assign high importance to influence building through arguments and take longer time. They also give high importance to agreement drawing matters, while Japanese give it low importance and less time.

Profiling

It pays to build up a profile of the company with which one is negotiating. This requires information about

- Ownership and legal status; history
- Equity structure, current financial circumstances
- Size, its markets and distribution network
- Strategic interests and scope, suppliers, customers, partners, competitors, industrial relations and technology
- Organization structure, systems and culture
- General/national structures, systems, culture.

This profile should be updated from time to time.

GUIDELINES FOR SUCCESSFUL NEGOTIATIONS

For conducting successful negotiations, it is important to practice following guidelines:

1. **Separate people from the problem:** Address problems, not personalities. Avoid attacking your opponent personally; if the other person feels threatened, he/she will defend his/her self-esteem and make problem solving more difficult. Separate the people from the problem. Maintain a rational, goal-oriented frame of mind; if your opponents attack you personally, don't react emotionally. Let the other person blow off steam; try to understand the problem behind the aggression.
2. **Emphasise win-win solutions:** Even in apparent win-lose situations, win-win solutions are possible. Look for integrative solution, create additional alternatives, such as low-cost concessions that might have high value to the other party; frame options in terms of the other party's interests; look for alternatives that allow your opponents to declare victory.
3. **Find underlying interests:** A key to success is finding the 'integrative' issues; often they can be found in underlying interests. We are used to identifying our own interests, but a critical element in negotiation is to understand the other person's underlying interests and needs. With probing and exchange of information we can find the commonalities and minimise differences. Understanding these interests is the key to 'integrative bargaining' to find a win-win solution.

   A key part in finding common interests is problem identification. It is important to define the problem in a way that is mutually acceptable to both sides. This involves depersonalising the problem so as not to raise the defensiveness of the other person.
4. **Use an objective standard:** Keep the result based on some objective standard. Make your negotiated decision based on principles and results, not emotions or pressure. Find some objective criteria that both parties can use to evaluate alternatives, without succumbing to assertiveness or pressure.
5. **Understand the other party:** Often we tend to focus on our needs, our goals and our positions. To successfully negotiate and resolve conflict, it is important to focus also on the other person. We need to understand what the other's goals, needs, positions and underlying interests are. We need to think about the personality of the other person, how far we can push, and how open or concealed we should make our position. Acquire as much information about the other's interests and goals: what are the real needs verses wants; what constituencies must be appeased; what is his or her strategy? Be prepared to frame solutions in terms of his or her interests.
6. **Negotiation as a sequence of events:** A negotiation usually involves a number of steps including the exchange of proposals and counter proposals. The negotiators are expected to make offers and concessions in good faith. The goal here is not only to solve the problem, but also to gain information that will enable us to get a clear notion of what the true issues might be and how the 'opponent' sees reality. Through offers and counter offers there should be an information exchange that might yield a common definition of the problem.
7. **The intangibles:** Intangibles are often the key factors in many negotiations. Some of these intangibles are:

(1) Personalities: Be conscious of your personality, your needs and interpersonal style, as well as the other person's personality. This will play a key role in understanding yourself. For example, how much you trust the other person and how much you want to conceal or reveal depend upon your personality.
(2) Physical space: Sometimes where the negotiation takes place can be important. The negotiating space must be comfortable for both the parties.
(3) Time pressure: Will the time pressure affect the negotiation process adversely? If so, you need to change this variable.
(4) Who has the authority to decide: In many cultures the person who takes the final decision on whether or not to accept the other side's offer is typically the leader of the negotiating team. For instance, company owners in the high power distance cultures of Greece and Latin America wish to keep personal control and not delegate. Individualist Anglo negotiators insist that headquarters give them the power to accept or reject proposals.
(5) This, however, is not the case everywhere. The real decision-makers may be absent. In China, the technical representatives often contribute most to discussions, but distant bureaucrats make the decision.
(6) Goals The important questions to explore are: what they must achieve; what they hope to achieve and what they should like to achieve. Goals on level 1, are most crucial; those on level 3 least. How far does this list match your own goals, in terms of what you must achieve? Further you should decide, what you are most willing to concede in order to achieve your essential objectives and what you are moderately less willing and what you are least willing to concede.

CULTURAL INFLUENCE ON INTERNATIONAL NEGOTIATIONS

National cultures influence negotiation in ten ways:

1. **Definition of negotiation:** What is negotiable, and what occurs when we negotiate can differ greatly across cultures. For example, American tend to view negotiating as a competitive process of offers and counter offers, while the Japanese view the negotiation as an opportunity for information-sharing.
2. **Negotiation an opportunity:** Americans perceive negotiation opportunity as distributive, while most other cultures perceive it as an integrating opportunity. Different cultures, thus approach negotiations from different perspectives and expectations.
3. **Selection of negotiators:** Different cultures select their negotiators using different criteria. These criteria can include knowledge of the subject-matter being negotiated, seniority, family connection, gender, age, experience and status. Different cultures weigh these criteria differently, leading to varying expectations and approaches being adopted by negotiating teams.
4. **Protocol:** Cultures differ in the degree to which protocol between the two negotiating parties is considered important or need to be followed. Protocol includes addressing each other properly, dress code, how visiting cards should be exchanged, and so on.
5. **Communication:** Cultures influence how people communicate, both verbally and non-verbally. Some body language signals may be presumed as highly insulting in one culture while quite innocuous in another. For example, placing feet on the desk in U.S. signals power or relaxation;

in Saudi Arabia and Thailand it is highly insulting. It is important to learn to communicate properly in different cultures so as not to anger, annoy or insult them.

6. **Time sensitivity:** The importance of time varies greatly across different cultures. Some are very punctual while others are quite relaxed and flexible about it.
7. **Risk propensity:** Cultures vary in the extent to which they are willing to take risks. Some cultures such as India, produce bureaucratic, conservative decision-makers while other cultures produce entrepreneurial ones.
8. **Groups versus individuals:** Group oriented cultures such as Japan or China, take time to reach group consensus in taking important decisions or changing stand, while in individually oriented cultures, the responses will come from individuals.
9. **Nature of agreement:** Cultures influence both concluding agreements and on what form the negotiated agreement takes. In U.S., the agreements are very detailed and considered most important part of concluding the negotiation, while in other cultures, it is the relationship arrived which is more important than clauses on paper in the agreements.
10. **Emotionalism:** Cultures differ in the extent to which negotiators display emotions. These emotions may be used as tactics or they may be natural responses to varying situations arising in the negotiations.

These aspects have been discussed next, in detail in the context of different countries and cultures.

An American Returns Without a Deal

An American company sent its VP to finally negotiate a big contract in Saudi Arabia. He planned his visit meticulously including return journey and fixed appointments and meetings, etc. well in advance. He had taken with him all the required facts, presentations and contract copy to be signed. When he arrived, he found that things are not going as planned. Meetings are being constantly postponed, disturbed by phone calls and by constant interference from visitors. People were nearly resting and no one was serious to discuss the matter at hand. He considered that the Arabs are not interested in the deal, hence informed his company accordingly and returned as planned. The real thing was that the Arabian company was very much interested in the deal, but it was the holy period of Ramzan and hence people were fasting in the day and taking business lightly. No doubt, the Americans lost a big contract.

IMPORTANCE OF TRUST

Trust between business partners is all important. Without it, you are unlikely to enter into negotiations or agree to a settlement. You trust the other side when you believe in their good intentions. This means accepting that they will:

- Negotiate in good faith (it is in their interests too, to do business with you);
- Exchange information that is needed to solve problems;
- Not resort to unethical behaviour, for example, by taping your communication with head office;
- Respect the secrecy of information and opinions expressed in confidence;
- Do their best to convince their members to accept any agreement that they make with you;
- Do their best to implement the agreement.

How far does one trust you? Behaviour is a more reliable guide than formal expressions of friendship. Where trust is high, negotiations are more likely to take a problem-solving approach and there is willingness to share information, even about profit schedules. Where trust is low, one depends upon persuasive agreements, threats and other forms of contentious behaviour.

Different cultures are more or less willing to trust the other side in a negotiation, and more or less suspicious. Harnett and Cummings (1980) divide the countries thus:

WILLINGNESS TO TRUST

Most trusting United States,
Thailand,
Spain,
South Africa,
Japan,
Least trusting Greece

According to Hofstede, two parties are willing to trust more if power-distance in their cultures is small. Employees in cultures with low need for uncertainty avoidance, trust the activities and motives of their own companies. They have greater readiness to compromise and resolve the conflicts with opponents. Such cultures indicate greater readiness to trust.

Rajan and Graham (1991) found that Russians respond to unknown outsiders with fear and suspicion, but with strong loyalty to those outsiders with whom they develop personal relationships. Despite their reputation for driving a hard bargain, Russians abide by the negotiated agreement and expect other side to do the same.

3-D NEGOTIATIONS

Three important barriers exist between success and failure in most serious negotiations. The first is tactics; the second is deal design and the third is set up. Each dimension is crucial, but much of the negotiation literature is devoted to the first two only. For instance, negotiation skills focus on how executives can focus on tactics-interaction at the bargaining table. The common barriers in this dimension include lack of trust, poor communications and negotiator's hard-ball attitudes. For this, one should learn how to read body language, adapting the style according to bargaining situation, listening carefully, framing your case persuasively, making offers and counter offers, managing deadlines, managing cross-cultural gaffes and others.

The second dimension (2-D), that of deal design or negotiator's ability to draw up a deal at the table that creates lasting value is also important. When a deal does not offer enough value to all sides - the negotiators work to diagnose underlying sources of economic and non-economic value and then craft agreements that can unlock that value for the parties. Does some sort of trade between sides make some sense and, if so, on what terms? Should it be a staged agreement, perhaps with contingencies and risk-sharing provisions? This deal is a more creative in concept and structure and one that meets the ego-needs as well as the economic ones.

Beyond the interpersonal and deal design challenges that executives face in 1-D and 2-D negotiations, lie the 3-D obstacles-flaws in the negotiating setup itself. Common problems in this often-neglected third dimension include negotiating with the wrong parties or about the wrong set of issues, involving parties in the wrong sequence or at the wrong time, as well as incompatible or unattractive no-deal options. 3-D negotiators, however, reshape the scope and sequence of the game itself to achieve the desired outcome. Acting entrepreneurially, away from the table, they ensure that the right parties are approached in the right order to deal with the right issues, by the right means, at the right time, under the right set of expectations, and facing the right no-deal options.

Former U.S. trade representative Charlene Barshefsky, who has negotiated with hundreds of companies, governments, and non-governmental organizations to spearhead deals on goods, services, land, intellectual property, characterizes successful 3-D negotiations this way: 'Tactics at the table are only the cleanup work. Many people mistake tactics for the underlying substance and the relentless efforts away from the table that are needed to set up the most promising possible situation once you face your counterpart. When you know what you need and you have put a broader strategy in place, then negotiating tactics will flow.'

3-D Negotiation in Practice

Even managers who possess superior interpersonal skills in negotiations can fail when the barriers to agreement fall in the 3-D realm. During the 1960s, Kennecott Copper's long-term, low-royalty contract governing its huge El Teniente mine in Chile was at high risk of renegotiation; the political situation in Chile had changed drastically since the contract was originally drawn up, rendering the terms of the deal unstable. Chile had what appeared to be a very attractive walkaway option-or in negotiation lingo, a BATNA (best alternative to negotiated agreement). By unilateral action, the Chilean government could radically change the financial terms of the deal or even expropriate the mine. Kennecott's BATNA appeared poor: Submit to new terms or be expropriated.

Imagine that Kennecott had adopted a 1-D strategy focusing primarily on interpersonal actions at the bargaining table. Using that approach, Kennecott's management team would assess the personalities of the ministers with whom it would be negotiating. It would try to be culturally sensitive and it might choose elegant restaurants in which to meet. Indeed, Kennecott's team did take such sensible actions. But, that approach wasn't promising enough given the threatening realities of the situation. Chile's officials seemed to hold all the cards. They didn't need Kennecott to run the mine; the country had its own experienced managers and engineers. And Kennecott's hands seemed tied. It couldn't move the copper mine, nor did it have a lick on downstream processing or marketing of the valuable metal, nor any realistic prospect, as in a previous era, of calling in the U.S. fleet.

Fortunately for Kennecott, its negotiators adopted a 3-D strategy and set up the impending talks most favourably. The team took six steps and changed the playing field altogether. First, somewhat to the government's surprise, Kennecott offered to sell a majority equity interest in the mine to Chile. Second, to sweeten that offer, the company proposed using the proceeds from the sale of equity, along with money from an Export-Import Bank loan, to finance a large expansion of the mine. Third, it induced the Chilean government to guarantee this loan and make the guarantee subject to New York state law. Fourth, Kennecott insured as much as possible of its assets under a U.S. guarantee against expropriation. Fifth, it arranged for the expanded mine's output to be sold under long-term contracts with North American and European customers. And sixth, the collection rights to these contracts were sold to a consortium of European, U.S., and Japanese financial institutions.

These actions fundamentally changed the negotiations. A larger mine, with Chile as the majority owner, meant a larger and more valuable pie for the host country. The proposal would result in more

---

Source: David A. Lax and James K. Sebenius, HBR, November 2003

revenue for Chile and would address the country's interest in maintaining at least nominal sovereignty over its own natural resources.

Moreover, a broad array of customers, government, and creditors now shared Kennecott's concerns about future political changes in Chile and were highly sceptical of Chile's capacity to run the mine efficiently over time. Instead of facing the original negotiation with Kennecott alone, Chile now effectively faced a multiparty negotiation with players who would have future dealings with that country – not only in the mining sector but also in the financial, industrial, legal, and public sectors. Chile's original BATNA to unceremoniously eject Kennecott was now far less attractive than it had been at the outset, since hurting Kennecott put a wider set of Chile's present and future interests at risk.

NEGOTIATING IN DIFFERENT CULTURAL ZONES

Based on discussions in this chapter and previous chapter on business communication and behaviour, we can broadly profile negotiation styles of major cultural zones. These are discussed below:

1. JAPAN (CHINA, SOUTH KOREA, TAIWAN, SINGAPORE)

Japan is a relationship-focused, formal, monochromic and reserved culture.

The Japanese negotiation process is based on maintaining harmony in relationships. Open conflict is avoided. Differences are resolved through cooperation and persistence. The Japanese strive for long-term relationship based on trust. Negotiations are conducted by teams and not by individuals. Communication is reserved and self-controlled. The context is highly complex. Spoken word is only one part; the total picture and the message may convey several levels of meaning. Much is expected to be understood without words. A lot can be achieved working behind the scenes where neither party is in danger of loosing face. The Japanese place more emphasis on exchanging extensive and detailed information. A meeting that might take three days in the West will probably take two weeks in Japan. Not being hasty is a sign of wisdom and sincerity. Further, consensus building (*ringi seido*) is valued. But, once decisions are taken Japanese will implement it faster than in the West; in fact, total time taken for negotiation and implementation would be less in Japan. The Japanese make life-long commitments. Contracts are not important; they can be changed as and when problems arise. 'Bottom up planning' ensures broad participation. The Japanese do not believe in bargaining and every rise in price has to be justified with facts and figures. They are conservative in approach, formal and observe certain rituals seriously.

2. GERMANY (UK, DENMARK, FINLAND, NETHERLANDS, CZECH REPUBLIC)

Germany is a deal-focused, moderately formal, monochronic and reserved culture.

Germans are planned and well organized negotiators. Conflict is seen as dysfunctional and a symptom of being unprepared. Direct in their approach, they pride themselves on speaking their mind. Clarity of understanding is the prime goal of communication and they readily get to point. They like to examine every small detail thoroughly. They tend to be uncomfortable with the effusive complements that are common in some other cultures. Visitors should use pleasantries such as *danke* (thanks) and *bitte* (please) liberally.

Germany is a strongly monochromic culture, i.e. *punktlichkeit* is very important. Their protocol is formal and they give attention to procedural aspects. Conservative in dress, they don't like anything too flashy or fashionable; these indicate lack of seriousness and discipline. The Germans are team oriented and their goal is to further the interests of the organization and government. They tend to keep a distance between themselves and their counterparts, as they feel the closeness might interfere with the negotiating process. Germans use low-context communication. Non-verbal cues and signals are not widely used and eye contact is important. They trust past performance to judge the individual rather than their intuition. Agreements are written and respected. They are 'risk averse' and less short-term oriented than their American counterparts. Decision-making is centralised and flows from top. They like to be addressed by designations or achievements.

3. FRANCE (BELGIUM, ITALY, SPAIN, HUNGRY)

France is a moderately deal – focused, formal, variably expressive and monochromic culture.

As people, 'the French constitute the most brilliant and the most dangerous nation of Europe, and the best qualified in turn to become an object of admiration, hatred, pity or terror but never of indifference' Alexis de ToqueVille said. The French are proud, at times displaying supremacy. They are rational about individual achievements and care little what others think of them.

In negotiations, the French follow their own logic based on previously established principles. They are thoroughly prepared and expect the same from other side. They believe that conflict can be constructive and help progress. They expect direct and honest arguments and due authority on the other side. Status conscious, social class is a key factor in selection of negotiators. The French are extremely formal and their attention to manners and respect is paramount in all business situations, even with friends in business. Negotiation issues are more important than relationships. The French tend to remain guarded about their personal lives and relationships. They quickly get down to business without wasting time. They are not receptive to hard-sell tactics and like to have a detailed contract to be signed, written in French. The French motivation to work is different from any other nation in the world. To the French, the only thing that really matters is the quality of life (*qualite de la vie*); the French work to live, do not live to work.

4. RUSSIA (POLAND, RUMANIA)

Russia is a relationship-focused, formal, polychronic and expressive culture.

Speaking with the experience of 35 visits to markets in Russia, Jenn Jensen, managing director of the Danish firm F. Uhren Roll Meat A/s, emphasises that 90 per cent of business in Russia is done face-to-face. You build your business on relationships. For Russians, negotiation is a competitive process in which their aim is to maximize their gains at the other side's loss. All Russian executives are trained in the art of conducting negotiations. They can be confrontational, blunt and combative negotiators and the process can be very slow or made slow. The decision-making is centralised and their approach is highly individualistic.

Russians are conscious of protocol and enjoy certain formalities like an after-dinner. They like to be addressed by their complete names. Hard bargainers, they use premeditated tactics to achieve the best alternative. They are cautious because they avoid uncertainties. Russians generally insist on formal signing of agreement and it is not uncommon for agreement to be renegotiated. Unlike East and South Asians, they are direct, saying what they mean and meaning what they say. In Russia, expect meetings to start a little late and run well beyond the scheduled time. Senior officials will keep several conversations going simultaneously. The Russians are quite and restrained at the beginning of a negotiation, but can display emotions and temper at critical moments. Winston Churchill rightly described Russia as a riddle wrapped in a mystery inside an enigma.

5. BRAZIL (ARGENTINA, MAXICO AND OTHER LATIN AMERICAN COUNTRIES)

Brazil is a relationship-focused, formal, polychronic and expressive culture.

Initial correspondence with the Brazilians should be in their national language Portuguese or Spanish. Establishing an atmosphere of trust is a precondition to a successful business relationship. Topics for small talks include football, Brazilian history and places to visit. Brazilians value deep, long lasting relationships. In southern Brazil, people value firm schedules and time, but in other parts of the country, clocks tick at different speeds. Waiting for an hour is not too long. Status is highly valued and, therefore, your dress and the hotel you stay in count. Warm and friendly, Brazilians tend to be talkative, and openly show emotions in public.

Conversational overlap is not considered rude. Brazil is definitely a high-context culture. As a sign of friendliness, they stand close maintaining physical and eye contact while talking.

Brazilians are widely known as tough bargainers, not afraid to turn down offers rather bluntly. Negotiation process can be very lengthy and they expect their counterparts to offer concessions. Wining and dining is expected and encouraged for establishing trust and relationship.

When arguing, Brazilians appeal to one's sensibilities and emotion. Arguments are persuasive, not because they are based on statistics and figures but because they are based on apparent common sense and are made with fervour and sincerity. Inference, assumptions and tradition are likely to play a part in persuasion.

Brazilian society is highly bureaucratic, hierarchical and class conscious with centralized decision-making.

6. NEGOTIATING IN ARAB WORLD (EGYPT, GREECE, OTHER MIDDLE EASTERN COUNTRIES)

Saudi Arabia is relationship-focused, polychronic and expressive culture.

The Arab world is conservative, traditional and strongly influenced by Islam, which pervades every aspect of life. One must learn Arab customs, practices and taboos. An Arab's honour, dignity and reputation are precious to him and are protected at all cost. Loyalty to the family is a paramount value; family needs often come before individual needs. Arabs readily express emotion and their language is marked by frequent exaggeration. They make use of elaborate and ritualised forms of greeting and leave talking. They avoid confrontation and saying 'no'. Time is flexible. When a meeting is in progress, people will come and go freely and telephone calls will be attended to.

Arabs attach a great deal of importance to status and rank. In meetings, respect should be shown to senior-most person. It is also important not to criticise any person publicly.

Mutual respect is to be shown at all times. Arabs often act on the basis of emotion rather than logic. They believe that every thing happens by the will of Allah. Most of the work is done through administrative channels and high contacts are useful. Decision-making is slow and most business is done face to face.

Arab negotiators tend to be enthusiastic bargainers and expect their counterparts to grant major concessions. It is wiser to build a wide margin into initial offer, leaving room for manoeuvre during the lengthy negotiating process. Entertaining and being entertained are essential parts of building a close relationship. Arabs will press you to eat more than you want to. Similarly, when hosting Arabs you must keep them pushing to eat and drink.

7. AUSTRALIA (CANADA, USA, NEW ZEALAND)

Australia is a deal-focused, informal, monochronic and variable expressive culture.

Australians are more reserved than their counterparts in southern Europe or Latin America. But, they are more direct and straightforward in their speech than the Germans, Dutch or Americans. Aussies are known for vociferous argument and even confrontations or open disagreements. Negotiators from Arab world or Japanese might consider this behaviour as hostile, while the latter's polite and mild behaviour is considered by Australians as an attempt to mislead or confuse them.

Australians are one of the most egalitarian and informal society in the world, surprising even the Americans. They consider Americans overly concerned with status, degrees, wealth or position in the corporate hierarchy. Visiting negotiators are advised to avoid impressing Australians by their titles or accomplishments. However their egalitarianism does not extend to women in business.

As regards their orientation to time, they are somewhat less monochronic than Germans or Americans. With regard to space bubble, they prefer an arm's distance like English or Americans and also direct eye contact. The best policy for success in sales presentations is moderation and soft selling. Instead of over-emphasizing your company's name, let your documentation, testimonials and third-party reports speak for you.

TOWARDS CULTURAL SYNERGY

Cultural synergy can be built when similarity and differences in cultural behaviour and assumptions are understood and utilized for problem solving and decision-making. Table 16.1 lists the national persuasion styles of Arabs, North Americans and Russians. The differences in persuasion styles among these three groups occur on eight dimensions: primary negotiation styles, conflict, making concessions, response to opponent's concessions, relationships, authority, initial positions and deadlines. Table 16.1 compares the negotiation styles and underlying cultural differences of the Japanese, North Americans and Latin Americans. In Table 14.1 dimensions, which range from emotional sensitivity to personal or impersonal decision-making are identified, including how concept of teamwork differs in these cultures.

BOX 14.1 THE WORLD-CLASS MANAGER

Mervyn Raphael, founder member, Performance Consulting International believes that global managers have the edge when it comes to being able to see the 'big picture'. However, he says , this is an innate ability. 'We once conducted an assessment for the employees of a very large company in India. During the course of the assessment, we found that their HR head had an amazing ability to link up different events in a pattern to create a roadmap for the company's future-a real global manager. Today he is the company's number two HR person in USA', Raphael says. A global manager is also moulded by an environment he works in, but the key characteristics of a global manager are that they're holistic thinkers, can network efficiently and are performance drivers. Tharun Raja of Hay Group says that following points differentiate global managers from regular ones, and make them successful across geographies:

- The ability to dream big, envision the future of the business and get others on the same page.
- The ability to predict changes on the business front and react proactively.
- The ability to deal with uncertainty and take key calculated decisions quick and fast.
- Entrepreneurial thinking and the drive to succeed in spite of adverse circumstances.
- Networking ability-professional and personal relationship to drive advantages for the organization.

Table 14.1 National Styles of Persuasion

	North Americans	*Arabs*	*Russians*
Primary Negotiating style and process.	Factual: appeals made to logic	Affective: appeals made to emotions.	Axiomatic: appeals made to ideals.
Conflict:Opponent's arguments countered with	Objective facts.	Subjective feelings.	Asserted ideals.
Making Concessions	Small concessions made early to establish a relationship.	Concessions made throughout as a part of the bargaining	A few, if any small concessions made
Response to opponent's concessions.	Usually reciprocate opponent's concessions	Almost always reciprocates opponent's ooncessions	Opponent's concessions are viewed as weakness and almost never reciprocated.
Relationship	Short term	Long term	No continuing relationship.
Authority	Short term	Broad	Limited
Initial position.	Moderate	Extreme	Extreme
Deadlines	Very Important	casual	Ignored

Source: *International Journal of Intercultural Relations*, vol, 1, E.S. Glenn, D. Wilmeyers, and K.A. Stevenson, 'Cultural styles of persuasion'.

Table 14.2 Negotiation Styles from a Cross-cultural Perspective

Japanese	*America*	*Latin America*
Emotional sensitivity highly valued. Hiding of emotions.	Emotional sensitivity is not highly valued. Straightforward or impersonal dealings.	Emotional sensitivity Valued; passionate.
Subtle power plays; conciliation.	Litigation; not as much as conciliation.	Great power plays; Use of weakness.
Loyalty to employer; Employer takes care of employees.	Lack of commitment to employer; breaking of ties by either if necessary.	Loyalty to employer, Who is often a family.
Group decision-making by consensus.	Teamwork provides input to decision-maker.	Decisions made by one individual.
Face-saving crucial; Decisions often made on basis of saving someone from embarrassment.	Decisions made on cost-benefit basis; face saving does not always matter.	Face-saving crucial in decision-making to preserve honour dignity.
Decision-makers openly influenced by special interests.	Decision makers influenced by special interests but often not considered ethical.	Execution of special interests of decision-maker expected and condoned.
Not argumentative; quiet when right.	Argumentative when right or wrong, but impersonal.	Argumentative when right or wrong, passionate.
What is in writing must be accurate, valid.	Great importance given to documentation as proof.	Impatient with documentation, seen as obstacle to general principles.
Step-by-step approach to decision-making.	Methodically organized decision-making.	Impulsive, spontaneous decision-making.
Good of group is the ultimate aim.	Profit motive or good of individual ultimate aim.	What is good for the individual is good for the group.
Cultivate a good emotional social setting for decision making; to know decision makers.	Decision-making impersonal; avoid involvements, conflict of interest.	Personalised approach necessary for good decision-making.

Source: Casse, P. training for the Multicultural Manager: A practical and cross-cultural approach to management of people, society for intercultural education & training,1982.

Review Questions

1. Explain the importance of negotiations in global business arena.
2. Discuss the anatomy of negotiations and detail key success factors which should be kept in mind while conducting successful international negotiations.

3. How will you prepare and plan for holding major negotiations for setting up a joint venture in India for a British organization?
4. Compare the persuasion style of people from Arab world with Americans.
5. Compare the negotiation style of people from Japan and Brazil.
6. Which countries are grouped as:

    (1) Relationship-focused, formal, polychronic and expressive.
    (2) Deal-focused, moderately formal, monochronic.
    (3) Relationship-focused, formal, less monochronic and reserved.
    (4) Moderately deal-focused, formal, variably monochronic.

7. Explain how to create Cross-Cultural Synergy in a diverse working group?
8. Discuss the competencies required in global managers. Which were of them can be developed through training and which are innate?

Assignment

Select some multinationals and interview their managers on the challenges they face and how they have handled adverse situations. Summarise the interview findings and present them in the class.

Role play

Five students should form a team of Japanese auto company executives conducting negotiations in Brazil with Latin American family firm's executives for a joint venture in that country. Both sides should prepare their positions in advance and try to reach a settlement through give and take. Let a group of students act as observers, who should analyse the individual roles in conducting successful negotiations to the class including the mistakes made by teams.

PART 3

15. Organizing International Structures
16. Employee Relations and Employment Practices Across Countries
17. Managing International Projects and Teams: A Human Resource Perspective
18. Frontiers of IHRM and Corporate HR Strategies for Competitive Advantage

Chapter 15

Organizing International Structures

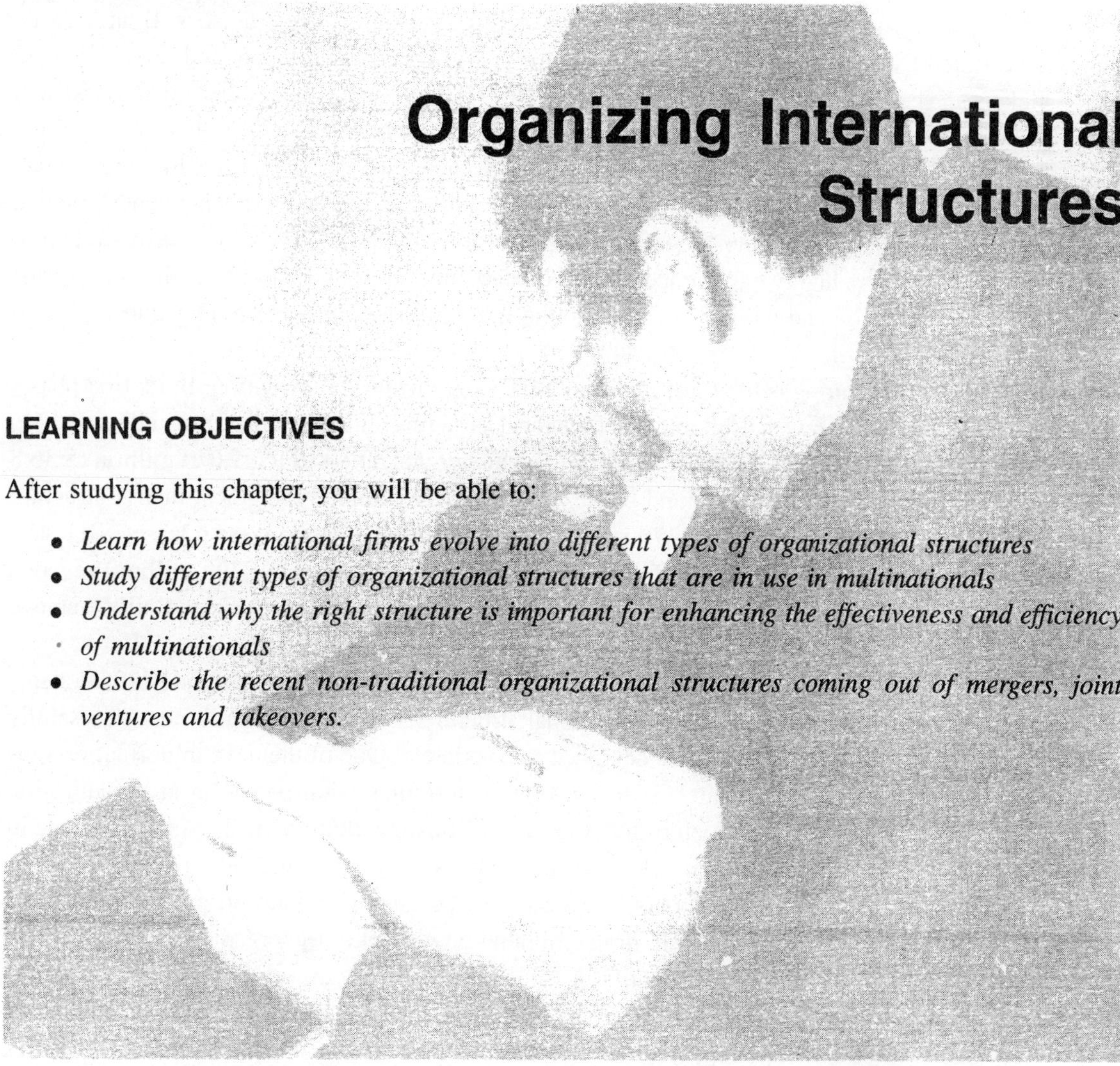

LEARNING OBJECTIVES

After studying this chapter, you will be able to:

- *Learn how international firms evolve into different types of organizational structures*
- *Study different types of organizational structures that are in use in multinationals*
- *Understand why the right structure is important for enhancing the effectiveness and efficiency of multinationals*
- *Describe the recent non-traditional organizational structures coming out of mergers, joint ventures and takeovers.*

OPENING CASE
NIIT (India's global IT solutions company)

NIIT, India's global IT solutions company, is nurturing an ambitious growth plan to allow it to increase its sales 8-fold within 6 years, and to reach its target of becoming a Rs. 10,000 crore ($ 2200 million) company. The company did for nine months intense planning, during which the top management team examined the firm's business process, organization structure, and employee aspirations and beliefs. The result was the 'Fast Forward' plan. A key element of the plan is to change the organizational structure. The proposed organizational structure will consist of Independent Business Units (IBUs) and a Corporate Centre. The Independent Business Unit Heads (IBHs) will be accountable to the NIIT board for strategy, targets and performance, and will be equipped with an Advisory Board. The Advisory Board, to be constituted by the IBH, will be responsible for providing external inputs and cross business linkages. The Advisory Board members from the NIIT (typically from other businesses) will enhance the synergy unique to the NIIT business model, while outside members will enforce the crucial outside perspective. The IBUs will have their own staff functions like the Human Resources, Finance and Commercial.... The IBHs will have increased independence coupled with increased accountability. The Corporate Centre will pursue NIIT's long-term strategies. It will have a few highly experienced heads of staff functions, and will act as the brains trust of the organization and will be available to the IBHs to draw upon the NIIT values, wisdom and experience.'

This re-structuring is the third phase in NIIT's organizational evolution. In its first phase, in 1989, the company had adopted a divisional structure. That restructuring allowed it to grow from a Rs. 169 million ($ 3.7 million) revenue organization to Rs. 1,670 million ($ 36.8 million) one by 1995. In the second phase, in 1995, NIIT adopted the global matrix structure and grew to a turnover of Rs. 12,370 million ($ 272.7 million). In the press release, NIIT says it expects the new structure 'to help NIIT scale the Rs. 100 billion ($ 2200 million) revenue mark it has set for itself for the next six years, just as earlier structures helped NIIT achieve new revenue levels.'

As the NIIT example shows, when companies grow larger in size, and shift strategy, there is a need to change their organizational structure. For an organization to successfully implement its strategy, it should be designed appropriately. One of the most important reasons why organization design is vital, is that it often determines what people in an organization pay attention to, and thereby determine, the sort of decisions that are made. As we will see in this chapter, if an organization is based on functions, needs of the functions are focused upon; and when it is based on customers, the needs of the customer take priority. Organization design also plays an important role in determining how quickly the organization can respond to its environment, and how innovative it can be. How an organization is designed also has cost implications – some designs are efficient while others have duplication of personnel. Obviously, there are important trade-offs. At the micro-level, organization design influences the motivation of employees. When an organization is designed poorly, strategic initiatives go astray because no one is responsible for them, information and knowledge are not shared, resulting in all sorts of coordination problems, and turf wars take place. Costs may increase, or innovation may decrease.

The case also shows that structure plays a key role in influencing organizational performance.

INTRODUCTION

Structure is a social creation of roles and relationships, which facilitates effective control and coordination by clarifying authority-responsibility-accountability and role-clarity, both vertically and horizontally across the boundary of the organization. If organizations are appropriately structured, they provide a climate of cooperation, job satisfaction and innovation. Inappropriate structure can create conflicts lack of teamwork and obstacles to change, and people may resist control or pursue their own agenda at the cost of the organization. As a result, many multinational organizations are restructuring themselves regularly in response to local and global competition, joint ventures, mergers or acquisitions, divestment, diversification and integration and strategic alliances. NIIT's case shows structure generally follows strategy. However, structure also influences formulation and implementation of strategy. Organization structure is one of the major determinants of organizational efficiency and effectiveness.

Structure also plays a key role in domestic firms and its role in global firms is crucial, because it presents greater complexity and differentiation, technological uncertainty and thus requires greater integration. International structures need to have, greater capacity for environmental adaptation, problem-solving, knowledge and innovation management across the global subsidiaries. Organizations being open systems depend for their survival and growth upon their environments. Their capability to respond to environmental changes depends upon their decision-making processes and local adaptation, which are influenced by their structure.

In this chapter we first discuss how structure changes when firms go international. Next, we have reviewed different options of structure design with their suitability for particular contextual factors. Constraints and benefits of each type of structure are also discussed. The role of the corporate headquarter in managing the subsidiaries is also discussed. Finally, structures that promote innovation and use of IT have also been explained. Recent structural development in multinationals, such as heterachy, transnational, the keiretsu, the networked structure, the infinitely flat spider's web, starburst have been explained with examples.

STRUCTURAL IMPERITIVES OF GLOBAL FIRMS

The organization structures of many international firms are often similar to those used domestically by providing sufficient information processing for coordination and control while focusing employees on specific functions, products or geographical areas. However, significant differences may arise depending on the nature and scope of overseas businesses and headquarters' approach for controlling the operation. The main objective of a global firm is to meet the needs of both the local market and the home office strategy of globalization. Structure is also influenced by the type of industry as some industries face high pressure for localization while others face high pressure for globalization as shown in Fig.15.1.

The pressure for globalization (globalization strategy) means that product design, manufacturing and marketing strategy are strandardised throughout the world. For example, Japanese companies designed and marketed similar low-cost, fuel-efficient cars throughout the world in the same business format. Pressure for localisation (multidomestic strategy) means that competition in each country is handled independendly of other countries. Thus, a multidomestic strategy would encourage product design, assembly and marketing tailored to the specific needs of each country. Some firms have found that their products do not thrive in the single global market, for example, firms dealing with personal care products and toothpaste.

On the other hand some firms design products for global markets, such as Coca-Cola, but tailor-marketing and advertising according to specific countries. The globalization or multidomestic strategy is thus primarily influenced by the type of industries and the nature of products. Service industries need more multidomestic strategy than manufacturing ones. These relative pressures change over tivem as the organizations grow and respond to respective country environments and competition.

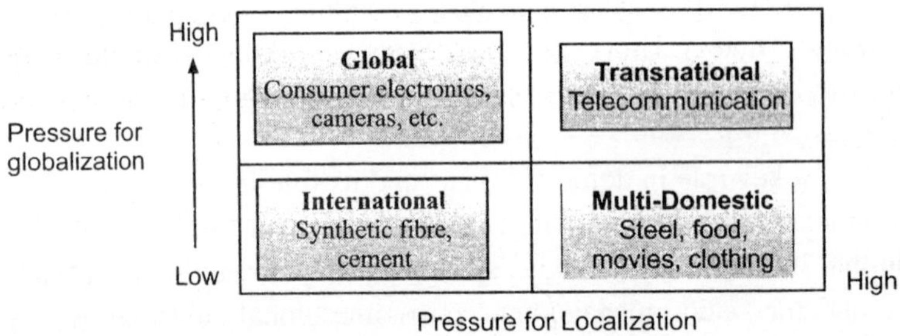

Fig. 15.1 Globalization and Localization Matrix

Source: Adapted from information found in Paul W. Beamish, J. Peter Killing, Donald J. LeCraw and Harold Crookell, *International Management: Text and Cases* (Homewood, Ill: Irwin,1991, p. 99.

Most multinationals grow through certain stages in structural change over the time in their operations. This rate of change is, therefore, industry-specific and also is influenced by several other factors, such as pressure of stakeholders, technology and size, etc. But the most important factor is the complexity and the rate of change in their domestic as well as international environment. The usual structural changes are desired next.

INTERNATIONAL STRUCTURE (EXPORT STAGE)

An export, import or franchising set-up is a common initial stage of international operations, particularly for firms with technologically advanced products or locally made goods of high quality produced by the firms for export. The sales are through foreign agents or distributors until a critical sales volume is reached. In the initial stage, the company appoints an export manager who reports to chief of marketing in the company and all operations concerning exports and imports are controlled by the home office. The export manager deals with foreign agents and distributors, gaining knowledge of foreign markets.

At this stage, the key success factors are: modifying the product to meet the requirement of foreign markets, maintain quality acceptable to the customer, ensure timely delivery and follow up all the required paperwork and procedures.

As the firm develops expertise in foreign markets and if overseas sales continue to increase, agents and distributors are replaced gradually by direct sales with the establishment of branch offices in the foreign market countries. This stage occurs due to problems with agents and distributors or gaining more confidence in international sales activity or the desire to have greater control or give extra thrust to exports. At this stage, the company creates an export division or a corporate home office, and the export division head reports directly to the CEO. The export head becomes at par with the chief of marketing in the company or other functional heads. Export managers of other countries where the company is doing its business also report to him.

When the international sales increase further, the local government and growing markets exert pressure on the company for setting up on-site manufacturing facilities. This prompts the company to set up subsidiaries in the concerned foreign countries. This new structural arrangement is shown in Fig.10.2. Each subsidiary is responsible for operations within its own geographic area, and subsidiary managers report directly to the export division, V.P. (international) at the corporate office. This arrangement is useful because it takes a great deal of burden off the CEO for monitoring and supporting the different subsidiaries in different foreign markets.

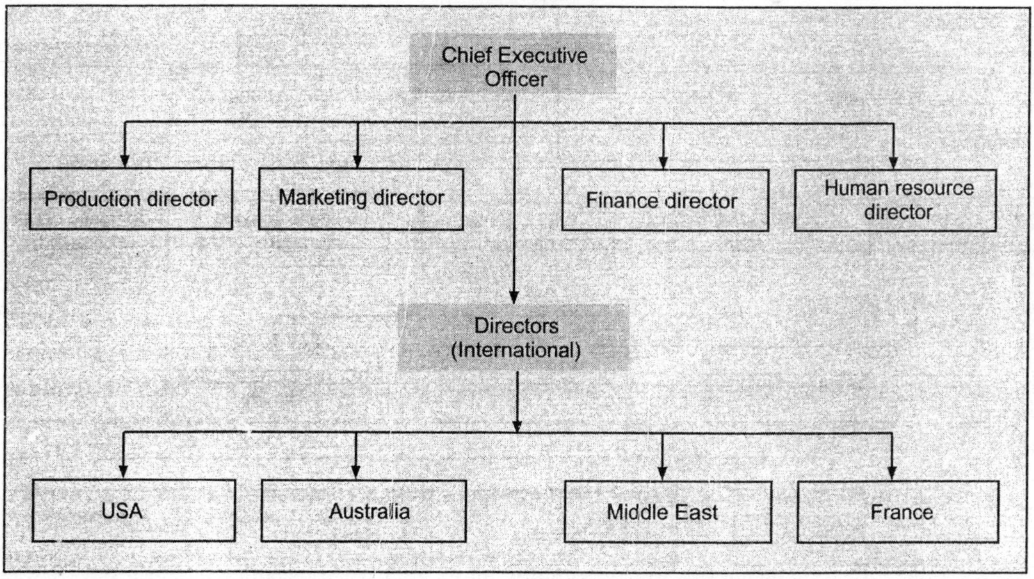

Fig. 15.2 Creation of International Business Function

The human resource issues that arise at this stage are: selecting heads of these foreign subsidiaries and staffing them with PCNs (parent country nationals) or HCNs (host country nationals) according to management philosophy. In the beginning, PCNs are usually posted at important positions because a firm has more confidence in them to implement proven home office human resource policies and practices. This approach is known as the ethnocentric approach.

The other important issues that need attention are: selecting entry strategy, assessing practical and economic risks, foreign exchange management and developing appropriate supply chain globally. Other issues of expatriates' selection, training, compensation and performance management are also important. The role of the foreign subsidiary manager, whether he is a parent country or host country national is to:

- Transfer managerial and technical know-how to the subsidiary from the parent company;
- Communicate, coordinate and implement corporate policies;
- Assist the corporate office in strategizing by keeping the HQ informed of political, economic and firm-related developments, opportunities and threats in its market and offering appropriate advice;
- Liaison with the local government and other important functionaries and build the goodwill of the company and strengthen its brand;. and
- Handle other activities, including strategic alliances or joint ventures, which the company might be planning in the region.

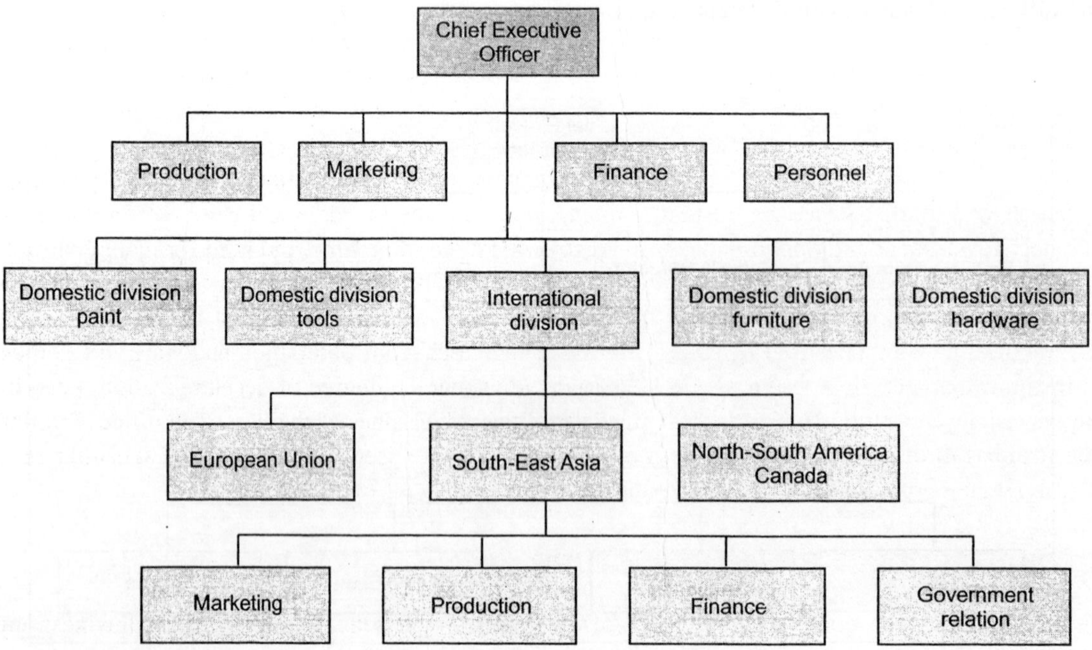

Fig. 15.3 An International Divisional Structure

A number of **advantages** are associated with the use of an international structure:

1. The grouping of international activities under one senior executive at the headquarter ensures that the international focus receives priority attention.
2. It allows the company to develop an overall unified approach to international operations.
3. It helps the firm develop a cadre of internationally experienced managers.

However, the **problems** with this structure are:

1. The structure separates the domestic and international managers which can result into two camps with divergent objectives.
2. As the international operations get larger, the home office may find it difficult to think and act strategically and to allocate resources on a global basis.
3. Most research and development efforts are still domestically oriented, so ideas for new products and processes in the international market are not given enough weightage in R & D priorities.

GLOBAL STRUCTURES

When companies start acquiring and allocating resources on the basis of global opportunities and threats, they need to adopt structures either on the product, geographical area pattern or functional pattern. This global perspective signifies a major change in management strategy and it is supported by the requisite changes in the organizational structure, which can be on the basis of product or geography or function. At this stage the firm is also standardizing the product, diversifying and globalising its supply-chain, raising capital resources in international markets and enhancing its technological capabilities by technology transfers and strategic alliances. Relationships with governments and regulators also require increasing attention. Because of increasing size of the firm, the international division becomes overstretched, affecting efficiency of operations and communications. Therefore, tensions of all sorts may crop up between the subsidiaries and international division at headquarters.

Further, demand for local responsiveness increases at the subsidiary unit levels because of differences in market structures, distribution channels, customer needs, local culture or pressure from the host government and opportunities for investment. At the same time, the need for more centralized global integration by headquarters comes from having multinational customers, global competitors, and increasingly rapid flow of information and technology, and from the quest for large volume for economies of scale. The level of competition also increases from other multinationals and domestic firms in its markets. As a result, the firm has to decide about the degree of decentralization, i.e. which key decisions are to be made at the subsidiary level and which ones at the corporate office. Similarly, the firm has to decide the type and form of control to be exercised in managing the subsidiaries and also how the corporate office can add value to the management of subsidiaries.

GLOBAL PRODUCT-BASED STRUCTURE

In this structure, the company treats each of its major products as distinct strategic business units (SBUs). Product divisions at the corporate office are given worldwide responsibility for production, finance, marketing and management of supply-chain for each product or product line. These product-based divisions also have internal functional support. The structure is shown in Fig. 15.4.

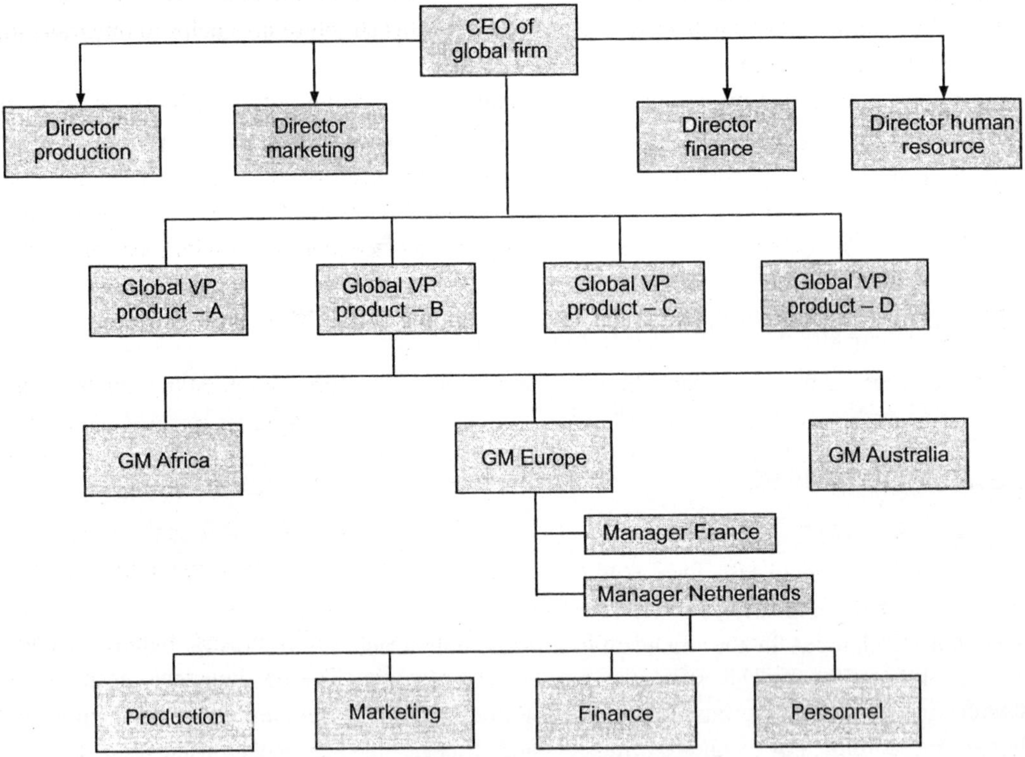

Fig. 15.4 A Global Product-Based Structure

On the global basis the firm can strategise the shift of products as they reach different life cycle stages from one market to another, according to their acceptability and scope. For example, if colour TVs are in maturity stage in advance countries, then it can shift them to developing countries and black and white TVs to the underdeveloped countries. Another major advantage is that this structure provides a direct link from customer to policy-makers to direct the research and development of new products that serve the need of global customers. It also helps to integrate the marketing, production and finance functions

The logic behind this type of structure is that products and services of the company should be sufficiently distinct in production technologies, requiring different marketing skills to deal with different types of customers and markets. Each product division is treated as a separate profit centre for accounting and finance purposes. The products are generally in the growth stage of product life cycle stage, hence they need to be carefully promoted and marketed. The corporate headquarters will usually maintain control in terms of budgetary constraints, approval of certain decisions such as launching of new products, total profit and contribution.

This structure has certain advantages. If the firm is very diverse (for example, it produces products using wide variety of technologies or has wide variety of customers), the need to customise the product to the specific demands of the buyer becomes important. It can lead to client satisfaction because product responsibility and contact points are clear. Different units can adapt to differences in products, cultures and market practices in various regions. This structure also helps to integrate supply chain globally on product basis.

The first disadvantage of this structure is duplication of personnel within each division, making it expensive. The second disadvantage is that product managers may pursue currently attractive markets and neglect other areas with better long range potential. The third disadvantage is that many country managers spend too much time trying to tap their local markets rather than the international markets because it is more convenient and easier, as they become more experienced with local operations.

GLOBAL AREA-BASED STRUCTURE

In this arrangement, a multinational prefers to divisionalise the foreign operations on the basis of geography, rather than on product basis. Corporate structure at the headquarter remains same as in the case of product-based divisionalisation. This signifies a major change in the thinking of the company, because the international operations are now put on the same level as domestic operations. This structure offers the advantage when economic and political environment in different countries where the firm is operating is fast changing and requires the operations to be adapted to the pressures of the environment and governments in those countries.

This structure is useful when the product range is not very different and, therefore, common resources in a country can be shared to support all the operations. The headquarter is responsible for the transfer of excess resources from one country to another as required, and to establish coordination and control among different countries for achieving synergy and overall goal achievement.

This arrangement is also suitable when products are in the maturity stage and have narrow product lines. These product lines are often differentiated on the basis of the geographic area or when they have huge demand concentrated in some countries and much less in other countries. This structure allows the area manager to integrate marketing, production and finance functions in a given area to achieve economies of scale and scope. Firms that are producing automobiles, beverages, containers, cosmetics, food or pharmaceuticals often use such a global area structure.

The main disadvantage of the global area structure is the difficulty encountered in reconciling a product emphasis with a geographic orientation. For example, if a product is sold worldwide, a number of different areas are responsible for the sales. The lack of centralized management and control can result in increased cost and duplication of efforts. A second disadvantage is that divisional groups often ignore development efforts because they are selling goods that have reached the maturity stage. Their focus is not on the latest technologically superior goods that will win in the market in the long-run but on those goods that are proven winners and are now being conveniently marketed worldwide.

GLOBAL FUNCTIONAL STRUCTURES

They are not very common except in mining and construction fields. Here the global operations in different countries continue to be divided on the basis of functions such as marketing, finance, operations and human resource. Subsidiary functional heads report directly to corporate functional heads.

GLOBAL MATRIX STRUCTURE

When a multinational is trying to integrate its operations across on more than one dimension, such as product as well as geography, or customers or technology, it resorts to matrix structure. As shown in Fig. 10.5, both product division and area division share joint responsibility. This means both executives jointly decide allocation of resources and other important matters but the matrix manager is held responsible for results.

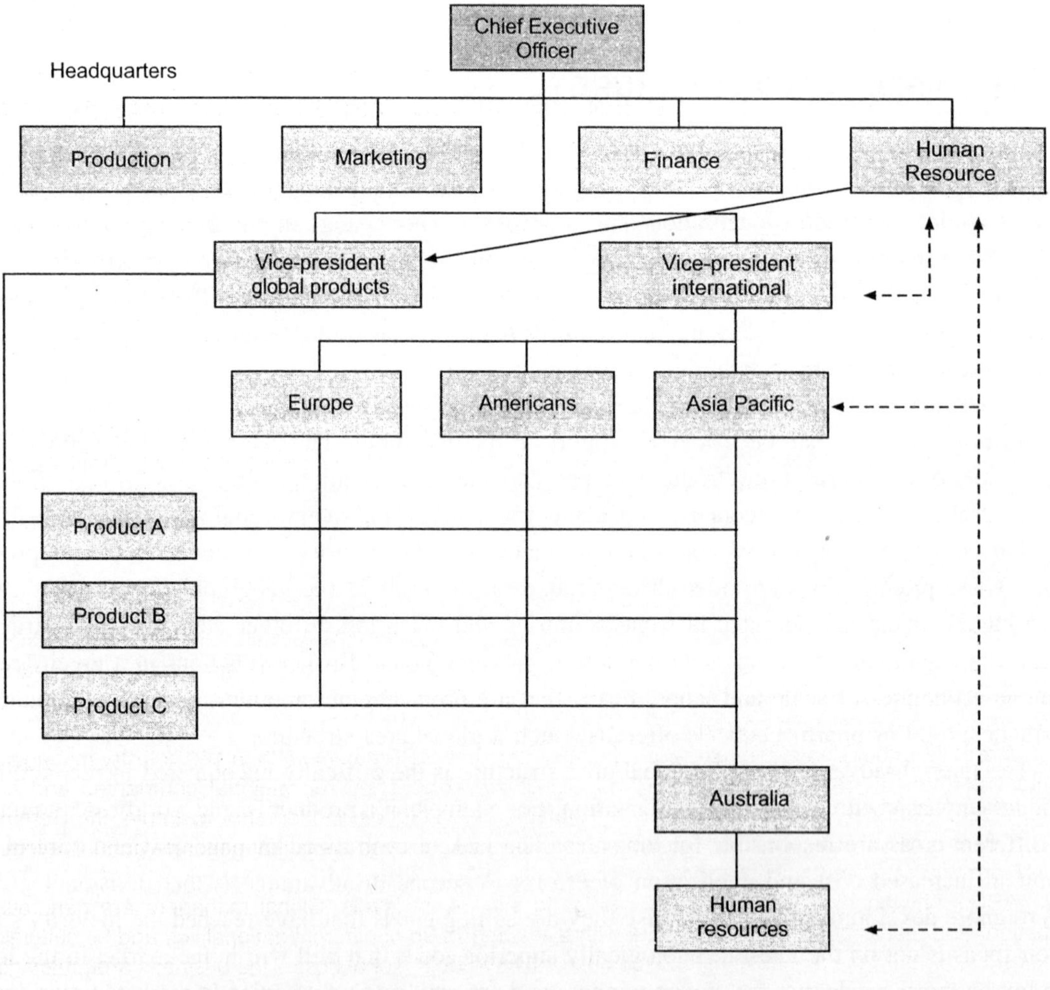

Fig.15.5 The Matrix Structure

In this structure there are pressures from horizontal matrix managers for equal allocation of resources however the vertical managers are supposed to balance this by taking into account relative importance of products or projects based on organizational priorities and other long-term considerations. This structure reflects the process of decision-making and results in higher quality of decisions. It also results in better customer focus on final results or on response to local needs.

However, there are several shortcomings associated with this matrix. First, as the design complexity increases, coordinating the personnel and getting everyone to work towards common goals often become difficult. Second, some employees experience dual authority, which is frustrating and confusing. Matrix managers need excellent interpersonal and conflict-resolution skills. This matrix also forces managers to spend a great deal of time on meetings. If managers do not adapt to the information and power-sharing required by the matrix, the system will not work. Managers must collaborate with each other rather than rely on vertical authority in decision-making. Proliferation of communication channels creates information logjams. And barriers of distance, culture and language make it virtually impossible for managers to resolve conflicts and to clarify the confusion.

BOX 15.1 BERNEVIC, THE FORMER CEO OF ABB, DISCUSSING THE MATRIX, SAID,

ABB is an organization with three internal contradictions. We want to be global and local, big and small, radically decentralized with centralized reporting and control. If we resolve these contradictions, we create real organization advantage. This is where the matrix comes in. The matrix is the framework through which we organize our activities. It allows us to optimise our business globally and maximize our performance in every country in which we operate. Some people resist it. They say that the matrix is too rigid and too simplistic. But what choice do you have? To say you don't like matrix is like saying you don't like factories or you don't like breathing. It is a fact of life. If you deny the formal matrix, you wind up with an informal one, and that in much harder to reckon with. As we learn to master the matrix, we get a truly multidomestic organization.

ABB owns 1,300 subsidiary companies divided into 5,000 profit centres located in 140 countries. ABB's average plant has fewer than 200 workers and most of the company's 5,000 profit centres contain only 40 to 50 people, meaning almost everyone stays close to customer. For many years, ABB used a complex global matrix structure similar to one shown in Fig. 15.2 to achieve worldwide economies of scale combined with local flexibility and responsiveness.

At the top is the CEO with eight top executives, who hold frequent meetings around the world. Along one side of the matrix are sixty-five or so business areas located worldwide, into which ABB's products and services are grouped. Each business area leader is responsible for handling business on a global scale, allocating export markets, establishing cost and quality standards, and creating mixed-nationality teams to solve problems. For example, the leader for power transformers is responsible for 25 factories in sixteen countries.

Along the other side of the matrix is a country structure; ABB has more than 100 country managers, most of them citizens of the country in which they work. They run national companies and are responsible for local balance sheet, income statements and career ladders. For example, the German president is responsible for 36,000 people across several business areas that generate annual revenue in Germany of more than $ 4 billion.

ABB's philosophy is to decentralize things to the lowest levels. Global managers are generous, patient and multilingual. They must work with teams made up of different nationalities and be culturally sensitive. Finally, the president of local companies, have both global boss – the business area manager – and the country boss, and they learn to coordinate the needs of both J. Barlett and Ghoshal, conclude that the most successful multinationals today focus less on searching for the ideal structure, and more on developing the abilities, behaviour and performance of individual managers. This creates 'a matrix in the minds of managers' where individual capabilities are captured and the entire firm is motivated to respond cooperatively to a complicated and dynamic environment.

Source: W.Taylor, 'The Logic of Global Business: An Interview with ABB's Perey Barnevik, *Harvard Business Review*, March-April 1991, pp. 95-96.

EMERGING MULTINATIONAL STRUCTURES

The structure has so far been viewed from headquarter-subsidiary relationship, from coordination and control, flow of resources, information, decision-making and problem-solving perspectives. However, in the large mature multinationals these flows are multidimensional, i.e. from the headquarter to a subsidiary, from one subsidiary to other subsidiaries, and also from a subsidiary to the headquarter itself. The mergers, takeovers, joint ventures and strategic alliances are also giving way to newer variations in organization structure design. These can be considered under four types: the heterarchy, the transnational, the network firm and the keiretsu.

THE HETERARCHY

The heterarchy structure, as proposed by Hedlund (1986), recognises that a multinational might have a number of different kinds of centres apart from the traditional centre referred to as 'headquarters'. He argues that the competitive advantage does not necessarily reside in any one country, rather it may be found in many countries. Therefore, each subsidiary centre may simultaneously be a centre and a global coordinator of discreet activities, thus performing a strategic role not for just itself, but for the multinational as a whole. For example, some multinationals may centralize research and development in a particular subsidiary. In a heterarchical multinational, control is less reliant on the top-bottom mechanisms of previous hierarchical modes and is more reliant on mutual cooperation and coordination, organization culture and widely shared awareness of central goals and strategy.

From the organizational effectiveness perspective, the success of heterarchy type structure depends solely on the ability of the multinational to formulate, implement and reinforce the required human resource policies and practices. The organization vision and corporate culture play no small part. Hedlund recognizes that this structure demands skilful and experienced professionals as well as sophisticated reward and punishment systems and shared leadership. The use of staff transfers as an informal control mechanism is quite important.

THE TRANSNATIONAL

The term 'transnational' has been coined to describe a new organizational structure that is characterized by interdependence of resources and responsibilities across all business units regardless of national boundaries. The transnational tries to cope with the large flows of components, products, services, resources, people and information among its subsidiaries, while simultaneously recognizing the distributed specialized resources and capabilities of each business unit. It demands a complex process of coordination and cooperation involving strong cross-unit integrating devices, a strong corporate identity, and a well-developed worldwide management perspective. The role of human resource is once again very critical and similar as in matrix or heterarchy. They all need transnational or global managers who can think and act across national and subsidiary boundaries. Staff transfers also play a crucial role in integration and coordination. Unilever, for example, is more like a transnational organization today.

BOX 15.2 BARTLETT AND GHOSAL DEFINE THE TRANSNATIONAL IN THE FOLLOWING WORDS:

Among the companies we studied, there were several that were in the process of developing such organizational capabilities. They had surpassed the classic capabilities of the multinational company that operates as decentralized federation of units able to sense and respond to diverse international needs and opportunities; and they had evolved beyond the abilities of the global company with its facility for managing operations on a tightly controlled worldwide basis through its centralized hub structure. They had developed what we termed transnational capabilities, the ability to manage across national boundaries, retaining local flexibility while achieving global integration. More than anything, this involved the ability to link local operations to each other and to the centre in a flexible way, and in so doing, to leverage those local and central capabilities equally.

HRM, and p.48.

THE NETWORKED FIRM

Some scholars (U. Anderson, M. Forsgren, C. Pahalberg, and P. Thilenius, 1990) suggest viewing certain large and mature internationalised firms as a network in situations where:

- Subsidiaries have developed into significant centres for investments, activities and influence and cannot be regarded at the periphery;
- Interaction between headquarters and each subsidiary is likely to be dyadic, taking place between various actors at many different organizational levels and covering different exchanges, the outcome of which is important for effective global performance;
- Such multinationals are loosely coupled political systems, rather than tightly bonded homogeneous, hierarchically bonded systems. This runs counter to the traditional structure where linkages are described formally via the organization's structure and standardized procedures. They operate informally through interpersonal contact, socialization shared vision and goals;
- One subsidiary may act as a nodal unit linking a cluster of satellite organizations. Thus one centre can assume responsibility for other units in its country or region.

The management of multi-centred networked organization is complex. Apart from the intra-organizational network (comprising headquarters and the numerous subsidiaries), each subsidiary also has a range of external relationships with local suppliers customers, competitors, host governments and alliance partners. Efficient management of both intra-organizational and inter-organizational spheres, and of the total integrated network is crucial to global corporate performance.

It involves a less hierarchical structure, featuring five dimensions: delegation of decision-making authority to appropriate units and levels; geographical dispersal of key functions across units in different countries; de-layering of organizational levels; de-bureaucratisation of formal procedures; and differentiation of work, responsibility and authority across the networked subsidiaries.

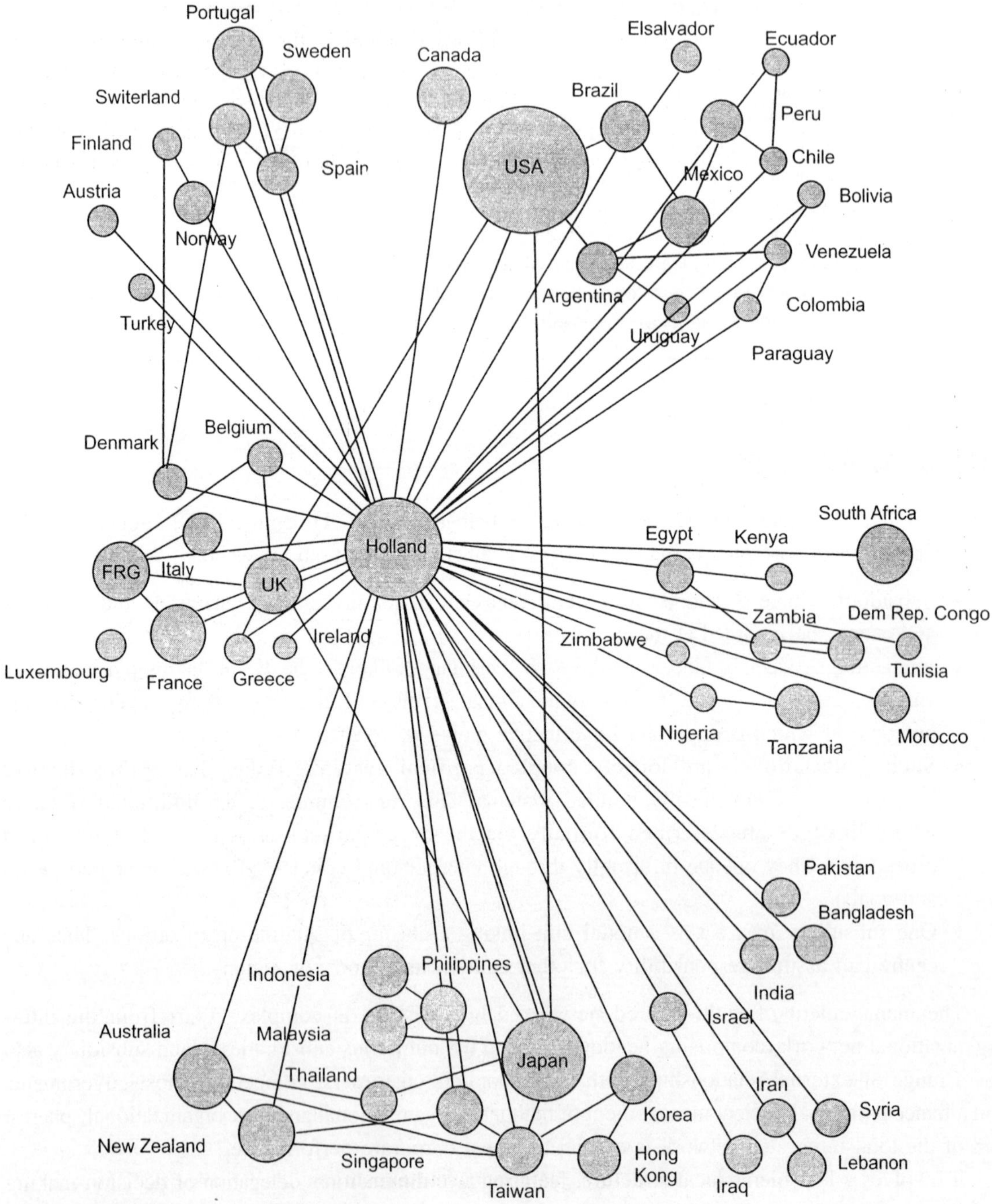

Fig. 15.6 The Networked Organization

THE KEIRETSU

Still another type of newly emerging organizational arrangement is the kieretsu, which is a large, often vertically integrated, group of companies that cooperate and work closely with each other. A good example is the Mitsubishi Group, shown in Fig. 15.7. This keiretsu consists of 28 core members who are bound together by cross-ownership, long-term business dealings, interlocking directorates, and social ties (many of the senior executives are collegemates or schoolmates or family members and

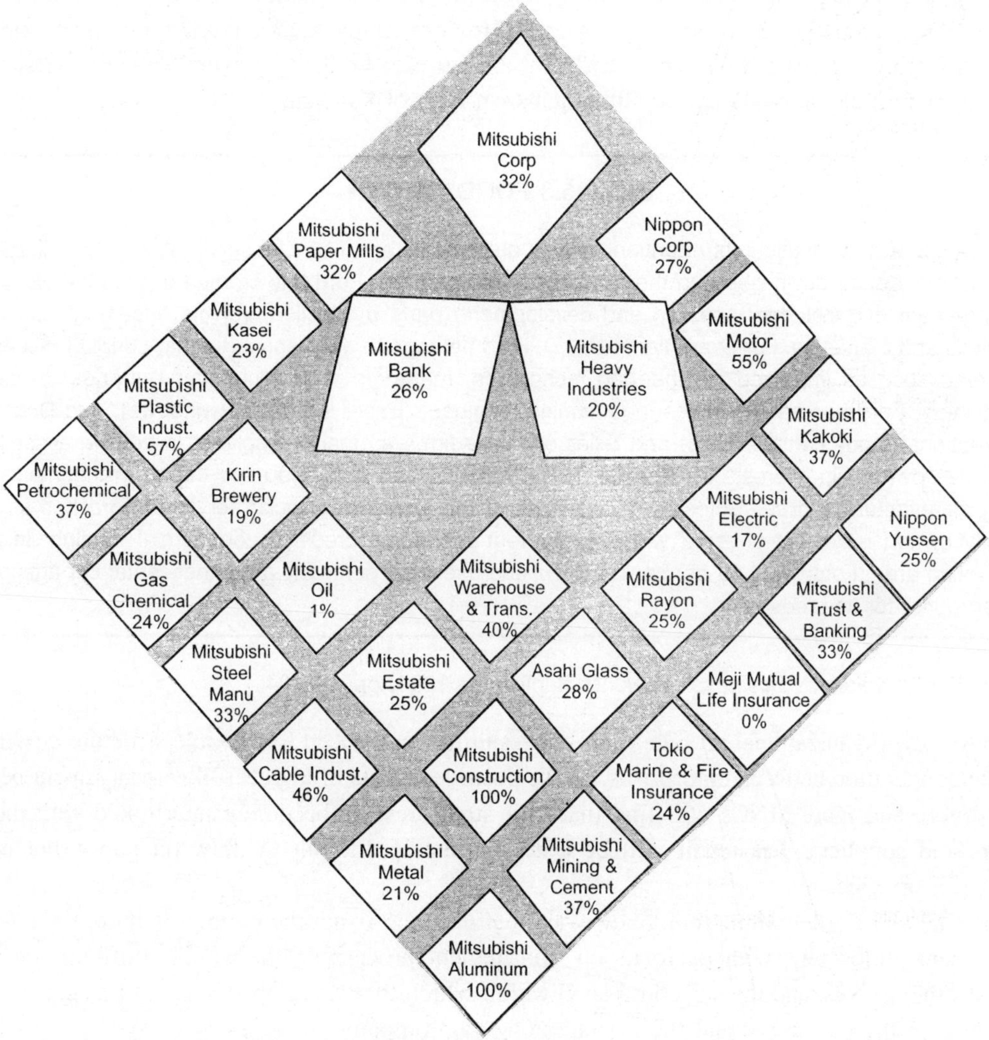

Fig. 15.7 The Mitsubushi Keirestu

'Percentages refer to the shares of each company that are hold by other members of the group

Source: Adapted from information found in William J. Holstein et al.' Mighty Mitsubishi is in the move'. *Business Week*, 24 September 1990, pp. 98-104.

relatives). In this keiretsu, there are three flagship firms in the group: Mitsubishi Corporation, which is a trading company; Mitsubishi Bank, which finances the keiretsu's operations; and Mitsubishi Heavy Industries, which is a leading worldwide manufacturer. In addition to the firms, as shown, there are hundreds of other Mitsubishi-related companies that contribute to the power of the keiretsu.

This form of organization has been cited by some international analysts as the reason why Japanese multinationals are so successful. For example, although keiretsu companies in Japan account for less than one per cent of all Japanese firms, they account for 78 per cent of the value of all shares on the Tokyo Stock Exchange, 68 per cent of all Japanese investments made in the U.S. high-tech firms. Quite obviously, these keiretsus are very powerful. However, Japanese are not the only ones using this organizational arrangement. In a sense, Birla Group can also be thought as an Indian keiretsu. Even large American multinationals are creating their own type of keiretsus.

BOX 15.3 FORD MOTOR

Ford Motor is now focusing its attention only on automotive and financial services, and has divested itself of most other businesses. In the process of reorganizing, Ford has created a giant keiretsu-like arrangement that includes research and development, parts production, vehicle assembly, financial services and marketing. For example, in R & D, Ford belongs to eight consortia that conduct research in areas such as improved engineering techniques, materials and electric-car batteries. In parts production, Ford has equity stakes in Cummins (engines), Excel Industries (windows), and Decoma International (body parts, wheels) and relies on these firms as major suppliers. In vehicle assembly, Ford has ownership interests in Europe, South America and Asia, and uses these arrangements to both manufacture and sell autos in these parts of the world. In financial services, Ford has seven wholly owned units that cover a wide gamut from consumer credit to commercial lending. In the marketing area, Ford owns 49 per cent in Hertz and uses this company and other rental car agencies as an outlet for its production.

Source: 'Ford's Keiretsu', *Business Week*, 24 September 1990, pp. 98-104.

These new organizational arrangements are resulting in the need for flexible structure designed to promote cooperation between enterprises. As the positive effects of keiretsu-like arrangement begin to spread, more and more MNCs will find that their structures are becoming interlinked with those of partners and suppliers. The result will be a design that is difficult to draw on paper, but is very effective in practice.

Ghoshal and Bartlett argue that a new way of structuring is not the issue, it is more the emerging management philosophy, with its focus on management processes: 'the actual configuration of the processes themselves, and the structural shell within which they are embedded, can be very different, depending on the businesses and the heritages of each company.'

These less hierarchical and networked structures that are evolving require coordination and human resource processes of high-level involvement, taking into account cultural variables of each unit and national culture. Human resource management and information systems play a crucial role in the control and coordination processes. Controlling is achieved by well-designed financial systems, organization culture and well-designed management information systems.

GLOBAL STRUCTURES THAT LEVERAGE KNOWLEDGE

The main function of organization in today's hyper-competitive environment is to develop and deploy, attract, leverage and disseminate organization's intellectual capital effectively. The knowledge of the organization, in order of increasing importance, includes:

1. Cognitive knowledge or know-what,
2. Advanced skills or know-how,
3. System understanding and trained intuition or know-why,
4. Self-motivated creativity or care-why.

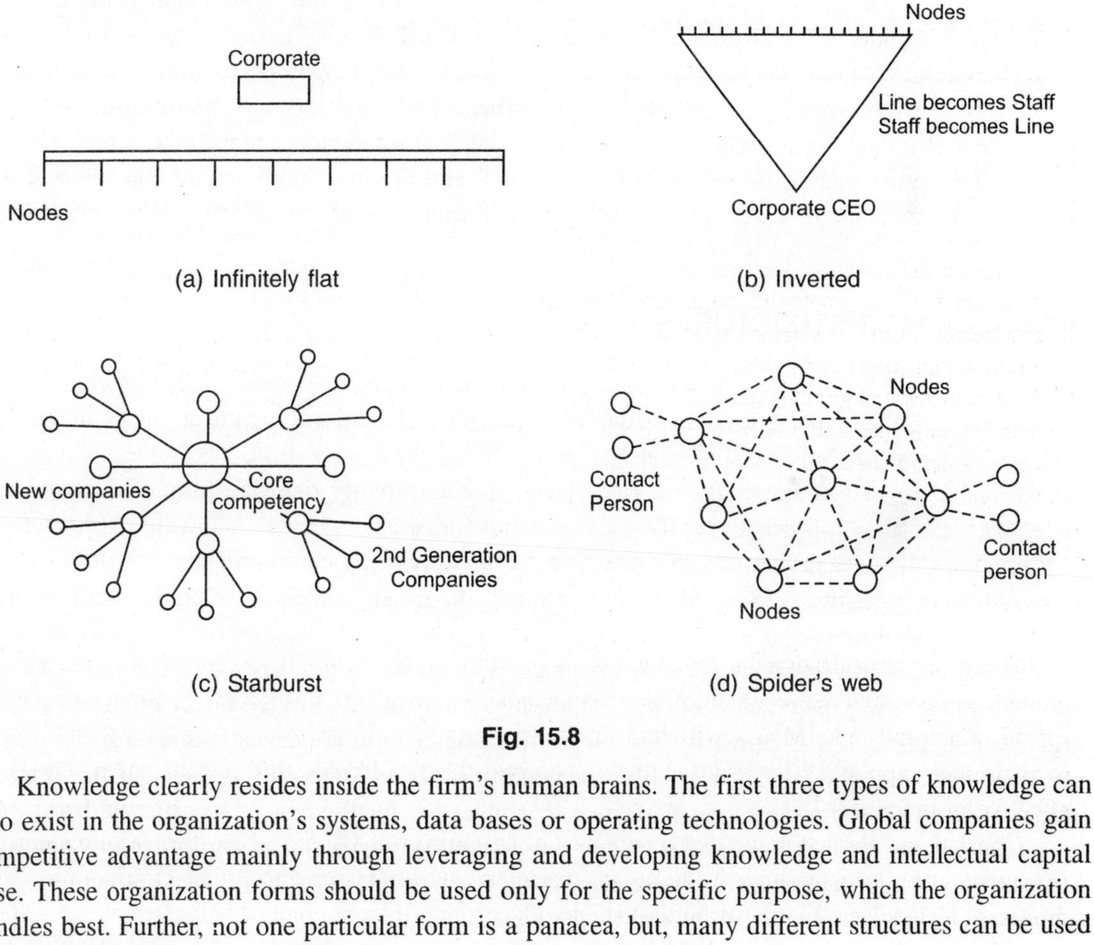

Fig. 15.8

Knowledge clearly resides inside the firm's human brains. The first three types of knowledge can also exist in the organization's systems, data bases or operating technologies. Global companies gain competitive advantage mainly through leveraging and developing knowledge and intellectual capital base. These organization forms should be used only for the specific purpose, which the organization handles best. Further, not one particular form is a panacea, but, many different structures can be used to advantage within the same firm. These organizational forms are:

1. Infinitely flat.
2. Inverted.
3. Starburst.
4. Spider's web.

Table 15.3 summarises the primary differences between these organizations and their utility in leveraging the knowledge. The key variables in choosing these forms are:

- Locus of control: where deep knowledge of the firm's particular core competence primarily resides.
- Locus of customization: where intellect is converted into unique or novel solutions.
- Direction of intellectual flow: the primary directions in which the value-added knowledge flows.
- Method of leverage: how the organization leverages its knowledge.

All the structural forms tend to push responsibility outward to the point at which the company contacts the customer. All tend to flatten the oganisation and remove layers of hierarchy. To some extent, hierarchies will also exist in them. All seek faster, more responsive, action to deal with the customization and personalization demands of an affluent and complex market. All require breaking away from, traditional thinking about command and control from the top, and management of physical assets as the key to success. However, each differs substantially in its purpose and management with very different methods of nurturing technologies and support systems to achieve its performance goals.

INFINITELY FLAT STRUCTURES

They are so-called because there is no inherent limit to their span. The primary locus of knowledge is at the centre, e.g. the operations knowledge of a fast food franchising organization, or in the huge body of data and analysis capability at the centre of the brokerage firm. The nodes of customer contact are the locus of customization. Knowledge flows primarily one way from the centre to the nodes. The leverage is arthmatic, i.e. the total amount of leverage is equal to the value of knowledge, as many times the number of nodes that use it. One centre presently can coordinate anywhere from 20 to 18,000 individual nodes. Examples include highly dispersed fast food, shipping, mail order, or airline flight operations.

Several other characteristics are also important. The nodes themselves rarely communicate with each other, operating quite independently. The centre rarely needs to give direct orders to the line organization. Instead, it is primarily an information source, a communications coordinator, and a reference desk for unusual inquiries. Lower organization levels generally connect to the centre to obtain information to improve their performances, rather for instructions or specific guidance. Most operating rules are programmed into the system and changed automatically by software. Many operations are even monitored electronically. These organizations are single-layer hierarchical structures where human command and control is replaced by electronics.

For example, Merrill Lynch's 480 domestic offices connect directly the parent central information office to satisfy the bulk of their information and analytic needs. Although regional marketing structures also exist, business is conducted as if each of Merrill Lynch's more than 17,000 branch offices contact directly to the head office. Technology permits the company to capture data and manage directly through information. Local brokers manage their own small units and accounts independently as if they alone provide the total service on a local basis.

Infinitely flat organizations operate best when the activity at the nodes can be broken down and measured to the level of its minimum repeatable transaction elements. Response time can be instantaneous, and the organizations can support any desired degree of centralised or decentralised autonomy. Control can be exercised at the most detailed level. The system can eliminate most of the routine jobs, and free employees for more personalised or skilled work, which is decentralised, individually challenging and quite rewarding.

Well-designed systems simultaneously offer highest responsiveness, maximum level of efficiency, and great consistency in quality. Such has been their effect on firms, like Fidelity Securities, Federal Express, Domino's Pizza. However, they also provide some management problems. Lower-level personnel wonder, how to advance in career path when there is no 'up'. Those at the centre have very different skills set than those at the nodes. Traditional job evaluation system breaks down, and new compensation system is needed based on professional capability, individual performance and customer satisfaction. Reward system needs to include a great variety of titles, intangible performance measurements and rewards. Constant training and updating is needed from the central office. There is tendency for the system to rigidify with time, if companies continue to use the same measurement and control systems. Consequently, external scanning system, constant customer sampling and personal observation systems are essential to supplement the structured 'hard information' linkages of these very flat organizations.

INVERTED STRUCTURE

In this type, the locus of both corporate knowledge and customisation is at the nodes and not at the centre. Hospitals and consulting firms are typical examples. The nodes tend to be highly professional and self-sufficient. Accordingly, there is no need for direct linkage between nodes. Critical knowledge about operations gets diffused informally from node to node or formally from node to the centre, the opposite of infinitely flat structure. The centre efficiently distributes logistics, analysis or support to nodes but does not give orders to them.

In inverted organizations, the former line of hierarchy becomes a support function, only intervening in extreme circumstances. The function of line managers become bottleneck breaking, culture development, communication of values, developing special studies, consulting on request, institution image building, expediting resource movements and providing service economies of scale. Hierarchy may exist within some departments to ensure efficiency and quality. Generally, what was line management now performs essentially staff function.

A well-known example of an inverted organization was SAS after Jan Carlzon became its CEO. He utilised the concept of inverting to empower SAS's contact people in ground and flight operations to bypass its heavily entrenched bureaucracies. Another is Nova Care the largest provider of rehabilitation package in the U.S. and one of the fastest growing health care companies of the last decade. With its central resource-well trained physical, occupational, and speech therapists in short supply, Nova Care provides the infrastructure for over 4,000 therapists, arranging and merging contracts with nursing homes and chains, handling accounts and credit activities, providing training updates, and stabilizing and enhancing therapists' earnings. However, the key to performance is the therapists' knowledge and their capacity to deliver this to patients.

The inverted organization works well when:

1. Servicing the customer at the point of contact is the most important activity in the enterprise.
2. The person at the point of contact has more information about the individual customer's problem and its potential solutions than anyone else.

Experience suggests, because they present unique problems, inverted organization should be used sparingly, and not just for empowerment. While seeming to diminish line authority, line managers' role often increases in importance in this structure, as they perform more influential activities, such as strategic analysis, resource building or public policy participation.

The inverted organization poses certain unique challenges. The apparent loss of formal authority can be quite traumatic for former line managers. They often don't stay updated on details about the firm's own control systems and their empowerment without adequate information can be extremely dangerous. A classic example is the rapid decline of People Express, which enjoyed highly empowered and motivated people, but lacked the systems or computer infrastructure to enable them to self-coordinate as the organization grew.

THE STARBURST STRUCTURE

Another highly leveragable structure, the starburst, serves well when there is highly specialized and valuable intellect both at the nodes and the centre. Starbursts are common in creative organizations that constantly spinn off more permanent, but separate, units like shooting stars from their core competencies. These spin-offs remain partially or wholly owned by the parent organization and usually can raise external resources independently, and are controlled primarily by marketing mechanisms. Some common examples of this structural form include: movie studios, mutual fund groups or venture capitalists, etc.

In this structure, the centre retains deep knowledge of some area such as plastic moulding technology for Nypro, managing no-load funds for Vanguard, or risk taking and resource-assembly skills for movie studios. Unlike holding companies, Starbursts, contain some intellectual core of competency. They are not merely banks or portfolio managers. The nodes are essentially separate permanent business units, having continuing relationship with the given marketplaces or production knowledge. The nodes may in time spin out further enterprises from their own core.

The flow of knowledge is typically from the centre towards the outer nodes. The organization rarely transfers knowledge from one node laterally to another. But nodes do provide feedback to the core, specialised information that other nodes may find useful without direct competition. The nodes multiply the number of outlets using the firm's core competencies and leverage: (1) through their access to specialized market expertise; and (2) through independent relationships and external financing they can generate as separate entities.

Starburst organizations work best when the core embodies an expensive and complex set of competencies and houses a few knowledgeable risk takers who realize they cannot micro-manage the diverse entities at the nodes. They work well in very ambiguous environments where it is difficult to estimate outcomes without undertaking a specific market research. Usually, they occur in environments where entrepreneurship is critical. To be effective the nodes require the economy of scale and new opportunity to spin-off that only a large centre can provide. In addition to maintaining the core competency, the corporate centre generally manages the culture, sets broad priorities, selects key people and raises resources more efficiently than could the nodes. Unlike conglomerates, Starbursts maintain some cohesive, constantly renewed, and critical intellectual competencies at their centre.

The classic problem of this organizational form is that managements often lose faith in their freestanding 'shooting stars.' After some time they try to consolidate some functions in the name of efficiency or economy of scale – as some movie studios, HP, TI, 3M, did to their regret – and only recover by reversing such policies. Starbursts also encounter problems if their divisions move into heavy investment industries or such capital-intensive mass production activities that one unit's needs can overwhelm the capacity of the core, as HP's computer division overwhelmed its test equipment groups.

INTEGRATING DIVERSE FORMS

Each organization form performs best for a specific set of intellectual tasks. Hence most large enterprises will require a mixture of these basic building blocks, combined with more traditional hierarchical structures. The critical non-organizational element in integrating and leveraging these diverse forms within the same firm is a software framework that can mix, match and manipulate 'the smallest replicable units' of tasks, customized data, or transactions across all units. For example, in some industries, such as banking, publishing, communication, structural design or medical research, it has become possible to disaggregate the critical units of service production into digitised sequences, electronic packets, data blocks, or 'bytes' of information that can be endlessly combined or manipulated for new effects and to satisfy individual customers and operating needs. These micro-units permit the highest possible degree of segmentation, strategic fine tuning, value adding, and customer satisfaction at the lowest cost-in the marketplace.

In keeping with the exponentiality of knowledge, systems that capture such data from the outset can build up a detailed information base that later provides insurmountable competitive edge. By constantly updating, analyzing and sharing data patterns from all detailed sources, successful IT systems automatically capture and disseminate the highest level of experience available within the enterprise. They also provide the basis for laterally integrating the wide range of different organization forms now available.

Table 15.1 Summarising Characteristics of Different Structures

Characteristics	*Infinitely Flat*	*Inverted*	*Starburst*
Definition of node	Individual	Individual	Business units
Locus of intellect	Centre	Nodes	Centre and nodes
Locus of customization	Nodes	Nodes	Centre and nodes
Direction of flow	Centre to nodes	Nodes to centre	Centre to nodes
Method of leverage	Multiplicative	Distributive	Additive
Example	Brokerage firms aircraft operations	Hospitals, construction, engineering	Major movie studios, mutual fund groups

(*Contd.*)

Table 15.1 Contd.

Characteristics	*Infinitely Flat*	*Inverted*	*Starburst*
Type of intellect – cognitive know-what	Deep knowledge and information at centre	Primary intellect at nodes, support services from centre	Depth at centre, technical and markets at the nodes
Advance skill know-how	Programmed info system	Professionalized skills informally transferred from node to node	Transferred from centre to nodes then node to node via the core
System knowledge know-why	Systems experts at the centre, customer knowledge at the nodes	System and customer expertise at the nodes	Split between central technical competency at the core, systematic market knowledge at nodes
Motivated creativity care-why	Frees employees from routine for more skilled work	Great professional autonomy	Entrepreneurial incentive
Examples	Merrill Lynch 17,000 branches	SAS airlines Nova Care	Thermo Electron TCG; Nypro,

ROLE OF CORPORATE HEADQUARTER IN MANAGING SUBSIDIARIES

The role of corporate headquarter in the development and management of subsidiaries is crucial for the growth of the enterprise as a whole. Corporate parent has to take the view on how it will relate to and seek to enhance, the strategies of subsidiaries and add value to their functioning. This is quite significant because different subsidiaries play different roles. Subsidiaries may be playing a receptive (global), active (transnational) or autonomous (multi-domestic) roles. They may be implementers, integrated players, local innovators or global innovators in the context of knowledge inflow and knowledge outflow. Or they may be contributors, strategic leaders, implementers of blind roles when judged from their competence and their importance.

There are different approaches, as shown in Table 15.2 that are adopted by various corporates (parents) in managing their subsidiaries. There are parents who seek to operate in a portfolio management style. They have slim corporate head office staff seeking to balance investments in business by reviewing acquisition targets, buying wisely and divesting poor performers. A second role is as a restructurer of businesses, for example, the role taken by Mittal Steel or Hanson Group. They focused on acquisition of businesses not doing well but having inherent value and turning them around by restructuring the organizations and revamping their operations. The corporate skills will be in the area of identifying such targets and restructuring and transforming them. They will frequently move senior executives from the head office to subsidiaries for this purpose.

A parent may also seek to add benefits to businesses by helping with the interrelationships between the businesses themselves. This is sometimes called managing synergy. The corporation may seek to transfer skills and competencies from one business unit to another. These could be competencies learned in the management of one value chain, which are relevant to the value chain of another business. It could be the marketing skills that can be transferred to other less sophisticated businesses, for example, by moving experienced marketing executives. Another approach is the sharing of activities. Marriot sought to share activities across hotels, restaurants and airport facilities. Such shared activities included the ability to provide and learn from standardised hotel procedures and to benefit from shared procurement and distribution. They were supported by an organizational structure that encourages integration and cooperation.

Table 15.2 Role of Corporate Headquarter in Managing Subsidiaries

Portfolio managers	• Identifying and acquiring undervalued assets • Divesting low-performing subsidiaries quickly and good performers at a premium	• Autonomous subsidiaries • Small low-cost corporate staff • Incentives based on subsidiary results
Restructurers	• Identifying restructuring opportunities • Intervention in subsidiaries to transform performance • Sale of subsidiaries when restructuring is complete or when market conditions are favourable	• Autonomous subsidiaries • Turnaround skills of corporate staff • Incentives based on acquired subsidiarys' results
Skill transferrers	• Transferring skills to give competitive advantage to subsidiaries • On-going transfer of skills • Identification of appropriate skills to transfer	• Autonomous but collaborative subsidiaries • Corpoarte staff as integrators • Cross-subsidiary task forces • Incentives based partly on corporate results
Activity sharers	• Sharing activities to provide competitive advantages to subsidiaries • Identification of benefits of sharing which outweigh costs • Overcoming subsidiary's resistance to sharing	• Subsidiaries encouraged to share • Strategic planning at different levels • Corporate staff as integrators • Incentives based on corporate results

Source: Adapted from M. Porter, 'From Competitive to Corporate Strategy', *Harvard Business Review*, May-June 1987.

GLOBAL EXPANSION THROUGH STRATEGIC ALLIANCES

One of the most popular ways companies get involved in international operations is through international strategic alliances. The average large U.S. Corporation, which had no alliance in early 1990s, now has more than 30 alliances globally. Companies in rapidly changing industries, such as media, entertainment, pharmaceuticals, biotechnology and software, might have hundreds of these relationships.

Typically alliances include licensing, joint ventures, and consortia. For example, pharmaceutical companies such as Merck, Eli Lilly and Pfizer-cross-license their newest drugs to one another to support industry-wide innovation and marketing to offset the high fixed costs incurred on research and distribution.

Companies often seek joint ventures to take advantage of partner's knowledge of local markets, to achieve production cost savings through economies of scale, to share complementary technological strengths, or to distribute new products and services through another country's distribution channels.

A type of consortium, 'the global virtual organization', is increasingly being used and it offers a promising approach for meeting worldwide competition. The virtual organization refers to a continually evolving set of company relationships that exist temporarily to exploit unique opportunities or attain specific strategic advantages. A company may be involved in multiple alliances at any one time. Oracle, a software company, is involved in as many as 15,000 short-term organizational partnerships at any time. Some executives believe shifting to a yirtual approach is the best way for companies to be competitive in the global marketplace.

Review Questions

1. A small manufacturing firm believes that there is market for hand-held tools that are carefully crafted for local markets. After spending 2 months in Europe, the president of this firm believes that his company can create a popular line of these tools. What type of organization structure would be of most value to this firm in its initial efforts to go international?
2. If the same company finds a major market for its other products in Europe and decides to expand in Asia also, would you recommend any change in organizational structure? If yes, what would you suggest? If no, why not?
3. If the company finds after 3 years of international effort that it is selling more than 60 per cent of its output overseas, what type of organizational structure would you suggest for the future?
4. Explain the conditions that favour matrix structure and what are its problems and what is required to make this structure successful?
5. Explain the following structures in detail:
    1. The Heterarchy.
    2. The Transnational.
    3. The Networked firm.
    4. The Keiretsu.
6. Discuss the roles of corporate parents in managing the subsidiaries of different kinds.

Assignment

Explore organizational structure of a manufacturing MNC and one in services sector, also one in pharmaceutical business and the other in information technology by surfing their websites and explain the logic of differences in their organizational structures.

Chapter

16

Employee Relations and Employment Practices across Countries

LEARNING OBJECTIVES

After studying this chapter, you will be able to:

- *Framework of industrial relations in countries*
- *Trade unions and collective bar group with MNCs*
- *Employee relations approaches and role of HRM in MNCs*
- *Understanding psychological contract and its effect on employee attitude*
- *Industrial relations practices in major economics of the world including HR related cultural practices.*

OPENING CASE
European Union and the Social Charter

In terms of human resource management the Social Charter is the key body of EC legislation as its proposals will have a considerable impact on employee relations at international, national and local levels. Much of the Social Charter is an amalgam of the articles embodied in various treaties which jointly created the EC, such as, The Treaty of Paris 1952 and the Treaties of Rome, 1957. The Social Charter states that:

> the completion of the internal market must offer improvements in the social field for workers of European Community, especially in terms of freedom of movement, living and working conditions, health and safety at work, social protection, education and training whereas, in order to ensure equal treatment, it is important to combat every form of discrimination, including discrimination on grounds of sex, colour, race, opinions and beliefs, and whereas in a spirit of solidarity it is important to combat social exclusion.

The main twelve provisions of the social charter are:

1. Free movement. The right to free movement within the community to all workers without needing visas or work-permits.
2. Employment and remuneration. All employees should be fairly remunerated. Workers should have an equitable wage, i.e. a wage sufficient to enable them to have a decent standard of living (often interpreted as 'minimum wage'). Workers subject to atypical terms of employment (part-time workers) shall benefit from the equitable wage in line with full-time employee remuneration.
3. Improvement of living and working conditions. The process must result from an approximation of conditions as regards, in particular, the duration and organization of working time and forms of employment; the process must cover such aspects of employment as collective redundancies and bankruptcies; every worker must have weekly day of rest and annual paid leave and a contract of employment.
4. Social protection. Every worker in the community shall have the right to adequate level of social protection and shall regardless of status, enjoy an adequate level of social security benefits. Persons outside the labour market (those who are ill, retired or unable to work) must receive sufficient resources and social assistance in keeping with their particular situation.
5. Freedom of association and collective bargaining. Employers and employees have the right of association to protect their social and economic interests (employers' association and trade unions). There is also the right not to join them. There is also the right to negotiate and conclude collective agreements. There shall also be the right to collective action (strikes and lock-outs) subject to national legislation.
6. Vocational training. Every worker must have access to and receive vocational training, with no discrimination on grounds of nationality.

7. Equal treatment for men and women. Regarding access to employment, remuneration, working conditions, social protection, educational training and career development.
8. Information, consultation and participation of workers. These must be developed along appropriate lines, taking account of the practices in force in the various member states. This shall apply especially in companies or groups of companies having establishments or companies in several member states. These processes must be implemented when technological changes take place having major implications for the workforce; in connection with restructuring operations or mergers; in case of collective redundancies; when trans-frontier workers in particular are affected by employment policies adopted by the undertakings where they are employed.
9. Health protection and safety in the workplace. Appropriate measures must be taken to achieve further harmonization of conditions in the area.
10. Protection of children and adolescents in employment. The minimum employment age must not be lower than the school-leaving age, neither of which must be lower than 15 years. After completing compulsory education young people must be entitled to receive initial vocational training of a reasonable duration.
11. Elderly persons. Every worker must at the time of retirement be able to enjoy resources affording him or her a decent standard of living, and those not entitled to pension must be provided for.
12. Disabled persons. All disabled person must be entitled to additional concrete measures aimed at improving their social and professional integration. These measures must concern vocational training, ergonomics, mobility, means of transport and housing.

The implementation of Social Charter has proved more controversial than the debate over what it should contain, still it has greatly influenced the employee relations in organizations operating within the EU.

INTRODUCTION

The employee relations management in the global business has undergone a dramatic change. The traditional approach in most domestic organizations has been characterized by collective bargaining, where the dialogue has been between the trade union and management, the trade union representing individuals, and management exclusively representing the organization. The formal agenda for bargaining is restricted to pay and working conditions, with neither side seeking more from a formalized contractual relationship. This traditional approach has undergone a sea change with the arrival of globalization, knowledge workers and multinational enterprises.

The industrial relations climate in any country is evolved over a long period out of the struggle between the labour and capital, religious and cultural ethos, and class conflict, nature of governance and its legal system, apart from the socio-economic development and many other factors. We have tried to group these practices in this chapter according to important countries, representative of their region.

In this chapter, first a model of industrial relations is discussed, followed by collective bargaining. Next, employee relations policies and practices of multinationals and their attitudes towards trade unions are explained. After this, we have analysed the 'psychological contract of employees', their perspective and the role of HR professionals. Finally, we have described the societal climate and employee management practices prevalent in important countries of the world so that these practices are understood in the context of entire social, political and cultural backgrounds prevailing in the countries concerned. In the opening part, the politico-social environment of the European Union is described which largely guides and decides the employment policies of organizations operating within the EU.

FRAMEWORK OF INDUSTRIAL RELATIONS

Industrial relations in the final analysis are the outcome of how power is being shared between employees and the management in major industrial units and industries across any country, although considerable differences exist in individual undertakings. The sharing of power primarily depends on the nature of labour markets, political and economic situations prevailing and the legal system. Poole (1986) has attempted to construct a theoretical framework to explain these influences. He sees workers' participation and control as being the central manifestation of power. This is linked with 'underlying or latent power resources and a series of values which either buttress particular power distribution or facilitate their successful challenge or change.

Finally, 'values about participation and control are shaped by the existing levels of workers participation and control, latent power, government action and ideologies'. While this framework, as shown in Fig. 16.1, pinpoints the major factors influencing the styles of employee participation and control, it cannot clearly demonstrate how these factors interact to produce such systems. Nevertheless, it is a useful model to aid the understanding of these complex processes. In the words of Poole (1986:28):

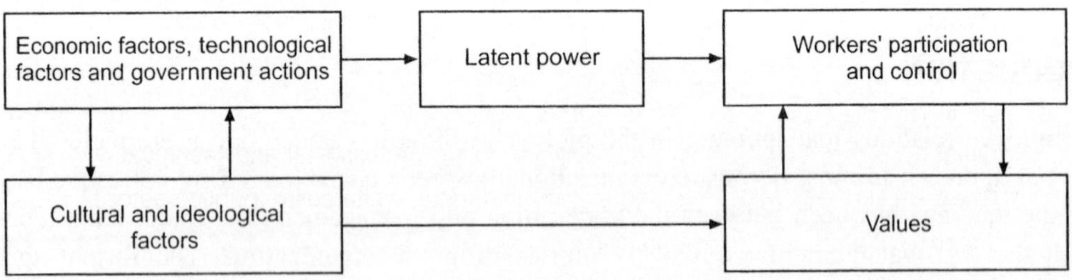

Fig. 16.1 Poole's Model of Industrial Relations Climate

> Worker participation and control are reflections of the latent power of particular industrial classes, pairs or groups and the 'value' climate which may or may not be favourable to participation experiment. These values, thus, mediate between certain structural factors associated with latent power and their realization in the form of workers' participation and control. It will also be seen that the principal structural factors associated with the latent

power of the main industrial classes, parties or groups are 'economic factors', such as levels of the employment, the profit margins of particular companies, the levels of competition, the degree of industrial concentration and periods of economic disintegration, technological factors, such as the approximation of the technology of a company to a given point on the 'technical scale', the degree of complexity and education involved in any given task and the effects of the micro-electronic revolution; and finally, various forms of government action such as legislation on labour issues, its intervention in the working of the economic system and so on.

A comparative study of industrial relations in different countries shows that industrial relations phenomena are a very faithful expression of the society in which they operate, of its characteristic features and of the power relationships between different interest groups. Industrial relations cannot be understood without understanding the way in which rules are established and implemented and decisions are made in the society concerned.

An interesting example of the effect of historical differences may be seen in the structure of trade unions in various countries. Poole has identified several factors as shown in Fig. 16.1 above and also mentioned below, which might underline these historical differences:

- The mode of technology and industrial organization at critical stages of the trade union development;
- Method of trade union regulation by government;
- Ideological division within the trade union movement;
- The influence of religious organizations on trade union development; and
- Managerial strategies for labour relations.

BOX 16.1 TRADE UNION STRUCTURES IN LEADING WESTERN COUNTRIES

Australia	general, craft, industrial, white collar
Belgium	industrial, professional, religious, public sector
Canada	industrial, craft, conglomerate
Denmark	general, craft, white collar
Finland	industrial, white collar, professional and technical
Great Britain	general, craft, industrial, white collar, public sector
Japan	expertise
Netherlands	religious, conglomerate, white collar
Norway	industrial, craft
Sweden	industrial, craft, white collar, professional
Switzerland	industrial, craft, religious, white collar
United States	industrial, craft, conglomerate, white collar
West Germany	industrial, white collar

Source: M. Poole, *IR: Origins and Patterns of National Diversity*, London 1986.

COLLECTIVE BARGAINING

Collective bargaining remains an important part of the employee relationship, although the same is declining in general in all countries and more steeply in MNCs for a variety of reasons. However, in terms of the number of employees covered and the scope of agreements concluded, it remains an important channel for establishing terms and conditions of employment and productivity norms. Collective agreements are reached after the negotiations and agreements are recorded in the presence of the Labour Officer and many of them are informally concluded and followed. There are three perspectives on collective bargaining:

- Unitary perspective. For those (MNCs) who view the firm as an essentially cooperative system where management and labour share a 'unitary' outlook, a union presence and collective bargaining procedures are unnecessary. If the management is working efficiently and remains sensitive to the individual's employment conditions, any collective voice attempting to influence the working environment is superfluous. Moreover, the introduction of collective bargaining and potentially critical force into the employment relationship will lead to conflicts and questioning of legitimacy of the managerial prerogative.
- Pluralist perspective (PSUs). This perspective largely supports the collective bargaining process as a channel to institutionalize the conflict situations. Where labour and management have some conflicting aims within the employment relationship, collective bargaining process offers the opportunity to establish the areas of commonality, negotiate about issues of disparity and inevitably, on some occasions, take industrial action (strike) to re-establish power relations to reach new consensus.
- Radical perspective. The major critique of the collective bargaining process is that it focuses very narrowly on terms and conditions of employment without changing the capitalist structure of market economy. There is no recognition of the essentially exploitative nature of labour-capital relationship. As such, the collective bargaining obscures or prevents any threat to political, social or economic challenge to capital.

In this connection there are some vital issues that are being raised but they are beyond the scope of this book for a meaningful discussion. These issues are:

1. Is HRM compatible with collective bargaining?
2. Will HRM bypass collective bargaining?
3. Can collectivism and individualism coexist in a society or organization?
4. Should local governments remain neutral in the conflict and allow the parties to settle the dispute or provide support to one or the other party?

EMPLOYEE RELATIONS AND MULTINATIONALS

Because of differences in industrial relations the climate in different countries and subsidiaries of MNCs, and management practices also differ. While in general, for the above reasons, the labour management matters are delegated to subsidiaries but central intervention and degree of centralization cannot be ruled out. The degree of centralization or decentralization in labour policy depends on following factors:

1. The degree of inter-subsidiary production integration. Higher is the inter-subsidiary production higher will be the degree of centralization.
2. Nationality of ownership of the subsidiary. A number of studies have revealed that U.S. firms tend to exercise greater control over labour relations than do British or the European firms. U.S. firms were less likely to recognise trade unions and preferred not to join employers association. They have developed specialised HR function at plant levels and tend to pay higher wages and offer more fringe benefits than local firms. Ethnocentric MNCs are likely to centralize more than polycentric ones. Similarly geo-centric MNCs are likely to ensure global coordination of labour policies.
3. MNCs' prior experience in labour relations. European firms have tended to deal with labour unions at industry level frequently via employer's association level rather than at firm level. The opposite is truer for U.S. firms.
4. Subsidiary characteristics. Subsidiaries that are formed through acquisitions of well-established indigenous firms are likely to be given much more autonomy over labour relations than are green field sites. Greater strategic intervention is expected in those subsidiaries which are of strategic importance by the corporate and where the subsidiary is more dependent for resources on the headquarters. Finally, poor subsidiary performance tends to be accompanied by increased corporate involvement.
5. Nature of Issues. Those matters which have repercussions on the image and performance of the MNC as a whole will certainly be decided at the headquarter.

TRADE UNIONS AND MULTINATIONALS

Trade unions limit the strategic choice of multinationals in three ways: by influencing wage levels to the extent that cost structures may become uncompetitive, by constraining the ability of multinationals to vary employment levels at will, and by obstructing global integration of their operations by using the influence of their local governments and other means. For multinationals, varying employment levels are more important than the rise in wage levels, because they depend for their operations more and more on technology rather than on labour. Similarly, moving facilities and manufacture of parts and components from one location to another is also equally important to remain competitive globally. They also phase out old products faster and introduce new products more regularly.

Similarly, unions also perceive multinationals as a threat to their bargaining power because of their influence across and large resources. Various concerns of unions against multinationals can be summarized as under:

- Formidable financial resources. The budget of some multinationals is larger than the budget of some nations. The economic pressures which a union can exert on a domestic firm are much more than over a multinational.
- Alternative source of supply. This may take the form of an explicit dual sourcing policy to reduce the vulnerability of the multinational to a strike by any national union.
- The ability to move production facilities to other countries. An important concern of employees and unions is that job-security may be threatened if an MNC seeks to produce or source from

other countries where the relative cost may be lower or better skills may be available or for any other reason.

- Remote location of decision-making authority in case of dispute. The union leaders find it difficult to travel and put their case across effectively.
- Production facilities in many industries cause, therefore, less pressure on multinationals to bargain and settle the dispute.
- The capacity to stage an investment strike or refusal to modernise or expand facilities in a location which is prone to labour unrest.
- Superior knowledge and expertise of labour relations.
- Lack of information and data about multinational operations with the union on which to conduct bargaining.

Table 16.1 Union Memberships for Selected Countries

	Union Density		*Proportionate Changes in Union Density (%)*	*Rank Order of Union Density*	
	1985	1995	1985-95	1985	1995
Australia	46	33	–28	2	4
Canada	35	35	0	6	3
France	15	11	–27	9	10
Germany	36	30	–16	5	5
Italy	42	38	–10	4	2
Japan	29	24	–18	7	7
Korea	12	13	+8.3	10	9
Sweden	85	83	–2.2	1	1
UK	45	29	–35	3	6
USA	18	15	–12	8	8

Source: ILO unpublished data (1996); Australia ABS Cat. No.6325.0; Korea NSO

Collective Bargaining with MNCs and International Regulation

There is increasing pressure by unions and other leftist organizations for the regulation and control of MNCs by the U.N.O. and other international bodies. For this the purpose, International Confederation of Trade Unions (ICFTU), the International Labour Organization (ILO), the United Nations Conference on Trade and Development (UNCTAD) and the Organization for Economic Cooperation and Development (OECD) have been set up to assist local unions and governments to bargain and deal with MNCs.

A key section of these guidelines is the umbrella or 'chapeau clause' that precedes the guidelines issued for MNCs. This clause states that multinationals should adhere to the guidelines within the framework of law, regulations and prevailing labour relations and employment practices, in each of the countries in which they operate. This means compliance with local law supersedes the guidelines.

MANAGING PSYCHOLOGICAL CONTRACT

The manner in which the organizational dialogue takes place has undergone dramatic change within the multinational organization. The traditional approach in most domestic organizations has been characterised by collective bargaining, where the dialogue has been between the trade union and the personnel in an industrial arena, the trade union representing individuals, and almost exclusively the personnel function representing the organization. The formal agenda for bargaining restricted to pay and working conditions, in line with Taylor's view that the basic employment relationship is no more than the straight exchange of a 'fair day's work for a fair day's pay', with neither side seeking more from a formalized contractual relationship. This traditional approach has undergone a sea change with the arrival of globalization and knowledge worker.

Knowledge about different employee relationship practices and HRM environment in multinational organizations is relevant in the sense that international HR managers need to be alert to such matters as:

- What some of the expectations of local nationals might be;
- Issues of congruence or incongruity with company philosophy;
- Differing legal requirements around the world;
- Motivational and cost aspects of the differing practices;
- What foreign practices are particularly innovative and might have application in ;introducing them to other subsidiaries in other countries.

It is necessary that these practices are understood in the context of entire social, political and cultural background prevailing in the country concerned. The industrial relations climate in any country is evolved over a long period out of the struggle between labour and capital, religious and cultural ethos, and class conflict, nature of governance and its legal system apart from socio-economic development and many other factors. We have tried to group these practices first according to important countries representative of the region they belong to.

Psychological Contract. In multinational environment where employees are posted far and wide with little personal contact between the headquarter and the controlling superior, it is very important for the motivation and performance of an employee how he perceives the support provided by the headquarter and his boss. Psychological contract is in addition to the terms of his employment and constitutes an integral part of employee relationship. The psychological contract represents an implicit contract to execute the employment contract according to a set of values, beliefs and norms. The employment contract, also called 'transactional contract', comprises the specific, short-term, monetisable obligations, while the psychological contract is characterised by broad, open-ended, long-term obligations based on both exchanges around monetisable elements and socio-emotional elements like loyalty and support. It is about the employee's beliefs which he holds regarding promises made, accepted and relied upon between themselves and the employer. The two contracts, psychological and transactional, together constitute what is called a 'social contract'. Perceived violation of the psychological contract by an employee results in his poor performance and affects his sense of loyalty and commitment.

The environmental changes due to globalization and other socio-economic, political and technological changes over the period have altered the individual work values, psychological needs of employees and also organizational work values, which are given in Table 16.2:

Table 16.2 Dominant Values in the Workforce

Category	*Entered Workforce*	*Age Now*	*Individual Work Values*	*Organizational Work Values*
Protestant work ethics	1945-59	55-65	Hard work, conservative, loyal to organization,	Command, control, efficiency, compliance, dehumanisation
Existentialism	1960-70	40-45	Quality of life, non-conforming, seeks autonomy, loyal to himself	Team work
Pragmatism	1980-89	30-39	Success, achievement, ambition, hard work, loyalty to career	Efficiency, cost reduction, growth and diversification, win the competition
Generation X1	1990s	Under 30	Lifestyle, self-development, loyalty to peers and friends	Empowerment, organizational learning, collaborations

EMPLOYEE PERSPECTIVE

Recent research undertaken to discover how a particular group of employees, viewed the employment relationship in a multinational high-tech company revealed a number of perspectives on 'psychological contracts' (Parkinson, 1999). Although the formal contract of service was the same, there were at least four different types of perspectives based on intangible or informal psychological contract. These perspectives emerged based on what they are looking for in that relationship, whether the focus is on the purely formal aspects of employment or on looking for a wider involvement in the organization. The second factor that seemed to influence the relationship was that how active they were in pursuing their career. These perspectives/psychological contracts are:

1. **It is not broken (passive and organization):** This first view comes from those having relatively long service in the organization. While everything is going well, there is a feeling of inertia with the career. The job is enjoyable and the career seems to manage itself. Although they have some career direction, yet they expect the organization or their line manager to take responsibility of their career. This group is looking for achievement, recognition and enjoyment from their work, and any career decision happens only to avoid being in situation where they are unable to obtain these states or until something goes wrong with the fulfilment of their psychological contract.
2. **I know what I am talking about (active-individual):** Those in this group are focused on building their skills and are prepared to change organizations to pursue their career or set up their own. They have a sense of self-reliance through constantly developing and practising

their skill base, which enables them to move easily between companies. The sense of identity that comes from their skills has given many of them the confidence to set up on their own at various stages of their careers. They see the new job as an alternative to using their technical skills. Another factor in common was having had a 'bad experience' previously, with the subsequent impact on wariness in future relationships with the organizations.

3. **A desire to get on (active-organization):** Members of this group positively look for challenges and are concerned about being recognised for their efforts. Expecting both to contribute and receive in the employment relationship, they feel that by contributing and being loyal to the organization at a higher level, they will receive back the means to manage their career actively and be more in control of their lives. They do not want to compromise on lifestyle issues and are highly aware of the problem of balancing family life with a career. These people have had a clearer idea of what they wanted to do from early on, and have recognized the need to plan their careers, moving to take up next challenge rather than waiting until something goes wrong; but when it does, they suffer a personal sense of failure and sadness.
4. **I come to work to earn money (passive-individual):** This group views the relationship as the traditional basic exchange of a 'fair day's work for a fair day's pay', where motivation is the extrinsic rewards of pay and benefits and the security of a large organization. They would see their career as something that happens to them, particularly early on, having often drifted into their first job, allowing themselves to be pushed along by circumstances and other people, often ending up in situations they would otherwise have sought. With no specific career goals to pursue, their main drivers are extrinsic rewards and security; and outside the formal terms of their employment contract they prefer to keep their relationship with the organization at a minimum.

In some companies HR function manages only the formal contract while line managers manage the informal contract. Increasingly HR professionals are expected to help line managers in this critical role. Overlaid with the global workforce, the pressure is on managers to find different ways of developing a relationship with their workforce. Golzen has highlighted that successful leaders manage relationships through 'emotional intelligence' which is also indicative of the importance of interpersonal skills; as he suggests: Social skills at a personal level translate into the ability of companies to handle diversity, both within their own workforce, and in their global activities. Some employees think that, 'To me the organization is my manager and my manager's manager'.

ROLE OF HR PROFESSIONALS

In applying the employment research to employee relationship there are three key roles for HR professionals:

1. To clarify the expectations and obligations that make up the organizational part of the employment relationship at the macro-level, through the formal process of delivering corporate communications to employees and enabling feedback on how it has been received through instruments, such as attitude surveys or focus groups and in order to deliver a consistent

organizational message, each aspect of the communication process must be reviewed to ensure that the various filters, whether they be cultural, organizational or individual, have been understood and adjusted for. This is particularly important in mergers or restructuring or changes from unionized workforce, etc.

2. The second is related to the first; it is HR's role to ensure that line managers, who represent the organization as far as employees are concerned, have both the ability and the motivation to deliver those **consistent corporate** messages. It is necessary to ensure that messages and communications from managers and various management practices to employees are consistent with those that organization wants to send to an increasingly diverse workforce.
3. The third role for HR professionals is in supporting and advising line managers to develop skills they need to manage the informal relationship with their staff, particularly in terms of the design of performance management processes. In designing management development programme, they should see that emphasis in on development of 'soft' skills and interpersonal skills which are considered outside the domain of operational management.

EMPLOYEE RELATIONS IN IMPORTANT COUNTRIES

China

China is one of the world's oldest civilizations and with 1.3 billion people, the largest country in terms of population. The country has been under the Communist Party rule since 1921 and has experienced at least two major cultural and economic changes between then and now. After World War II, the party under Mao Zedong established a dictatorship that, while ensuring China's sovereignty, imposed strict controls over everyday life and security. Starting from 1978, his successor Deng Xiaoping gradually introduced market-oriented reforms and decentralised economic decision-making. Political controls, however, remain tight even while economic control continues to be relaxed. China is a very large and diverse nation with a variety of ethnic groups, languages and religious cultures. There are however, like India, some common cultural threads going through many of the values and attitudes that people hold: a long imperial history, and traditional heritage with 'Han' as a prominent ethnic group with overwhelming influence of the Confucian philosophy. All these have left their imprint on the national culture and at the micro-level on employee-management relationship and HRM practices.

As Fang (2000) points out, the Chinese culture has been moulded, among others, by Confucianism (551-479 BC). Among the values Confucianism espouses are: moral cultivation, importance of interpersonal relationships, family orientation, respect for age and hierarchy, need for harmony and concept of saving face. One of the fundamental Chinese tenets is the yin-yang philosophy which accepts the simultaneous existence of opposite values and beliefs within a person, and by implication within a culture. Fang succinctly interprets the yin-yang philosophy within the context of cultural 'values attributed to the Chinese, "The Chinese are, as many cross-cultural studies point out, reserved, long-term oriented, high context and collectivist. But substantial evidence shows that the Chinese are also expressive, short-term oriented, low context, individualistic given circumstances....The Chinese, for instance, can be extremely expressive on festive occasions and when they are being put in a contest setting.'

In addition, unlike the Japanese, their work organizations do not seem to be a part of their in-groups. It is more loyalty to particular individuals rather than to organizations as Yager (1994), in his study of foreign joint ventures in China, found that Japanese managers were almost baffled by Chinese workers' display of a lack of pride in and identity with their employer organizations. Traditionally, Chinese personal networking (guanxi) has been important to success, using extended family and other developed relationships and connections to gain cooperation and to get things done. However, this trait has not been so effective in developing large organizations and in running joint ventures. But it has been very effective in building small enterprises.

Yager et al. found that this had some implications for industrial discipline which means that workers follow a regimen in their jobs and the will of supervisors to exercise sanctions in controlling worker behaviour that was non-existent among Chinese workers. A sense of responsibility to the employer organization, consistency in work performance and follow-through also seemed to be unusual. There was the pervasive need to build identity to the organization. A combination of guanxi and personal loyalty has other interesting implications for labour relations as well. It is, for instance, very common for Chinese managers who leave their company to join another one to invite their subordinates to follow them to the new company. Similarly, it is common for employees to stay in a company mainly because they have strong personal ties with their superiors.

The centrally planned political economic structure of the society has also had profound implications on the ways in which employees behave in their workplace and on their relationship with their superiors and managers. For example, until recently, a Communist Party hierarchy existed in every plant or firm. Every plant manager had to live under the shadow of the party boss. Although the formal party control has been relaxed, the plant's trade union leaders behave in the same way as if they have the power to veto even top management decisions. It is worth noting, however, that China has no independent trade unions truly comparable to those in Western or any other democracies. Local government exerts a lot of control and influence over people and their affairs. For example, people are not free to live wherever they choose. They must obtain a residency permit before they can live officially in a city other than their home town. Local government plays also an important role in the transfer of people across companies. For instance, the local labour bureau can stop a transfer from one organization to another if the bureau believes that the requirements of the original employment contract were not met. Also, if the foreign companies located in China wish to recruit Chinese national managers, they need to obtain permission from the local government.

Chinese managers, especially the older ones who lived through the Cultural Revolution, are usually not proactive or bold when making decisions and they often do not offer independent opinions on particular decisions. One study found that Chinese managers reposed much stronger reliance on widespread beliefs as a source of guidance in their decision-making than did managers in other nations (Smith et al.1997). Moreover managers are reluctant to share information and to take risky decisions; they also worry much more about political relationships in the organization than they do about the organizational goals and how to achieve them (Li et al. 1999).

Employees often avoid problems until they are impossible to ignore. When problems are finally addressed, solutions are based on precedents and usually involve a reference to authority. The managers, on their part, tend to rely on rules and procedures. As Weldon and Vanhonacker (1999) point out, the tendency to avoid problems and lack of creativity have been attributed to various facets of Chinese culture, including traditional socialisation practices, where obedience, impulse control and acceptance of social obligations are encouraged, while independence, assertiveness and creativity are not encouraged. According to Weldon and Vanhonaker, the following factors have also contributed to this state of affairs:

- The education system, in which students are taught what to think.
- The hierarchical society, where status and precedent must be respected.
- Experience in state owned enterprises, where managers made few decisions and were rarely held accountable for results.
- The volatility of political life under Mao and continuing political campaigns: However, since 1978 and the opening of the economy to the outside world, a great deal has changed. Weldon and Vanhonacker, for instance, observe that younger people in China, who did not experience Mao's reign, worked in state-owned enterprises and they grew up in the market-oriented economic environment of contemporary China (as opposed to the planned economy their parents experienced prior to economic reforms). The evidence shows that socialisation practices have changed too; parents are now more tolerant of assertive children and feel less strongly that a child must always obey strict rules and regulations and are more tolerant of children who talk back. Together these changes could produce a generation of young people more likely to adopt a proactive and responsible approach to work.

A scholar who interviewed a senior manager of a major multinational company which was in the process of setting up a joint venture with China, described, how he saw the situation with regard to the Chinese employees' work-related attitudes and their productivity in the context of communist system:

> A standard joke making the round is 'How many Chinamen does it take to light a bulb?' The answer is four in my experience. We needed a light bulb changing in the house and we had four people coming to change it, one at the top of the ladder to put it in, one to hand the bulb up to him, one to hold the ladder and one to supervise, you know. So, they do employ everybody but not everybody is all that productive.

The challenge facing this company, the manger told, was not to change the cultural attitudes and values of their Chinese workforce, but to help them unlearn unproductive working practices, and replace them with those which are more conducive to greater efficiency. In addition, what the company was aiming for was to recruit young employees who are basically more adaptable and who have not been subject to traditional working practices. The company would then train these employees to work in a different way. The belief was that the Chinese would not have any problem with this approach, because they needed to be competitive in the world market, so they would be keen to learn the way their foreign partners did things and did maybe within 20 or 30 years, they would be doing it even better (see Tayeb, 1998, for more details).

Scandinavian Countries

Scandinavian countries have inherited the liberal traditions of western Europe, and yet have a distinctly different culture from the rest of Europe. They share the language and pragmatism of the British but their culture has a special Nordic flavour (Leesam and Neubauer, 1994) that is a result of the similarities in their political, social and cultural life. They are economically, technologically, and industrially advanced welfare states, directed towards greater social and economic equality and towards a collective role in framing 'public policy'. People's attitude towards the state is more positive than in the rest of Europe and the state is viewed more as a service organ than an authority system. The business environment is more export-oriented and industrial relations are highly regulated and cooperative. Female participation in the workforce is very high, about 85 per cent, and they hold one-third of supervisory roles. Wage differences between men and women are nearly same. Their culture lays strong emphasis on pragmatism rather than on intellectual fascination. Human considerations, in fact, carry more weight than strict efficiency requirements. Business decisions in personnel matters are generally more emotional than rational. Their MNCs do not sacrifice human considerations unless in crisis. Scandinavians are highly individualistic as well as egalitarian. The 'Jante's law' leads to a strong tendency to uniformity in behaviour and conformity to the social pressure to curtail personal ambitions or any sense of superiority. The four top commandments of the Jante's law are:

1. Do not think that you are very important.
2. Do not think that you are worth as much as others.
3. Do not think that you are wiser than others.
4. Do not think that you are better than others.

No doubt that power-distance is least in these countries and their culture is most feminine on Hofstede's cultural dimensions. It induces a mindset that encourages individuals to be humble, and yet responsible for making independent assessment and questioning management decisions before accepting them. In case of failure the whole group is held responsible rather than individuals.

The egalitarian values also suppress individual competitiveness and there is a strong impetus in Scandinavian management for consensus and cooperation that often require long discussions and bargaining for an acceptable compromise. Naturally, then, open conflicts are avoided. If a conflict does arise, a person talks to those involved in the conflict and this is followed by getting them to talk to each other directly. If this fails, arbitration is resorted to. Ikea, worth $ 4 billion, and Nokia are the largest MNCs reflecting Scandinavian culture. Scandinavians are more individualistic, value their privacy more, and are least likely to go out and help their bosses in non-work matters. They value achievement over family and see an organization as a functional rather than an authority system.

Some characteristic labour practices are mentioned below:

- Self-directed work teams are commonplace in the Swedish auto industry, along with frequent job rotation and enrichment.
- The workers get full pay for all sick days, with average of 26 days in a year, as compared to only 15 days in Europe and 10 days in the US. Swedish firms report that it is not unusual for one-fourth of all employees to be absent on a given day.
- It is estimated that 80 per cent of all wage earners are organized into trade unions. Further, the labour market features a high level of vocational training, which includes both apprenticeship programmes and retraining of adult workers.

- Ikea keeps minimum sales staff. Customers load and put the merchandise together themselves.
- Management practices reflect simplicity and humbleness. All managers spend a week working in stores serving customers, working in the restaurants and so on. There are only seven layers between the president and the entry-level person.
- All employees dress casually. They all travel coach class on their own time, stay in less expensive hotels. The chairman stays in the same hotel.
- The egalitarian values of Scandinavian culture are best reflected in the mission statement of Ikea, 'We shall offer a wide range of home furnishing items of good design and function, at prices so low that the majority of people can afford to buy them.'

Japan

Japan's success in the international market in the past few decades has encouraged many researchers and managers to learn about the country's culture and the ways in which its companies are managed. The role of the state in Japan's industrialisation is quite significant. The state established strategic industries and handed them over to the private sector that developed them into large 'zaibatsus'. After the Second World War, Zaibatsus were dismantled but were reborn as 'keiratsus'. These enterprises were promoted by the Ministry of International Trade and Industry (MITI). The Japanese keiratsus grew by developing a cluster of vertically integrated companies with cross holdings in each other with strong in-house banks for financial support. They became increasingly professional; the ownership was separated from management by hiring competent managers as 'adopted sons' (mukoyoshi).

Another major influence was Confucian philosophy and practising Buddhism although the official religion is Shintoism. Confucian values of harmony, loyalty, hard work and respect for elders created high power-distance and collectivist culture. Japanese collectivism permeates every nook and corner of the Japanese society. The derivative of uchi (i.e. my house), also means a place of work, organization, office, or school. The Japanese feel naturally belonging to them. It represents a communal spirit that mobilizes work groups to function effectively. This integration of communal and functional characteristics of work groups constitutes the spirit of Japanese capitalism (Yamamoto, 1992) that is driven by personal and emotional sharing, cooperation and harmony (wa) and loyalty to each other. The in-group members (miucht) or friends or colleagues are clearly distinguished from strangers. Trust that takes the form of assurance reflects the Japanese belief that they can continue to depend on personal connections for preferential treatment among in-group members.

The Japanese are very hardworking and have 'infinite capacity for hardship and pain (Buruma, 1985). They also have a strong sense of duty and indebtedness running across generations. There is an absence of westernstyle horizontal social class system in Japan. For example, a shop floor technician does not identify himself with all the technicians in the county or with the working class in general. Rather, he identifies himself with his workplace and all those people who work for it. Japanese enterprise wide unions are manifestation of this vertical system. Status is signalled in different ways, such as the extent to which one bows when meeting others, seating arrangement at tables and the time given to people to speak in groups and the terms one uses to address seniors.

Trade unions are company-based. For example, Toyota, Nissan and Hitachi have their own unions in contrast to Western countries where coal miners, firefighters, pilots, etc. have their own unions. Another characteristic of Japanese enterprises is the 'ringi' method of decision-making. This involves a great deal of informal consultation and problem-solving, leading to preparation of written proposals which is circulated first to those who will be affected by the implementation of the proposal and then to senior management.

Quality circles are another vehicle for employee participation and continuous improvement (kaizen). A QC is a small group activity in which ordinary blue and white collar workers, usually employed on similar work and led by their supervisors, volunteer to participate. Such volunteers are trained in problem identification and problem-solving techniques. Their success is supported by collectivist culture and life-time employment (nenko) practices. This practice creates a stable work environment with no fear of losing jobs. The promotions and salary structure are seniority-based with a component for merit-based pay based on company profits. Team work and consensus style of management are often regarded as a distinctive characteristic of Japanese companies.

Japanese companies operate a rigidly hierarchical system but the barriers between levels are absent as shown in the Box 16.2.

Japanese employees work much longer hours than workers in other industrial societies, but this pattern is shifting due to competitive pressures and the changing attitude of younger people. In 1992 a five-day week replaced a six-day one. In the US or the UK, work is divided into tasks and then assigned to individual workers. The Japanese prefer to assign work to groups and to let the group figure out how to carry it out. Another version of autonomy is Sony Corp.'s progamme of 'self promotion' in which enterprising engineers are encouraged to seek out projects of interest to them without informing their supervisors. If they can land a new position elsewhere in the company, the supervisor is expected to allow the transfer. Sony employs 400 women engineers in Japan.

BOX 16.2 JAPANESE SYSTEMS AND PRACTICES IN MARUTI UDYOG

All employees from the lowest to the MD used to wear a uniform of the same colour and quality of the fabric and tailored by the same source. They eat same food in the same canteen although food and tables for the Japanese are different. They commute in the same bus without any separate seats for managers. They gather together in the morning and exercise together before starting work. Irrespective of their positions, all employees get the facility of quality medical treatment in the same hospital and the medical reimbursement scheme is same for all. If an employee dies or retires, one of his dependent was given a job in the company. In case of death or marriage, or on similar occasions, Maruti personnel visit the family and extend necessary help.

Source: Sinha, 2000, p.13.

Every year several hundred employees of Japanese firms are sent to the US and Europe to pursue MBA degrees, primarily to develop their understanding of Western business practices including knowledge of the English language. However, MBA degrees do not have much value as promotions are based on seniority. In 1986 the Japanese Diet passed legislation barring sex discrimination. Today, women constitute 40 per cent of the Japanese workforce.

BOX 16.3 WHO IS RESPONSIBLE?

Jean Safari was investigating a serious error made by a Japanese worker at a Japanese subsidiary of a US multinational. A component had been inserted upside down and the entire batch had been pulled out of production to be reworked. The cost of this was very high. Jeans asked Japanese plant director about which employee had made the error. Had she been identified? What action was being taken against her? She was amazed when the director claimed not to know. 'The whole work group has accepted responsibility,' he told her. As to the specific women responsible, they have not told me, nor did I ask. Even the floor supervisor does not know and if he did, he would not tell me either, 'But if everyone is responsible then in effect no one is responsible Jean argued. They are simply protecting each other's bad work.'

'This is not how we see it' the manager was polite but firm. 'I understand the women concerned was so upset that she went home. She tried to resign. Two of her co-workers had to coax her back again. The group also knows she was responsible and she feels ashamed. The group also knows she is new and that they did not help her enough to look out for her, or see that she was properly trained. This is why the whole group has apologised. I have their letter here. They are willing to apologise to publicly.'

Arabian Countries

Arab world extends from Persian Gulf to Morocco in North Africa with strong bond and share the common language, religion and history. These oil producing countries have attracted enormous amount of Foreign Direct Investment and seen major political conflicts in history for the control of oil wealth.

The Arabs are highly collectivist with a strong sense of loyalty to their group, whose membership goes well beyond the immediate family, to embrace extended family, relatives and friends. Researchers argue that the Arab nations group orientation can be traced to their Bedouin tradition, which, in turn reinforces customs, such as consultation, obedience to seniors, loyalty, face to face interaction and networks of personal connections. The loyalty to the group has to some extent resulted in a low level of tolerance for new ideas and challenges of accepted wisdom. Respect for the elders is also fostered by Islam, which in addition encourages dedication to work, cooperation and harmony.

The above characteristics are reflected in organizations having hierarchical and centralised structures, with paternalistic authoritarian management style. Research evidence (Weir, 2000; Mellahi, 2003) shows that subordinates, although they expect to be consulted with, do not expect to participate in the actual decision-making as equal partners, which is the prerogative of their senior managers. Senior positions are usually held by older people, promotions and pay are more likely to be related to the employees' degree of loyalty to their managers than to their job performance. However, the younger generation managers, most of whom have received higher education either at home or abroad, are more in favour of Western style professionalism than their older colleagues. In Bahrain, for instance, as Weir (2000) points out, the well-educated emerging managerial elite is developing a realistic self-image, setting strict performance standards and taking advantage of opportunities for professional self-renewal. It demands, within the context of the authoritarian and autocratic power structures of Bahraini organizations, inclusion in the decision-making process.

The Bedouin tradition of chieftains holding council meetings, Majlis, which the commoners also attend or bring in their petitions, appears to have been carried over to work organizations as well. Here, senior managers get together on a regular basis with employees and supervisors from various levels. Managers normally communicate with their colleagues and subordinates through personal contact, conversation and networking rather than written memos and letters.

The cultural traits of the Arab society are summarised in Box 16.4.

BOX 16.4 ARABIC LEGACY, BEDOUIN WAY OF LIFE

1. Highly collectivist within their group (tribe or extended family) and highly individualist with the other groups.
2. Loyalty to tribe, pride in tradition, dynasty and tribe.
3. Dependence on relatives and friends.
4. Emphasis on consultation in decision-making within the same tribe or extended family but authoritarianism with outgroup.
5. High uncertainty avoidance: low tolerance for new ideas, low degree of initiative for bringing about change, fatalism, unquestioning acceptance of conventional wisdom, and obedience of justified authority.

One of the main features of many Arab companies is the extensive use of expatriates, both at highly technical and professional levels, because of shortage of home-grown experts, and at the shop floor manual work level, mainly because the locals are not prepared to do low-paid, low-esteemed menial jobs. These expatriates engaged for manual jobs are usually Indians, Pakistanis, Malaysians, Filipinos or citizens of other Arab countries. Expatriates recruited for senior technical and professional positions are mostly from the advanced industrialised countries of Europe and North America.

At high-level positions, the expatriates are very well paid, and in many cases their pay is exempt from income tax, and their families enjoy living in comfortable and well-appointed accommodation, but their contracts are on a short-term basis with no guaranteed job security or contract renewal. At the shop floor level, there exists harsh discrimination against their local counterparts (Harry, 2003). There is also widespread discrimination against women, both domestic and expatriates, especially in terms of job opportunity, recruitment, promotion prospects and pay.

With a few exceptions, no serious independent labour union movement has developed in the Arab world. In these countries where workers are permitted to organize their unions are either created by the ruling single party system or are closely controlled by the government.

Muna's (1980) seminal study, whose findings are valid to this day judging by the research evidence produced since 1980, highlighted other Arab work-related values and attitudes. The Arab executives whom he interviewed admired certain characteristics in expatriates and wanted to see them trained by their employees. These are high value and respect for time; productivity and hard work; technical know-how and competence; organized and systematic approach to work consciousness and dedication to work; discipline; accuracy and precision. These are, it appears, the work-related characteristics which Arab managers long for and which they miss most in their people.

Muna also detected the following characteristics among the Arab employees:

- Lack of industrial mentality: aversion to systems and procedures: lack of organization, especially delegation; non-professional attitudes toward business.
- Individualistic approach to work: a preference to work alone rather than be in a team; a tendency to take sole credit for good deeds and to pass the blame to others or to circumstances when things go wrong.
- Dislike of manual work by Arab nationals: young men demand only clerical and administrative work.
- Nepotism and a strong socio-cultural pressure to hire relatives:. None of the countries had a system of democracy, which is a continuation of socio-cultural characteristics of the larger social system of which organization is a part.
- A dislike of committee meetings and team work in general: Further, subordinates view a participative management style as a sign of weakness on the part of the senior manager; they expect to be consulted but not to make the final decision.

The HRM practices are summarized in Box 16.5.

BOX 16.5 MAJOR HRM AND OTHER EMPLOYEE-RELATED VALUES AND PRACTICES OF ARABS

1. Management culture based on talking and not writing.
2. A strong preference for participative and consultative style but managers tend to adopt an authoritarian management style.
3. The last word is always the manager's word.
4. Explicit decision-making culture based on interpersonal connections.
5. Network takes precedence over loyalty to the firm.
6. Productivity and performance largely disconnected from pay and promotion.
7. Lack of relevant human resource management policies and management development and planning. Loyalty to individuals and paternalistic and hierarchical organizational relationships.
8. Widespread lack of Western style management practices, such as assessment centers.
9. Extensive use of Western expatriate managers and expatriate employees from India, Pakistan and Malaysia.
10. Gender discrimination and some degree of occupational segregation.
11. No serious independent labour union movement/trade union activity.
12. Discrimination between locals and expatriates.
13. Respect for seniority.
14. A strong preference for power and dominant role and less for achievement and support.

UK

The UK, as its full name implies, is the United Kingdom comprising four nations, Scotland, England, Wales and Northern Ireland, each with certain distinctive cultural characteristics. However, they also share many common values and institutions which bind them together. Box 16.6 summarises those common features that are relevant to the focus of this chapter.

The British are highly individualistic, yet they engage well in collective action, for instance, they will freely disagree with certain government policies. This disciplined individualism is manifested in the UK's strong trade union traditions, whose roots can be traced to the 18th and 19th centuries. Union membership is craft-based and cuts across firms and organizations. As a result, there are likely to be several unions in the same factory, bargaining not only with employers but also compete against each other. The British unions, unlike their counterparts in some other European countries such as France and (pre–1989) Poland, are more pragmatic in their approach. They fight for better pay settlements and better working conditions within the present economic and social system, rather than engage in class struggle and ideological battles to overthrow the system. They see their role as one of representing the workforce and pushing for objectives that are consciously desired by the workers themselves. Since the 1980s, a combination of decline in membership and anti-union legislation has greatly diminished the powers of trade unions.

BOX 16.6 BRITISH NATIONAL CULTURAL CHARACTERISTICS

1. Individualism: autonomy, liberty, love of privacy, yet caring for the community.
2. Small power-distance: yet deference and acceptance of inequality, class consciousness.
3. Aggressive, yet caring and friendly.
4. Reserve: shy, self-control and self-discipline, tight upper lip but alert ears and eyes.
5. Conservatism: dislike of change and uncertainty, aversion to risk, lack of ambition.
6. Tenacity: resilience, resourcefulness.
7. Pragmatism: social, political realism, compromise, flexible unwritten constitution, common law, prepared to bend the law when it does not suit them.
8. Chauvinism: dislike of foreigners, xenophobia.
9. Honesty: trustworthy, and trusting yet clever.
10. Past-orientation: love of age-old tradition and belief that the present is a culmination of past developments, ambivalence towards new technology.
11. Dislike of open conflicts.

Individualism appears also to influence the relationship between employees and their bosses and their work organizations. This relationship is strictly contractual. British employees, unlike, for instance, their Japanese counterparts, do not expect their superiors to look after them and to help them in their personal difficulties. This would be an invasion of their privacy. To them a manager who is concerned with the employees' well-being is one who, for instance, provides them with up-to-date equipment so that they can perform their tasks better. In other words, managers and workers have an impersonal and task-oriented relationship with one another (Tayeb, 1994).

British employees, similar to the Americans, are career-oriented and join another company if better prospects beckon. However, unlike in America, managers tend to spend much less on employee training. As a result, the British workforce has far lower productivity rates than the Americans, and indeed, the workers in many other leading economies.

In Hofstede's (1980) study, Britain scored low on power-distance relative to many other nations, but people do not really care as much about equality as they do about liberty. Both inside and outside the workplace, the Britons are deferential to their seniors; opposition to authority is usually indirect and sometimes wrapped up in humour, rather than direct challenge. Yet, at the same time, they do not like to be ordered about and hate to be dictated to. In effect, they respect authority only when it is used well.

BOX 16.7 HRM VALUES AND PRACTICES IN THE UK

1. Leadership style: persuasive.
2. Job satisfaction derived from personal sense of achievement and the superior's recognition of individual's contributions.
3. Preference to have freedom to choose their own approach, using individual skills and abilities.
4. Expectation from subordinate; commitment, initiative, owning, responsibility and honesty.
5. Deference to authority.
6. Comfortable with minimal amount of rules and authority.
7. Flexibility yet preference to work according to rules.
8. Well-educated, skilled and adaptable work force.
9. Learning style: mostly by trial and error or doing rather than learning theory.
10. Short-term perspective: low expenditure on training, resulting in low productivity rates compared to many leading economies.
11. Some evidence of discrimination among employees on the ground of age, gender or ethnicity, 'glass ceiling'.
12. Formal in communication and interpersonal relationship at work.
13. Ethnocentric attitudes towards foreigners.
14. Conservative approach towards new technology.
15. Contractual, non-emotional relationships at workplace.
16. Strong trade union tradition: mostly craft unions.
17. Pragmatic trade unions: fight for better pay and working conditions, not ideologically-based class struggle against managers, absence of serious trade union challenge to management's prerogatives and right to manage.
18. Expectation of government involvement in employee relationships.
19. Like most of Europe, the UK does not have laws barring age discrimination, and it is common practice for employers to run ads seeking workers under the age of forty.
20. Forced early retirement is common.
21. Annualized hour systems, under which a worker's hours are calculated for a full year, are spreading and now include about 8 per cent of the British employees. Such systems, negotiated with unions, give employees the security of a monthly pay cheque, but permit flexible scheduling of 5-day work weeks so that companies can operate seven days a week without paying overtime.

The acceptance of power inequality is also noticeable in British class consciousness. Almost everybody one speaks with can place themselves in one class or the other. Managers and other white-collar employees have normally greater advantages over manual workers in many respects, such as power, status, pay, physical working conditions, and eating places, rules for lunch and tea breaks and holidays. Shop-floor workers and low-rank office clerks are subject to a tighter control at work. They have to clock in and out at specific times, work in some cases, e.g. on an assembly line conveyor belt, at a pre-determined speed, and produce a specified number of units per hour and so forth. The managers, by contrast, can come in and go out of the company premises whenever they like and can do their job as they see fit, provided that they achieve their performance targets. Their holiday entitlements, pension schemes, bonuses, share options and the like are disproportionately far greater than those of the shop-floor employees. This dual-treatment tradition has created a hostile 'them and us' attitude among the workforce which has for a long time bedevilled the British industrial relations. The HRM practices are detailed in Box 16.7:

The USA

The US, a nation of immigrants, is truly a 'melting pot' in terms of the diversity of ethnic background and cultural heritage of its people referred to hereafter as Americans. However, like many other culturally diverse countries, such as India or China, one can identify certain characteristics which are common in Americans. A summary of major American cultural values and attitudes and some of their manifestations in American companies is listed below:

National Culture of the USA

- Highly individualistic: self-focused, preference to act as individuals rather than as members of a group, yet can be collectivist in the face of a common threat.
- Small power-distance: egalitarian: tend not to treat people differently even when there are great differences in age or social standing.
- Masculine: ambitious, competitive, goal-oriented, achievers.
- Low uncertainty avoidance: risk-takers, entrepreneurial.
- Low-context: directness, expressive in communication, do not talk around things, tend to say exactly what they mean.
- Open: friendly, informal.
- Ethnocentric: believe their culture and values are superior to all others.
- Future-oriented: strong belief that present ways of doing things inevitably are to be replaced by even better ways.
- Readiness to change: try new things, a predisposition to believe that new is good.
- 'Can do' attitude.

As the list shows, prominent among American national cultural characteristics is individualism. Americans are independent, ambitious and individualistic, place a high value on freedom and believe that individuals can shape and control their own destinies. But, as Lawrence (2000) points out, American individualism is not expressive and it is not about being different; rather it focuses on achievement, and, above all, on economic achievement. People pursue mainly their own interests and those of their immediate family; the in-group definitely does not include the workplace. The primary commitment and loyalty of the individuals do not, therefore, lie with the company or any other larger groupings of which they may be members. This is, in contrast to this, with the Japanese culture. The Americans, however, do display a high level of collectivism and group-orientation in the face of a common threat, for instance, as we all witnessed in the aftermath of the 11 September 2001 terrorist attacks on the World Trade Center's twin towers in New York, and on happy and festive occasions, such as the annual National Independence celebrations on 4th July.

Individualism informs and inspires American management and the ethic of personal achievement which runs through it: hard work and long hours when necessary, individual employees' readiness to take decisions, personal initiative, strong presentation of personal image, promotion and high incomes as reward for success (Lawrence, 2000). In addition, the individualistic nature of the society encourages managers to promote on the basis of merits as opposed to status, hierarchy or gender. And unlike, for instance, many Arab countries where reward and promotion are on the basis of loyalty, in the US the reward system is performance-oriented and status is based on how well people perform their functions.

The emphasis on individual freedom and success includes freedom to pursue one's career progression by moving from one company to another in pursuit of success. A by-product of employees' careerism is the system that hires and fires people at will and when market conditions justify it. For instance, in heavy-engineering firms, such as steel, cars and aerospace, employees are routinely laid off in a slump and rehired when business picks up. Also, large American companies typically hire people to fill particular jobs. Their senior managers know that Americans are mobile people, who have a limited commitment to any particular employer or part of the country. As a result, jobs are clearly defined and so are the skills needed to fill them. This is again the opposite in many large Japanese companies, where the relationship between the employee and the company is based on long-term commitment on both sides and employees are trained to be 'all-rounder' rather than specialists to perform only certain types of jobs.

In this connection, the starkly different approaches which Mazda and Chrysler adopted in reaction to the common threat of bankruptcy in the early 1980s, are interesting. Mazda viewed its workforce as an asset that had to be retained at all cost. Instead of cutting jobs, the firm's managers agreed to a 25 per cent salary cut and a loss of bonuses for four years. Chrysler, in contrast, cut its blue-collar workforce by 28 per cent, its white-collar staff by 7 per cent and its executives' pay by ½ per cent (*The Economist*, 24 November 1990).

This kind of attitude to employees is exemplified also in the advice given a few years ago to Germany by the American newsmagazine *Time*. The magazine identified high unemployment as one of the major problems of the German economy, and advised the politicians to accelerate labour-market reform to allow easier hiring and firing of workers (*Time*, 14 September 1995, p.28), a policy which goes against the grain in Germany's social-market economic system.

In organizations, in which Americans prefer participative management, superiors are usually approachable and subordinates are more willing to question authority. Americans live more easily with uncertainty, compared with many other nations, a characteristic which facilitates participation in decision-making and risk-taking. (US scored 46 on uncertainty avoidance in Hofstede's 1980 study, well below the average for the sample.) Together with individualism, tolerance for uncertainty also accounts for the entrepreneurial and 'go-getter' spirit and competitiveness which underpin the business culture of the country.

BOX 16.8: PEPSI-COLA

Pepsi-Cola operating in over 150 countries with over 250,000 employees, represents the largest segment of American business, with sales over $ 7 billions. It is a pay-for-performance company. This means that compensation is always tied up to individual results. A written performance appraisal is required before any compensation adjustment can be made. The appraisal may be written in the local language, but no matter where or how it is done, the language of appraisal is always focused on the individual's performance against assigned accountabilities. The appraisal form also requires a specification of areas for improvement within each area of separate accountability. To make the appraisal as culturally neutral as possible, accountabilities are specified in terms of what must be accomplished.

Source: Fulkson and Schuler, (1992, p. 264.

A prominent feature of the US business culture is its anti-trade unionism. A vast majority of American employees work in the non-unionized sector, and the power of employers in both organized and non-organized sectors is very high in both political and economic spheres. Also, the opposition of employers to unions has been especially intense since the mid-1970s. Throughout most of the non-unionized sector, redundant workers can be laid off in whatever order the employer desires, and employment contracts terminated for any or no reason. Furthermore, the conditions under which employment takes place are essentially employer-determined, limited only by labour-market forces and the protective labour legislation (Wheeler, 1993), notably the minimum wage law. In addition, many, especially large, American companies prefer to deal with their employees through human resource management policies and practices rather than recognition of unions. HRM, in fact, has replaced the need for workplace unionisation as far as these companies are concerned.

Americans dislike rules and regulations but do use them in their organizations and in the society at large. This is a culture characterised by, among others, a written constitution, clearly defined roles and functions, minutely spelled out and legally enforced business contracts and a greater use of written formal rules than many other cultures, a culture which took up Weber's (1947) bureaucratic model and turned it into a model of professionalism.

The Americans' professionalism is also reflected in their business education; they invented MBA and MBO (management by objectives) and coined the term HRM, and arguably invented modern management. The interactive system based on MBO is common in American organizations, and can produce beneficial results, such as high output, greater corporate awareness and employee commitment to the company, but can also lead to greater bureaucracy and overproduction in certain areas. However, although MBO schemes have been used by some companies elsewhere outside the US, they do not fit in with the culture of many countries (Hofstede, 1980) and have not been enthusiastically embraced by them.

American companies have some of the highest employee working hours, productivity rates and employee training expenditure in the world. They take training of their employees at all levels very seriously even though the trained employees may later leave if another company offers them better pay, working conditions and promotion prospects.

Most US multinational companies tend to have ethnocentric policies in their HRM, and indeed in many other aspects of their management, in relation to their foreign subsidiaries. They normally allow a limited amount of deviation from their centrally-determined strategy, especially with respect to host-country legal requirements, where compliance is not negotiable. They also allow local managers some discretion to make modifications in the implementation of their strategy. For instance, the overall decision on training strategy and policy is taken at the HQ but subsidiaries can choose whether to provide their training programmes in-house or contract them out (Tayeb and Dott, 2000).

HRM and other employee related values and practices in the US

- Prefer participative leadership style.
- Superiors are approachable.
- Subordinates are willing to question authority.
- Status based on how well people perform their functions.
- Performance-oriented.
- Promotion and reward based on merits as opposed to status, hierarchy or gender.
- Live more easily with uncertainty, sceptical about rules and regulations.
- Value punctuality and keep appointments and calendars.
- Much more concerned with their own careers and personal success than about the welfare of the organization or the group.
- Value success and profit.
- Acceptance of conflict.
- System-driven: conviction that all problems can be solved, system and energy will overcome any obstacles.
- Proactive: take initiative, aim high, 'go for it'.
- Result-oriented.
- Professional: educated and well-trained.
- Strong devotion to managerial prerogative.
- Hire and fire policies.
- Communication skills, informal, direct, explicit, often aggressive.
- Emphasis on entrepreneurship and innovation.
- Legalist approach to contracts.
- Informality, yet a preference for written rules and procedures.
- Dislike of trade unions.
- Preference for HRM over unionization.

South Korea

Korea's rapid industrialization began in the 1950s at the end of Japanese occupation. The state sold out enemy properties to 'chaebols' and helped them to grow rapidly by giving special favours, such as import licence and exemptions from taxes. The chaebols also grew rapidly because the founders consisted of a group of men with outstanding leadership, sharp vision, great determination and unfailing devotion (Chen,1995, p.162). As the Korean economy grew, there were many opportunities in diverse areas and because of that chaebols and their affiliates grew fast. At one point of time in 1980s they contributed 36 per cent of Korea's GDP. Fukuyama (1955, p.133) reported that large numbers of founders, their children and their relatives occupied the top 100 chaebols. According to one study, half of the offspring of top 100 chaebols married persons from a similar background, while the remaining married the elite of the Korean society.

Although some of the Confucian values are markedly same in Japan and Korea, their functions are strikingly different because of highly hierarchical blood-related paternalism in the Korean culture. For example, the value of harmony is common, but Japanese 'wa' reflects group-oriented harmony, while Korean 'inhwa' implies harmony between superiors and subordinates. The family in Korea means blood relations mostly.

Chen made a comparative analysis of Japanese and Korean management systems. Age and gender carried weight in both cultures. Training for moulding the mindset of employees was equally important in both, but in Korean companies it also aimed at inculcating traditional cultural values. Korean employees were more concerned about their wages, working conditions and job security. Authority was far more centralized in Korean companies than in Japanese companies. Nearly 80 per cent of the authority is concentrated in upper echelons of management. Communication is mostly top-down while it is both-ways in Japan. Korean subordinates hesitate to disagree with their superiors because they do not want to antagonise them. In Japan, reciprocal mutual obligations between employees and the employer presented a contrast to the Korean way of obligations of the employees to the organization.

There was also difference in the structure and role of trade unions. The Japanese system of in-house trade unions did not exist in Korea. Further, Korean managers felt freer to lay off unwanted workers than the Japanese. The Korean concept of 'that is good enough' forms a sharp contrast to Japanese 'kaizen'; a continuously increasing process is a way of life and nothing is good enough. Korean long-term planning is much shorter and more general than their Japanese counterpart. Many Korean companies prefer quick actions to detailed planning and are dominated by the 'go for the first and fix it later' mentality.

BOX 16.9 A KOREAN STRATEGY FOR EFFECTIVE MANAGEMENT-KIMCO, A KOREAN SUBSIDIARY

VP Kimco explained the core of Kimco's culture like this:

Every individual in this company gets a numerical target that he must achieve. There is no escape. Targets are often raised requiring people to stretch a bit. This might cause stress. But stress is inevitable if we had to compete in the market. We see that nobody gets overworked because of overwork. Of course, we can't help if family obligations interfere with work and cause overstress. We give full autonomy and empower employees to keep improving themselves and to keep performing their best within the budget given to each department.

We do not allow anybody's mind remain free and unutilised anytime of the day; even during lunch or in buses there are quizzes and discussions about realising targets, improving on one's previous achievements, and so on. While working on lines, workers are often asked : How can we become champions in the market? Kimco has 'no excuse' (for not realising the target) but forgetting (mistakes) management. Those who perform well are amply rewarded and those who fail have to admit before others and promise to improve. We take good care of our employees, but they must perform and keep improving their performance.

Review Questions

1. Explain the reasons for differences in industrial relations environment in different countries and how it impacts HRM policies of multinationals.
2. What factors decide the degree of centralization or decentralization of powers in dealing with the labour of subsidiaries by the MNC headquarters?
3. Compare and contrast the labour management practices and cultural environment of China with Japan.
4. Compare and contrast the labour management practices and cultural environment of Scandinavian countries with Arabian countries.
5. Do you find a link between economic growth of nations and their cultural values? If so, which values in your opinion promote economic growth and which ones retard the same? Support your answer with examples.
6. Why has India been not clustered with any group of countries with regard to its cultural and HRM practices? In which areas it is similar to both East and West?

Assignment

Try to collect information about the ILO and other international organizations mentioned in this chapter. Try also to find out various guidelines made regarding multinationals and study their compliance in practice.

Chapter

17

Managing International Projects and Teams: A Human Resource Perspective

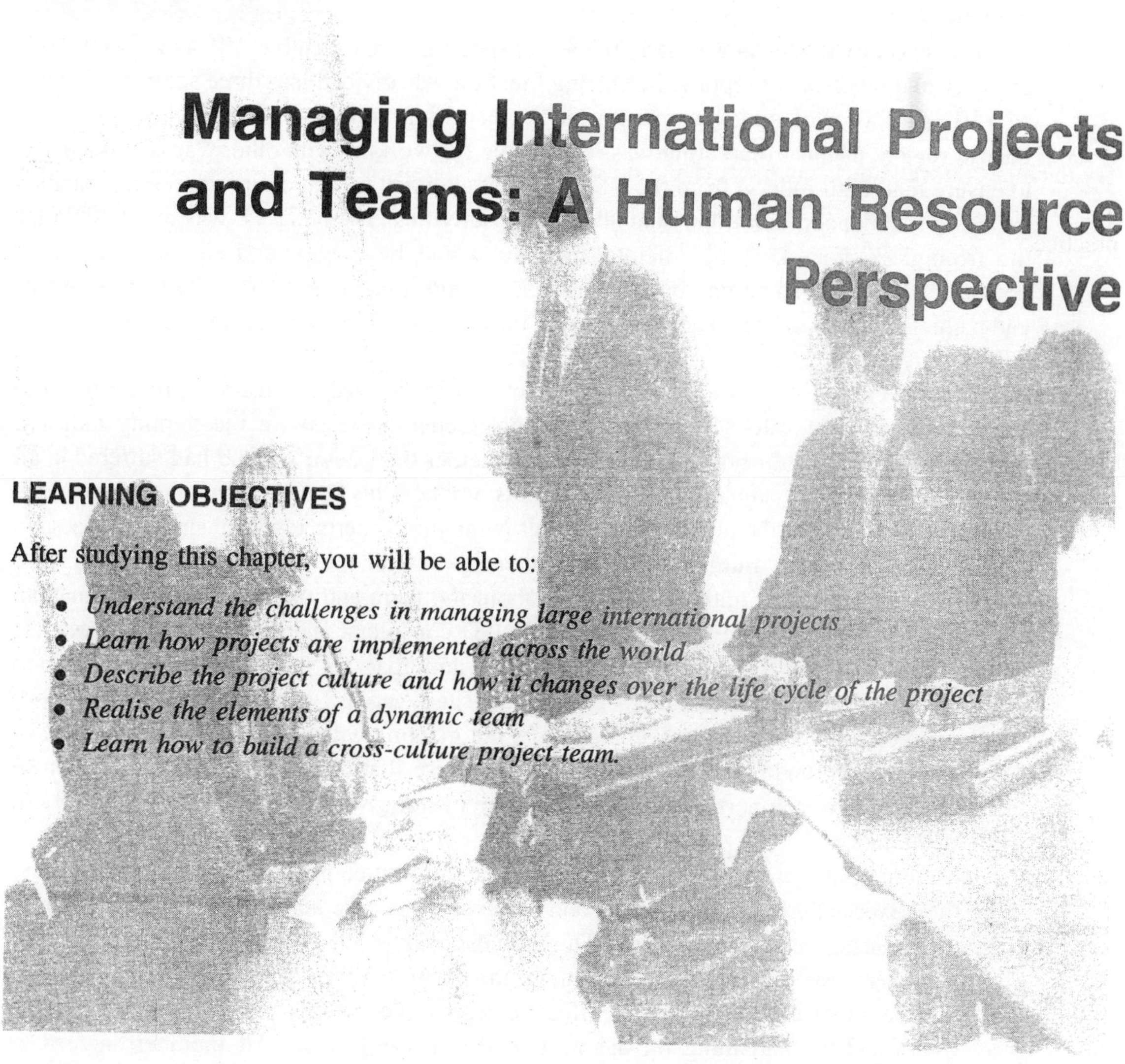

LEARNING OBJECTIVES

After studying this chapter, you will be able to:

- *Understand the challenges in managing large international projects*
- *Learn how projects are implemented across the world*
- *Describe the project culture and how it changes over the life cycle of the project*
- *Realise the elements of a dynamic team*
- *Learn how to build a cross-culture project team.*

OPENING CASE
Building the Executive team at Caesars Tahoe

Caesars Tahoe is a casino, hotel and entertainment complex in Nevada, US. As part of the Caesars Tahoe's world chain, including Caesars Place in Las Vegas, Caesars in Atlantic City, and the riverboat Caesars Indiana, the company enjoys a reputation as a 'high-end' experience. Its history is laced with stories of celebrities, athletes and some of the wealthiest people in the world winning and losing millions of dollars. Originally established as an alternative to Las Vegas Desert, Caesars is the third largest in terms of floor-space and number of rooms, but it has the largest showroom for headline talent and highest gambling limits. The company was sold to Park Place Entertainment in 1997 when management decided to focus on nongaming properties.

The executive team at Caesars Tahoe consisted of an executive VP and GM for the property and seven direct reports. Marketing function was divided into three segments headed by a VP. Far East marketing was responsible for recruiting 'million-dollar' players from South Pacific region; national marketing was responsible for working with other Caesars properties to ensure that 'high-rollers' from the US were well attended to, and casino marketing handled the more traditional promotional and advertising activities. The hotel VP was responsible for the front desk, housekeeping, maintenance, food and beverages, and so on. The casino operations VP managed all gambling operations. In addition, there is VP for human resources and a chief financial officer. There was a high turnover of executives and the current GM was 13th in 20 years.

The GM contacted an external OD consultant to help the executive team improve teamwork and clarify the core values of the organization. General changes in the gaming industry, higher than the normal turnover, concerns over whether the Caesar's brand had suffered in all the corporate portfolio adjustments and conflicts amongst his senior managers prompted his call. His own vision for the property included growing the property, re-establishing the Caesar's brand and investing in human resources. Interviews with the members of the executive committee confirmed his initial descriptions about the team and the organization's situation.

In consultation with the GM, the corporate OD consultant and the human resources VP, an agenda was developed that addressed the vision and goals for the propery, team processes roles and action plans for the future. A two day off-site meeting was arranged at a local resort. The workshop kicked off on the evening before the meeting with a welcome and overview of agenda by the GM and a stakeholder mapping exercise that clarified the current mission of the property. Team members were excused for the evening with the thoughts of the exercise fresh in the minds.

On the morning of the first day, the executive committee members were encouraged to share their expectations for the meeting and to develop specific norms that would guide their behaviours during the 2-day meeting. This process was aided by an exercise in which the group members shared their experiences about the best team they had ever worked on and in that way identified characteristics of effective teams. The norms and characteristics were placed on flipcharts and hung on the wall of the meeting room. All members agreed to behave according to the norms and to assess periodically how well the norms were being followed. The consultant agreed to provide feedback on norm compliance during the session.

The group then participated in the problem-solving exercise that prompted members to collaborate on a task. The task generated important data about the group's functioning. Those observations were discussed, as were insights about the team gleaned from an interpersonal style instrument completed by members before the meeting. The nature of conflicts among the members also was discussed. From this new basis of group understanding, the executive committee began to discuss their hopes and visions of the property. The first day ended with several unfinished lists of value statements, core purposes and thoughts about the strategies and markets served by the organization. An evaluation of the day asked for an overall rating and comments about what the group should stop, start and continue to do.

The next day began by feeding back the data from evaluation, which suggested most people were satisfied with the accomplishment of the first day, but that important issues still needed to be addressed. Although the agenda called for a flow similar to that of the day before, moving back and forth between team-related activities and discussions about the property's future, the consultant wrote several important topics on a flipchart and asked the group to identify the most important agenda items. Quickly they decided that they wanted to finish the core value work and then discuss their core purpose.

The consultant facilitated the conversation that was now clearly under the control of the group members. Within a couple of hours the group had produced a list of core values, developed the process for involving the rest of the organization in creating a final list of values, and crafted a core purpose that described the essence of the organization. Based on this work, the group moved to some initial discussion about its vision for the future. In addition, the group generated a list of key action items, necessary to realize that vision. This was specially tricky given the uncertain demands of the new owner, but the group decided that it was important to have clear strategy for themselves so that any demand from a new parent could be evaluated. Members also reasoned that that the parent might ask them what they thought was possible and they wanted to be ready.

The meeting ended with the completion of a responsibility chart to clarify task completion expectations and accountabilities among the team members. A final evaluation of the meeting included process observations by the team members about how they have worked together and statements about their satisfaction with the results of the meeting. They all agreed that they had made important decisions and were leaving with substantial results.

INTRODUCTION

Projects serve the basic need of society and help it to usher in change. Whether it was the construction of pyramids in Egypt, the landing of man on the moon, the setting up an international space station, the Normandy landing, the construction of the Euro tunnel or developing an atomic bomb in record time with a totally new technology and dropping it on Hiroshima in total secrecy – none of these was possible without tne management of human resources in an outstanding manner. Such international projects in future can be managed more efficiently if lessons learnt from the past project management can be applied.

CHALLENGES IN MANAGING INTERNATIONAL PROJECTS

Successful project management calls for performing the basics of planning, organising, controlling with specific challenge of managing, the scope, schedule, cost, quality, communications and human resources. A great deal of attention is also needed in the area of contract management, risk management and organization of supply chain and logistics. The primary factors in global projects are cross-cultural settings that call for special attention, as nationals from different nationalities will be working together. Other factors are functional redundancy, and political factors such as managing local and national governments and complying with their legal requirements. Procurement of plant, equipment and building materials in a systematic manner and sequence from different countries at the right time and place is highly important. However, the most important part is to identify the required competencies and skills, procure them for the required period, integrate them into motivated teams and finally redeploy or dissolve them on completion of the project. Some of these are explained below:

- Functional redundancy means the duplication or overlap of certain functions or activities at headquarters and projects, like account keeping or information management. This may be necessary because of contractual agreements involving technology transfer, requiring 'national counterparts' to be ready when the project is handed over. Further, when projects end, there may be surplus in some categories and when projects are in the middle stage, there may be shortage. Ignorance of language and organizational complexity of the project may also be responsible for creating functional redundancy. Therefore, special attention is required for managing the human resources function in the projects.
- Political factors in international projects are a strong influence and are plagued with countless unknowns. Apart from fluctuations in international politics, it is local politics which places a major roadblock in attaining project success. This calls for strengthening communication and relationships with all stockholders including the government and important public personalities.
- The expatriate way of life refers to the habits and expectations, including the physical and psychological needs, of the people who are posted in a strange country with unique customs and way of life. Substantial differences would mean making special provisions for a group of people who would otherwise refuse to relocate to the site, or, if transferred temporarily, will remain highly unmotivated.
- Language and culture include the system of written, spoken or other social forms of communication. Included in language and culture are systems of codification and decodification of thoughts, beliefs and values common to a given people. Language includes all the subtleties of communication.
- Additional risk factors may include personal risks, such as kidnapping, local epidemics and faulty medical care, rapid swings in political and economic situations and weather uncertainties. These different risk factors require analysis and subsequent management so that they do not adversely affect the project.
- Supply management encompasses all contracting, procurement and logistical challenges that must be faced in international projects. This is a very complex job requiring new solutions and

innovation, as normal domestic solutions may not work. Therefore, it requires highly qualified personnel and some partially redundant management systems for follow-up procedures.

- Local laws and customs may even affect personal habits, such as abstaining from drinking in Muslim countries.

HOW PROJECTS ARE MANAGED ACROSS THE WORLD

Globalization affects all areas of endeavour, including how projects are managed. In spite of some commonalities, there remains a basic difference in the way business is performed in different lands. Various systems and models are in place for generating and transferring knowledge in different parts of the world. In very general terms, the basic models may be called the European, the North American and the Japanese. The characteristics of their models are as follows:

- The European model: Europe has highly structured, formal and centralised systems for generating and disseminating technical knowledge. Responsibilities are clearly defined, with specific national organizations charged with generating research, while other organizations take care of transferring the results to industry. The Swedish system is a typical example, with the National Swedish Institute for Building Research being responsible for knowledge generation, and the Swedish Institute for Building Documentation being responsible for dissemination. Government and industry often jointly finance national systems in Europe.
- The North American model: The system in North America is less formal than in Europe. There is, in fact, little coordination in the construction research effort in North America. In contrast to the European model, advanced construction knowledge is mainly generated at the university level. Broad-based engineering or trade associations, such as the American Society of Civil Engineers, largely perform the dissemination to the industry. Committees made up of volunteers carry out the technical work in these associations.
- The Japanese model: In the Japanese model, research is concentrated in the big six integrated companies that dominate the Japanese construction, where technology development is considered a significant competitive tool. Therefore, as much as $100 million is invested annually by the 'Big Six' in research, which is considered proprietary and subject to commercial confidentiality. Companies invest in research to attain competitive advantage.

Another factor that influences managing projects internationally is the increasingly active role being played by owner organizations in the management of their projects. In the case of developing countries, this interface often reflects a national policy aimed at attaining greater managerial and technical capability so as to be less dependent on the developed world. Owners in such countries have a need for contracting services toward getting their projects completed as well as transferring experience to their own organizations.

INTEGRATING CULTURES

In international projects, success depends primarily on giving proper emphasis to those factors that are particularly vulnerable in cross-cultural settings and on building a team capable of dealing with the challenges presented. It is common practice in bi-national projects to have formal authority shared by two people, one from each country. This shared authority ranges from an integrated partnership managers to a lead-manager/back-up manager situation. Such projects are products of hard politi processes that involve long and difficult negotiations. In most cases each side has a different perception about the adopted solution, and during the project phase each side may try to 'win back' some of the points initially 'lost' at the negotiation table. This sets the stage for conflict during the implementation phase of the project. The need for strong communication management becomes immediately evident in such a setting. Sometimes, agreements are worded diplomatically and contain writings 'between the lines', which complicate the situation even further.

A MODEL OF INTER-CULTURAL TEAM BUILDING

The challenge in international team building boils down to creating a convergence of people's differing personal inputs towards a set of common final outputs. This means developing a process that facilitates communication and understanding between the people of different national cultures. Making this process happen signifies the difference between the success and failure of international projects.

People's inputs are their personal and cultural values, beliefs and assumptions. They also include patterns of thinking, behaving and feeling. Expectations, needs and motivations are also part of people's inputs into any given system. The outputs are the result or benefits produced by a given system. They may be perceived as a combination of achievements benefiting the individuals, the team, the organization, and the outside environment.

The secret is to transform the way people do things at the beginning of the project into more effective behaviour as the project moves along. This transformation initially involves identifying the inter-cultural differences among the parties. Once this is done, a programme of inter-cultural team building is called for in order to make the transformation take place. The result of the team-building process is influencing the behaviour of the group toward meeting the project's goals. Inter-cultural team building thus calls for developing and conducting a programme that will help transform the participants' inputs into project outputs. The opening case has highlighted the OD process for building teams.

DEVELOPMENT OF A PROJECT CULTURE

Experience in managing bi-national projects indicates that for cultural convergence to take place, managers of both sides need to understand the culture of the other, analysing the different patterns that make up that culture. This means learning about the other country's history, geography, economy, religion, tradition and politics. Both sides, therefore, need to become aware of the basic differences involving educational levels, professional experience, experience on this kind of project, knowledge of language and host-country's way of life.

Aside from this information, which can be readily obtained and assimilated, other perceptions must be taken into account, such as beliefs, feelings, informal behaviour patterns, group norms and values. All these factors strongly affect behaviour of project managers and team members. These dimensions can be mapped on a grid (Fig. 17.1), where the *y*-axis will depict all these dimensions, and on the *x*-axis we can do the assessment of the two groups on a scale from 0 to 5. These assessments, of course, will be subjective but will provide sufficient insight to both groups about each other. Based on the analysis of differences, behaviour standards need to be developed. The objective is to define a desirable behaviour or a project culture. In other words, cross-cultural team building must take place so that individuals' inputs can be channelled to meet the project goals.

Forming a culture is a project by itself; therefore, it must have an objective, a schedule, resources and a development plan. The objective of building a project culture is to attain a cooperative spirit, to supplant the 'our side versus your side' feeling with a strong 'our project' view. The project culture is developed around the commonalities of both groups, identified in the analysis shown below. Other different traits must be sorted out through training programmes.

Characteristics	Country-1					Country-2				
		Minimum		Maximum			Minimum		Maximum	
	1	2	3	4	5	1	2	3	4	5
Gregariousness			X				X			
Technically-oriented				X					X	
Consensus-oriented					X			X		
Project experience			X					X		
Rational behaviour					X					X
Non-nationalistic behaviour			X					X		

Fig. 17.1 Evaluation of Cultural Patterns of Two Countries Involved in a Joint Venture

ELEMENTS OF A DYNAMIC TEAM

The success of a project depends as much on the project leadership as on the dynamics of the project team. A dynamic team is a high-performance team, one that utilises its energy to meet cost and time schedules and solves uncertainties that arise in project implementation by joint problem-solving and combined effort. All dynamic teams have certain characteristics which can be assessed or developed through team-building exercises. Each team functions as under:

Clearly States its Mission and Goals

A team requires a clearly stated purpose, and goals which are specific, measurable, agreeable, resource and time-bound. It is not enough to merely understand what needs to be done at the moment, but to understand the overall focus of the team.

Operates Creatively

Experimentation and creativity are signs of a dynamic team. Such teams take calculated risks by trying different ways of doing things. They are not afraid of failure, and they look for opportunities to implement new processes or techniques. They are also flexible and creative when dealing with problems and making decisions.

Focuses on Results

The ability to produce what is required and when it is required is the true test. A dynamic team is capable of achieving results beyond the sum of its individual members. Team members continually meet time, budget and quality commitments.

Clarifies Roles and Responsibilities

A dynamic team clarifies roles and responsibilities for all its members. Each team member knows what is expected of him or her, as well as the roles of fellow team members. A dynamic team updates its roles and responsibilities to keep up with project life cycle demands, objectives and technology.

Is Well Organized

A dynamic team defines protocol, procedures and policies from the very beginning. The structure allows the team to meet the demands of the project or task in hand.

Builds upon Individual Strengths

Leaders of project teams regularly catalogue their teams' knowledge, skills and talent. Team leaders are aware of their team members' strengths and weaknesses, so they can effectively draw upon individual competencies.

Supports Leadership and Each Other

Dynamic teams share leadership roles among members. Such teams give every member the opportunity to 'shine' as the leader. The team members also appreciate formal supervisory roles, because the formal leaders of a dynamic team support team efforts and respect individual uniqueness.

Develops Team Climate

It has members who enthusiastically work well together with high degree of involvement and group energy. Collectively they feel more productive and find team activities renewing their interest and spirit. Such a team develops a distinct character of its own.

Resolves Disagreements and Communicates Openly

It deals openly with conflict when it occurs. The members resolve it by mutual discussion and by solving the problem on win-win basis or by consensus. Each person solicits suggestions from other members, fully considers what they say, and then builds on their ideas.

Makes Objective Decisions and Evaluates its Own Effectiveness

In such teams 'continuous improvement' and 'proactive management' are the operating principles.

PROJECT CULTURE OVER THE LIFE CYCLE OF THE PROJECT

Culture begins to establish itself right from the early stages of the project. The participative process in the development of the work breakdown structure and the project activities network can stimulate the 'our project' spirit. It is also then that the first problems arise. Problems at this stage are relatively easy to solve, because enthusiasm on the part of team members is high. The cultural model to be established at this stage is that of cooperation of all parties in the spirit of 'all for one, one for all'.

If some individuals at this stage don't show efforts towards integration or show uncooperative attitudes, project managers should seriously consider taking them off the project because if they create problems in blue-sky conditions, they may be impossible to work with when stormy weather appears. On the other hand, emerging team leaders need to be identified with and motivated early for the project.

During the maturity stage of the project, when the organization is well defined and each unit takes care of its own tasks, the culture becomes competitive as project groups try to show efficiency in relation to other groups. Problems arise at this stage because of unbalanced workloads. Some groups may claim to be overworked while others have little work to do. Strong coordination and regular follow-up meetings are required during these intermediate project stages.

The final stage of the project is particularly difficult in terms of cultural integration. There is less work to do, and people are leaving to go on to other new projects. At this stage project managers are hard-pressed to maintain the spirit of the remaining group. This is the time for managers to show their leadership capabilities to make sure that the final activities of the project are performed with the same efficiency as the previous ones.

TEAM LEADERSHIP

Leadership can be a crucial issue in negotiating the team's relationship with the organization and beyond the organizational boundaries. Leadership is oftern a fluid concept within a team and particularly in virtual teams where people are called on to manage people whom they see only infrequently.

Expectations about the role of the team leader are likely to differ in international teams. A number of international surveys suggest that, in most countries, subordinates find the following characteristics undesirable, where their leader:

- Is individualistic and self-centered.
- Is non-egalitarian, dominating, distant and elitist.
- Is punitive and vindictive.
- Is narcissistic, cynical and arrogant.
- Saves face.
- Is secretive, cunning.

Conversely, almost universally desired characteristics appear to be where the leader:

- Is visionary, a team-builder.
- Is rational, analytical, intelligent.
- Is team-oriented and collaborative.
- Has integrity.
- Is decisive.

In broad stereotypes, the UK looks for casual leadership, whereas French teams may expect more directive, autocratic leadership. Swedish teams may expect their team leaders to be the first among the equals, whereas Germans may expect a formal hierarchy with consensus. Asian teams may expect a leader to offer consensus, whereas Latin and Arab cultures may expect a more familial approach from their leader. Clearly, in a multinational team, the leader should ideally be at least sensitive to different expectations and flexible in approach.

A key element of a successful international team is leadership development, because the selection of international teams is often ad hoc. HR can play a useful role in assisting those responsible for setting up teams in the selection of team personnel and team-building and leadership development training.

Review Questions

1. Discuss the role and responsibilities of the human resource department in implementing successful international projects.
2. Do you think that integration of two cultures is necessary and possible for successful implementation of joint venture projects? If yes, how one should go about it?
3. Discuss the impact of project culture on the life cycle of a project.
4. Describe various team-building exercises and the characteristics of ace (most successful) teams.

Chapter

18

Frontiers of IHRM and Corporate HR Strategies for Competitive Advantage

LEARNING OBJECTIVES

After studying this chapter, you will be able to:

- *Recent thinking in organization theory and its change implications*
- *Challanges before corporate HR in global organizations and capability required*
- *The variables that influence strategic thinking and IHRM enablers*
- *Corporate HR strategic practices in global organizations.*

OPENING CASE
Seiko Instruments

The Seiko group, established in 1937, consists of three distinct companies – Seiko Corporation, Seiko Instruments Inc. (SII) and Seiko Epson Corporation. They operate independently but function as a cohesive unit as regards the design, production and marketing of timepieces that established the Seiko name. The company has 70 subsidiaries worldwide and over 10,000 employees. Through its global network, Seiko Corporation markets the timepieces produced by SII and Seiko Epson. In 1988, Seiko completed the world's first automated assembling system for multipurpose, small-lot production of watch movements.

HR Strategy

The organisation's structure is constrained by British standards in some respects, in common with other Japanese companies operating in the UK. The general manager, who is Scottish, has worked on the site for over 10 years and in all these years there have been only two visits by a personnel representative from Japan. The main objective of these visits for the HQ to survey the Japanese employees working overseas.

The Corporation's stance is basically that in the overseas countries, the personnel function should operate entirely autonomously. It's fairly bizarre to have identical policies and procedures in sites as in diverse location as Japan, China, Thailand, Malaysia and UK. Generally the company tries to treat the employees fairly well and it is left to the local personnel to follow local standards and customs.

'If it wasn't for Mr. X (a Japanese senior manager) you wouldn't know that you worked for a Japanese company. There isn't really anything Japanese about it at all. I say to people: you will probably find this company is not like your typical Japanese company.'

Most personnel policies of the Scottish site are made locally; the site is given targets and a free range to achieve them 'the Scottish way'. The company's policy is to respect local ways – they try to adapt to local management practices 100 per cent within the Scottish location. People management is designed mainly by the General Manager. They have constructed a policy manual and a handbook containing mostly local practices. They are first written in draft, involving all the managers at this stage, agreed upon, and then formalized. Then they are placed on the notice boards and employees are notified. Revisions are initiated as required by legislation, for example, changes in working practices. The GM has spent some time working in the USA (California) with Seiko and has introduced Californian practices into the site. Quality is the only common ingredient in all Seiko plants throughout the globe.

Recruitment

All recruitment is done from the Scottish site. In Japan they select school leavers for operators. Initially, the Japanese Manufacturing Manager had a preference for school leavers and teenagers and wanted the Scottish site to recruit them. He was involved in selecting the first 90 employees who fulfilled this age criterion. When these 90 recruits were assessed on, for example, how they behaved with their elders on site, they were considered unreliable and found 'unaccustomed to this kind of work.' Absenteeism was a problem at this stage. He believed that they had 'no work ethic at this age.' The personnel manager, who at the time was the only personnel manager of a Japanese company in Livingston said, 'I will not employ school leavers and teenagers.' He thinks the policy of recruiting school leavers works only in Japan because youngsters are more obedient and better educated.

Overseas Training

Watch manufacturing has been in operation for over four years. A lot of initial training was done in Seiko's subsidiaries in Singapore and the Far East; a lot of overseas trainees came over and worked with the operators for about three months. The on-site practices have been refined over the years. Production supervisors go over to Japan every year to learn new practices and processes. If the Scottish site had a disastrous manufacturing problem, a Japanese would come over. Recently, they had had an engineering problem in the printer's section and quality people came over from Japan. They stayed for a week to sort things out.

What has been brought from overseas is mainly knowledge. When the watch manufacturing was set up there were no processes in existence. 24 employees were sent to Japan to learn how to operate the equipment. They came back and increased the number of people in the area and developed their own systems. The senior manufacturing engineer goes to Japan for training and looking at business opportunities and to Singapore for the transfer of production lines and further training. Generally, no one goes to Japan for training, although things are changing – they are becoming more interested in what Scotland is doing with regard to technical processes. Scotland has taken Japanese ideas and is now running some of their machines more efficiently.

Training Differences between Scotland and Japan

In Scotland, the company encourages people to develop at operator level, both in-house and in colleges and other educational establishments and finance their education.

In Japan, because employees remain in the company for a long time, they have large, established internal training and recognized formal qualifications. They have extensive support resources, for example, engineering and technical support. Rank-and-file employees do not go to college or university, because they are not available to everyone at the company's expense, but sometimes managers do attend short courses in these establishments. However, company pays up to 50 per cent of the cost of outsourced English classes if the employees wish to learn the language.

Team Working

The subsidiary management has introduced the Japanese way of team working. The local managers know the Japanese practices, such as 'total quality management' and 'quality circles', and use them in a modified way. The management does not push Japanese quality initiatives; they are happy for the employees to apply the tools they prefer. Also, in Japan, they run quality circles after working hours on a voluntary, non-paid basis but the Scottish managers are not able to implement them here because operators want them to be paid overtime. In addition the managers believe that such practice as twice daily exercise in the office, customary in the Japanese sites, will not work here 'because the company is not a school or army'.

Consensual Decision-Making

The GM's observation from working in Seiko plants in Japan is that the Japanese style of consensual decision-making offers unsatisfactory compromises. He says decisions take time to be made. Also, if junior Japanese managers are involved they will not speak their mind because they feel inhibited for cultural and traditional reasons. In the Scotttish site employees are more frank.

Pay and Benefits

These are decided locally. There is considerable competition for skilled local workers. Seiko competes against the likes of Motorola and Sky for employees. Consequently, their pay is competitive with rewards for hard work. They also offer paternity leave, pensions, life insurance and sick pay.

Industrial Relations

The Scottish site is not unionized, but the Japanese site has company-based unions. Moreover, in Scotland, there are grievance removed procedures in place to enable the employees to file claims against their boss, but such a system does not exist in Japan. Senior managers believe that the history of local trade unions still makes the employees suspicious of the management even today. The management has to work harder to gain trust and get people to buy into and get them to come up with new ideas and work on problems themselves. In Scotland they make employees redundant if they have to. In Japan, Seiko does not do this. The company offers job for life and, if need be, transfers employees to holding divisions rather than make them redundant.

INTRODUCTION

In this final chapter, we have looked at several issues and trends that are influencing the processes and practices of HRM in multinational oganisations. In this book we have focused on IHRM approaches and processes in large multinationals in the context of current organisation theory. However, organization theory itself is undergoing change. As said by Winston Churchill, 'We are shaping the world faster than we can change ourselves, and we are applying to the present the habits of the past.' We will look at the contemporary organization design and challenges posed by dynamic and complex environmental changes where resources are scarce and difficult to hold. We will look at HR processes in small and medium enterprises operating in the global arena (mini-multinationals). We will look at new thinking how global companies gain competitive advantage and the new role of IHRM. It is important to recall the words of Rosabeth Moss Kanter (*World Class: Thriving locally in the global economy*, 1995), who said, 'Success in the global economy derives not just from meeting high standards for competition in world contest, but also from strong relationships – networks that link to global markets and networks that build collective local strengths. In the future, companies that flourish will be best partners to their customers, suppliers, employees, and allies in joint ventures. Their leaders will know how to create productive partnerships that span companies, sectors, countries, or communities. Companies need collaborative advantage.

CONTEMPORARY ORGANIZATION THEORY AND LEADING CHANGE

Today's organizations and managers may be seen as shifting from a mindset based on mechanical systems to one based on natural and biological systems. These changing beliefs and perceptions affect how we think about organizations and the pattern of behaviours within organizations. For most of the 20th century Newtonian science, which suggests that the world functions as a well-behaved machine, continued to guide managers thinking about organizations. The environment was perceived as orderly and predictable and the role of manager was to maintain stability. And growth was the primary criterion for organizational success.

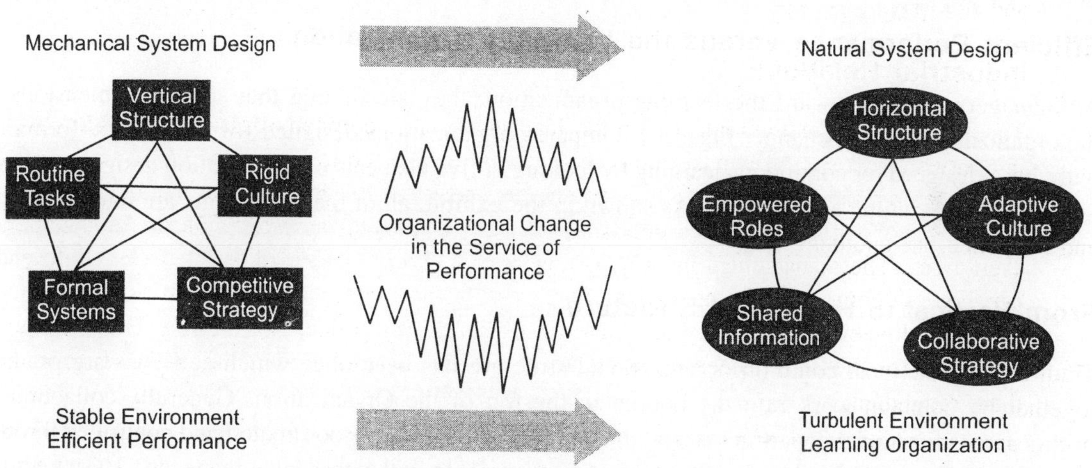

Fig. 18.1 Two Organization Design Approaches

Source: Adapted from David K. Hurst: Crisis and Renewal: Meeting the Challenge of Organizational Change (*Boston, Mass: Harvard Business School Press*, 1995).

Global organizations became larger and more complex and boundaries between functional departments and units become distinct. Internal structures grew more complex, vertical and bureaucratic, and communication was primarily through formal memos, letters and reports. Managers did all the planning and 'thought work', while employees did the manual work in exchange for wages. The environment for today's organizations is anything but stable. With the current economic and financial turbulence managers can no longer maintain an illusion of order and predictability. The chaos theory suggests that the relationship in complex adaptive systems – including organization – is non-linear and made up of numerous interconnections and divergent choices that create unintended effects and render the universe unpredictable. The world is full of uncertainty, characterized by surprise, rapid change and confusion. Managers cannot measure, predict or control in traditional ways the unfolding drama inside or outside the organization. However, chaos theory also recognizes that this randomness and disorder occur within certain larger patterns of order. The chaos theory suggests that organizations should be viewed more as natural systems than as mechanical systems. This requires radical change in restructuring and rethinking about organization design and management. An ecosystem of a MNC is shown in Fig. 18.2.

Although-the stakes might not be as high, business and nonprofit organizations today also need greater fluidity and adaptability. Many managers are redesigning their companies toward something called the **learning organization.** The learning organization promotes communication and collaboration so that everyone is engaged in identifying and solving problems, enabling the organization to continuously experiment, improve, and increase its capability. The learning organization is based on equality, open information, little hierarchy, and a culture that encourages adaptability and participation, enabling ideas to bubble up from anywhere that can help the organization seize opportunities and handle crises. In a learning organization, the essential value is problem solving, as opposed to the traditional organization designed for efficient performance.

Efficient Performance versus the Learning Organization

As managers struggle toward the learning organization, they are finding that specific dimensions of the organization have to change. Fig. 18.1 compares organizations designed for efficient performance with those designed for continuous learning by looking at five elements of organization design: structure, tasks, systems, culture, and Strategy. As shown in the exhibit, all of these elements are interconnected and influence one another.

From Vertical to Horizontal Structure

Traditionally, the most common organizational structure has been once which activities are grouped together by common work rain the bottom to the top of the Organization. Generally collaboration occurs across functional departments, and the whole organization is coordinated and controlled through the vertical hierarchy, with decision-making authority residing with upper-level managers. This structure-call be quite effective. It promotes efficient production and in-depth skill development, and the hierarchy of authority provides a sensible mechanism for supervision and control in large organizations. However, in a rapidly changing environment, the hierarchy becomes overloaded. Top executives arc not able to respond rapidly enough to problems or opportunities.

In the learning organization, the vertical structure that creates distance between managers at the top of the organization and workers in the technical core is disbanded. Structure is created around horizontal workflows or processes rather than departmental functions. The vertical hierarchy is dramatically flattened, with perhaps: only a few, senior executives in traditional support functions such as finance or human resources self-directed teams are the fundamental work unit in the learning organization. Boundaries between functions aye practically eliminated because teams include members from several functional areas. In some cases, organizations do away with departments altogether. For example,·at Oticon Holding A/S, a Danish company that introduced the world's first digital heating aid, there are no organization charts, no departments, no functions, and no titles. Employees are continuously forming and reforming into self-directed teams that work on specific projects."

From Routine Tasks to Empowered Roles

Another shift in thinking relates to the degree of formal structure and control placed on employees the performance of their work. Recall that scientific, management advocated precisely defining each job and how it should be performed. A task is a narrowly defined piece *of* work assigned to ' a person. In traditional organizations, tasks are broken down into specialized, separate parts, as in a machine. Knowledge and control of tasks are centralized at the top of the organization, and employees are expected to do as they are told. A **role,** in contrast, is a part in a dynamic social system. A role has discretion and responsibility, allowing the person to use his or her discretion and ability to achieve an outcome or meet a goal. In learning organizations, employees play a role in the team or department and roles may be continually redefined or adjusted. There are few rules or procedures, and knowledge and control of tasks are located with workers rather than with supervisors or top executives. Employees are encouraged to take care of problems by working with one another and with customers. The U.S. Army again provides an excellent example. Four-star General John Abizaid, who took charge of U.S. Central Command (all of the forces in the Middle East) in July 2003 has long advocated an expanded role for soldiers in the field. He knows that today's soldiers have to do more than Just shoot rifles and follow orders. During the peacekeeping operations in Iraq, low-ranking soldiers on a daily basis have to use intelligence, emotional understanding, and cultural sensitivity to defuse potentially dangerous situations.'

From Formal Control Systems to Shared Information

In young, small organization, communication is generally informal and face-to-face. There are few formal control and information systems because tie top leaders of the company usually directly with employees in the day-to-day operation of the business. However,, when organizations grow large and complex, the distance between top leaders and workers in technical increases. Formal systems are often implemented to manage the growing amount of complex information and to detect deviations from established standards and goals.

In learning organizations, information serves a very different purpose. The widespread sharing of information keel): the organization functioning at an optimum level .The learning organization strives to return to the condition of a sill-all, entrepreneurial firm in which all employees have complete information about the company so they call act quickly. Ideas and information ale shared throughout the organization. Rather than using information to control employees, a significant hart of a manager's job is to find ways to open channels of communication so that ideas flow in all directions. In addition, learning organizations maintain open lines *of* communication with customers, suppliers, and even competitors to enhance lea riling capability. At. Jet Blue Airways, CEO and founder David Neeleman promotes widespread information sharing by regularly going on flights to talk with employees and customers. Neeleman believes this is where he gets his best ideas for improving Jet Blue.' Information technology also plays a key role in keeping people cross the organization connected.

From Competitive to Collaborative Strategy

In traditional organization designed for efficient performance, strategy is formulated by top managers and imposed on the organization. Top executives think about how (lie organization can best respond to competition, efficiently use resources, and cope with environmental In the learning organization, in contrast, the accumulated actions Of all informed and empowered workforce contribute to strategy development. Since all employees are in touch with customers, suppliers and new technology, they help identify needs and solutions and participate in strategy making. In addition, strategy emerges from partnerships with suppliers; customers, and even competitors, Organizations become collaborators as well as competitors, experimenting to find the best way to learn and adapt. Boundaries between organizations are becoming diffuse, with companies often forming partnerships to compete globally, sometimes joining in modular or virtual network organizations that are connected electronically.

From Rigid to Adaptive Culture

For an organization to remain healthy, its culture should encourage adaptation to the external environment. A danger for many organizations is that the culture becomes fixed, as if set in concrete. Organizations that were highly successful in stable environments often become victims of their own success when the environment begins to change dramatically. This is what happened at Xerox Corp., as described in the opening case, when managers became stuck in the Burox culture and were unable to respond to rapid changes in the technological environment. The cultural values, ideas, and practices that helped attain success were detrimental to effective performance in a rapidly changing environment.

In a learning organization, the culture encourages openness, equality, continuous improvement, and change. People in the organization are aware of the whole system, how everything fits together, and how the various parts with one another and with the environment. This whole-system mindset minimizes boundaries within the organization and with other companies. In addition, activities and symbols that create status differences, such as executive dining rooms or reserved parking spaces, are discarded. Each person is a valued contributor and the organization becomes a place for creating a web of relationships that allows people to develop and apply their full potential. Consider QuikTrip, a chain of convenience stores, where most of the top managers started out at the store level, and everyone is considered a vital part of the chain's success. 'The purpose of QuikTrip,' says CEO Chester Cadieux 11, 'is to give our employees the opportunity to grow and succeed.' The emphasis on treating everyone with care and respect creates a climate in which people feel safe to experiment, take risks, and make mistakes, all of which encourages learning.

No company represents a perfect example of a learning organization, although many of today's most competitive organizations have shifted toward ideas and forms based on the concept of a living, dynamic system.

As illustrated in Fig. 18.1, today's managers are involved in a struggle as they attempt to change their companies into learning organizations. The challenge for managers is to maintain some level of stability as they actively promote change toward the new way of thinking, to navigate between order and chaos.

One organization that is transforming into a learning organization is Mexico's Cementos; Mexicanos (Cemex).

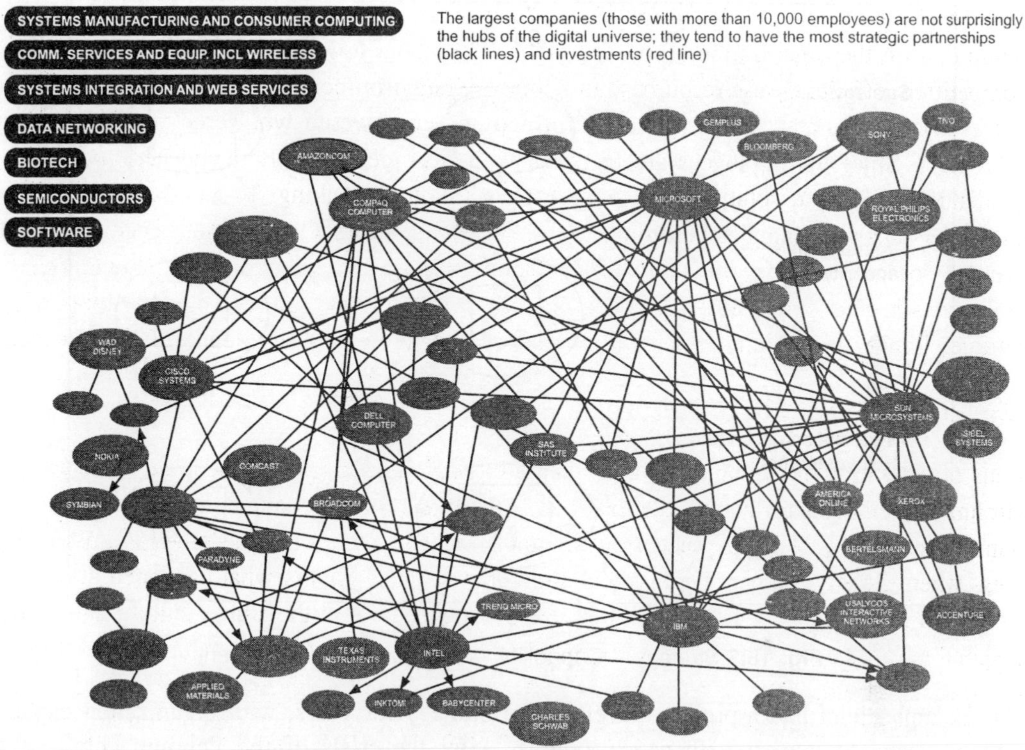

Smaller companies that have no relationships with the hubs are not featured.

Fig. 18.2 An Organizational Ecosystem (based on 1999 data)

THE NEW FRONTIERS OF IHRM

In recent years, an ascent view of organizations has emerged. Rather than defining organizations as 'bundles of capabilities' (Ulrich and Lake 1990; Stalk et al, 1992). This transition shifts the focus from rules, procedures, policies and levels of management and other hierarchical mechanisms to a focus on:

- Core competencies (Prahalad and Hamel, 1990; Gallon, Stillman and Coats, 1995).
- Agility (Dyer and Shafer, 1998).
- Culture (Barney, 1986).
- High performing work practices (Delaney and Huselid, 1996).

An effective organization is now defined by its ability to respond to business demands. The age-old adage 'structure follows strategy' is being replaced by 'capability follows strategy' (Ulrich, 1997).

The logic of this converging and emerging view of organization is portrayed in Fig. 18.3. As suggested in the figure, as an organization shifts its strategy from cell 1 to cell 4, it must also redefine required capabilities (cell 5) and HR investments (cell 6) to align with the emerging strategy.

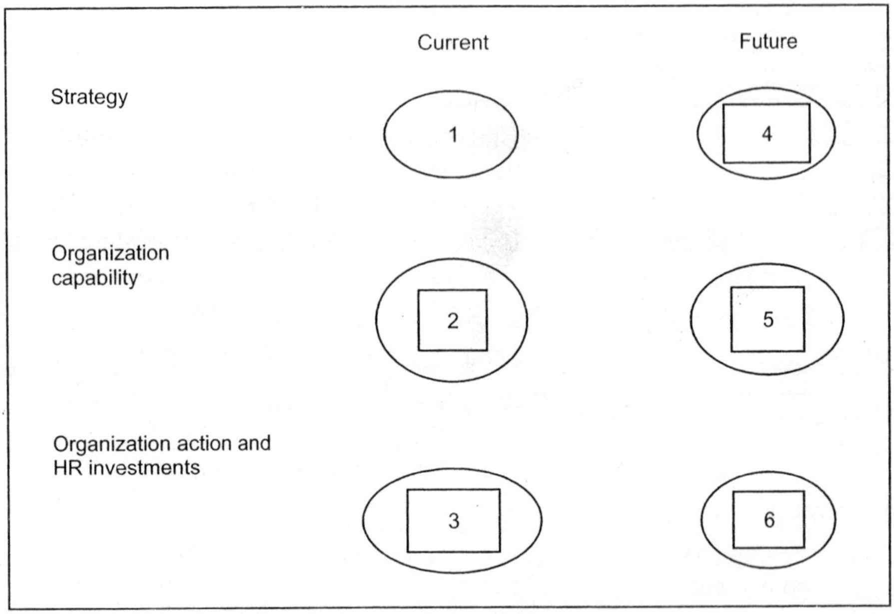

Fig. 18.3 Strategy – Capability – Organization Assessment

For example, Intel had a product development strategy for years, with organization capabilities focused on speed to market with new products. After the crisis of the Pentium chip – a small mathematical error that an Intel chip produced was highlighted by the media, and Intel's response concentrated on the technical specification at the expense of the customer, with subsequent loss of credibility – Intel's management realized that their strategy should not be product but customer or brand. So they began to find ways to build the brand (Intel Inside) that would attract and retain customers. This strategic shift required a new set of capabilities for Intel's success, such as building customer intimacy, leveraging brand across products, forming alliances with distributors and quality. Embedding these new capabilities enabled Intel to turn its strategy into practice. Once these new capabilities were identified, Intel executives and HR professionals could make HR investments (cell 6) that drove these capabilities; for example, they began:

- To hire individuals with customer focus.
- To develop training and development experiences focused on customers.
- To create incentive schemes that encourages customer-oriented behaviour.
- To redesign performance appraisal system with high focus an customer service.

These HR practices are bundled together to deliver required critical capabilities. A capability focus entails rethinking the organizational implications on global strategy. For example, strategic decisions, like which market we choose to enter and how? what activities we do there (production, marketing or research and development), etc.? If these decisions are taken with a focus on 'capabilities' to succeed, then we will also be asking: where do we find right people and how do we compensate and train them? In the team, charged with developing a global strategy, either the line manager or HR professionals (or both) must ask 'what capabilities are required to compete in this global market?''

CAPABILITIES FOR GLOBAL STRATEGY

There is a set of capabilities that must be created for a global strategy to successfully implemented The capabilities are so organized that each set represents important tensions to be managed successfully. Overall it is that of being able to think simultaneously in two different directions, such as, 'thinking globally and acting locally'. However, at a more detailed level, some capabilities enable global leveraging while others ensure maximum local adaptation. Thus six capabilities enable the firm to compete globally and adapt locally. They are summarized in Table 18.1 and explained below:

Table 18.1

	Global Integration	*Local Adaptaion*
1.	Determine the core...	Determine the non-core...
2.	Achieve consistancy...	Allow flexibility...
3.	Build global brand equity...	Honour local customs...
4.	Get leverage and scale (Bigger is better...)	Get smaller...smaller is better
5.	Share knowledge and learning ...	Experiment and create new knowledge
6.	Create global perspective or mindset.	Ensure local accountability...

1. **Determining the core versus determining the non-core:** It is not possible that same thing is simultaneously integrated globally and adapted locally. Hence the first critical capability is being able to determine what is 'core' to the organization and should be integrated and standardized throughout its worldwide operations, and what is non-core.
   Issues core to the organization relate to principles that give the firm a global identity. For example, Disney has identified a set of core principles on which its theme parks function. When Walt Disney created the first theme park in Anaheim, California, he did so in order to provide a **'clean, safe and fun experience for families'.** The experience he set out to create was in stark contrast to the seedy carnivals of the time. This core principle remains the same throughout all Disney's theme parks. The world is just too big and too diverse to entertain the notion that every policy or practice, let alone product or process, can be the same everywhere. Senior managers must also determine what is non-core and therefore open to local adaptation. Identifying practices, policies and so on that are clearly non-core can eliminate the time and energy that otherwise go into debating and politicking over the issues. It will ensure autonomy to all unit managers in different parts of the world. Clearly, not everything can – or even should – be classified from the outside as core or non-core. Some issues will be grey or will only be decided on a case-by-case basis. For example, alcohol was not served or allowed in Disney parks for the reason that it might endanger the safety of families. But over time

review and adjustment is required in what is determined as core or non-core. For example, now wine is allowed in Paris and beer in Tokyo.

2. **Achieving consistency versus allowing flexibility:** After the core is determined, it is necessary that it is implemented by people consistently across the world. This consistency in human behaviour in diverse cultures and countries is not easy to ensure. This capability centers on understanding what guides people's behaviour when no one is looking. But the world is too big a place for any corporation to monitor employee behaviour constantly and correct anything undesirable in it.

   Consistency in behaviour requires that first people should know that this is core value of our organization and why it is core. Neither the 'what' nor 'why' can create understanding unless the word comes to life through stories and examples. And examples alone will not guarantee consistency unless a corporate culture of commitment is ingrained. In other words, both head and heart must be engaged. How such a corporate culture is created has been discussed in this book exhaustively in Part-2. Disney selects the individuals who already believe in its core values and carefully interviews them to ascertain whether they are already disposed towards providing their guests with friendly service and towards believing in the importance of cleanliness. The intensity of orientation programme is increased for those who are selected. For those issues which are non-core, flexibility and adaptation must be allowed. And this requires tolerance of differences. Interestingly, P&G found greater success in Asia when it abandoned its traditional bottles and put its shampoo in single-use packets.

3. **Building global brand equity versus honouring local customs:** Building a global brand equity is essential for global integration of all units across the world. The key criterion to decide what is 'core' rests on the logic of what is important to its customer. It is the customers who decide whether the 'consistency' discussed above is important or not. If customers and their needs are critical to determining what is core, then building equity in the minds of customers relative to that core is equally critical. The Richard Branson's Virgin brand has four key dimensions:

   - A positive buying experience.
   - Experiencing outstanding service.
   - Seeing continuous improvement in products or service.
   - Receiving economic value for the transaction.

   Despite the need for building global brand equity, differences in local customs persist. These differences affect everything, from how laundry is done to how contracts are negotiated. Hence the HR manager has to make special effort in understanding local customs and their origin and drivers. They have to advise management which customs are likely to persist and which are amenable to harmonization over time. For example, Americans in Indonesia tried to use their practice of fixed-time break for coffee for heavy equipment drivers, which did not work as the custom there is to enjoy 'pan' whenever friends meet. Another famous example is of Unilever's famous Sunlight soap, introduced after studying the way ladies wash clothes in India.

4. **Getting leverage (bigger is better) vs getting focus (smaller is better):** The business world has entered an era of the mega-corporation. Merger mania has given rise to behemoths, such

as, the City Group. The dream of every organization is to become a member of the Fortune 500 list – to grow fast and grow large. Wal-Mart, for example, employs more people than the US military. In most cases, bigger translates into greater geographical coverage. Both economies of scale and scope are the focus behind getting bigger. They hope to cut costs by using their size to get better deals from suppliers and by harmonizing their IT systems. Their size should also allow them both to reduce the combined total amount spent on research and development and also to leverage what is invested and generated across a larger product and the sales base.

In their search for global efficiencies and economies, firms often forget that they are competing with local firms (Unilever vs Nirma). They forget that these local firms must succeed at home as they have no foreign market options. Hence they compete fiercely in a fight for their life. Although they may lack many of the advantages of global firms, they have advantages of their own. They often know the inner working of the relevant government and have close personal relationships with powerful officials. They have years of experience of serving local customers and have developed an insight into their minds. Small organizations have flat structures and an organic, free-flowing management style that encourages entrepreneurship and innovation. Today's biotechnological drugs, for example, were all discovered by small firms. Moreover, the personal involvement of employees in small firms encourages motivation and commitment, because employees personally identify with the company's mission. Most of the 100 firms on *Fortune* magazine's list of the fastest growing companies in the US are small firms characterized by an emphasis on being fast and flexible in responding to the environment.

The challenge before the HR manager is that to design an organization that is both big and small. The solution is what Jack Welch called the 'big company/small-company hybrid' that combines a large corporation's resources and reach with a small company's simplicity and flexibility.

5. **Sharing learning versus creating new knowledge:** Global success requires both the ability to leverage learning across a firm's worldwide operations and an ability to create new knowledge wherever incubation conditions exist. The larger the organization, the greater is the potential of cost and revenue benefits from sharing knowledge. Consequently, maintaining a competitive position as the firm globalizes requires developing the ability to share knowledge throughout the firm's far-flung operations.

   However, sharing of knowledge is resisted. Local managers resist incorporating best practices from outside for fear of an erosion of their power base. Most of the time, people do not openly admit that they are resisting the adoption of the best practice or other shared learning because they feel threatened. General Electric (GE) creates many forums for sharing global knowledge. It.

   - Uses written and live-case studies in its development programmes from many countries.
   - Deploys best-practice teams to codify the best practice that can then be shared.
   - Uses groupware technology to connect people from different countries to share ideas.
   - Transfers people from one country to another either permanently or on temporary assignments to transfer knowledge.

These activities allow good ideas generated within one country to be shared with others. although sharing learning across a global organization is no small task. For many firms it is easier than creating new knowledge on a worldwide basis. Many firms are concentrating on research and development (R&D) for innovating new products and improving process efficiency. However, many firms are experiencing undistributed knowledge creation, particularly if research and development labs are located in a few selected centres only. People assume that innovation is the responsibility of R&D only. Yet the world is too large and contains too many bright and capable people to contribute towards new knowledge creation and innovation. HR professionals face the challenge to motivate the capability in employees to generate new ideas and willingness to share learning.

Two distinct approaches to knowledge management are outlined in Fig. 18.4. The first approach deals primarily with the collection and sharing of explicit knowledge (is formal, systematic knowledge that can be codified or written down and passed on to others in documents for general instructions) largely through the use of sophisticated IT systems. Explicit knowledge may include intellectual properties, such as patents, licences, work processes, specific information on customers, suppliers or competitors, benchmark information and so on. With this people-to-document approach, knowledge is gathered from the individuals who possess it and is organized into documents that others can access and reuse.

The second approach focuses on leveraging individual expertise and know-how – tacit knowledge – by connecting people face to face or through interactive media. Tacit knowledge includes personal experience, rules of thumb, intuition and judgment. It includes professional know-how, individual insight and experience and creative solutions that are difficult to communicate and pass on to others. With this approach, managers concentrate on developing personal networks that link people together for the sharing of tacit knowledge. The organization uses IT systems primarily for facilitating conversation and person-to-person sharing of experience.

Organisations typically combine several methods and technologies to facilitate the sharing and transfer of both explicit and tacit knowledge.

6. **Creating global perspective versus ensuring local accountability:** This last capability requires viewing the organization from global perspective, leading to a sense of belonging to the worldwide entity and at the same time fervent feeling of personal accountability and responsibility. Creating a global mindset is extremely difficult [only 11% of all US heads of HR have international experience (Black et al, 1999)]. In a study of over 130 senior executives in 50 firms across Europe, the US and Asia, eight out of ten said that an international assignment was the most powerful developmental experience in shaping their global perspective.

   Firms at the same time must also create a sense of local accountability and ownership in their people. For example, Shell assigns global accountability for overall firm's results, and the officers at the corporate set direction for the whole enterprise. However, within the broad directives local managers are accountable and responsible for their operations.

   If the above six capabilities are critical, then the role of HR professionals is to:

- Raise, define and clarify the capabilities required to win globally, and
- Invest, design and deliver HR practices that ensure these capabilities.

RAISE, DEFINE AND CLARIFY CAPABILITIES

First the HR professional may engage the global corporate strategy team in a profile and assessment of which capabilities are more critical for the firm's particular global strategy. Fig. 18.3 is a diagnostic that the HR professional in concert with line managers may raise in the strategy discussions. For example, if the answers tend towards globalization side (in Fig. 18.3 letters), then the firm should invest in HR policies and processes that encourage co-ordination, integration and standardization; if towards the localization side (the numbers), a focus on local requirements would prevail. If both, then it is important for the HR executive to help the team to identify the specific nature of the duel pressures. Although it is possible that a specific activity would simultaneously experience both. Analyzing the specific pressures and relative importance of capabilities is one of the more difficult but valuable contributions HR executives can make to the development and subsequent implementation of global strategy.

For this business to succeed, where should we rank on each capability?

GLOBAL INTEGRATION									LOCAL ADAPTATION
	IMPORTANCE								
	High			Neutral			High		
Determine the core	A	B	C	D	4	3	2	1	Determine the non-core
Achieve consistency	A	B	C	D	4	3	2	1	Allow flexibility
Build global brand equity	A	B	C	D	4	3	2	1	Honour local customs
Give leverage and scale	A	B	C	D	4	3	2	1	Get focus, smaller is better
Share knowledge/learning	A	B	C	D	4	3	2	1	Create new knowledge
Create a global mindset	A	B	C	D	4	3	2	1	Ensure local accountability

Fig. 18.4 Profiling Critical Capabilities

Second, the HR professional may invite discussion about which of the six capabilities are more critical for business to win and succeed and which require more investment. For example, for a firm with with strong local market presence (Unilever-HUL) but inability to share ideas would probably focus on the knowledge and learning capability as the most salient capability going forward. This would then have implications for the HR investment necessary to build global learning into the firm.

Third, in managing paradoxes inherent in these capabilities the firm should create a forum where dialogue continuously occurs.

Fourth, paradoxes embedded in global vs local capabilities may be sequentially managed. For example, when entering new market with a new product, the focus may be on flexibility, learning local customs, being focused, creating new knowledge, and local accountability. However, over time, the localization capabilities may need to be adapted to gain global leverage.

Finally, HR professionals may create measurement systems (balance scorecard) to monitor how well each of the desired capabilities is being delivered.

INVEST IN DESIGN AND DELIVER HR PRACTICES

HR professionals have the expertise to invest in HR practices that build the desired capabilities. They can use the worksheet shown in Fig. 18.5. In selecting, prioritizing and designing HR practices they should see that that are aligned to each other and accordingly deliver appropriate programmes which are integrated with each other. For example, if hiring local employees becomes important for adapting to local customs then the training, compensation and communication practices must also encourage this capability.

Table 18.2 HR Investments for Global Integration and Local Adaptation

HR Investment Domain *Capability* 1	*Critical* *Capability* 2	*Critical* *Capability* 3	*Critical* *Capability* 4
Staffing Hiring new talent and orienting them, contracting with outside talent and retaining them. **Developing** Designing and delivering training. Systematically rotating talent. Building succession plans. Using career development **Performance management** Setting individual/team goals Designing financial and non-financial rewards Designing and delivering benefit programmes. Removing poor performers. **Communication** Crafting communication plans. Holding communication forums. **Governance** Shaping organization structure. Building dynamic teams. Clarifying decision-making logic setting.			

Source: J. Stewart Black and Dave Ulrich, *Organization Capability*, 1990, Wiley, New York.

THE MAP OF IHRM TERRITORY

IHRM is having a much wider periphery today. It encompasses all the HR areas and is practised by all line and unit managers. This is due to the network nature of global firms in which decentralization, empowerment and development of all managers are essential. This structure requires intensive communication, involvement and commitment of middle management and other employees deeper with the organisation. Thus to gain competitive advantage it is essential to integrate structure, strategy and culture with HR policies. A flexible model describing the map of IHRM's territory, developed by Beer and his associates (1984) at Harvard University is given in Fig. 18.5.

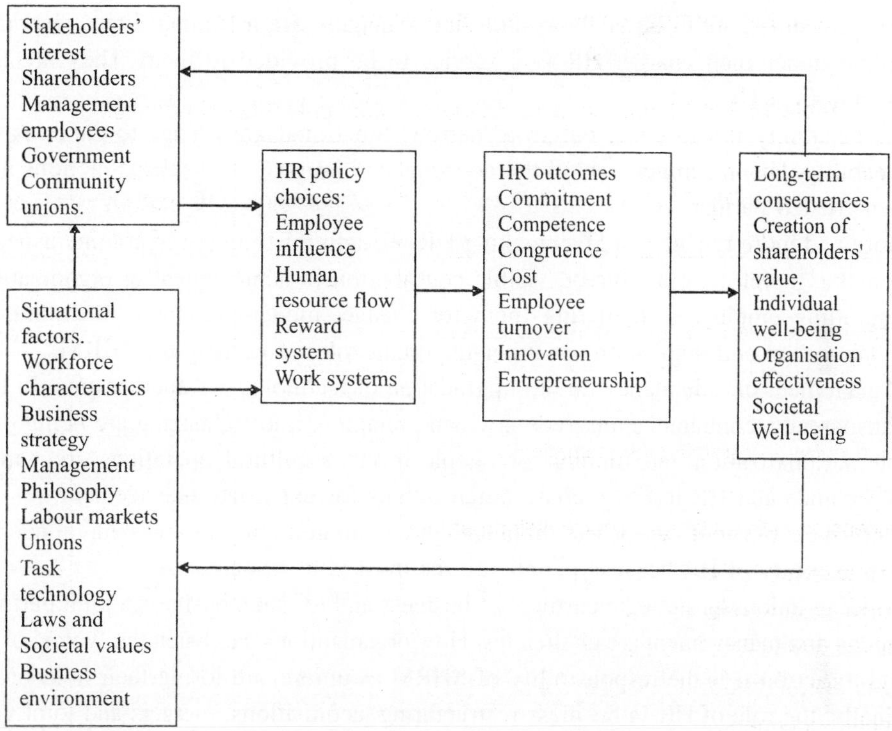

Fig. 18.5 The Map of IHRM Territory

The model is comprehensive to encompass all the variables that influence the desired outcomes by HR professionals and are properly linked.

EMERGING TRENDS AND ISSUES

In post-industrial society dominated by multinationals, information technology, globalization, and services, the field of people management has changed from reactive personnel management to proactive human resource management to value creating function, which is strategic in nature. The trends in SHRM and issues, it is trying to provide answers are as follows:

1. Each organization has its own situational realities, characteristics and challenges. The business strategy and the role, strategy and process of HR therefore have to be customized. It is generally felt that the competitive pressures increasingly demand speed, flexibility, process

integration, team building and concern for quality and customer care. There should be more focus on results and social responsibility of business. All the stakeholders have to be taken care of HR interventions in the area of selection, performance management, compensation and employee relations have to be strategically managed to meet specific organizational situations.

2. HR roles are changing with decentralization, de-layering and downsizing. Corporate and HR roles are emerging to be advisory and line managers are assuming direct responsibility the people under their charge. HR is a service to be provided to them. They are the internal customers of HR.
3. HR capability has to come out from narrow, functional knowledge to encompass business capability. HR has to understand the concerns and languages of other functions and become their trusted partner.
4. More and more reliance on IT is making HR self-administering in its routine aspects. HR has to make, therefore, more direct, visible contribution in achievement of organizational goals.
5. Upgrading employees, preparing them for change, modernization of the mind, leading to collaboration and innovation are other important roles, emerging for SHRM.
6. Management of redundancy due to upgradation of technology is another area. In this context transparency, communication, redeployment, retaining and rightsizing are being emphasized.
7. Internationalization and training of people in cross-cultural operations are gaining added importance and HR has to prepare organizations for expatriate management.
8. Employee burnout, work-life balance and management of stress have become prime responsibility of HR because people are the most vital resource.
9. Building unions as strategic partners of business and to make business a joint partner between unions and management are challenges. How organizations can listen the 'voice' of employees and to act on it is the responsibility of SHRM as unions are losing their hold on MNCs.
10. Finally, the role of HR in business restructuring, acquisitions, mergers and joint ventures has become the most important strategic responsibility of HR function.

HR practices that distinguish successful firms

Pfeffer (Universalism: Concept of HRM) enumerates seven human resource practices that seem to distinguish between high-achieving firms and poor performers. They are as follows:

1. **Selectivity in recruiting-hiring the best:** Hiring the right people means more than just securing employees who possess the knowledge, skills and abilities required to perform a particular job; these people must also be able to acquire new knowledge and skills as jobs and environment change. In addition, employees must find that the work is satisfying and that overall organisational climate and reward structure meet their needs. They spend a great amount of resources and effort in selecting the best and better than their competitors. They select people for values and culture compatibility too. This is their core competency, and in labour markets where there is a shortage of employees it results in 'war for talent' which they always win.

2. **Incentive pay:** If employees are expected to behave in extraordinary ways and add value to the firm, sharing that gain with employees meets the workplace justice and fairness. Some form of performance-contingent pay is required if employees are expected to be persistent in their effort to add value to the firm. If employees believe that their contributions are instrumental in enhancing firm performance and increasing profitability, they will want to share in the benefits. How this is done, again, is strategic and important. (Individual level or group level or unit level or company level and in what proportion?). We believe the key is to link rewards to the particular behaviours required of employees and to make sure that all relevant behaviours, like dependability, quality and quantity of output, generation of new ideas or cooperation are encouraged.
3. **Employee ownership:** Employees can share the ownership of firm by holding the company's stock. By making employees shareholders the company reduces the conflict between capital and labour. This puts the performance-pay contingency at the organisational level.
4. **Training and skill development**: High–performing firms display a greater commitment to training and skill development than their counterparts. This core HRM activity is related to 'Kaizen'. However, knowledge and skill acquisition will not lead to improved firm performance unless employees are allowed and encouraged to use job-related knowledge and skills when performing their jobs. Thus, firms must take care to select people who are willing to learn and adapt and also establish rewards that encourage employees to participate in training.
5. **Cross-utilisation and cross-training:** Training and development should also lead to 'flexibility' so that employees are utilized even during production slowdowns. When people are able to perform multiple jobs or are multi-skilled, they represent a reserve of talent and are more likely to appreciate how their work and output levels affect the work of other employees in jobs related to their own.
6. **Symbolic egalitarianism:** If the goal is to increase communication between and across organisational levels, a case can be made out for reducing sub-divisions in job grades and other areas of inequality. Firms must signal with practices and policies that are all equal.
7. **Wage compression:** The relative pay differences between people at various organisation levels can have profound effects on employee perceptions. These perceptions, in turn, can affect wide variety of employee attitudes and behaviours. Current theory and empirical evidence suggest that if the goal is to increase the level of cooperation and team orientation, pay differences between jobs should be reduced. Note that this concerns pay distinctions at the level of job, not at the level of individual. That is, incentive pay is distinguished from pay hierarchy compression. This of course depends on HR strategy to be adopted.

CORPORATE EXAMPLE OF IHRM PRACTICES

The Hindustan Unilever (HUL) is India's largest fast moving company in FMCG industry. R&D and marketing are the key thrust areas in HUL. Yet it has accorded highest importance to HRM. Its HR philosophy is reflected in its mission statement (in part):

- People first and everything is next ring of trust and confidence is critical.

- Review and revise continuously.
- Don't hesitate to overresource when called for or when you find worthy people.
- Continue to recruit quality resource for the organization rather for the job perspective only.
- Planning for speed is very important. Closely monitor and be vigilant about expected synergy.
- Communicate, communicate and communicate.
- Top management is seen to be fair and equitable in dealing with people issues.
- Reward system to recognize efforts as much as possible.

Influence of HR Enablers at HUL

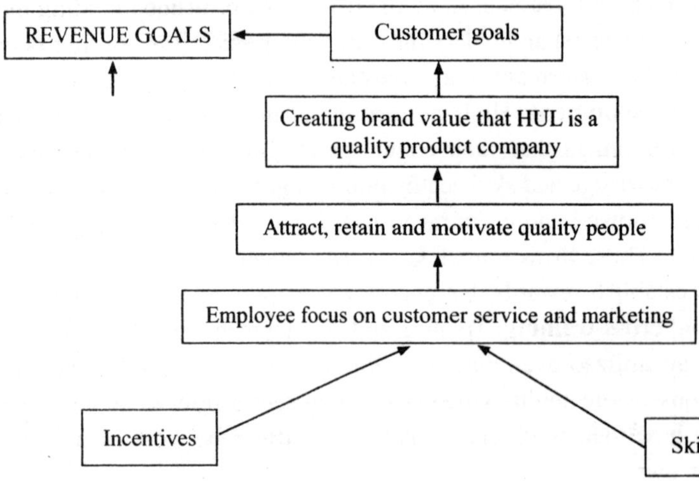

ABB

ABB faced following HR challenges: Labour unrest, low productivity, old, demotivated employees, aggressive unions; loss making business.

An attitudinal survey was conducted focusing on: self-introspection, team building, interpersonal relationship, attitudinal change and creativity. Organizational culture diagonastic survey assessing: organizational support, achievement motivation. Controls and roles: In implementing TQM, **key areas of improvements** identified were: reduced control orientation; cross functional team building, transparency in communication process; flexibility of operations and enhanced organizational support: empowerment: Total employee alignment was attempted through: shared vision, personnel development programmes, building teams, enhanced internal customer orientation and focus on continuous improvement in cost, quality and service. Open communication system: upward, downward and horizontal was strengthed.

Results: the revenue tripled in three years, material cost as percentage of revenue dropped by 27%, drop in manpower by 19%, revenue per employee increased by 340% and salaries were increased by 17%.

We can summarize the strategic decision-making by leading global companies on HR processes in Table 18.3.

Table 18.3 Strategic Decision-making Categories

	Resourcing	*Performance Management*	*Rewards*	*Management Development*	*Employee Rel]ations*
Staffing	Including all those activities related to internal movement of people across positions must match for the 'jobs' and external hiring of people must match both organization and job. Hire from most prestigious institutions and groom their career.	It contributes to two processes: (1) human resource planning and develop current pool of Talent. Development process in varying forms like, promotion, recognition, opportunities to learn, responsibility, security, respect from peer groups, co-employees etc.	Rewards in relation to performance, financial/ non financial	Activities to ensure that individuals are properly equipped with skills/ knowledge to perform jobs	
Strategic issues	Promotion system flow of people to match the business strategies.	Designing an appraisal system supportive of the corporate and business strategies.	Designing a reward system to provide balance support to short-term and long- term goals	Job improvement career planning succession planning Women managers Expatriation career templates	Activities oriented towards establishing a degree of participation and collaboration with management, unions and employees.
Strategic Choices	Make vs buy Little recruiting above entry level vs sophisticated recruiting at all levels	Process-oriented system Identification of training needs vs staffing needs Individual/group	Compensation oriented towards performance External competitiveness Cash vs non-cash	Formal vs informal Extensive vs limited Skills-building vs skills identification	Development of an ER policy. Flow of people to match the business strategies. Match key

(*Contd.*)

Table 18.3 Contd.

	Resourcing	*Performance management*	*Rewards*	*Management development*	*Employee rel]ations*
	Assessment centre approach			Multiple career paths Continuous learning	executives to business strategies. Individual vs group representation. Employee involvement process. Strict regulatory compliance and go above it. Ethical conduct all round.

CONCLUSION

I conclude this book by quoting Kanter (1992: 39) which best defines the new frontiers of international human resource management:

'Our company faces competitive world markets and rapidly changing technology. We need the flexibility to add or delete products, open or close facilities, and re-deploy workforce.' Although we cannot guarantee tenure in any particular job or even future employment, we will work to ensure that all our people are fully employable and sought out for new jobs here and elsewhere. We promise to:

1. Recruit for the potential to increase in competence, not simply for narrow skills to fill today's slot.
2. Offer ample learning opportunities, from formal training to lunch-time seminars, the equivalent of a month a year.
3. Provide challenging jobs and rotating assignments that allow growth in skills even 'without' promotion to higher jobs.
4. Measure performance beyond accounting numbers and share the data to allow learning by doing and continuous improvement.
5. Retain employees as soon as jobs become obsolete.
6. Recognise individual and team achievements, thereby building external reputations and offering tangible indicators of value.
7. Provide three months sabbaticals or extended internship every five years.
8. Find job opportunities in our network of suppliers, customers and venture partners.
9. Tap our people's ideas to develop innovations that lower costs, serve customers and create markets – the best foundation for business growth and continuous employment.

This is the task for global HR professionals and for the most of the organizations here and in future.

Insert and scan Box Nos. companies grooming leaders for global roles.

Review Questions

1. Discuss why has HR function become so crucial for large multinational organizations.
2. Explain the competencies required in HR professionals in large organizations.
3. Bring out the best HR practices in leading organizations in services and manufacturing organizations.
4. How HR strategies and corporate strategies are so interrelated and interdependent?
5. What are the pressures and tensions that HR managers have to balance in winning global success for their organizations?

Assignment

Select any global firm and study its HR practices and assess people's satisfaction with them. Suggest any change that you would like to make if you are its HR vice-president.

Index